D0212548

FILM AND RADIO PROPAGANDA IN WORLD WAR II

Film & Radio Propaganda in World War II

Edited by K.R.M. Short

THE UNIVERSITY OF TENNESSEE PRESS
Knoxville

First Edition

Published in the United States of America in 1983 by
The University of Tennessee Press, Knoxville 37996–0325

Library of Congress Cataloging in Publication Data

Main entry under title:
Film and radio propaganda in World War II.

Includes bibliographical references and index.
1. World War, 1939–1945 – Propaganda – Addresses, essays, lectures. 2. Radio in propaganda – Addresses, essays, lectures. 3. Moving-pictures in propaganda – Addresses, essays, lectures. I. Short, K.R.M. (Kenneth R.M.)
D810.P6F5 1983 940.54'88 82-23838
ISBN 0–87049–386–8

CONTENTS

For Mary Jane

PREFACE

'Propaganda' is one of those ambiguous words which has the problem of being both a pejorative term in common usage and an umbrella term amongst its professional users. If one reads through the extensive number of definitions to be found in dictionaries, encyclopedias and the writings of social science, an extremely wide range of emphasis can be discovered without any one definition proving conclusive. The oft-raised question of whether propaganda was (or is) a good thing or not is usually answered by commentators in the negative, although the alternative has its able defenders.

Nazi Germany accepted the word propaganda as a positive concept in its Ministry of Popular Englightenment and Propaganda, although Goebbels himself wanted to call his Ministry that of 'Information' only to be overruled by Hitler. The writings of contemporary Soviet historians continue to feature the word propaganda as one of the proper methods for the process of informing and through it motivating its citizens to action in support of the state. They couple this word with 'agitation' as the alternative method which relies on symbolic and emotive stimulus. On the other hand, during World War II the United States had its Office of War Information, Great Britain had a Ministry of Information, France had a Commissariat général à l'Information, soon upgraded to a ministry, and Japan organised its activities through a Central Information Bureau. But is there a theoretical difference between propaganda and information? Erik Barnouw, actively involved in American information activities during the war, has recently written:

> Much of what we radio writers did during those years, whether called fiction or non-fiction, I now feel can be described as *propaganda*, but we zealously avoided that word. Propaganda was what others did, especially the Germans. Our work had other names. Programmes I wrote for CBS in the 1930s and for NBC in the 1940s were *public service* programmes. What I did for the Office of War Information, which I briefly served as a short-wave commentator early in the war, was by definition *information*. At the Armed Forces Radio Service, where I

> organised and headed the Education Unit, our programmes were presumably *education*. Since the activity was in a division of the War Department that was, for a time, called the Morale Services Division, I guess we were also performing a morale service. In another segment of the Army, where friends of mine were in action, broadcasts were *psychological warfare*.[1]

If we take this American analysis, 'propaganda', 'information' and 'education' were much the same thing in the wartime context; they meant *persuasion* by whatever method was most applicable to the purpose in hand and best suited to the social and educational background of the persons to be persuaded. The British definition of the purpose of their Ministry of Information as 'propaganda with the truth (facts)' reflects the same realisation of the interchangeability, and utilitarian nature of the words propaganda and information in the time of total war.

Philip Taylor's article, 'Propaganda in International Politics, 1919–1939', which was written as an introduction for this collection, traces the development of propaganda as a concept and a practice from its inception in the later stages of World War I. Here the media available to those early propaganda/information organisations were basically limited to the popular press read by the masses or to the dropping of leaflets on the enemy front lines or homeland. The British Ministry of Information's apparent success in breaking down the morale of the Central Powers and enticing the United States into the war as an associate power, stimulated the development of the techniques of propaganda in nations such as the Soviet Union, Italy and, of course, Nazi Germany. In France, Britain and the United States such activity was viewed with the greatest of suspicion and there was a shared belief in the Western democracies that the manipulative power of propaganda as practised in 1916–18 was so enormous as to threaten the very existence of democratic society. Furthermore, the use of propaganda as an international tool of diplomacy was considered unnecessarily provocative and contrary to the received rules of foreign relations. The Soviet Union, enjoined by Lenin to use propaganda to 'defend the revolution', also used it through the mechanism of the Third International to extend the revolution. The effect was such upon the capitalist nations that they were scarcely aware that Stalin's Russia after 1930 was committed to a different first priority: 'Socialism in One Country'. Nevertheless the rise of virulent fascism forced the democracies to organise their defences against both Hitler and Mussolini's adverse propaganda. This assault coincided with the related technological revolutions of the sound cinema and the radio which together revolutionised the potential for influencing the mass electorates of Europe and America – the former with its ability to seduce its pliable, dark-shrouded audiences and the latter with its capability to transcend the political and geographical boundaries which earlier had blocked the use of the press against belligerent powers.

Propaganda techniques of the 1930s exploited these new media both domestically and internationally, but not to the exclusion of the press, which remained of primary importance even in that era of developing mass audio-visual communication. The exclusion here of the press or the process of censorship, both basic to any comprehensive treatment of propaganda, is not to diminish their importance. Hopefully treatments of those two aspects of propaganda will follow on. Nor does this book stress Nazi propaganda – a topic which has spawned an enormous literature, much of it currently available in English. Rather the emphasis in this collection of essays has sought to redress the imbalance so markedly in favour of Goebbels' life-work. In order to see Nazi propaganda in perspective it is necessary to understand French, Italian, Russian and Japanese propaganda effects in addition to that generated by the members of the Grand Alliance itself. The 15 articles collected here reflect a consensus that propaganda was a persuasive process initiated by governments, industries (such as the American motion picture industry), interest groups, political lobbies, as well as individuals. This domestic-oriented persuasive process had as its target the national population, the masses who represented the democratic electorates of the west, as well as those in nations with far more limited political rights. The initiator of the propaganda campaign sought to achieve electoral or revolutionary support for particular policies or the maintenance of a government in power, as in the case of the Soviet Union, Japan or Nazi Germany. Latterly, the British Ministry of Information and the American Office of War Information were both seen by political parties in wartime opposition (respectively the Labour and Republican parties) as a potentially effective means of keeping the Conservative leader, Churchill, and the Democratic party leader, Roosevelt, in power after the defeat of the Axis powers.

The transmission of propaganda was directed to the mass

electorates through the three basic channels of press, cinema and radio. For example, cinema was the particularly favoured form of entertainment and escape of the British working classes, while initially radio was the medium of the educated and educable it soon grew into the prime information media for all during the war. Generally speaking radio easily reached the rural citizen, but the cinema by its very nature offered less opportunites of propaganda in the countryside. The urban target was the propagandist's prime objective, for its concentration of population offered greater potential in political and economic power. The main thrust of propaganda or information diffusion was domestic and sought essentially during the war in the words of the Office of War Information, to 'achieve enthusiasm for America's war effort'.

The assessment of the population's attitude towards itself and the world was an important element in any propaganda agency's selection of content and persuasion. A Confidential Document (Report No. 21, Revised) of the Special Services Division, Bureau of Intelligence, Office of War Information (1 September 1942) summarised 'Attitudes Obstructing the War Effort' by claiming that Americans were 'apathetic', occupational groups were jealous of one another, many people mistrusted the government in Washington, many people mistrusted America's allies – especially the British – and, finally, that racial tensions regarding Negroes and Jews were on the increase. To counteract these negative attitudes was essential to the achievement of victory: 'HOW TO AROUSE THE EMOTIONS OF THE APATHETIC, AND DIRECT THE ENERGIES OF THE FRUSTRATED INTO THE WAR EFFORT, IS THE INFORMATIONAL CHALLENGE.' That was domestic information from the OWI, with an emphasis upon emotions and not intelligence or education which its Soviet or Nazi counterparts could have easily understood. Once the undesirable attitudes were defined it was the task of the propaganda organisation to mount campaigns to correct those opinions by replacing them with the governmentally-defined desirable ones. The channels of the mass media were the mechanisms by which the new points of view were to be communicated and by their very persuasive nature help in the effecting of the change.

There were points of similarity between the operations of all of the wartime propaganda organisations, Allied and Axis, but as this book will clearly illustrate, there were also major differences which must be recognised. First, the war situation clearly affected, if not dictated, the style that the propaganda took. Russian propaganda content was qualitatively different in the winter of 1941 (when the blitzkrieg reached almost to the heart of the Motherland) from 1944 when the massed Soviet armies were mauling the last vestiges of the Reich's defences; Dr Joseph Goebbels adopted a very different style and content in his propaganda of the period 1939–42, when he had tremendous victories to report and later when he had to resort to the cry for Total War and apocalyptic hopes of wonder-weapons to motivate the German people to fight on and defend the Homeland from the invading Bolshevik barbarians. Secondly, important distinctions need to be recognised between the propaganda of 'one-party' states and those preserving the multi-party political systems. The opposition parties, as mentioned above, could see beyond the war and were extremely nervous about the use of wartime propaganda/information agencies to perpetuate wartime political power. There was another facet, until now not widely recognised, that, unlike one-party states such as Japan, Russia, Germany and Italy, within the democratic propaganda agencies output a power struggle can be documented. Frenchmen were not unique in having to face competing propagandas, as strikingly documented in the articles by Rémy Pithon, Pierre Sorlin and Elizabeth Strebel. During the war years, French audiences, both cinema and radio, were exposed to propagandas emanating from Pétain's Vichy government and the Nazi-inspired Paris-based propaganda organisations, both of which demanded their allegiance. This was complicated by the ability of the same audience to covertly tune in on a third source of propaganda – the BBC's Political Warfare Executive controlled French Service. It was a problem to decide which world view to accept when the three sources carried on a trialogue with each other! The situation within the British Ministry of Information and the American Office of War Information was analogous. Nicholas Pronay's article, entitled '"The Land of Promise": the Projection of Peace Aims in Britain', strikingly documents how the left-wing documentarists dominated the MOI Films Division, producing films for the non-theatrical circuits of Britain which encouraged anti-National (Conservative-dominated) government voting in the drive for a planned Socialist economy. The Office of War Information document previously quoted noted that Jews and Negroes were being subjected to increased racial tension and articles by K.R.M. Short and Thomas Cripps deal with these two problems respectively. The first looks specifically at how the American motion-picture industry, dominated by Jewish studio executives, tentatively stepped through the minefield of American prejudice coming in direct conflict with members of its own faith as well as the directives of the Office of War Information. The quality of discrimination between Jews and Negroes (as they were then known) was marked by the economic and educational deprivation of the latter, thus the Hollywood liberals in conjunction with those in the Federal government and the black leadership had different problems from the Jews. In the second article Cripps makes a strong case for the contention that government films and their Hollywood counterparts performed the valuable service of giving visual substance to the black presence in American life and brought racism to the status of a national issue. On the other hand, he found that the conscience-liberals had in fact defined racism as a wartime phenomenon in their zeal to give the blacks a reason to fight.

It is possible to document the internal dissention of government agencies such as the MOI or OWI; it is also important to realise that such intra-departmental struggles were duplicated on the inter-departmental levels as in the *Commissariat général à l'Information*. The failure of either Churchill or Roosevelt to take propaganda seriously led to infighting on both levels within the respective governments in attempts to define national war aims and even greater difficulty, it would appear, came in efforts to co-ordinate the propaganda of the United States and Great Britain. While MOI films ran counter to its overall policy, such as was defined, a major conflict brewed up between the American War Department and the OWI, when the Army attempted to force Hollywood to put its *Why We Fight* series on general commercial release. David Culbert has carefully documented the development of that series under the heading 'Social Engineering for a Democratic Society at War'. The War Activities Committee of the Motion Picture industry was finally pressured into accepting *Prelude to War* (No. 1 in the *Why We Fight* series) for distribution but only after last ditch efforts of the OWI to protect the fragile agreement by which Hollywood was prepared to take limited advice from Hollywood OWI in return for protection from government film productions. *Prelude to War* may have been seen by millions of GIs but it was only shown to American domestic audiences literally over the dead body of the OWI.[2] Where there was not a clear doctrinaire party line on war propaganda, as in the case of Germany or Russia, a vacuum was created in which competing world views fought for domination. The main struggle took place in the domestic arena but it was also clear that the *realpolitik* manoevring of Churchill and Roosevelt as they compromised with 'Fascist' leaders such as Darlan and Badoglio, despite demands of unconditional surrender, left the anti-fascist liberal propaganda-makers in a quandry; one could not condemn them one day and praise them the next in a democratic war. *Volte face* might be a Soviet practice but it hardly fitted the principled expectations of the liberal Democrats of the OWI or the MOI.

While the continued competition for domestic votes in the post-war elections contributed somewhat to the confusion of western allied propaganda, no such problem existed under the Soviet constitution of 1936 which implicitly admitted the existence of a single party. The Communist Party defined the nation's war aims which are clearly projected in its newsreels, feature films, and documentaries, both collections and feature-length. No peacetime Utopia was offered, as in the cases of American liberals seeking Black or Jewish enthusiasm for the war effort or the British left-wing pursuit of a socialist society. The Soviet post-war dream was not that of a utopia in the making; rather it was the preservation of the classless society achieved. After the incomparable sacrifice of a generation, defence of the homeland allowed no sophistication. Sergei Drobashenko defines the party policy projected in the cinema as incorporating the principle themes of authority, authenticity, uncompromisingness, individualisation, social motivation and finally – a theme which echoes the American problems of Jews and Blacks – 'the unity of the various nationalities of the country'. there is no discounting the fact that the world's most effective propaganda machinery had been established with the success of the Bolshevik revolution and it had educated the Russian population with a thoroughness made possible by the Party's total domination of the nation. The most recent and perceptive definition of the Soviet commitment to propaganda appeared in an article by Drobashenko ('Palestine in Soviet Documentary Cinema') in the *Historical Journal of Film, Radio and Television*, vol. 2, no. 2 (October 1982). Referring back to Shub's *The Fall of the Romanov Dynasty* and Vertov's *Three Songs About Lenin*, he said:

> The main purpose of such films, as we have said, is propagandistic. This is political publicistics in the true sense of

> the word, that had deep roots in the history of the Soviet cinematography, with its own characteristic features, its own system of values and means of artistic expression. The authors of such films aim not only to describe, to inform, to present certain facts, but also to interpret all the material from a definite point of view, to influence the audience by the sum total of cinematic devices and means of expression they use, to reach to the spectator's heart, to move him emotionally, to carry across the idea of the film in a most effective, vivid form. The essential content, the ultimate significance of the documentary film becomes its impact on public opinion and, consequently, its role in directing the social behaviour of people.

The other viewpoint offered on film propaganda in the Soviet Union is offered by the American scholar Peter Kenez who, in his article, has taken great pains to stress that Soviet propaganda must be recognised as qualitatively different from the others dealt with in this book. In an introduction to his discussion paper delivered at Bellagio (see Acknowledgements), Kenez argued that 'the most significant and striking fact about the Soviet cinema world was its complete mobilization . . . The Americans and Russians seem to have been engaged in different wars. For the American people, protected by a fabulous industrial might and by the Atlantic and Pacific Oceans, war never grew into a life or death struggle.' Furthermore, although the Germans fought a total war, Kenez argued that this was not mirrored in the Nazi feature films. Whereas the total film output of the Russians was war-aims oriented, the majority of films which the Germans saw in these years had nothing to do with propaganda. He quite rightly pointed out that the Nazi power base was only seven years old when the war began and, perhaps even more important, Goebbels lacked the ideological richness of the Soviet version of Marxism, itself a comprehensive world view.

Peter Kenez's point of view concerning the non-propagandistic fantasy films which dominated Nazi wartime film production raises an important issue, in fact one that occupies a central position in several of the articles in this book. Is a fiction film propaganda? Does its existence in German cinema programmes evidence a lack of commitment on the part of Goebbels? When the Film Section, Information Services Division, Control Commission for Germany (BE) looked at the 700 feature and 2,500 short films produced between 1933 and 1945 it decided that all but 141 feature and 254 short films were devoid of the taint of Nazi propaganda. On the other hand the group of 96 films produced by the Order of the State propaganda Ministry (*Staatsauftragsfilms*) were clearly propaganda and thus banned in post-war Germany. David Welch's chronicle of Nazi wartime newsreel content highlights the propaganda decision of the Nazi government to primarily carry its propaganda contents in the newsreels rather than in the feature films; especially since the German audience had to be enticed by traditionally-styled entertainment films into the cinema where it would then be fed newsreel propaganda, in ever increasing doses as the war went on. Welch details how, as the character of the war changed, the war aims shifted from total victory and domination of Europe to simple survival. The conclusion offered is that, although Goebbels might have had limited success in arousing enthusiasm for total war through the newsreels, it was really patriotism and the desire to survive that brought forth the final efforts of the German people. Kenez demonstrates how all film in the Soviet war effort was propaganda; were only the *Staatsauftragsfilms* and the newsreels Nazi propaganda? The answer is in the programme and not the individual component. The Soviet people had been raised on ideologically laden cinema although, in the 1920s before Hollywood products were banned from Soviet Russia for ideological and foreign exchange reasons, its audiences clearly preferred Douglas Fairbank's *Robin Hood* to Sergei Eisenstein's *Battleship Potemkin*. Thus the Russian people learned the art of being entertained by ideologically oriented films. The German people had a 'free' cinema until 1933 and were far less malleable, as one would expect from a cultured and comparatively well-educated society. The German people got their requisite dose of propaganda with the newsreels, which became compulsory viewing with the feature films, and yet these very escapist films made an important contribution to supporting the Nazi regime.

Propaganda themes as elaborated in the newsreels, whether Nazi or Soviet, as well as the other producing nations, can be categorised into the political, economic, diplomatic, educational and ideological, although inevitably blurring occurs. Escapist entertainment via the feature film – taking the audience's mind off its troubles – can be an important factor in achieving social acquiescence and much of what was to be seen in the Italian, French and German cinema would fall into this category. What has not been given sufficient emphasis until now, is the importance of the totalitarian adoption and preservation of traditional values which were projected in films of the 1920s and 1930s and which preserved for audiences a sense of continuity and stability. In the two articles on the Italian cinema by Gianni Rondolino and David Ellwood it is stressed that the continuation of bourgeois superficiality – 'the white telephone idiom' – did nothing to detract from Italian support for Mussolini. Audiences went for escapist entertainment and the opulence of the screen world produced it. As the war wore on escape into the world of cinematic dreams became all the more compulsive, as indicated by rising attendances in those years. The situation in Russia was quite different from other one party states. What must be recognised is that feature films can deliver both potent and latent propaganda; the *Staatsauftragsfilms* were potent propaganda as evidenced by *Jud Süss*, the virulent anti-Semitic film of 1940, whereas the entertainment and escapist films were latent propaganda to the extent that they satisfied the emotional needs of a Nazi dominated society. Latent propaganda feature film is not didactic or activating, rather its function is escapist. Repressive governments do not have to fear people who have escaped into fantasy. Latent propaganda themes in escapist entertainment also are an indication of the extent to which the Nazi, Italian or Japanese regimes were an extention of, or modification of, established traditional national values. Vichy France's emphasis upon Travail, Patrie, Famille is an excellent example of how that particular Fascism or totalitarianism derived its ideology from the past; militaristic themes could serve fascism as effectively as could nationalism.

David Ellwood documents how most studies of the Italian fascist cinema agree on the failure of the Italian newsreels as propaganda vehicles, as well as deriding the 'white telephone' films which dominated the cinema. What has until now been ignored was the propaganda success of a group of what Rondolino describes as fictional documentaries produced by the Italian Navy and Air Force. He argues that the commercial success of these films points to their having a propaganda impact far out of proportion to their number. And yet these films really appear to promote a nationalism based upon military success, which would have been appropriate for the screen of a non-fascist nation. When the historian compares the Warner Brothers film *Flying Fortress* (1942) with the Italian *Un Pilota Ritorna* (1942) where does the difference lie? Nationalism dominates ideology when the chips are down, for the propagandist instinctively goes for those themes which will produce the most immediate response he desires, or to arouse the emotions of the apathetic, as the OWI put it in 1942. The continuity in Japanese society is reflected in Gordon Daniel's treatment of the wartime cinema with the added advantage of seeing how this was mirrored in domestic radio broadcasting. The extension of propaganda by short-wave transmission with different programming for Japanese troops in South East Asia, the occupied nations as well as progammes such as Zero Hour for Allied troops is described by Namikawa Ryo. Namikawa, a member of the wartime Central Information Bureau, describes the operation of the Japanese propaganda organisation, as well as detailing the difficulties of liberal opponents to the regime working for national survival.

Propaganda is a process which demands a high degree of organisation control and a flexibility which will enable it to meet changed circumstances with rapidity and accuracy. It seeks control of all information through censorship, command of all the media and the technological means to exclude competing propaganda from its national audience. Furthermore, it seems axiomatic that it will have access to coercive forces to silence any opposition which might rear its head, offering alternative views on the state of the nation or the world. At the very heart of such an integrated state lies a comprehensive and enforceable ideological view of society. This is the hall-mark of a totalitarian state but propaganda, or perhaps more accurately persuasion, is not limited to totalitarian states but belongs also to the world of the democracies. Whereas the totalitarian function of propaganda is to inculcate its beliefs to the exclusion of all others, democratic societies are by their very nature pluralistic. Studies of democracies at war makes the point that even at moments of national crisis competition amongst the various political, economic and social alternatives continued unabated and possibly even heightened in intensity. The general ideological conditioning of society, whether totalitarian or democratic, which was present in the pre-war world through such censoring bodies as the American Motion Picture Producers Association's Hays Committee, the British Board of Film Censors or the Communist Party Central Committe in Moscow, projected with varying degrees of effectiveness the norms of the respective national governing elite. It was not until the advent of war, however, that the democracies sought to directly control and refine the potential of their existent mechanisms for persuasion. These organisations both generally supported the state, as well as specifically campaigning for the acceptance of the target population of new attitudes. Such specific campaigns or programmes were an important part of the work of the British MOI and American OWI, even as they were for Goebbels' Ministry as it sought, for example, to promote the acceptance of euthenasia and the complete de-humanisation of the Jews.

Few nations have ever achieved the optimum conditions for the successful control of a nation's attitudes through propaganda; the experience of most nations, as indicated in this book, has been partial, lacking in consistency, and devoid of the power to ensure that its voice was the only one to be heard by its citizens. The failure of *propaganda*, which is a central function of a totalitarian state, is something to be heartily desired; a world in which *propagandas* compete for dominance and allegiance would appear to be our earthly lot.

Notes

1. Discussion paper, Bellagio Conference, April 1982; see acknowledgements.
2. See K.R.M. Short, '*Why We Fight*: The Office of War Information versus the U.S. Army', forthcoming.

ACKNOWLEDGEMENTS

This volume is the outcome of a conference on 'Film and Radio Propaganda in World War II: A Global Perspective sponsored by the *Historical Journal of Film, Radio and Television* (the official journal of the International Association for Audio-Visual Media in Historical Research and Education). The conference met at Easter 1982 through the auspices of the Rockefeller Foundation at its superb Bellagio Study and Conference Centre at the Villa Serbelloni on Lake Como, Italy. Organised by the editor of this volume and chaired by Erik Barnouw, the conference was composed of 16 contributors of pre-arranged papers with five commentators providing invaluable criticism and adding immeasurably to the vitality of the four days of seminars and discussions which, quite irresistably, flowed over into the very limited free time. Participants came from the United States, Japan, Germany, the Soviet Union, Italy, France, Great Britain, Switzerland and the Netherlands; three of the scholars had also personally taken part in the propaganda activities of Japan, the United States, and Great Britain during World War II. In an enterprise of this sort, the editor incurs a large number of debts, not the least of which is to the authors of the individual articles who throughout the summer laboured with the revisions required of their papers; papers which had been put through the fires of corporate criticism during the various seminars. The small group of commentators, which included Dorothy Barnouw, Jan-Christopher Horak, Frans Nieuwenhof, Wilhelm Van Kampen, as well as our efficient secretary, Antonella Cuccoli, deserve the thanks of all involved in the conference. A fifth commentator David Ellwood, subsequently graciously offered to write a survey of the current literature on Italian film propaganda which is included here.

Members of the conference would wish me to express our thanks, not only to the Rockefeller Foundation for putting its facilities at our disposal, but also to Villa Serbelloni's splendid staff, headed by Robert Celli. We are also grateful to the following organisations for providing travel grants for participants: the American Council of Learned Societies, Leeds University, Louisiana State University, the University of Copenhagen, Film

Art Institute, Moscow, the Bunka-Hoso Foundation of Tokyo, and Westminster College. The editor wishes to express his appreciation to the Twenty-Seven Foundation, Institute of Historical Research, University of London for the travel grant which made the research for his article possible. The Como Tourist Office and the local Bellagio tourist organisation were lavish in their entertainment of the conference and a special thank you is offered to Dr Alvise Zorzi, Secretary General of the *Prix Italia*, whose good offices were greatly appreciated and much admired.

Regretfully, restrictions on the length of this volume has necessitated the exclusion of two articles, Professor Michael Balfour's 'Personalities and Organisation in British Propaganda' and Karsten Fledelius's '"Signal": Nazi Propaganda and Photo-journalism'. The index was compiled by Julie Hounslow.

K.R.M. Short
Kidlington, Oxford

PART ONE: INTRODUCTION

1 PROPAGANDA IN INTERNATIONAL POLITICS, 1919–1939

Philip M. Taylor

As the crumbling stonework of the terraced steps at the Zeppelin field in Nuremberg would now appear to suggest, limestone is not the best of foundations on which to build a thousand-year Reich. Yet, to contemporaries, the Nazi Party rallies held there during the 1930s were awesome spectacles. Sir Nevile Henderson, who attended the 1937 rally shortly after his appointment as British ambassador to Germany, described Hitler's appearance in the following terms:

> His arrival was theatrically notified by the sudden turning into the air of the 300 or more searchlights with which the stadium was surrounded. The blue tinged light from these met thousands of feet up in the sky at the top to make a kind of square roof, to which a chance cloud gave added realism. The effect, which was both solemn and beautiful, was like being inside a cathedral of ice.[1]

This was the house that Reich architect Albert Speer and Propaganda Minister Joseph Goebbels built for the adoration of the Führer. The Nuremberg rallies represented the culmination of the annual celebrations of Hitler's rise to power and of the revival of Germany under his direction while, at the same time, providing the emotional climax of a sustained propaganda campaign conducted throughout the year. It was Leni Riefenstahl's intention, in her film of the 1934 rally *Triumph of the Will*, to allow those who had not been able to attend to join in the commemorations. Like the rallies themselves, the filmic record of them remain masterpieces of the Nazi concept of propaganda and of the role which mass meetings and the mass media could play, not only in preaching to the converted at home, but also in demonstrating to the outside world that Hitler enjoyed the full support of the German people. 'The Party is Hitler. But Hitler is Germany, just as Germany is Hitler', declared Rudolph Hess at the 1934 rally. If further 'proof' was needed, observers had only to note the overwhelming majority who voted for the Führer's policies in the series of plebiscites organised throughout the 1930s. There was, as yet, no sign of the contempt which Hitler was to develop for the German people during the final stages of World War II, nor of the contempt which many came to feel for him afterwards. For the moment, at least while peace prevailed, the recovery of Germany under Hitler appeared nothing short of miraculous – an impression driven home and abroad to great effect by Goebbels and his Ministry of Public Enlightenment and Propaganda.

The same had been true, if to a lesser extent, of Italian recovery under Mussolini, particularly before 1935. Had not the Duce succeeded where his predecessors had failed in making Italian trains run on time and in eradicating malaria from Rome by the draining of the Pontine marshes? To many observers, Mussolini's achievements, like those of Hitler, seemed to outweigh the more unpleasant gangster-like methods of their regimes, especially when it came to the removal of political opposition, as on such occasions as the Matteoti murder or the 'Night of the Long Knives'. In Mussolini's case power was in many respects more apparent than real. Italian military planning, for example, was more akin to Lewis Carroll than to Clausewitz. As John Whittam has written, Mussolini 'was so convinced by the power of words that he came to believe that even foreign policy and military objectives were attainable by the skilful deployment of an army of journalists rather than by the more orthodox formations'.[2] Indeed, Denis Mack Smith has examined Mussolini's entire foreign policy in terms of a massive propaganda exercise lacking any genuine basis in reality.[3]

We are certainly more used to thinking of Mussolini in terms of the fabrication of illusions which masked the harsh realities of Fascist dictatorships. One need only recall the movie-set façades with thousands of cheering Italians standing on concealed scaffolding which the Duce had erected to impress Hitler during his visit to Rome in May 1938, or the painted imitation cardboard trees lined along the processional routes. The competitive element in the relationship between the two dictators often provoked amusement among contemporary observers, something which was brilliantly portrayed by Charlie Chaplin as Adeonoid Hinkel and Jack Oakie as Benzino Napoloni in Chaplin's 1940 satirical masterpiece, *The Great Dictator*. During the war, mockery became a regular feature of allied propaganda. British Movietone, for example, parodied scenes from *Triumph of the Will* in the newsreel 'Germany Calling'

(1940) using trick photography of Riefenstahl's footage to the music of 'The Lambeth Walk'.[4] Alberto Cavalcanti lampooned Mussolini in his 1941 film, *Yellow Caesar*. However, such wartime exercises have tended to obscure the very potent nature of state-subsidised propaganda in the hands of the dictatorships during the inter-war years and, indeed, to diminish our appreciation of the enormous impact which it had upon contemporaries during a period in which illusions flourished. It was not simply a question of Miss Jean Brodie, Muriel Spark's fictional heroine, telling her girls of the classical qualities of the Italin Duce or of the obsession with the German Führer of Unity Mitford and many of her 'fellow travellers of the right'.[5] Admirers of both regimes, however silly, undoubtedly helped to foster a distorted image of fascist achievements, aiding their foreign policy objectives in the process. The claims made by the German government in 1934–5 and by such admirers as Charles Lindbergh concerning the size and offensive capacity of the Luftwaffe to deliver a 'knock-out blow' from the air were widely accepted in the years leading up to World War II. We know now that this strength was greatly exaggerated. But, at the time, such claims undoubtedly reinforced Nazi diplomacy at the expense of its adversaries.[6] So too did the belief that the Rome/Berlin Axis and the Anti-comintern Pact posed a genuine threat to the British of a three-theatre war, a scenario which was not to materialise in 1939.

Propaganda played a vital part in the peacetime diplomacy of both Italy and Germany. It was not just that both regimes to a considerable degree owed their existence to the successful employment of propaganda during their rise to power, or even that their maintenance was sustained with the aid of *agitprop* and the use of terror. They also regarded propaganda as an integral factor in their domestic and foreign policies or, in some instances, as an alternative to those policies.

Before turning to this matter, it is necessary to clarify the broader context in which propaganda could take root and flourish. Essentially, there are three main reasons why propaganda became a regular feature of international relations between the wars: (1) a general increase in the level of popular interest and involvement in political and foreign affairs as a direct consequence of World War I; (2) technological developments in the field of mass communications which provided the basis for a rapid growth in propaganda as well as contributing towards the increased level of popular involvement in politics; and (3) the ideological context of the inter-war period, sometimes known as the 'European Civil War', in which an increased employment of international propaganda could profitably flourish.

Propaganda, regardless of its precise definition, may well be an activity as old as man himself but its systematic or scientific employment in the service of government is basically a twentieth-century phenomenon. Propaganda is essentially about persuasion. The word itself has been much used and little understood. Perhaps, following Professor Medlicott's appeal made some years ago for diplomatic historians of the 1930s to abandon the use of the word 'appeasement' on the grounds that it had become such an emotive and prejudicial label for describing British foreign policy, a similar appeal should be made with regard to the word 'propaganda'. A major problem derives from the debasement of the word since World War I. Before 1914, 'propaganda' meant simply the means which an adherant of a political but chiefly of a religious doctrine employed to convince the unconverted.[7] The religious connotations derive from its semantic origins. Although the transmission of symbols dates from ancient times, the first remotely official propaganda organisation was established by the Papacy in the sixteenth century as a direct response to the forces unleashed by the Protestant Reformation. Pope Gregory XIII (1572–85) established a Commission of Cardinals to spread the true faith to non-Catholic countries and, shortly after the outbreak of the Thirty Years War, Pope Gregory XV made the Commission permanent in 1622 as the *Sacra Congregatio de Propaganda Fide* charged with the management of foreign missions. From the very outset, therefore, propaganda and external affairs were inextricably connected. The word soon came to be applied to any organisation established for the purpose of spreading a doctrine, religious or political. Its employment increased steadily throughout the eighteenth and nineteenth centuries, particularly at times of ideological struggle as in the American War of Independence and the French Revolutionary Wars.[8]

It was, however, between 1914 and 1918 that the wholesale employment of propaganda as an organised weapon of modern warfare served to transform its meaning into something more sinister. World War I was the first 'total war'. The conflict required the mobilisation of elements in the societies of the belligerent nations which had previously been generally uninvolved in, and unaffected by, the exigencies of national survival. Once the initial 'short-war illusion' had been shattered, propaganda began to emerge as the principal instrument of official control over morale. The Great War substantially narrowed the distance which had previously existed between the soldier at the front line and the civilian at home. War was no longer a question of relatively small professional élites fighting against like armies on behalf of their governments. It had become a struggle involving entire populations pitted against entire populations, which were now required to supply the manpower and the material and to endure the deprivations deriving from this total effort. The mobilisation of the entire resources of the nation – military, economic, psychological – in such a gargantuan struggle demanded that national governments develop the weapons of censorship, propaganda and psychological warfare. At home, propaganda was used to justify the need for continuing the struggle until victory was secured, often by the vilification of the enemy through atrocity stories, or to explain the need for personal sacrifices in the national interest. In enemy countries, it was used to persuade soldiers and civilians, by fair means and foul, that their sacrifices were unjust and unnecessary and to incite mutiny, revolt or surrender. Nor was neutral opinion excluded from what became a struggle for world sympathy; the United States especially was a happy hunting ground between 1914 and 1917 for propagandists striving to win the hearts and minds of the American public and its government with all the economic and military benefits which that could entail for the successful suitor. By 1918, all the belligerents had recognised the value of propaganda as a weapon in their national armouries.[9]

Although certain countries, notably Germany and France, had entered the war with at least some of the basic equipment required to engage in the war of words (having devoted considerable official energy to propaganda as an adjunct of their foreign policies since the 1870s)[10] the nation which finished the conflict with reputedly the most successful propaganda was Great Britain. This was despite the fact that in 1914 Britain possessed nothing that could even remotely be described as an official propaganda department. This impressive exercise in improvisation began with the creation of the Press Bureau and of the Foreign Office News Department and culminated in the establishment of a full Ministry of Information under Lord Beaverbrook and a separate Enemy Propaganda Department at Crewe House under Lord Northcliffe. The success of this operation was to have serious long-term consequences for British foreign policy during the inter-war years. In the United States, for example, the belief that the American people had somehow been 'duped' into involvement on the Allied side in 1917 by British propaganda emanating from the most secret of its propaganda organisations, Charles Masterman's War Propaganda Bureau at Wellington House, merely served to reinforce the arguments of those isolationist elements which advocated post-war withdrawal from the devious machinations of the Old World. Various scholarly studies of Britain's wartime propaganda published in the United States appeared to confirm these views. H.C. Peterson's book, for example, *Propaganda for War: The Campaign against American Neutrality, 1914–17* (significantly published in 1939) pointed to the methods of Masterman, Gilbert Parker and their fellow propagandists in helping to secure United States entry into the war on the Allied side and, by implication, warned against a repetition in another.[11] American sensitivity to foreign propaganda was highlighted by the passing of the 1938 Foreign Agents Registration Act which required all foreign publicists operating on American soil to register with the US Government.[12] The British had responded to such sensitivity by persistently refusing to inaugurate an official propaganda campaign in the United States despite the cautious work undertaken in the meantime by the British Library of Information at New York.[13] The British government did exhibit at the New York World Fair opened in 1939 with the theme 'Building the World of Tomorrow'.[14]

The experience of Britain's propaganda in World War I also provided defeated Germans with a fertile source of counter-propaganda. Adolf Hitler, for example, was sufficiently impressed with what he described as the very real genius of British propaganda that in *Mein Kampf* he paid tribute to propaganda's contributions to Germany's defeat. Admittedly Hitler was using this line of argument for propaganda purposes of his own. By maintaining that the German army (in which he had served with distinction) had not been defeated on the field of battle but rather had been forced to submit in 1918 due to the collapse of morale inside Germany (a process accelerated by Crewe House propaganda) Hitler was providing historical 'legitimacy' for his 'stab-in-the-back' theory.[15] But the fact remains that, regardless of the actual role played by British (or Soviet) propaganda in helping to bring Germany to her knees (and the evidence does point to a stronger case in so far as Crewe House propaganda directed against Austria–Hungary was concerned), it was generally accepted that Britain's wartime experiment was the ideal blueprint on which other governments should subsequently model their own propaganda apparatus. The very emphasis which the Nazis were to place upon propaganda merely served to perpetuate Britain's wartime reputation for success, a reputation originating in the testimonies of prominent enemy personalities during the final years of the war and strengthened by various scholarly and popular publications that appeared subsequently.[16]

It now appears that those right-wing elements in Weimar Germany who praised Britain's wartime experimentation may have misdirected their tributes. Although much research still needs to be done, it seems that propaganda emanating from the new Bolshevik regime in Russia did much more to undermine morale within the Central Powers during the final year of the war, particularly amongst the industrial classes. The Bolshevik leadership was certainly quick to appreciate the role which propaganda could play in international affairs. Shortly after their seizure of power in October 1917, they published various secret treaties negotiated by the Tsarist regime with the Allied governments. The embarrassment caused, for example, to the Allies by the publication of the 1915 Treaty of London, by which Italy agreed to enter the war on the Allied side in return for substantial territorial gains in southern and south-eastern Europe, is well known. The terms of the previously secret London treaty became public at a time when President Wilson's call for national self-determination as part of his Fourteen Point Peace Plan appeared to offer the Yugoslavs territory which had already been promised to the Italians by America's partners. Moreover, influenced by Trotsky's theories of world revolution, the use of propaganda to spread an international class-based ideology transcending national frontiers posed a significant threat to established regimes which were suffering from the intense socio-economic and political chaos of World War I. Comintern agents were included in the staff of Soviet diplomatic missions and, indeed, Soviet foreign policy and commintern propaganda became indistinguishable in the years following the October revolution.[17] For Russia's former allies, the replacement of 'Prussian militarism' by Bolshevism as the principal perceived threat to civilisation was clearly a development which required urgent counter-measures. The British Empire, for example, was a primary target for Soviet propaganda and clauses attempting to limit its conduct were inserted by the British government into the Anglo-Soviet Trade Agreement of 1921.[18] But such measures, by themselves, were insufficient to combat the post-war intensification of propaganda over and above even the wartime levels of expenditure. By 1930, the British government had become so accustomed to Soviet violations that it merely accepted that propaganda 'is to them a vital part of their proclaimed doctrines and intentions'[19] and nothing more than a protest was issued. In the meantime, however, the post-war struggle to recapture economic markets and to overcome the financial dislocation caused by World War I had been accompanied by a widespread increase in the use of propaganda. During the course of the 1920s propaganda was rapidly being converted into an instrument of peacetime commercial and ideological penetration by aggressive nationalistic regimes in the Soviet Union, Italy, Japan and, slightly later, Nazi Germany. In short, between 1914 and 1918, the British government had opened a Pandora's Box which unleashed propaganda on to the modern international arena.

Ironically, this new peacetime development was one in which the British largely remained disarmed bystanders, having chosen to dismantle their wartime machinery almost entirely in 1918. One observer noted in 1938: 'the very weapons used by democracy to defend itself successfully twenty years ago are now being turned against it'.[20] At the end of World War I, the British government had regarded propaganda as politically dangerous, financially unjustifiable and morally unacceptable in peacetime.[21] It had served as a distasteful but necessary evil of war and there was to be no room for it in Britain's attempt to return to normality. Some enlightened observers had recognised the implications of the wartime experiment and argued that there was room for propaganda in the modern democratic state. Sir Charles Higham, for example, had written in 1916:

> Advertisement, honourably used, developed along subtle yet dignified lines, may yet prove the chief factor in the Government of the future; which, in a great democracy, must tend ever to substitute arbitration for force and enlightenment for coercion.[22]

Such views gained only gradual acceptance in Britain where

'propaganda' remained a pejorative word, associated with subversion of freedom of thought and deed. It was, as one official wrote in 1928, 'a good word gone wrong – debauched by the late Lord Northcliffe'.[23] Yet the hollowness of those illusions which prompted the dismantling of Britain's elaborate wartime propaganda machinery were to be gradually exposed during the course of the inter-war years when totalitarian propaganda presented democracy with no alternative but to re-enter the field it had done so much to pioneer. Once opened, the lid of the Pandora's Box proved impossible to close. Another Foreign Office official wrote in 1937:

> The emergence of the totalitarian State in Europe has presented us with new and urgent problems. To deal with them a new outlook is required. We are faced with competition on a formidable scale in many parts of the world and that competition is taking new forms to which this country has hitherto been unaccustomed. One of these forms is what is commonly known as propaganda, powerfully and deliberately directed to promote the political and commercial influence of the national State.[24]

This development had grown to such serious proportions by the mid 1930s that the government was responsible for the foundation of the British Council in 1934 and for the inauguration of the BBC foreign language broadcasts in 1938 in an attempt to combat this totalitarian challenge to democracy.[25]

However, there were also various domestic forces working for the gradual acceptance of propaganda as an instrument of the modern democratic state. World War I, as we have seen, introduced the concept of 'total war'. For the British, the introduction of conscription, the recruitment of women into the factories, Zeppelin raids on the south coast, the bombardment by the German High Seas Fleet of east coast towns like Scarborough and the attempt of the German U-boats to starve Britain into submission all contributed towards a higher level of public participation in the conduct of modern warfare. With the advent of air power, the role of the English Channel serving as a giant anti-tank ditch was no longer adequate protection against the possibility of aerial attack, a vulnerability that was to be driven home during the 1930s by films such as Alexander Korda's *Things to Come* (1936) and by newsreels showing the bombing of civilians in Manchuria,

Abyssinia and Spain.[26] However much they might have wished to do so, successive British governments could not follow the American example of withdrawing into isolation safe in the knowledge that military technology was not yet sufficiently advanced to jeopardise the geographic isolation and corresponding American security from European attack. Indeed, one of the major problems which faced George Creel's Committee on Public Information during 1917–18 had been how to make the geographically remote struggle in Europe of immediate ideological relevance to the majority of the American people.[27] The same problem was to face President Franklin D. Roosevelt between 1939 and 1941.[28] Yet in Britain, the widely held assumption that the bomber would always get through made such attitudes a luxury neither the government nor the people could afford.[29]

Under such circumstances, a greater level of popular involvement and interest in foreign affairs was inevitable. World War I had to be justified to the nation as a whole because the entire nation was actually fighting it or else suffering from its consequences – whether in the form of the German submarine campaign against Allied shipping or the Allied blockade of the Central Powers.[30] While the economic weapon thus emerged as the fourth arm of defence, propaganda became the fifth arm.[31] The impact of these developments, combined with the lessons to be drawn from the alarming frequency of mutinies within the new mass conscript armies, as well as the outbreak of Bolshevik revolution in Russia, Central Europe and elsewhere, led to a heightened appreciation of the role which the masses would henceforth play in the survival of the state – or, alternatively, in its destruction. Foreign affairs would no longer be confined to kings, nobles and aristocrats centred around a small court. The creation of a League of Nations as an expression of 'the organised opinion of mankind' and calls for open diplomacy ensured that public opinion would in future play a greater role in the determination of foreign policy-making than it had ever done before 1914. Moreover, that opinion was not only becoming more literate and educated – i.e. more capable of forming its own judgements – but it was also becoming more directly involved in politics with the broadening base of political power.

With the 1918 Representation of the People Act and the further extension of the female franchise ten years later, Britain was only really beginning to approach full parliamentary democracy during the inter-war years. The number of people entitled to vote had risen to about five million by 1885 and, by the time of the 1910 elections, the figure had only reached slightly more than seven and a half million. The 1918 Act trebled the size of the electorate while the 1928 Act brought the total to 29 million, about 90 per cent of the adult population, by the time the Labour government was elected the following year. Political parties responded to these developments by experimenting in mass persuasion; the Conservative Party, for example, began using a small fleet of travelling cinemotor vans in the mid 1920s which toured the country showing political films and cartoons.[32] By the 1930s, a major problem for any British government was not merely confined to whether it should seek to influence opinion but mainly to ensure that the means to do so provided by the new technological advances in communications was exercised for recognisably national, rather than simply sectional or party, interests. This was the purpose of the National Publicity Bureau established in 1935 by the MacDonald–Baldwin government to explain its policies to the general public, something which it may well have done during the election campaign that year but which it clearly failed to do over the Hoare–Laval Plan.[33]

It is often assumed that democratic regimes purport to follow public opinion and that totalitarian regimes set a standard and enforce conformity to it. As one observer noted in 1938:

> In countries where the herd instinct is highly developed, and individualism is discouraged, propaganda is the normal method of evoking or formulating public opinion. But in countries where individualism is cherished, propaganda, though recognised as a necessary evil, is relegated to a 'second best' position in the formulation of public opinion.[34]

In fact, the difference is less clear cut. During the inter-war years, democratic regimes were forced, albeit reluctantly, to recognise that propaganda had indeed become an essential feature of modern political and international affairs. They may have comforted themselves in the belief that propaganda was something other people did and that what they were doing was really 'publicity', 'political advertisement' or 'national projection' but they could hardly fail to recognise the implications of doing nothing in so far as this new peacetime weapon was concerned. In Germany, Hitler was able to secure power by legal, if not wholly democratic, means and, like the Bolsheviks in Russia and the Fascists in Italy, he owed a large part of his success to propaganda. The extension of party political propaganda onto the national and then the international scene presented a serious challenge to the democracies whose governments had previously depended upon a consensus of opinion, however limited. It was a challenge which was made all the more threatening in view of the new means of international communications provided by science and technology.

If World War I had demonstrated the power of propaganda, the 20 years of peace that followed witnessed the widespread utilisation of the lessons drawn from the wartime experience within the overall context of the 'communications revolution'.[35] 1927 was a particularly momentous year. It was the year of Charles Lindbergh's historic solo trans-Atlantic flight, thereby heralding the beginning of the end of the North American continent's geographic remoteness from Europe. With the rapid development of civilian aviation routes extending across the globe, the world was becoming more familiar and accessible. The telephone also helped this process; in 1927 communication was established across the Atlantic by radio-telephone. In the same year, the British Broadcasting Company became the British Broadcasting Corporation and, within five years, the BBC had initiated its Empire Service designed to enable the far-flung peoples of the British Empire to remain in close and constant touch with the mother country. 1927 also witnessed the arrival of the commercially successful talking motion picture with *The Jazz Singer*. Radio and the cinema, both in their infancy during World War I, were the first truly mass media and their implications for both politics and propaganda were far-reaching. In Glasgow, Baird demonstrated the transmission of colour television pictures in 1927, although this particular medium was not to receive the attention its real significance deserved until the late 1940s.

During the inter-war years, the gradual replacement of cables by wireless as the chief means of international communication and propaganda was a more immediately significant development. Even so, cables remained important. The emergence of London during the late nineteenth century as the major news capital of the world, at the hub of a vast global cable network, had served to provide Britain with enormous advantages in the transmission of international news and views – advantages so clearly demonstrated within hours of the outbreak of war in 1914 when the British severed the direct German trans-Atlantic cables. However, with the advent of wireless, together with the continued reluctance of the British government to subsidise the Reuters News Agency to the same extent that the French subsidised the Agence Havas or the Germans the Wolff Bureau (which became the DNB under the Nazis), a situation was created whereby the leading British news agency found it increasingly difficult to compete with its leading continental and American rivals – Associated Press and United Press. Various pre-war agreements between the news agencies were allowed to lapse and there followed a keenly fought battle between the national news agencies, including Stefani of Italy and ROSTA (after 1935, TASS) of the Soviet Union, which made it apparent that trade no longer followed simply the flag. It followed news, information and views, let alone propaganda, tinted by the very source from which it originated. It was a battle in which British news was being swamped to an alarming degree.

Radio offered one means of compensating for the paucity of British news and views that contributed to Britain's commercial prosperity in an increasingly competitive world. Yet this was in turn linked to technological considerations. Short-wave transmissions over long distances were only being developed during the 1920s; Australian broadcasts were heard in Britain for the first time in 1927.

The potential of radio as an instrument of international communication had long been appreciated. Marconi had considered it to be 'the greatest weapon against the evils of misunderstanding and jealousy'.[36] Yet such a view was based upon a fundamentally optimistic view of the way in which states regard one another. Radio provided governments with an ideal instrument of political propaganda in the age of the politicised masses. It had been used during the 1914–18 war but its impact had been limited because transmissions had largely been confined to morse code. Nevertheless, its potential had been sufficiently well appreciated that the allied peacemakers at Versailles prohibited German broadcasting from Nauen, Hanover and Berlin or the construction of any new stations for a period of three months after the peace treaty had been signed.

In the 1920s, radio was used intermittently in international disputes. During the 1923 Franco–Belgian invasion of the Ruhr, for example, a radio 'war' did break out between the Berlin and Eiffel

Tower stations. The German government was quick to recognise the value of radio as a means of enabling those Germans who had been separated from their homeland by the terms of the Versailles treaty to keep in touch and to retain their sense of nationality. During the 1930s the lofty BBC ideal that 'Nation Shall Speak Peace Unto Nation' had given way to the exploitation of broadcasting as an instrument of aggressive propaganda. Radio was used by Germany and Poland in the dispute over the Upper Silesian question; a broadcasting non-aggression pact was signed in 1931 by the two countries.[37] Out of the 30 European national broadcasting systems in existence in 1938, 13 were state-owned and operated, 9 were government monopolies operated by autonomous public bodies or partially government controlled corporations, 4 were actually operated by government but only 3 were privately owned or run.[38] Under such circumstances, radio propaganda became a regular feature of international relations and an instrument of national policies.

This development had become apparent with the transmissions from Radio Moscow (established in 1922 and greatly extended in 1925) when the Soviet Union developed the world's first short-wave station. For Lenin, radio was 'a newspaper without paper . . . and without boundaries'.[39] With the advent of Hitler in Germany, radio propaganda was used to spread the doctrine of National Socialism and to make the new regime more respectable abroad before embarking upon an ambitious foreign policy.[40] Prior to the Saar plebiscite of January 1935, propaganda transmitted from the Zeesen radio station was used to great effect while radio propaganda was a central feature of the German propaganda assault on Austria between 1934 and 1938:[41] 'The primary aim was to create a Fifth Column of convinced believers in the Nazi cause and to use them as a lobby to back up the work of the German embassies.'[42] In peace, as in war, the Nazis used radio as an 'artillery barrage' to weaken the morale of the enemy before the attack.

The special qualities which made radio such an effective instrument of international propaganda were simple. It relied upon the spoken word and was thus more direct in approach and personal in tone than any other available medium. It was also immediate and extremely difficult to stop when jamming devices were inefficient. Radio was capable of reaching large numbers of people, regardless of their geography, literacy, political and ideological affiliations or of their social status. Moreover, because there were no territorial (as distinct from technological) limitations to its range, radio enabled the propagandist of one nation to speak directly and immediately to large numbers of people in another from the outside. This latter quality proved important during World War II.

Whereas the totalitarian regimes used radio as an instrument of ideological and nationalistic expansion, the League of Nations was concerned with the value of broadcasting in the cause of peace. During the World Disarmament Conference (1932–4), the Polish government proposed a convention on 'moral disarmament' and, as a result of this initiative, the League Assembly requested member states to encourage the use of radio 'to create better mutual understanding between peoples'.[43] After several years of deliberation, in 1936, a League convention *Concerning the use of International Broadcasting in the Cause of Peace* was signed by 28 states (but only ratified by 19) which attempted to outlaw aggressive radio propaganda, mis-statements and incitements to insurrection or war. Instead, radio was to be used 'to promote a better knowledge of the civilisation and conditions of life in one country, as well as of the essential features of the development of its relations with other peoples and of its contribution to the organisation of peace'.[44] Such high-sounding aims could well have been written by an official of the British Council, established just over a year earlier to conduct cultural propaganda. However, the real significance of the convention (which came into force on 1 April 1938) lay more in the spirit of its intent than its effect, for its articles were framed in terms so vague that only serious violations could be punished. Moreover, Britain, France and the Soviet Union were the only great power signatories; the absence of the two countries whose radio propaganda was at that time causing the most serious international concern – Germany and Italy – rendered the convention virtually impotent.

The British government was forced to depart from the spirit, if not the letter, of the convention when it initiated broadcasts in foreign languages in 1938. This decision was a response to the escalation of anti-British radio propaganda during the Abyssinian crisis when the Italian government had been quick to exploit the role which a successful marriage of radio propaganda and totalitarian ideology could play in the cause of an aggressive foreign policy. The Italian broadcasts, transmitted from Radio Bari and from the short-wave transmitter in Rome (2R04), exacerbated existing tensions and grievances in the Middle East, particularly in Palestine and Egypt, by portraying Britain as the imperialistic oppressor and the Duce as the protector of Islam. Broadcasting in seven languages including English, Greek and Arabic, the Italian programmes were carefully structured to meet local requirements and were presented by Arab employees with a command of the local dialects. 'Never before in time of peace', wrote one observer, 'had such a sustained campaign of invective and abuse been launched by one country against a supposedly friendly power'.[45] The need for counter-measures was urgent, while the issue threatened the success of the so-called Anglo–Italian 'gentleman's agreement' that was eventually signed in May 1938.[46]

Radio was not the only medium used for international propaganda purposes, although it was the most important. At his famous meeting with Lord Halifax in November 1937, Hitler maintained that nine-tenths of all international tension was caused by the press.[47] The captive press in the Third Reich did, of course, play the tune orchestrated by the Nazi state.[48] In democracies, where vague notions of free speech were cherished, direct control was more difficult. The French press, however, was notoriously prone to political influence, including subsidies from foreign governments. In Britain, the situation was less extreme although Fleet Street was amenable to government influence.[49] But, given the nature of British newspaper proprietorship during the 1930s, Fleet Street generally shared the same common interests of the British government on foreign policy issues, particularly regarding the policy of appeasement. After the Munich agreement was signed, only one British newspaper proved critical of Neville Chamberlain's policy.[50] Even so, with the exception of *The Times*, the British press was frequently erratic in its attitude towards Germany.[51] Hitler's resentment of it was merely compounded during the May weekend crisis of 1938 when Fleet Street heralded the British government's warning to Germany not to march against Czechoslovakia as a great diplomatic triumph. Hitler, who had no plans for such a move at that time, was furious. The extent to which the British press (as distinct from the *démarche* itself) contributed to Hitler's subsequent instructions for the modification of Case Green and the seizure of the Sudetenland by 1 October 1938, must remain a matter for historical conjecture. Yet the lesson was clear enough. Governments resented the manner in which the press of a foreign country gave adverse publicity to their policies. If that press was state controlled, it was simply held to be a reflection of the government's views. If it was not, it was frequently, often erroneously, held that the democratic press reflected public opinion within the society in which it operated.

Film, also, was an effective medium of international propaganda. Considerable work has already been done on informational films such as newsreels and documentaries[52] and historians are examining feature films as sources for the history of the society which produced them.[53] Like the press, national film industries 'acted as propaganda for and endorsement of its country's "way of life" within the country in question and abroad'.[54] The role of feature films in the context of international propaganda between the wars is best illustrated by the example of Hollywood's movies in promoting American culture, commerce and political ethos abroad. By the end of World War I,the United States owned over half of the world's cinema houses. In 1923, 85 per cent of films shown, for example, in French cinemas were American. Whereas in 1914 25 per cent of films shown in British cinemas were British, by 1925 the figure was only 2 per cent.[55] Even by 1939 America owned about 40 per cent of the worldwide total of cinemas thus providing American film producers with an enormous advantage over their foreign competitors. This global distribution network ensured the projection of American society and culture, as seen through the eyes of Hollywood, and was to create significant commercial repercussions. 'Trade follows the film' became a popular maxim for economic expansionists during the 1920s and early 1930s[56] and European countries with less well-developed film industries soon began to express concern at what was felt to be the significant and unfair advantages provided by Hollywood for American commerce. In Britain, the *Morning Post* declared in 1923:

> If the United States abolished its diplomatic and consular services, kept its ships in harbour and its tourists at home, and retired from the world's markets, its citizens, its problems, its towns and countryside, its roads, motor cars, counting houses and saloons would still be familiar in the uttermost corners of the world . . . The film is to America what the flag was once to Britain. By its means Uncle Sam may hope some day, if he be not checked in time, to Americanise the world.[57]

Within a few years, the problem had grown to such proportions that the British government passed the 1927 Cinematograph Act largely to protect the British film industry. Exhibitors were legally compelled to show a proportion of home-produced films, but the problem remained. In 1930, one official wrote:

> It is horrible to think that the British Empire is receiving its education from a place called Hollywood. The Dominions would rather have a picture with wholesome, honest British background, something that gives British sentiment, something that is honest to our traditions than the abortions which we get from Hollywood . . . The American film is everywhere, and is the best advertisement of American trade and commerce. Trade follows the film, not the flag.[58]

Until such people as Alexander Korda could go some way towards rectifying the absence of British feature films with 'wholesome, honest British background' with productions like *The Private Life of Henry VIII* (1932), *Sanders of the River* (1935) and *The Four Feathers* (1939), the burden fell mainly on the Empire Marketing Board (EMB). This was Britain's first official peacetime propaganda agency established in 1926 whose pioneering work with British audiences was extended after 1930 to encompass the Empire itself as well as foreign countries. Nevertheless the documentary-type films produced by the EMB and, following its demise in 1933, other like-minded official agencies established to project Britain abroad such as the British Council and Travel Association were inadequate to combat the American domination of the entertainment film world, even if they did elicit universal critical acclaim from intellectual circles. Despite the recommendations of the Moyne Committee and a further Cinematograph Act in 1938, the British government was unable to legislate against American domination of the home market: it was claimed that 'every successful feature film which Hollywood [sends] across the Atlantic [is] a piece of propaganda for American civilisation, all the more powerful for not being labelled as such'.[59]

In one respect, this was a most ungracious comment. During the 1930s, Hollywood fell in love with British history and the British imperial legend. A glance at the Warner Brothers' films starring Errol Flynn with distinctively British themes is sufficient to illustrate this point: *The Charge of the Light Brigade* (1936), *The Prince and the Pauper* (1937), *The Adventures of Robin Hood*

(1937), *Dawn Patrol* (1938), *Elizabeth and Essex* (1939). Moreover, the final speech in *The Sea Hawk* (dir. Michael Curtiz in 1940), spoken by Flora Robson playing Queen Elizabeth I, is a classic piece of pro-British propaganda in the context of the year 1940:

> And now, my loyal subjects. A grave duty confronts us all. To prepare our nation for a war that none of us wants – least of all your Queen. We have tried by all means in our power to avert this war. We have no quarrel with the people of Spain or of any other country. But when the ruthless ambitions of a man threaten to engulf the world, it becomes the solemn obligation of all free men to affirm that the earth belongs not to any one man but to all men and that freedom is the deed and title to the soil on which we exist. Firm in this faith, we shall now make ready to meet the great armada that Philip sends against us. To this end, I pledge you ships – ships worthy of our seamen. A mighty fleet hewn out of the forests of England. A Navy foremost in the world, not only in our time, but for generations to come.

The substitution of Hitler for Philip II and the Luftwaffe for the armada (for those who made the obvious connection) make this Hollywood production a useful propaganda contribution for Britain's struggle against Nazi tyranny at a time when Roosevelt was struggling to overcome American neutrality.

Before the war, however, other countries struggled unsuccessfully to combat Hollywood's dominance by introducing quota systems and, later, import licensing schemes. At the same time, they attempted to bolster their own native film industries. Germany increased its film output so that in the period between 1923 and 1929, 44 per cent of feature films shown in Germany were home produced. The French were less successful; the corresponding figure for the same period was 10 per cent. In 1928, therefore, a quota system was introduced whereby one French film had to be shown for every seven imports. Yet, as *Le Matin* argued:

> The truth is that the Americans are trying to make Europe give way to their ideas and rightly believe that the propaganda in motion pictures which permits American influence to be placed before the eyes of the public of all countries is the best and least costly method of spreading their national influence.[60]

Accordingly, under the Herriot decree of February 1928, the exhibition of all films in France was put under the control of the Ministry of Public Instruction and Fine Arts. Hollywood retaliated to these and other measures by buying into foreign film industries and by producing multiple-language films, although this latter development proved costly and had to be abandoned as the impact of the Great Depression began to be felt even in Hollywood. It did not really matter anyway. Hollywood remained dominant.

A much more powerful weapon in the hands of those European governments which felt threatened by this dominance was censorship. Such a weapon had proved particularly effective in checking the spread of subversive ideas portrayed in Soviet films. Eisenstein's *Battleship Potemkin*, for example, was denied commercial distribution in Britain and in several other countries on the grounds that it might incite the working classes (the section of the community which most supported the cinema) to imitate the example of their Russian counterparts. The film was successful in Weimar Germany where it was premiered in April 1926, despite the wishes of the armed forces to see it banned because of its 'inflammatory' nature. The German version of the film was nevertheless cut substantially. Censorship acted as a form of negative propaganda affecting the image which domestic audiences were exposed to concerning foreign societies, while suppressing unpalatable images of events at home. Recent research into film censorship has demonstrated that this was just as significant, if not more so, in peacetime as it was to prove in war, in democracies as in dictatorships.[61]

These, then, are some of the technological and sociological reasons which helped to make propaganda an established feature of international politics between the wars. But, by themselves, they provide only a partial explanation as to why governments chose to adopt propaganda as an additional instrument of their political and diplomatic machinery and, moreover, why it was to prove so effective an instrument. A further reason was the ideological context of the inter-war years – the so-called European Civil War.[62] This concept rests upon the notion that Europe during the first half of the twentieth century was beginning to resemble a single polity, in part due to the 'shrinking world' produced by the communications revolution. Indications of this were the general acceptance of rules and conventions which governed inter-state relations, innumerable international conferences and the creation of such bodies as the International Postal Union, the Conference of Ambassadors and even the League of Nations itself which, following the refusal of the United States to join and the deliberate exclusion of the Soviet Union until 1934, resembled a largely European organisation, based, of course, in Geneva. But the conflict was not merely confined to the European state system; it also operated between separate elements in a common European society. On a more human level, most European nations had experienced the tragedy of the 1914–18 war; they shared a macabre brotherhood of the trenches and a communal revulsion toward war, commemorated throughout Europe each year on Armistice Day with the survivors standing before war memorials, cenotaphs and tombs of unknown soldiers. Lewis Milestone's film, *All Quiet on the Western Front* (1930) (banned in Germany[63] and released, significantly, 18 months before the World Disarmament Conference) was a near universal rejection of militarism as a means of solving disputes. Thus, within this overall context, the socio-political unrest which greeted the end of World War I, the challenge to democracy in the streets of Italy and Weimar Germany, the Vienna riots and the Stavisky riots of 1934, the movement of Italian troops and British warships through the Mediterranean in 1935, the bombing of Spanish cities in 1936 and 1937, the German invasion of Austria in 1938 and of rump Czechoslovakia in 1939 were all seen as part of the same process embracing all Europe, namely a civil war between the forces of 'oligarchy, aristocracy, authoritarianism, Fascism and those of popular democracy, socialism, revolution'.[64]

Europe as a single entity, as a political community, may, of course, have existed more in the minds of its governing and intellectual classes who perceived such a development during the inter-war years than in the relatively inarticulate minds of the masses. Yet such factors as the universal fear of indiscriminate civilian bombing were common to all peoples and governing elites could ill-afford to ignore such a factor in the formulation of their foreign policies. If, during the 1920s, they had been concerned with what they perceived to be the threats posed by Bolshevism or the insidious spread of American popular culture through the new mass media, they were to meet an more serious challenge to their survival in the following decade in the form of an expansionist Nazi Germany.

Propaganda offered a potentially important weapon in this international battle for hearts and minds and, in many respects, accentuated the problem. As Sir Austen Chamberlain said shortly before his death: 'This attempt [by propaganda] to create what in the phrase of the day – which I am bound to use, though I dislike it – is a kind of ideological division of the world, is, I think, bound to fail.'[65] Although both sides used propaganda in this struggle, the weight of historical attention has tended to concentrate upon the totalitarian regimes. Certainly, during the 1920s, the democracies were slow to respond. Most of them shared a common fear of the new Bolshevik regime in Russia but it was not simply because of the advent of a regime based upon an international class-based ideology that transcended traditional views of foreign policy: nor was it because the Communists were dedicated to the overthrow of those capitalist societies which had barely survived World War I. This new challenge was driven home by the aggressive use of propaganda in conjunction with domestic agitation. The Soviet Union had been the first government to establish, in the form of the Comintern – 'The General Staff of the World Revolution' – a large-scale peacetime propaganda organisation designed to supplement the work of Russian foreign policy. Soviet propaganda took no account of national frontiers; it tampered with foreign opinion as part of its attempt to promote an international class community dedicated to the overthrow of established capitalistic governments. Those governments, following the failure of their intervention during the Russian Civil War, responded in a variety of ways – international legislation, counter-insurrection and deliberate exclusion of the Soviet Union from the international community – but rarely did they take up the gauntlet thrown down by the Comintern and respond by counter-propaganda. Censorship was regarded as a far more effective weapon. However, following the ascendancy of Stalin over Trotsky during the 1920s and the acceptance of 'Socialism in One Country' over the policies of the Third International, Soviet propaganda became a less serious challenge to the western democracies in that its militant activities were replaced by a more opportunistic strategy. Hitler's rise to power in January 1933 prompted a further revision of Soviet policy. The entry of the Soviet Union into the League of Nations in 1934 and the return to an unsatisfactory version of the old Franco–Russian alliance in 1935 was followed by the seventh World Congress of the Commintern which called for foreign communists to co-operate with socialist and even liberal parties in the popular front against fascism. In 1938, Eisenstein was commissioned to make *Alexander Nevsky* as part of Russia's psychological preparations for the coming war. With the signing of the Nazi–Soviet Pact in August 1939, this thirteenth-century spectacle of the war between the united peoples of Russia and the invading Nazi-like Teutonic Knights was withdrawn from public exhibition until Operation Barbarossa converted Eisenstein's allegory into reality. The change in the international atmosphere similarly affected Germany's anti-comintern stance; the hostile *Friesennot* (1935) was banned within a fortnight of the Nazi–Soviet Pact and was only to be re-released in 1941 as *Dorf im roten Sturm* (*Village in a Red Attack*).[66]

In the meantime, the democracies had begun to respond to Nazi propaganda in a way they had been reluctant to do during the 1920s. The battle was by no means confined to political propaganda. Even international sporting occasions were transformed into propaganda exercises. The case of the 1936 Olympic games and Leni Riefenstahl's film *Olympiad* is well known, but even the England–Germany football matches of December 1935 and May 1938 became propaganda events. Although Germany lost on both occasions, the Nazi press described the loss in 1935 as an 'unqualified political psychological and sporting success' for Germany: the 1938 British victory was regarded by the British ambassador in Berlin as a triumph for Britain's prestige in Germany (not least because the England team gave the Nazi salute before the match started).[67]

The British did in fact enter the field of cultural propaganda very late in the day (the United States was even later[68]). Following the government sponsored activities of the Russian VOKS,[69] the Italian Dante Alighieri Society and IRCE,[70] the French Alliance Française[71] the Japanese Kokusai Bunka Shinkokai and the German VDA,[72] the British Council had been formed in 1934 to project Britain's cultural achievements. The philosophy of the Council was that 'mutual understanding is the basis of mutual tolerance on which alone can be built a sure and lasting peace'.[73] By the late 1930s, however, cultural activity was assuming a distinctly political purpose. One British official noted in 1935:

> It would be difficult to deny that the impression made on the world by an exhibition of Fine Arts goes beyond the walls of the exhibition buildings themselves and enhance the respect and admiration felt for the country that produced such works'.[74]

A notable example of this political dimension of cultural propaganda was Picasso's painting, *Guernica*, which came to represent fascist barbarity in Spain. As one art historian has written:

> As a propaganda picture, Guernica did not need to be a specific political statement. The mass media supplied the agreement by which it became one, and Picasso knew exactly how and where to insert his painting into that context – through the Spanish pavilion at the Paris World Exhibition, where it was shown in 1937 as a virtually official utterance by the Republican government of Spain.

The same historian also argued that the 'mass media took away the political speech of art' and that *Guernica* was 'the last modern painting of major importance that took its subject from politics with the intention of changing the way large numbers of people thought and felt about power'.[75]

It is certainly true that the Spanish Civil War served to polarise the various ideological conflicts of the inter-war period. Both sides learned a great deal about propaganda from the conflict. The Germans, for example, decided to retain the screaming engine noise of the Stuka dive-bombers because the Spanish experience demonstrated the terrifying impact created upon soldiers and civilians on the ground. On the very limited experience of 1917–18, British rearmament rested on the highly dubious assumptions that offence was the best form of defence, that the ratio of casualties to bombs would prove abominably high and that bombing would cause panic, industrial and social disruption on such a scale that morale would collapse. Hence the importance of propaganda and the decision as early as 1935 to initiate plans for a wartime Ministry of Information. The British were thus confirmed in their belief that the bomber would always get through. Most observers failed to see that the Luftwaffe at that stage was being designed principally as an army support unit. Hordes of German bombers could not appear over British cities without fighter support and that required control of the Low Countries in order to provide the bombers with short-range fighter protection. And when the Blitz did begin, it was learned that wholesale bombing often served to strengthen rather than shatter civilians morale. More significant, perhaps, were the short-term diplomatic implications of the Spanish Civil War. With

Mussolini's adherence to the anti-comintern pact in 1937, the war seemed to demonstrate that the Duce's announcement of a Rome–Berlin Axis in the previous year really did represent a new alignment in European diplomacy following the debacle of the Abyssinian crisis and the collapse of the Stresa front. Although it was ostensibly designed to combat the Soviet Union (thus guaranteeing considerable support in the west), the anti-comintern pact, so it was believed, could quite easily be converted into an anti-British combination directed against the Empire's far-flung possessions. If the Manchurian crisis had exposed British weakness in the Far East, the Abyssinian crisis had demonstrated Britain's inability to defend her interests simultaneously in two or more theatres. Following the strengthening of Germany's position in western Europe with the remilitarisation of the Rhineland in March 1936, the outbreak of the Spanish Civil War four months later shifting tension in the Mediterranean from east to west of Malta, and the renewal of war in the Far East in July 1937, the possibility of a three-theatre war reinforced Britain's need to appease one or more of the anti-comintern powers. However, all was not as it appeared. The Rome–Berlin Axis and the anti-comintern pact were perhaps the most effective exercises in myth-making of the 1930s. They gave the impression that Rome, Berlin and Tokyo were acting in collusion when, in reality, this was far from the case. All three powers were following their own objectives within this loose alignment and all three clearly benefited from the diversions caused by the others. But they rarely acted in harmony.[76]

Granting Britain's lack of determined allies and military strength before the Axis Illusion, it is difficult to understand the repeated failure to conduct any serious propaganda during the 1930s in the two countries that might have helped Britain to deter Hitler – the Soviet Union and the United States.[77] There were, of course, many reasons why this did not happen. Following the experience of World War I and subsequent American sensitivity concerning foreign propaganda, the British had considered, not entirely without justification, that 'hands across the water' propaganda might do more harm than good. The Soviet Union presented different problems. As the pariah of international politics for most of the inter-war period, it was extremely difficult for many British politicians to accept that the Soviet Union could play a positive role in a peacetime anti-Hitler coalition. It was also a difficult regime to penetrate from a propaganda point of view. Yet the price of this reluctance even to try to overcome the numerous difficulties involved was to prove a high one. The major problem for British propaganda following the political decision to guarantee Poland in March 1939 was how to make the gesture credible as a deterrent (if that was its real purpose): that meant involving the Russians.[78] Were the Moscow negotiations that took place in the summer of 1939 a genuine attempt to add military credibility to the Polish guarantee, or were they largely a British propaganda exercise? In Soviet eyes, at least, the despatch of a relatively minor official (Lord Strang) on literally a slow boat to Moscow gave the impression that the British were not treating the negotiations seriously. The Nazi–Soviet Pact was the price which the British had to pay for their apparent insincerity.

E.H. Carr claimed that

> the success of propaganda in international politics cannot be separated from the successful use of other instruments of power. . . It is an illusion to suppose that if Great Britain (or Germany or Soviet Russia) was disarmed and militarily weak, British (or German or Soviet) propaganda might be effective in virtue of the inherent excellence of its content.[79]

In other words, propaganda is dependent for its success upon the realities of power from which such factors as 'influence' and 'prestige' derive. However, during the inter-war years, Britain was both relatively and absolutely in a process of decline. Commitments inherited from a bygone age were fast becoming liabilities in the face of increasingly hostile actions on the part of Germany, Italy and Japan. The broadening gap between Britain's worldwide responsibilities and her capacity to defend the very source of her strength was exploited repeatedly by Axis powers who were quick to recognise the value of aggressive propaganda as a tool of their foreign policies. Moreover, Britain herself was vulnerable to attack, particularly from the air, in a way that she had not been before. She simply no longer enjoyed that position of supremacy which had enabled her to remain successfully aloof in splendid isolation for long periods in the past. In the 1930s, therefore, Britain was forced to re-enter a field she had done so much to pioneer in World War I, partly to perpetuate the appearance of power in the eyes of foreign observers at a time when hostile propaganda was beginning to expose the harsh realities of British decline. She suffered from all the disadvantages of a former champion attempting a come-back against younger opponents who had studied their mentor wisely. When the British government was forced to consider rearmament in 1934–5, caught as it was between financial restraints and the demands of national defence, it responded 'by seeking to create the image of power without investing in its more costly substance.'[80] And although the British would not have considered themselves to be in the business of myth-making, such policies as 'showing tooth' to Japan in the Far East and creating a 'shop-window' deterrent against Germany were tantamount to the same thing, despite their financial expediency. Furthermore, coupled with the physical threat was an assault by the new totalitarian regimes upon democracy as a viable political philosophy in a fierce war of ideas. The very fact that there was felt to be a need to project British achievements on behalf of the democratic principle was not only symptomatic of Britain's declining influence in international affairs but it was also a reflection of the virulence of the totalitarian challenge and its successful employment of propaganda within the overall context of the European Civil War. Truth was a casualty long before the actual fighting began.

Notes

1. Sir Nevile Henderson, *Failure of a Mission* (London, 1940), p. 71.
2. John Whittam, 'The Italian General Staff and the Coming of the Second World War' in Adrian Preston (ed.), *General Staffs and Diplomacy before the Second World War* (London, 1978), p. 79.
3. Denis Mack Smith, *Mussolini's Roman Empire* (London, 1976).
4. Frank Capra used footage from the same film in the first of his *Why We Fight* series, *Prelude to War*. For further details, see David Culbert's essay in this volume.
5. R. Griffiths, *Fellow Travellers of the Right* (London, 1980).
6. In 1938, a story circulated in Berlin that the British had so many aeroplanes that they blackened the skies, those of France were so numerous that they blotted out the sun but when Hermann Göring unleashed the Luftwaffe, even the birds would have to walk. See R. Parkinson, *Peace For Our Time* (London, 1971), p. 10.
7. W. Irwin, *Propaganda and the News: or, What Makes You Think So?* (New York, 1936), p. 3.
8. Robert B. Holtman, *Napoleonic Propaganda* (Baton Rouge, 1950); Philip Davidson, *Propaganda and the American Revolution, 1763–83* (Chapel Hill, 1941).
9. On Britain: Sir Campbell Stuart, *Secrets of Crewe House* (London, 1920); J.D. Squires, *British Propaganda at Home and in the United States from 1914–17* (Cambridge, Mass., 1935); Cate Haste, *Keep the Home Fires Burning* (London, 1977); M.L. Sanders and Philip M. Taylor, *British Propaganda in the First World*

War (London, 1982). On the USA: George Creel, *How We Advertised America* (New York, 1920); George Viereck, *Spreading Germs of Hate* (New York, 1930); Stephen Vaughn, *Holding Fast the Inner Lines* (Chapel Hill, 1980). There is no satisfactory account of French propaganda but see G.C. Bruntz, *Allied Propaganda and the Collapse of the German Empire in 1918* (Stanford, 1938) and Hansi (Jean Jacques Waltz) and Henri Tonnelat, *À Travers Les Lignes Ennemies* (Paris, 1922). Germany suffers from the same problem, but see Wilhelm Ernst, *Die Antideutsche Propaganda durch das Schweizer Gebiet im Weltkrieg, Speziell die Propaganda in Bayern* (Munich, 1933).

10. Paul Gordon Lauren, *Diplomats and Bureaucrats* (Stanford, 1976); Ruth E. McMurray and Muna Lee, *The Cultural Approach* (Chapel Hill, 1947).

11. See also, S. Rogerson, *Propaganda in the Next War* (London, 1938).

12. One writer commented the previous year: 'The self-respecting American is down on all propagandists, as the self-respecting housewife is down on vermin.' Jay Nock, 'A New Dose of British Propaganda', *The American Mercury*, 42 (1937), p. 482. The Foreign Agents Registration Act was observed mostly in the breach.

13. Philip M. Taylor, *The Projection of Britain* (Cambridge, 1981), pp. 68–80.

14. G. Ainsworth, 'The New York World Fair: Adventure in Promotion' *Public Opinion Quarterly*, 3 (1939), pp. 694–704; John Grierson, 'World's Fair and Royal Visit Are Our Greatest Opportunities in 1939', *Kinematography Weekly* (12 January 1939), p. 44.

15. It is worth noting that Hitler did not invent the theory. Nor did Ludendorff. Shortly after the conclusion of the Armistice, General Sir Neill Malcolm attempted to articulate Ludendorff's explanation for German defeat by using the phrase 'stab-in-the-back' to him and Ludendorff seized upon the phrase. Lindley Fraser, *Germany between Two Wars; A Study of Propaganda and War Guilt* (London, 1944), p. 16.

16. In addition to those works already cited in note 9, see: H. Wickham Steed, *Through Thirty Years* (London, 1924); H. Lasswell, *Propaganda Technique in the World War* (London, 1927); Arthur Ponsonby, *Falsehood in Wartime* (London, 1927); *The Times History of the War* (London, 1921).

17. R.K. Debo, *Revolution and Survival* (Toronto, 1979).

18. S. White, *Britain and the Bolshevik Revolution* (London, 1979). For other examples of attempts to curb Bolshevik propaganda by treaty see, H. Lauterpacht, 'Revolutionary Propaganda by Governments', *Transactions of the Grotius Society*, 13 (1927), pp. 143–64; Lawrence Preuss, 'International Responsibility for Hostile Propaganda against Foreign States', *American Journal of International Law*, 28 (1934), pp. 649–68.

19. P[ublic] R[ecord] O[ffice, London], CAB 23/65, 64 (30) 1, 28 October 1930.

20. R.S. Lambert, *Propaganda* (London, 1938), p. 131.

21. For further details see Philip M. Taylor, 'British Official Attitudes Towards Propaganda Abroad, 1918–39' in Nicholas Pronay and D.W. Spring (eds.), *Propaganda, Politics and Film, 1918–45* (London, 1982).

22. C.F. Higham, *Looking Forward* (London, 1920), p. 63. See also M.T.H. Sadler, 'The Meaning and Need of Cultural Propaganda', *The New Europe*, 7, no. 84 (23 May 1918), pp. 121–5.

23. Angus Fletcher to Sir Arthur Willert, 10 May 1928. PRO, FO 395/437, P 732/732/150.

24. Foreign Office memorandum, 19 February 1937. PRO, FO 395/554, P 823/160/150.

25. On the British Council see Philip M. Taylor, 'Cultural Diplomacy and the British Council, 1934–39', *British Journal of International Studies*, 4 (1978), pp. 244–65; Diana Eastment, 'The Policies and Position of the British Council from the

Outbreak of War to 1950', University of Leeds, Unpublished PhD thesis, 1982. On the BBC Foreign Language Service see C.A. MacDonald, 'Radio Bari: Italian Wireless Propaganda in the Middle East and British Countermeasures, 1934–38', *Middle East Studies*, 13 (1977), pp. 195–207.

26. A. Aldgate, *Cinema and Hitory: British Newsreels and the Spanish Civil War* (London, 1979).

27. Vaughn, *Holding Fast the Inner Lines*.

28. R.W. Steele, 'Preparing the Public for War: Efforts to Establish a National Propaganda Agency, 1940–41', *American Historical Review*, 75 (1970), pp. 1640–53.

29. U. Bialer, *The Shadow of the Bomber* (London, 1978).

30. M. Howard, 'Total War in the Twentieth Century: Participation and Consensus in the Second World War' in B. Bond and I. Roy (eds.), *War and Society* (London, 1975).

31. H. Wickham Steed, *The Fifth Arm* (London, 1940). Some confusion exists as to the accuracy of this label. It follows the army, navy, air force and the blockade. Propaganda is occasionally described as the 'fourth arm' following political, military and diplomatic activity in wartime. Given that it became a weapon, the former description is more appropriate.

32. T.J. Hollins, 'The Presentation of Politics: The Place of Party Publicity, Broadcasting and Film in British Politics, 1918–39', University of Leeds Unpublished PhD thesis, 1981.

33. D. Waley, *British Public Opinion and the Abyssinian War, 1935–36* (London, 1975); R.D. Casey, 'The National Publicity Bureau and British Party Propaganda', *Public Opinion Quarterly*, 3 (1939), pp. 623–34.

34. Lambert, *Propaganda*, pp. 17–18.

35. A. Briggs, *The Communications Revolution* (Leeds University Press, 1966).

36. Cited in J. Hale, *Radio Power: Propaganda and International Broadcasting* (London, 1975), p. xiii.

37. J.B. Whitton and J.H. Hertz, 'Radio in International Politics' in H.L. Childs and J.B. Whitton (eds.), *Propaganda by Short-Wave* (Princeton, 1942), p. 7.

38. Cesar Saerchinger, 'Propaganda Poisons European Air, *Broadcasting* (15 April 1938), p. 20.

39. Cited in Hale, *Radio Power*, p. 17.

40. Z.A.B. Zeman, *Nazi Propaganda* (2nd edn., Oxford, 1973), pp. 85–140.

41. Zeman, Ch. 5; Whitton and Herz, 'Radio in International Politics', pp. 12–15.

42. Hale, *Radio Power*, p. 3.

43. Taylor, *Projection of Britain*, p. 190.

44. Ibid.

45. A.J. Mackenzie, *Propaganda Boom* (London, 1938), p. 139. On Japan see NHK, *50 Years of Japanese Broadcasting* (Tokyo, 1977).

46. K. Middlemas, *The Diplomacy of Illusion* (London, 1972), pp. 211–3.

47. *Documents on German Foreign Policy*, Series D, Vol. 1.

48. Oron J. Hale, *The Captive Press in the Third Reich* (Princeton, 1964).

49. James Margach, *The Abuse of Power: The War between Downing Street and the Media from Lloyd George to James Callaghan* (London, 1978).

50. W.W. Hadley, *Munich: Before and After* (London, 1944).

51. F.R. Gannon, *The British Press and Germany, 1938–9* (Oxford, 1971).

52. On newsreels see Aldgate, *Cinema and History*; N. Pronay, 'British Newsreels in the 1930s, I: Audiences and Producers', *History*, 56 (1971) and 'II: Their Policies and Impact', *History*, 57 (1972). On documentaries see P. Swann,

'The British Documentary Film Movement, 1926–46', University of Leeds, Unpublished PhD thesis, 1979.

53. See Pierre Sorlin, *The Film in History* (Oxford, 1980); K.R.M. Short (ed.), *Feature Films as History* (London, 1981).

54. Keith Reader, *Cultures on Celluloid* (London, 1981).

55. D.J. Wenden, *The Birth of the Movies* (London, 1975), p. 147.

56. Sidney Box, *Film Publicity* (London, 1937), especially Chapter 1 entitled 'Trade Follows the Film'. See also John Grierson, 'One Foot of Film Equals One Dollar of Trade', *Kine Weekly* (8 January 1931), p. 87.

57. Cited in Robert Sklar, *Movie Made America* (London, 1975), p. 219.

58. Quoted by Swann, 'The British Documentary Film Movement', p. 195. See also Peter Stead, 'Hollywood's message for the world; The British response in the 1930s', *Historical Journal of Film, Radio and Television*, 1 (1981), pp. 19–33.

59. Lambert, *Propaganda*, p. 63.

60. Cited in Wenden, *The Birth of the Movies*, p. 159.

61. N. Pronay, 'Film Censorship in Liberal England' in Short, *Feature Films as History*; N. Pronay, 'The Political Censorship of Films between the wars' and 'The British Newsmedia at War' in Pronay and Spring, *Propaganda, Politics and Film*; J. Richards, 'The British Board of Film Censors and Content Control in the 1930s, I: images of Britain', *Historical Journal of Film, Radio and Television*, 1 (1981), pp. 95–117; 'II: foreign affairs', *Historical Journal of Film, Radio and Television*, 2 (198), pp. 39–49; J.C. Robertson, 'British Film Censorship Goes to War', *Historical Journal of Film, Radio and Television*, 2 (1982), pp. 49–65.

62. For this interpretation, I have relied heavily upon D.C. Watt's 'The Nature of the European Civil War, 1919–39' in his *Too Serious a Business* (London, 1975).

63. Modris Eksteins, 'War, Memory, and Politics; The Fate of the Film *All Quiet on the Western Front*', *Central European Review* (1980), pp. 60–82.

64. Watt, 'The Nature of the European Civil War', p. 13.

65. *Parliamentary Debates* (Commons) 5th series, Vol. 321, 2 March 1937, col. 238.

66. F. Isaakson and L. Furhammer, *Politics and Film* (London, 1971).

67. James Beck, 'Football as Propaganda: England v Germany, 1938', *History Today*, 32 (1982), pp. 29–34.

68. In 1938, the State Department set up a Division of Cultural Relations, (nearly four years after the foundation of the British Council under the auspices of the Foreign Council) although private endowments, particularly from the Rockerfeller Foundation and the Carnegie Corporation, were meanwhile potent forces for the spread of American culture overseas. PRO, FO 395/575, P 2438/80/150.

69. F.C. Barghoorn, *The Soviet Cultural Offensive: The Role of Cultural Diplomacy in Soviet Foreign Policy* (Princeton, 1960).

70. A. Haigh, *Cultural Diplomacy in Europe* (Strassburg, 1974).

71. McMurrary and Lee, *The Cultural Approach*.

72. On Japanese cultural propaganda see R.S. Scharanks, 'Japan's Cultural Policies' in J.N. Morley (ed.), *Japan's Foreign Policy, 1868–1941: A Research Guide* (New York, 1974). On the VDA, see Zeman, *Nazi Propaganda* and McMurray and Lee, *The Cultural Approach*.

73. Sir Angus Gillan, 'The Projection of Britain on the Colonial Empire' in Sir Harry Lindsay (ed.), *British Commonwealth Objectives* (London, 1946).

74. Alfred Longden, 'British Art Exhibitions at Home and Abroad', 31 October, 1935. PRO, BT 60/44/3, DOT 5215/1935.

75. Robert Hughes, *The Shock of the New* (London, 1979).

76. D.C. Watt, 'The Rome–Berlin Axis: Myth and Reality', *Review of Politics* vol. 22, no. 2 (1960).

77. D.W. Ellwood, '"Showing the World What it Owed to Britain": Foreign Policy and Cultural Propaganda, 1935–45' in Pronay and Spring, *Propaganda, Politics and Film*. But see my counter-arguments in *Projection of Britain*, pp. 172–5.

78. Cf. S. Newmann, *The British Guarantee to Poland: March 1939* (Oxford, 1976).

79. E.H. Carr, *Propaganda in International Politics* (Oxford, 1939). See also Urban J. Whitaker Jr, *Propaganda and International Relations* (San Francisco, 1960) and my forthcoming book on *Propaganda in International Politics, 1900–1982*.

80. R.P. Shay, *British Rearmament in the 1930s* (Princeton, 1977), p. 46.

PART TWO: ASPECTS OF THE ALLIED EXPERIENCE

2 'THE LAND OF PROMISE': THE PROJECTION OF PEACE AIMS IN BRITAIN

Nicholas Pronay

The experience and the lessons drawn from World War I played a significant part in the conduct of World War II in Britain. Many of the leading political figures and senior civil servants of 1939 had already served in high positions both during World War I and in the aftermath of that singularly traumatic war. Although younger men tended to come to the fore after May 1940, this was certainly not true for the single most important person: Winston Churchill. Churchill had been a cabinet minister several times over before World War I, intimately associated in fact with many aspects of war-planning in the years before 1914, and he had served in the Cabinet both during the opening and closing periods of the Great War. Perhaps even more importantly, he was also a leading member of the Coalition government of Lloyd George and then Chancellor in the Conservative Government which faced the General Strike. He was thus personally involved in government during the 1918–29 period when government and political establishment alike grappled with the manifold legacies bequeathed by the political conduct of World War I.

During the next ten years 'in the wilderness', Churchill had the time and the inclination for reflecting on the political, and of course also the military, conduct of the war and for preparing himself more or less consciously for the next war. He thought deeply about the lessons of the Great War and came into office with the fruits of that thinking. In so far as this enabled Churchill to organise a war-cabinet/government system, with himself as Minister of Defence as well as Premier, which was very unlike indeed the peacetime pattern in Britain but which functioned exceptionally flexibly and effectively, this accumulation of experience and reflection which put the second war into the perspective of the first was an invaluable asset.[1] But in so far as it acted as a barrier to recognising some of the particular needs and conditions operating in Britain during World War II, it proved to be a mixed blessing.

A particular case in point was the question of 'war aims'. As a leading member of the government of the 1918–29 period Churchill was particularly sensitive to the consequences of the liberal dispensation of promises concerning the post-war world which Lloyd George's government made or permitted to be made. Emotive phrases, propelled by Lloyd George's genius for oratory, even where the actual phrase may not have originated with him, or indeed may have come from the other side of the ocean, 'a war to end war', 'making the world safe for democracy', 'a land fit for heroes to live in', 'homes for heroes' have rebounded upon the governments of the post-war period. Taken as 'promises' they were not and could not be fulfilled. They created disappointment, bitterness and contributed significantly to that alienation between at least sections of the working class and the government which so deeply frightened and concerned the ruling elite, of whichever particular party affiliation, in the inter-war years.[2] One thing, therefore, that Churchill had drawn as a binding lesson from World War I and which he was determined to put into practice in World War II was that the government should not make declarations of post-war aims.

When he took office in May 1940, in the midst of what was recognised by all as the greatest emergency which had faced Britain for centuries, and which therefore gave him a measure of political freedom and power, as well of course as responsibility, of a magnitude which had not been accorded to an English Prime Minister since the younger Pitt, he could therefore make clear this determination with absolute force and in characteristically powerful language. 'You ask what is our policy? I will say "it is to wage war, by sea, land and air, with all our might and with all the strength that God can give us: to wage war against a monstrous tyranny never surpassed in the dark lamentable catalogue of human crime." That is our policy. You ask what is our aim? I can answer in one word: victory – victory at all costs, victory in spite of all terror, victory, however long and hard the road may be; for without victory, there is no survival.'[3] He never deviated from this policy. There were war aims: victory, but there would be no peace aims. As Paul Addison put it: 'In his view the peace would have to be framed after the war was won or almost won.'[4]

It was natural that he was often tempted, cajoled, or even pushed to formulate 'peace aims'.[5] As a good politician, for Churchill proved that in wartime conditions he was that too, he avoided making an issue of his determination not to have a repetition of 'homes for heroes' at home or 'war to end war' in foreign policy, put out by *his* government. The more so, because he was more conscious than some others with a less experience-bred sense of politics that between himself and the Conservative Party on the one hand and Attlee and the Labour Movement behind him on the other there were more fundamental differences on post-war aims than some of his younger colleagues in his own party could perceive. Churchill was more aware than he is perhaps given credit for, for recognising that while the Labour Right and the Conservative Left may indeed have been made up of people who represented the basic philosophies of neither parties, but who shared a common belief in 'big government', the country behind them was divided on more fundamentally irreconcilable lines. He was therefore conscious that if his Coalition War Cabinet were to address itself to drawing up peace aims the highly effective unity of the War Cabinet would inevitably become jeopardised. The political and personal harmony of the War Cabinet functioned undisturbed so long as its central commitment was to win the war of survival by the total mobilisation of Britain's human and economic resources. If, however, they began to discuss peace aims, however alike they may have been in their *étatist* proclivities themselves, they would have to come under the respective influences of their rank and file. Whether this was a major conscious consideration in Churchill's mind, a mind which more than most others in English political life then operated on two levels – rational and intuitive – need not be discussed here. It may well be that he was principally determined to avoid the declaration of peace aims by the government as he had learnt from World War I that vague and general pronouncements would cause trouble later or because he believed that 'talk of the future would divert attention from the terrible urgency of the immediate crisis, and stir up political controversy' or even because 'he found such questions humdrum, gruel after the champagne of grand strategy'.[6] The fact is that he prevented it by procrastination, by sidetracking the issue into committees made up of people whom he wished to be kept quiet[7] and out of the way, or by simply rigging cabinet agenda in such a way that the issue could never be fully discussed. The presentation of peace aims through the government's machinery of communications was thus, as a matter of policy, avoided during World War II.

Yet, by the close of World War II, significant sections of the British people had been treated to visions of a grandiose post-war

Utopia which exceeded anything promised during World War I. By 1945, it had been articulated for them in considerable detail, related to particular regions or groups within the country, increasingly ensloganised and constantly repeated, just as *Mein Kampf* advised that propaganda should be. Moreover, it had been given a clear and specific party-political identification: if you want this wonderful future, you can only have it if you vote Labour and if you are prepared to fight for it as well as vote, if necessary. It is one of the strangest paradoxes of World War II that under one of the most powerful governments ever in Britain, exercising the most widespread control over all aspects of economic and social life and especially over the mass media, which far exceeded the control exercised over it in World War I, and under a government which was particularly conscious of the lessons of wild promises in wartime, the exact opposite of one of its principal policy decisions actually came to pass in practice.

Moreover, these expectations and the specific programme of how they should be realised were brought to the people through that medium which was especially suited to creating visions of the future, to make dreams appear real and realisable and which also had particular powers of simplifying problems and emotionalising issues and policies: the film.

This paradoxical situation came about for two reasons. First, because the absence of officially produced peace aims left a vacuum which do-it-yourself propaganda was bound to try to fill, but that was not in itself a reason for the highly particular and single-party-oriented projection which actually occurred. An official absence of peace aims should have left a situation which produced a Babel of voices instead of specific expectations, and thus furthered the basic Churchillian aim. What he failed to realise was that this policy would have required encouragement to all sorts of Conservative sympathisers to produce schemes and to debate those of others, rather than the heavy discouraging of any such effort. For only his own supporters would heed that command, the other side would not. Churchill's own peace-aim, a continuation of the Coalition government for a period of 'post-war reconstruction', depended on the willingness of Labour and thus was an unrealistic policy: he did not have the power to make it continue. The Churchillian reading of the 'lessons' of World War I thus resulted in a mistaken policy which itself was bound to give some advantage, at least to those who would not be willing to loyally abide by the policy of postponing argument about what should be done after the war until victory was certain. Such arguments would nevertheless be produced and would, under Churchill's policy, lead to some predominance of the debates of the other side.

But that such arguments could be actually embodied into film, *the* most potent medium for making Utopias appear real prospects under the apparently watertight controls over film, was due to a remarkable group of people indulging in a characteristically British game of 'open conspiracy'.

The controls over film were particularly tight under the wartime scheme of censorship. Film, in fact, had long been recognised in Britain as the most potent medium for Utopian propaganda, for the projection of a better world in place of the one which the powers-that-be were providing for the audience. Consequently (the traditions of the free press notwithstanding) the cinema had been placed under the most comprehensive and effective system of censorship operating anywhere outside the totalitarian parts of the world which, although differently conducted, was in its over all effectiveness just about as good as the systems operating within them. The details of the operation of political censorship in Britain before 1939 need not concern us here.[8] The effect was, quite simply, that anyone was free to make a film about anything they wished – but only films which, in the opinion of a full-time professional body of long experience, did not carry political messages conflicting with those of the government in any fundamental way could be shown to the 'great audience'. Since making films with sufficient technical quality to have any effect whatever on the audience was incomparably more expensive than writing or even printing books in the conditions of the 1930s and 1940s, the exemption from censorship which allowed the showing of more or less any film to small non-paying audiences ('non-theatrical exhibition') operated chiefly as a useful *propaganda* device: few could afford to lose the sums involved and those were rarely to be found on the 'other side'. In wartime, the system of censorship was, of course, further tightened rather than relaxed – and made virtually watertight by declaring film-stock to be a strategic material obtainable only by licence.[9] Moreover, a massive film-propaganda operation to boost morale and provide instruction was mounted by the Ministry of Information which should have largely accounted for all the 'spare' capacity for film making and stock. It was however through official films commissioned by, or produced under the direct control of and distributed by, the Ministry of Information – and that under two successive Conservative Ministers of Information – that this peace aim propaganda came to be presented to significant sections of the population.

How this remarkable fact came to pass can be briefly told. At the outbreak of war, the Chamberlain government was a badly weakened, shaken and easily harassable government. The 'man of peace' who claimed to have saved peace for our time, was very much on trial as war leader in the House and in the country alike. By not seeking immediately to form a Coalition government – for amongst other good reasons because his sharp political personality and economic policies during the 1930s had ruled out the chance of Labour serving in his cabinet – he also put the official Conservative Party on trial beside him. Thus he and his party were obliged to avoid conflict over the wartime activities of the government as much as possible. The Ministry of Information immediately emerged at the outbreak of war as just such a potential source of embarrassment and political rows because it made a singular mess of the teething troubles of the new wartime Ministries, as they hatched from the incubators of pre-war contingency planning.[10] Under the circumstances it was inevitable that Chamberlain would not wish to put up a fight to protect it from its critics. On the contrary, he wished to accommodate as many of them as possible by sacrificing whichever official's head was being bayed for – even if the mess was *far* from being solely due to their own inadequacies. Thus the carefully and intelligently chosen Head of the Films Division came to be one of the sacrificial victims when, for no fault of his own or even of his staff, the initial film coverage of the war proved to have left much to be desired.[11]

Sir Joseph Ball would indeed have been an excellent choice for that post and had been carefully selected for it – but only under a strong and confident government. In 1939 Sir Joseph Ball had more experience of propaganda in general and the place of films in it than any other man in Britain, and he had also acquired over many years excellent personal relations with the majority of the heads and senior staff of the major production studios, film distributing organisations and the newsreel companies. Moreover, he had that other vital asset for a propagandist; he was in the confidence of the Prime Minister politically and personally. Under Ball film propaganda would have been in safe hands and could be relied on to realise the policy objectives of the government. But these very qualities made him an embarrassment to a weak and shaken government: through his experience of propaganda in general, and film propaganda in particular, he had been appointed Head of the National Publicity Bureau (the National Government's highly effective propaganda organisation) and Head of the Conservative Party's Research Department and party publicity/propaganda organisation.[12] He was thus a natural target for the Opposition for claiming that the Films Division under him was not going to serve genuinely national purposes but party ends. A strong government would have brushed aside such inevitable kinds of attacks, but a shaken and weak government could not. To such a government he became a liability to be sacrificed as soon as an attack built up upon him. He was replaced by a rank amateur without *any* political affiliations with a pleasant, well-liked personality: Kenneth Clark. The Films Division, not surprisingly, failed to produce virtually anything at all under him (once again not altogether his fault, for he *was* learning fast, but due to a variety of circumstances beyond his control). So when professionalism came to be the grounds on which the Films Divison, and indeed the MOI and the government itself, were to be judged, Kenneth Clark was replaced by Jack Beddington. Beddington remained in office from 1940 to the end of the war.[13]

Beddington was a man with unusual qualifications and contacts. He was a professional: a successful Public Relations Officer for a great oil company, Shell, and he *had* used film for public relations purposes on a substantial scale. But his experience and contacts were limited entirely to the specialised world of promotional film and within that largely confined to the highly self-contained 'documentary' film. It was the only kind of film-making of which he had any personal managerial experience. As far as it is recorded, the only film-makers or producers Beddington had actually known at all well were members of the Documentary Movement, people who were very much outsiders, distrusted and disliked by the commercial cinema world; sentiments which they heartily reciprocated. Beddington had no previous political experience or involvement. He had shown no interest whatever in politics either before he became Head of the Films Divison or after he returned to Shell. Did he have any clear political views himself? If he did, they are certainly not recorded: he does not turn up in the extensive correspondence of either Conservative Central Office or Labour's Transport House and what little he published himself is entirely non-political. This is not necessarily, however, the end of the story. He was a man who spent much of his working life in promoting Shell as a responsible, national institution of expertise and service to the community, rather than as an ordinary profit-oriented oil company. In fact he built up such an image for Shell, partly through the Shell Film Unit which spent a lot of Shell's profits (in sum rather than in proportion of its gigantic profits, that is) on making films about marine life or indeed about any other worthy subject under the sun with the only 'advertising' being a discreet credit 'Shell Film Unit' over its famous sea shell emblem. If would thus be inconceivable if Beddington did not himself have a corporatist mentality. It was a mentality shared by the people of the Documentary Movement. It was therefore natural that Beddington would get on particularly easily with documentary film-makers who, as a rule, were also socially and educationally of his own class and background, unlike the much more mixed, brash, *nouveau riche* entrepreneurial characters of Wardour Street.

To remedy his utter inexperience with the commercial cinema, Beddington was teamed up with Sydney Bernstein, who was in effect his second in command although the managerial side of the job was run by Beddington himself.[14] Bernstein was everything that Beddington was not: a self-made entrepreneur from an East-End background who built up a large chain of cinemas (the Granada chain) and who knew the sharp world of the film distribution trade inside out – and who was also interested in getting involved in film production if and when an opportunity presented itself.

It might be expected that Sydney Bernstein would balance Beddington's antagonistic inclinations towards the aggressively private-enterprise, entrepreneurial and indeed capitalistic mentality of the commercial cinema world. But, the later Lord Bernstein was one of that curious breed, like others of a similar background, such as Lord Kagan and Robert Maxwell (and, in earlier days, Isidore Ostrer himself):[15] that is a socialist millionaire, or – before his Granada Television made him one in fact – a socialist millionaire in the making. Bernstein was a dedicated member of the Labour party, a chief financial supporter of it, an articulate and politically passionately committed man of the Left and, later, a member of its inner councils.

It was thus not surprising that, although the Parliamentary Select Committee on National Expenditure recommended in 1940, the discarding of the employment of Documentary films (and film-makers) by the Films Divison and the scrapping of their cherished 'non-theatrical distribution' scheme in favour of concentrating the funds given to the Films Division on commercial-type film productions and on the also commercial newsreels,[16] the Films Division under Beddington and Bernstein avoided compliance with these recommendations. Although, tactfully, only two of the well-known members of the Documentary Movement were formally employed in Mallet Street itself by the Films Division – Sir Arthur Elton as Head of Production and Thomas Baird in charge of non-theatrical distribution and, later, other posts – 74 per cent of all films produced by or commissioned by the Films Division for distribution inside Britain between August 1940 (when the Select Committee's recommendations were made) and the end of the war, were either written, directed or produced (or all three) by members of the Documentary Film Movement.

The views of the Documentary Film Movement are so well known that it is unnecessary to repeat them here at length. They were certainly not a completely single-minded group politically – but the spectrum of their views was not very wide. It ranged from the committedly and knowledgeably 'pure' Marxism of Ralph Bond and the somewhat more esoteric 1930s-Cambridge-undergraduate-style Marxism of Basil Wright on the Left, to the elitist, étatist, social-reform ideals of Sir Arthur Elton and Edgar Anstey which would nowadays be associated with the Social Democratic Party.[17] It may have been a spectrum, but it certainly excluded all shades of blue. Moreover, the reality and potential depth of the difference between the Marxists and the 'Social Democrats' was largely obscured during the exciting and anticipatory years of the Labour Movement during the war. It was a period when Sir Stafford Cripps and Ernest Bevin would contentedly work together in the coalition government and indeed came to hold the two highest offices – that of Foreign Secretary and Exchequer – in the Labour government, despite the expulsion of the former from the Labour Party for being a revolutionary Marxist Socialist in 1938. The differences, small as they were or appeared to be within the Left (and therefore among members of the Documentary Movement), during the war were further minimised by the fact that as people they were about the same age, had known each other closely for many years and shared a youthful devotion to John Grierson, who had played the guru to them with amazing force and success. Here therefore, was, a natural proximity of political outlook and personal contact as well as a temporary glossing-over of ideological differences which led to remarkably cohesive and integrated propaganda by the members of the Documentary Movement.

How did Beddington and Bernstein get away with the fact that 74 per cent of film production paid for by a Ministry which was supposed to be particularly 'non-partisan' in a period of informal 'Party truce' and which was under Conservative ministers in a Coalition government, was in fact made by a committedly single-party and partisan group of film-makers? Basically, it was done by a skilful exploitation of the administrative weaknesses of any large organisation, aided by some particular factors relating to film itself. The Ministry of Information was a huge, bloated organisation engaged in a multitude of tasks. Its first and most vital function was the control of the news and information which were to reach the public. Censorship for security and morale was a mammoth job, politically and militarily sensitive and indeed crucially important. It was carried out on a virtually 24–hours routine which also involved constant and high-speed decision-making amidst the fast-flowing and ever-changing conditions of global warfare. Its second main function was the production of news: getting information out of the Service Departments, the Ministry of Home Security (air raids) and the Foreign Office, and then the augmentation of such basic information with follow-up, 'human interest' and interpretative materials for feeding the voracious needs of a public accustomed to a vast flow of 'news'. It also had to, very importantly, monitor public opinion. None of these primary functions involved the Films Division directly, for film censorship was carried out by the Censorship Division itself in co-operation with the British Board of Film Censors. All the Production Divisions – ranging from Posters to the Films Division – were inevitably therefore much lower in the sights of the Minister and the top MOI officials than the Censorship/News/Intelligence Divisions engaged in their hectic daily and vital activities.

Provided, therefore, that the Films Division was efficiently run so that neither the Treasury auditors not the Administrative officers had occasion to call the ministerial eye upon it – including a sensible absence of too many of the wrong sort of names on its Establishment[18] and provided that it could present a reasonable list of completed productions, showing that it was active and effective, with sensibly relevant-sounding synopses, and produced at fair intervals a film which was successful and well-received in the *general* cinemas (such as *Desert Victory* or *Western Approaches*) nobody would much enquire into its 'non-theatrical' documentary films. Such films were understood in any case to be rather 'arty' and 'precious' films beloved by the intelligentsia – and, like the intelligentsia itself, both a bit 'lefty' and harmlessly inconsequential. The dismissal of the Films Division's work as 'a nice little flash in the cultural pan' by Ian MacLain in his monograph on the Ministry of Information, based on the perspective given by the papers of the central political and administrative leadership of the Ministry, is most revealing. So is the fact that there is no chapter or section dealing with it at all in the book.[19] Equally revealing, if anything more so, is the fact that M.L.G. Balfour, who himself had been a member of the top echelon (Secretary of the Policy Committee) before he moved to work at high level in the Political Warfare Executive and who ended his propaganda career directing the 'political re-education of Germany' after 1945, also has nothing to say about the Films Division's activities during the war, in his own massive and scholarly book.

Beddington was well experienced in these ways of huge organisations; for him, as Director for Publicity for Shell, exactly the same considerations applied concerning how he spent whatever budget the Board gave him and which in fact allowed him to play patron to artists and film-makers in the 1930s.

The nature of the medium itself contributed to this happy state of affairs for the 'documentary boys'. Since cinemas open just when MPs get down to the parliamentary day – and when newspapers are in the busiest period of *their* daily routine – both politicians and journalists tend to be, in any case, quite unaware of what is in the cinemas, particularly in the run-of-the-mill working-class picture houses. In 1936 Neville Chamberlain did not know whether to be pleased or not when at a social gathering someone told him that on the screen he looked like Groucho Marx for he had never as much as heard of the Marx Brothers and had to make quick enquiries: the results of which he then reported to his sister Hilda.[20] As late as September 1943 a leading journalist, Joan Lester, wrote the following piece for her regular column.

> One section of film fare is rarely mentioned in columns such as this . . . this week I made it my business to see a current newsreel and had a surprise. As a journalist I earnestly believe that news is news and a matter for straight and accurate reporting . . . Here

> were remarkable and most interesting pictures of the work of the allied bombers. With them was a commentary to tell us that this was the second front in Europe, that it was not only crippling enemy war industry but holding down Nazi forces in Europe . . . hardly unbiased reporting I think you will agree . . . I think this is a matter for official attention . . .

Evidently she had not seen newsreels before! Interestingly, the piece did not strike the sub-editor of *Reynold's News*[21] either as manifestly containing nothing new for the people who bought the paper. It was therefore not surprising that neither the press nor the politicians were able to 'pick up' trends in films. And, of course, it is never what a single picture actually says, but rather what repeated exposure to regular sets of stereotypes and arguments can do that matters. As for them becoming aware of what was being shown not in cinemas within walking distance of the Houses of Parliament, but in factory canteens and the like the 'non-theatrical circus', there the chances of political detection were virtually *nil*.

The normally very efficient monitoring service of the Research Department of the Conservative Party's Central Office, which before the war kept a very close eye indeed on both the cinemas and the BBC, was for all practical purposes shut down at the beginning of the war. Chamberlain, confident and decently naïve as ever, agreed that its members might go to join the forces. Churchill had little interest in Party matters, let alone Party organisation, amidst the more congenial and exhilarating activities of being both Prime Minister and Generalissimo. Such complaints as were made by Conservatives relating to films in the cinemas therefore tended to come, naturally, from retired people, the archetypal retired major or colonel, whose views could therefore be dismissed as such.[22]

To insiders who both understood how film-propaganda actually operated and had the time and opportunity to watch what was being done, there was of course no mystery as to what was going on – but people with two such necessary qualifications were very rare indeed between 1939 and 1945. One such person however, was, Neville Kearney – a former Foreign Office News Department man turned Public Relations Officer for the Federation of British Industry before the war and head of the British Council's own Films Department since 1939. He had the further advantage of having personally known and watched the Documentary Film Movement's career all through the 1930s in his capacity as PRO for the

Federation of British Industry. Writing to a colleague in the Foreign Office in December 1940 about the changes and developments in the Ministry of Information, he observed:

> We seem to have a boxed compass or a complete cycle – 'Documentary Boys' controlling the the issue at the Ministry of Information, with their prototypes ranging far and wide . . . One cannot avoid the suspicion that the ultimate object is eventually to centralise in the hands of one body – i.e. Film Centre 'Documentary Boys' – the whole influence of films in the reordering of things social both during the war and when it comes to an end . . . the Films Division of the Ministry of Information itself is now largely composed of the same 'Documentary Boys', their satellites being selected to produce or direct all Ministry films or despatched to one place or another as advisers . . . it is ingenious, but seems to me all wrong. It also appears a little sinister.[23]

Two years later he wrote to Phillip Guedella:

> The 'Documentary Boys' are in clover . . . Those inside and those outside in the Ministry go into a huddle and think of every conceivable subject about which a film could be made – and then those inside proceed to get authority and dish out the films to those outside! It is a wonderful system.[24]

As for the Documentarists' own view that was summed up by Basil Wright, who, although not a member of the staff of the MOI until January 1945, directed, produced or scripted no less than 42 MOI films during the war:

> I believe absolutely that the revolutionary technique is now the only technique. Whether you like it or not we are undergoing a world social revolution here and now, and it is a revolution which must continue with increasing strength. For that is the only thing the people of Britain are fighting for. It is today the job of the documentary to integrate the immediate war effort with the facts and implications of radical social and economic changes which are part and parcel of it . . . [Then, turning to the future he concluded] Our films must be the shock-troops of propaganda. It is no longer policy to compromise with timidity – either amongst ourselves or in others.[25]

The films themselves followed a regular pattern. They began with the presentation of some wartime documentary actuality, shipbuilding at Tyneside,[26] the establishment of Pit Production Committees in the mines,[27] life in Wales/Ulster/Scotland[28] in war conditions, the working of various wartime social agencies[29] or of some particular group of people's activities such as an Air Raid Post[30] or a typical group of young people.[31] Thereafter came an emotive recapitulation of the 'dreadful conditions' of the pre-war years (sometimes with specific reference to broken World War I promises), of unemployed men contrasted with a host of urgent jobs which apparently could not be carried out for lack of money, such as better housing, hospitals, schools and so forth. Then a picture of how in wartime conditions it was apparently possible to find the resources for thousands of aeroplanes, tanks, ships etc. as well as for all sorts of social improvements *because* everyone was now employed and the human and financial resources of the country had been mobilised and organised. From which followed a two-stage argument. First, that it was 'manifestly' untrue that the country did not have vast resources, provided the government organised and mobilised those resources as opposed to leaving it to inefficient private industry and a private enterprise economy. Secondly, that if people do not want the same dreadful conditions to return they must make sure themselves that their wishes are carried out: sometimes this was presented in the form of telling the audience to use the power of its vote (tactfully without mentioning how) and sometimes in the form of presenting working-class activism and the threat of militancy as the methods for ensuring the creation of a fully planned economy. In the 1941/2 period the films emphasised 'the pre-war conditions *shall* never return' theme with vague threats of 'the people' this time not allowing Britain to go back to pre-war ways. From 1943 courage and openness increased and they increasingly spelt out not only the fully planned economy but the 'Vote For It' and 'be prepared to fight for it' argument as well.

Like all good propaganda, it thrived on repetition, both in its verbal and visual components, which makes extensive quotation from the soundtracks tedious and unnecessary. Perhaps the stylistically most arresting example of the 'never again' part of the argument though entirely typical in content, may be found in *Wales – Green Hill, Black Mountain*. Coming, as always, at the end of a film describing the scenery and lifestyles of different parts of Wales in wartime (*that* being what its official synopsis-scenario actually described it as) it concludes thus:

> The valleys grew rich but all the time the power and wealth of the world was rocking – rocking. Then days came when the pits stopped, the factories closed their gates, the furnaces died out, and the great sheet of smoke that floated over industrial Wales came down like blinds over the blind windows of the mean streets, came draping down over the houses without hope, the locked shop and the leaking roofs. At the corners lolled the old young men or they walked their thin whippets over the dirty grass or scrabbled on the tips for fishtails of coal.
>
> Remember the procession of the old young men,
> From dole queue to corner and back again.
> From the pinched back street to the peak of slag,
> In the bite of the winter and with a shovel and pack.
> With a droopey fag and a turned back collar,
> Stamping for the cold on the ill-lit corner.
> Dragging through the squalor with their hearts like lead,
> Staring at the hunger and the shut pit head.
> Nothing in their pockets, nothing home to eat,
> Lagging from the slag heap to the pinched back street.
> Remember the procession of the old young men,
> It shall never happen again.
>
> IT MUST NOT HAPPEN AGAIN. Already new industries are on their way to Wales. For the Rhonda Valley the Treforest Industrial Estate is one shape of Wales to come. Out of the sickening, deadening idleness must come the pride of LABOUR AGAIN. Out of the huddle of slum and valley must come the clean broad roads and the clean white houses.
>
> Britain at war asked these once denied, helpless and hopeless men, for all their strength and skill at the coal face and the dock side, at the foundry. So the world shall know their answer and the world shall never deny them again. [End-captions over soaring sound of Welsh choir.]

The flowing poetry worthy of Mayakovsky at Agitprop was appropriate style for Welshmen. Different tones were employed for different regions and traditions. For the North East (*Tyneside*

Story) a grittily prosaic monologue in dialect was delivered to the camera by 'a worker', complete with cloth cap and menacing pose and filmed from a low angle, which gave the conclusion of the film, nominally about the re-opening of a shipyard closed by the depression, as if it was an answer to the concluding line of the 'official' commentary itself: 'As long as Britain calls for ships the call will be answered by the ring of steel on steel in the shipyards of the Tyneside' ('worker' in camera).

> Aye, but wait a minute, Tyneside is busy enough today, old uns and young uns hard at work makin' good ships, but just remember what the yards looked like five years ago: idle, empty, some of 'em derelict, and the skilled men that worked in them scattered and forgotten. Will it be the same again five years from now?

For farm workers (*The Harvest Shall Come*) a fictional character, Tom Grimwood, was used. The Central Film Library Catalogue's description of the film encapsulates its format:

> The story of neglect and decay, relieved only during 1914–1918, and again today under the stress of war . . . Tom Grimwood . . . is typical of farm workers and of all workers, who expect that in the new world they are now fighting for all men everywhere shall have food and a job.[32]

Another variant was the 'discussion group' format. Perhaps the best example of this variety was *They Speak for Themselves*, in which an 'enquiry' was made into 'what young people think and feel in wartime'. (They were in fact actors.) The 'debate' worked its way around to deciding that their future is in their own hands as voters and that there is no need to be frightened of the word 'socialist'.

These kind of films belonged to the first half of the propaganda campaign. They prepared the ground. From mid–1943 onwards the campaign moved on to the second point: *how* a fully planned economy would be able to produce all that which was desired. In *Power for the Highlands*, for example, two soldiers of the famous 51st Highland Division, an engineer and a gillie, discussed the recent setting up of the North of Scotland Hydro Electric Board; a scheme planned back in the 1920s but shelved because of the economic crisis, but for which now, in the midst of the war with all the other thousandfold higher expenses, the money could nevertheless be found! Two American soldiers then join the discussion and sing the praises of the Tennessee Valley Authority. The lesson of it all was the limitlessness of the scope for public investment. In *Manpower* the recipe for the future was then presented in the planned use of labour. This film was also a good example of the use of simplification on the Hitlerian pattern. Portraying how it takes seven men and women working as civilians to make the weapons and equipment for one fighting man, the film tells the viewers, first, that 'manpower planning' in England during the war had achieved the highest productivity in the world. 'Manpower planning', it then proceeds to say, will therefore be able to produce the same massively wonderful results when concentrated on 'the urgent tasks of reconstruction' and, of course, it will completely abolish unemployment, as it did in wartime. Being a professionally made, skilfully cut film, all this appears to make powerful good sense especially to the viewer caught up in the wish-fulfilment atmosphere of the film-show: such is the power of the cinema! There was, of course, no mention of the fact that the full employment of wartime involved some four million people being 'employed' in His Majesty's Forces at rates scarcely better than the dole. Nor was there any reference to the possibility of problems arising out of what was in fact to be industrial conscription – which had been made possible in wartime only as a result of the suspension of basic *Trades Union* rights – such as protection from 'transfer of labour', the uprooting of worker and family or, from 'dilution of labour', the use of semi-skilled and unskilled people to do the job of men proud of their skilled status. No mention, naturally, was made of the fact that working men and women inside and outside the Trades Union movement had fought precisely against such practices and the right to be free from them for a century.

A constantly used allusive theme, which first occurred in 1942 in Paul Rotha's films and which he articulated with particular panache and developed into a slogan, though it was also a part of the others' work from 1943 onward, presented the following line of persuasion:

> We have learned how to turn out planes by the thousand and tanks, guns, shells, rifles, torpedoes, ships . . . and the machinery for the making of them . . . we have an equal capacity to turn out goods needed for a better way of living . . . If you

> could produce planes you can produce houses. That's logical. In war we got used to handle orders for millions of rifles, bombs and shells, so why should anybody jump out his skin at an order for so many millions of kitchens . . . But where is you guarantee of sustained demand? Without that nobody will place your order . . . Who ordered the guns and planes even though the demand could not last for more than a few years? Yes – *you know* who it was : *His Majesty's Government*. And those shells and rifles were not shoddy stuff, they were intricate, complex machinery, yet millions were made by half skilled and unskilled hands. These things have become possible in war. They are still more possible in peace . . . We have got the same machines and we know the new methods, so we can do it again for new housing . . . and this time we ARE going to do it right . . . It isn't only houses we want, it is whole neighbourhoods you understand : we'll need schools . . . health centres, clinics, libraries, nurseries, parks, theatres – the whole bag of tricks designed and carried out to a *proper plan*. We *know* how to do it – *and we are going to do it*! . . . It's ALL got to be done according to a Plan . . . What you are asking for, is a full Planned Economy. It is . . . Are you still wondering if we can afford it? You did not stop to wonder back in 1940 when the Nazis had one foot in the door . . .

This particular part of the 'argument', quoted here in its final, spring-of-1945 form, from what is probably Rotha's most definitive film, *The Land of Promise*, was plugged especially consistently, repetitively and in an emotive/simplified form in a series films made for exhibition in munition factories and other 'war-industries' from May 1942 onward, called *Worker and Warfront* which was produced by Paul Rotha Productions. Even by Documentary Film Movement standards, Rotha was a radical and this series was marked by some really hard-line propaganda making extensive use of Soviet propaganda film material; on one occasion actually explaining that the workers enjoyed truer freedom in the Soviet Union than in Britain.[33] It not only pushed the concept of 'proletkult' but also laid heavy emphasis on the importance of cadres coming along from the working class.[34] But, essentially, it stuck to the central argument that what is needed is a great central planning authority of experts replacing all the useless middle men of the private enterprise/ commercial/capitalist system.

Another component part of the campaign was directly electoral.

For example there was *New Towns for Old*, where a visitor from the south is taken on a tour of 'Smokedale' (in fact largely Sheffield). The visitor is given a run through of the usual warming-up process of 'ghastly conditions as the inheritance of the past' and his guide tells him that the whole of the residential part of the town must be moved far away from industry. The visitor, whose role is that of the straight man, asks that 'surely you cannot move a whole town?' whereupon he is told that some of that had already been done before the war because 'we have elected a new council, see' and then he is shown some of the new council-housing estates and blocks of flats. The (Labour) City Father who is taking the visitor round then explains all the plans for rebuilding 'Smokedale' on the same pattern a hundred times over. The film then concludes:

> Councillor: When this war is over we have got to rebuild all our big towns – all our big towns, like this.
> Visitor: At least you have plans for your town alright. But who is going to see that they don't stay just plans? Who is going to make them come true?
> Councillor: They are. You are. [Workers in vision.] You are the only folk who can make come true not only plans for this town but for every town – YOUR TOWN.

Town-planning was a particularly happy subject upon which propaganda for a fully planned economy and a fully planned society could be based. It was the one form of 'planning' which people had already come across: and it was one which, at least in this period still, had an unsullied reputation for making things better. Thus an endless procession of serious, bespectacled, pipe-smoking gentlemen were presented to the public surrounded by the paraphernalia of planning, with assistants in white coats sitting at drawing boards. In measured tones they explained that everything which was wrong with housing, living conditions, schools, location of industrial/commercial areas versus residential areas was due to towns growing up haphazardly with buildings being erected by 'speculators' of one kind or another. Pipe stems (much more humane than pointers) waved away whole districts of towns as being below par and then moved to large architectural models of buildings, districts, even whole towns. For the historian today these films call for an effort of historical empathy, when being shown in model form as the New Jerusalem, some of the glaringly obvious and dreadful post-war mistakes in town planning including several of the very blocks of flats which were blown up as uninhabitable a mere ten or twelve years after they had been completed, accompanied by the very arguments which have since become by-words for many of things which have gone wrong in Britain after the war. Yet one must remember that in 1944 all this amounted to a powerful case, at least through the simplifying nature and imaginative magic of the cinema, for placing the organisation of the whole country in similar hands, in a planned society.[35] Students today burst into spontaneous laughter when, for example, the GLC architect airily mentions in passing, that, of course, 'Many railway stations in London and the railway lines leading to them would be put underground' – without, naturally, making reference to the unimaginable sum of money and dislocation involved (*Proud city*). The reaction is the same when viewing films which emphasise that 'the planners' do consult 'the people', for the consultation process consists of explaining with long-suffering patience to 'ordinary people' – who are shown standing in front of a model of a post-war London with speechless wonderment – what is *going to be done* to their city! (*The People and the Plan.*)

Running through, as perhaps the most direct point of all these films for a planned economy and a planned society, is the theme of this 'vanguard party'. An intellectual leadership of 'planners and experts' backed by politicised working-class activists who will support and fight for them but who of course will take the lead from them. It is a hierarchy of reason in which there is no room for individual choice, taste or idiosyncracy. It is also totally stereotyped: there are 'the workers' who are identified only by their occupation: '*You were a plater, you were a corker, you were a burner . . .*' (and then as a result of the bad old days you got your own shop, you drove a baker's van or became an ice cream man, etc . . .) but come the new world: '*All you skilled MEN are needed in the yard again*' (*Tyneside Story*). You *will* return from being an individual making out for yourself and you will once again become 'a plater'.

As the end of the war, and the election, was coming closer, the propaganda arguments for a planned society and a planned economy were increasingly repeated and driven home by another interesting and ingenious device. Key visual/aural images from films, going back three or four years, were used as stock shots: as cueing devices in new films. For example, the litany '*Remember the procession of the old young men . . .*' had come to its visual crescendo by a shot of a large factory gate being slowly closed in *Wales – Green Hills, Black Mountain*. The words were unforgettable, and therefore the visual image which was associated with it also became so. That shot was now thrown in in film after film, cut increasingly shorter and shorter, as an evocative device for recalling the 'procession of the old young men' and what it stood for. In the same way every film which touched upon mining or miners, or indeed in general on the unemployment of the 1930s, used the shot of a couple of men with sacks in their hands standing at the side of a slag heap under billowing clouds of dust as the conveyor threw over them the stones, the dust and the small pieces of coal for which they were grubbing. In fact that shot used in *Wales – Green Hill, Black Mountain* was already a cueing device there, for it in fact went back to 1936 and had already been used in that way as a visual slogan by the Documentary Movement – even before the beginning of the war. Similarly, the little 'working-class lad', standing in front of the fireplace expounding on socialism in *They Speak for Themselves*, also kept coming back as the image of the 'conscious', proletarian youth – and of the argument of the humanity of socialism. A beautifully shot sequence about the assembling of a Lancaster bomber's fusillage in *Our Film* showing large lattice-work panels being intricately fitted together by women and apprentices became a standard cueing device, appearing in practically every one of these films in 1944 and early 1945, for the argument 'if they could build Spitfire bombers, delicate intricate mechanisms by thousands . . . why not hospitals, schools . . . ?' Whole long sequences of films were constructed entirely from cutting together these slogan-images for recalling in the minds of the audience what has already been input and stereotyped into them earlier – and then proceeding just to add the particular point, application, of that particular film. It was the use of these standardised, stereotyped components of memory fragments/analogy propaganda and the fact that they were used by *all* of the documentary film makers in their films – irrespective of whether it was an in-house or commissioned 'production of the MOI' or whether the film had nominally been only bought and distributed by the MOI – which shows more clearly than anything else how closely integrated the operation of this group was.

The distribution of these films, and the audience figures reached by them, is very difficult to establish. The Films Division made very high claims: one and a half million a week or, in another form, 13–

14 million in a year. As an annual estimate that is clearly excessive. As I have argued elsewhere[36] all work which has been done on the penetration of the non-theatrical film propaganda of the MOI, including my own, shows that as a short-term specific campaign-oriented device the non-theatrical distribution scheme was just as ineffective for wartime needs as the Select Committee on National Expenditure judged it to be in 1940. As far as the war effort was concerned, the country could have dispensed with the whole lot without an iota of difference. The real propaganda *war* was carried out in the commercial cinemas and by the newsreels, not in any significant way by the documentary film.

But, as a long-term conditioning propaganda, these figures may in fact tell a very different story. Coming to factories, working-men's institutes, church halls, adult-education classes and the like at regular intervals of every five weeks or so, and thus being projected not in an entertainment context but in a context designed to lead to 'structured discussion' afterwards (for they were accompanied by MOI lecturers drawn from the Left wing of the intelligentsia), it was in fact a classic Soviet-type, Agitprop operation. In that light the figures of attendance, which amount to about one and a half million for each *cycle*, may very well have significantly raised 'political consciousness' and helped to politicise a 'cadre' section of the working class and in particular its self-taught functionary-intelligentsia.

It was indeed a neat operation which had been, as Kearney had called it, 'ingenious and a little sinister'. After the end of the war, and with the Conservatives in the opposition, what had been so skilfully done during the war came to be recognised. Lord Boothby encapsulated that in his famous quip : The M.O.I. did not win the war, but it certainly won the election for Labour. It gave a firm resolve to the Conservatives to abolish the Crown Film Unit whenever they were to return to power, especially since the Labour government had not only retained it in existence but, now under Basil Wright, used it for much the same purposes.

It was also a game, though, at which two could play. It was through the cinema screens that the quintessential case against the 'planned society' was first put after the war, by Brendan Bracken's and Alex Korda's protegés from the days of Sir Joseph Ball onward, Pressburger and Powell. They had been commissioned by the MOI at the end of the war to make a film, a prestige production with money no object, which would help with Anglo-American relations by portraying our common ideals and such like. The funds provided came close to the cost of the whole Documentary campaign. They produced *A Matter of Life and Death*, in which there is portrayed two contrasting worlds: an untidy, messy, Earth on which little individuals are scurrying about blindly doing their own thing. Above Earth is Heaven : a perfectly organised, planned society conducted by superior intelligences. Earth and the doings of its infuriating, eccentric individuals which keep messing up the excellent schemes of their superiors in Heaven, was filmed in gorgeous colour – Heaven, and all its rational splendour, in grey monochrome . . .[37]

Appendix 2.1

Principal films dealing with peace-aims produced by the MOI or bought and distributed by the MOI 1940–5.

1940 *Health in War* – Harry Watt
Neighbours Under Fire – Ralph Bond and Basil Wright
The New Britain – Alexander Shaw

1941 *Dawn Guard* – Boulton Bros.
Post 23 – Donald Taylor, Ralph Bond
Scotland Speaks – Alexander Shaw
Wealth of a Nation – Donald Taylor (1938, re–dist. 1941 onward)

1942 *The Londoners* – Basil Wright
Mobile Engineers – Donald Taylor
Essential Jobs – Paul Rotha
The Great Harvest – Paul Rotha
New Towns For Old – Alexander Shaw
They Speak for Themselves – Paul Rotha
When We Build Again – Ralph Bond

1943 *The Harvest Shall Come* – Basil Wright
Our Film – 'Made and Financed by the Workers of Denham Studios'
The Crown of the Year – Edgar Anstey and Ralph Keene
Tyneside Story – Michael Hankinson and The People's Theatre Company
World of Plenty – Paul Rotha
Power for the Highlands – Paul Rotha
Wales – Green Mountain, Black Mountain – Donald Taylor

1944 *Manpower* – Alexander Shaw
Words And Actions – John Taylor

	Coalminer – Basil Wright
	Good Health to Scotland – S. Russel
	Highland Doctor – Paul Rotha
1945	*A City Reborn* – Donald Taylor
	Cotswold Club – Edgar Anstey and Donald Taylor
	Fuel For Battle – Donald Taylor
	New Builders – Paul Rotha
	The New Crop – Edgar Anstey
	The Plan and the People – John Taylor
	Proud City – Edgar Anstey
	Public Opinion – Sidney Box
	Teaching – Michael Hankinson
	Total War In Britain – Paul Rotha
1942–5	*Worker and Warfront* (for people in war-industries) 18 issues – Paul Rotha

Appendix 2.2

List of all those who were employed to produce, direct or write the script for ten or more films (excluding 'Trailers'), commissioned by, produced by or bought and distributed by the Ministry of Information in World War II.

Number of films	Names	
76	* Edgar Anstey	
53	* Paul Rotha	(Including 18 issues of *Worker and Warfront*)
47	* John Taylor	
43	* Andrew Buchanon	
42	* Basil Wright	
39	* Alexander Shaw	
35	* Donald Taylor	
32	Henry Cooper	
32	Gerald Sanger	(Newsreel compilations)
27	* Michael Hankinson	
25	Ian Dalrymple	
21	* Arthur Elton	
21	* Humphrey Jennings	
21	Sydney Box	
18	* Ralph Keene	
17	* Ralph Bond	
15	* John Eldridge	
15	Mary Field	
15	* Frank Sainsbury	
15	Margaret Thomson	

15	* Harry Watt	
14	James Carr	
14	J. Gardner Lewis	
13	* Gilbert Gunn	
12	G.T. Cummins	
12	Maxwell Munden	
12	* Hans Nieter	
11	* Donald Alexander	
11	Henry Cass	
11	Eugene Cekalski	(Polish Film Unit)
11	Francis Searle	
10	Michael Balcon	

Note: * Denotes member of the Documentary Movement. Where the same person both produced and directed and/or scripted a film it is counted as one only. Normally, a film had a separate Producer, Director and Scriptwriter.
Source: Frances Thorpe and Nicholas Pronay, *British Official Films in the Second World War* (Oxford, 1981).

Notes

1. This point is generally made in most accounts of Churchill's wartime premiership: for a treatment also linking Churchill's experiences during his long previous career and personality traits, see Ronald Lewin, *Churchill as War Lord* (London, 1973).

2. For a particularly well-documented and perceptive discussion of this frame of mind and its consequences for the politics of the inter-war and World-War II period see Keith Middlemas, *Politics in Industrial Society: the Experience of the British System since 1911* (London, 1977).

3. Randolp S. Churchill (ed.), *Into Battle: Speeches by the Rt. Hon. Winston S. Churchill, PC, MP* (London, 1941), p. 208.

4. Paul Addison, *The Road to 1945: British Politics and the Second World War* (London, 1977 edn), p. 126.

5. One of the more concerted efforts to push Churchill into formulating peace aims was made by the **MOI** under Duff Cooper and Harold Nicholson which got as far as several formal drafts of 'peace aims' being mulled over by all the members of the cabinet. For its fate see: Nigel Nicolson (ed.), *Harold Nicolson: Diaries and Letters 1939–45* (London, 1967), pp. 102–3, 126, 130.

6. Addison, *The Road to 1945*, p. 126.

7. The principal victims of this treatment included Arthur Greenwood and Lord Reith. See Reith's own bitter account: 'Planning in Vacuo' *et seq*. in J.C.W. Reith, *Into the Wind* (London, 1949)

8. For details and bibliographical references to the censorship and political control of the cinema in Britain during the inter-war years, see N. Pronay, 'The First Reality – Film Censorship in Liberal Britain' in K.R.M. Short (ed.), *Feature Films as History* (London, 1981).

9. For a balanced discussion of the unhappy and unintentionally farcical history of the **MOI** during the first period of the war see Ian MacLaine, *The Ministry of Morale* (London, 1979), Ch. 2.

10. For details see N. Pronay, 'The News Media at War' in N. Pronay and D.W. Spring, *Propaganda, Politics and Film 1918–1945*, (London, 1982).

11. For Sir Joseph Ball's career and his work with Chamberlain in Conservative Central Office, see T.J. Hollins, *The Presentation of Politics – the Place of Party Publicity, Broadcasting and Film in British Politics, 1918–1939*, Unpublished PhD thesis, Leeds University, 1981.

12. For an account of the history of the Films Division of the **MOI**, and for the circumstances and the personalities involved in the removal of Sir Joseph Ball and the replacement of virtually the whole of its staff, see F. Thorpe and N. Pronay, *British Official Films in World War Two: a Descriptive Catalogue* (Oxford, 1980).

13. Sidney Bernstein was Films Adviser to the MOI from 1940 to 1945: he also handled, amongst other things, the particularly tricky problems of liaison with the US film trade in Washington and then represented the Films Division on the Psychological Warfare Section of the Supreme Headquarters Allied Expeditionary Forces in Europe.

14. Isidore Ostrer controlled Gaumont British studios and it was he who in 1935 formally, if secretly, agreed to place it at the service of the government. Before 1931, however, Isidore Ostrer was a dedicated supporter of the Labour Party. He followed Ramsay MacDonald into the National Government camp.

15. *XIIth Report of the Select Committee on National Expenditure*, (HMSO, 21 August 1940), p. 10.

16. A guide to the political views which the leading members of the Documentary Movement *actually* held during the war can be found in *Documentary Newsletter*, which was published by the Documentary Movement between 1940 and 1947 for restricted circulation.

17. Only Sir Arthur Elton and Thomas Baird were employed by the **MOI** in positions of authority, while amongst the staff producers of the Crown Film Unit only Harry Watt, the most a-political of the Documentary Movement's leading members and who effectively broke with Greirson because he was not willing to confine film-making to visual propaganda sheets and Humphrey Jennings, the poet and artist of the Movement, were on the official pay-roll.

18. MacLaine, *The Ministry of Morale*, p. 279.

19. M.L.G. Balfour, *Propaganda in War 1939–1945: Organisations, Policies and Publics in Britain and Germany* (London 1979).

20. Alan Beattie, D.N. Dilks and N. Pronay, *Neville Chamberlain*, Inter University History Film Consortium, Archive Unit No. 1, (Leeds 1974), p. 11: 'Dorothy informs me that he is one of several Jew brothers who are familiar entertainers to film fans.'

21. *Reynolds News*, 3 March 1943.

22. Addison, *The Road to 1945*, pp. 133ff.

23. Kearney to Haigh, 2 December 1940, Public Record Office, Kew [*PRO*] BW63/2; quoted in Paul Swann, *The British Documentary Film Movement 1928–1945*, unpublished PhD. thesis, Leeds University, 1980, pp. 229–41.

24. Kearney to Guedella, 20 May 1942, *PRO* BW4/21; Swann, *ibid.*

25. 'Planning the Future', *Documentary Newsletter*, December 1942, quoted *British Film Yearbook 1946–1947* (London 1947), p. 71.

26. E.g. *Tyneside Story* (1943), co-produced by Michael Hankinson. The film was described at the time in the Catalogue of the Central Film Library: 'For years before the war shipyards with a long line of well-built ships to their credit lay derelict. The skilled men who knew how to build ships had found other jobs or been unemployed. Now they have been directed back into their yards. Women, too, have been trained to work in the yards. Today as the ships are launched the men ask what use will be found for their skills when the war ends?'

27. E.g. *Coalminer* (1944), produced by Basil Wright: CFL Catalogue description: 'At the outbreak of war Charlie Jones a Rhondda miner returned to the coal face at the age of 56 after 13 years out of work. In a talk with Arthur

Horner, President of the South Wales Miners' Federation, he discusses the miner's life, changed conditions in the pit and the part that Pit Production Committees can play in increasing output.'

28. E.g. *Wales – Green Mountain, Black Mountain* (1943), produced by Donald Taylor. CFL Catalogue description: 'Wales is a country of great contrast. On the green hills are the farms; in the valleys the black mining villages. Before the war, in many parts of Wales, young men waited in vain for work; now all who can work are working hard digging coal out of the rich mountains, rearing sheep on mountain slopes which new-sown grasses have made good pasture again. In town and village, in the mines, foundries and shipyards and on the farms, life throbs with work for all. Never again must there be young men with no work in derelict towns.' There was also a Welsh language version, *Ulster*, 1941/2, produced by Alexander Shaw.

29. *Highland Doctor* (1944), produced by Paul Rotha. CFL Catalogue description: 'Thirty years ago there were few doctors for the Highlands and Islands of Scotland. They could visit few patients because of the long distances and bad roads to be covered on foot, horse and by boat; and their fees were inevitably high. Doctor McWilliam recalls those days as he waits for the Air Ambulance which is to take a crofter's wife to a Glasgow hospital for a special operation. Today there are more doctors and nurses and they have cars; the roads have improved; the hospitals serving the district have been enlarged to receive patients brought in by ambulances; and the services are available at fees which people can afford. All this could only be achieved because the government initiated and subsidised the Highlands and Islands Medical Service.' *Power for the Highlands* (1943), produced by Paul Rotha.

30. E.G. *Post 23* (1941), produced by Donald Taylor. CFL Catalogue description: 'At their warden's post men and women get to know each other and the people living in their district. They see what they can do for each other in wartime and realise that the future will also depend on the co-operation of ordinary people like themselves.'

31. *They Speak for Themselves* (1942), produced by Paul Rotha. CFL Catalogue description: 'A report of a discussion by a group of young people of the war and the future for themselves in Britain.'

32. Central Film Library Catalogue for 1943, *Agriculture UK 383*.

33. *Worker and War Front*, No. 2 (July 1942).

34. See for example *Worker and War Front* No. 10, February 1944: 1. Ballet Rambert visits Midlands factory; 2. photographs for *British Ally* published in Moscow; 3. mechanics spend holiday at agricultural volunteer camp; 4. manufacture from paper of jettisonable fuel tanks for fighter aircraft.

35. See, in particular, *Proud City* (1945), produced by Edgar Anstey; *The Plan and the People* (1945), produced by John Taylor and *When We Build Again* (1942), produced by Ralph Bond.

36. Pronay 'The News Media at War'.

37. For a detailed discussion of *A Matter of Life and Death* see an article by John Ellis, 'Watching Death at Work: An Analysis of *A Matter of Life and Death*' in Ian Christie (ed.), *Powell, Pressburger and Others*, (London, 1978).

3 FRENCH FILM PROPAGANDA JULY 1939–JUNE 1940*

Rémy Pithon

Until the outbreak of World War II, France had no official propaganda organisation, although it had resorted to the weapons of propaganda during the Great European War of 1914–18.[1] Events in Eastern and Central Europe after the collapse of the Central Powers had convinced several leading French politicians that it would not be possible for France to remain aloof in the battle to win public opinion; and yet the inter-war governments of the Third Republic rejected the use of propaganda. Excepting the post of Minister for Propaganda given to Ludovic-Oscar Frossard in the three and a half weeks of the second Blum government (March to April 1938), the only official organisation created for something like propaganda activities during the 1930s was the *Service des Œuvres françaises à l'étranger*, a branch of the Ministry of Foreign Affairs. Concerned only with the diffusion of France's culture abroad, the intention was for the Service des Œuvres to protect France's reputation outside the country. It was not to spread ideas and there was no question of its addressing itself to the French nation.[2] It was not conceived of as an official organ of propaganda; moreover, the very term propaganda was banned. One section of the Service des Œuvres dealt, among other things, with the distribution and reception of French films abroad.

Facing the threat of the impending war with Nazi Germany, on 29 July 1939 Prime Minister Daladier issued a number of important decrees (the law on wartime national organisation dated from 11 July 1938); among other things he created a *Commissariat général à l'Information* (Department of Information) with poorly defined powers.[3] Its importance lay in its novelty; note also the cautious use of 'information', rather than 'propaganda' which the French governments associated with totalitarian government.

War broke out a month after Jean Giraudoux took office[4] as a director of the Commissariat général. Unexpectedly Giraudoux was given the daunting task of the organisation of information, in the widest sense of the term, for he was to control France's mass media, including its National Broadcasting, through censorship and the encouragement and the supervision of propaganda productions of every kind. Where censorship was concerned, the military had reserved itself extensive powers of intervention, amounting to encroachment of military authority on civil authority. This led to confusion over decisions and their application and it is often difficult to establish which body was responsible for a repressive measure. Archive documentation would perhaps help to clarify the problem, but many relevant records appear to have been destroyed during the war and verbal interventions leave no record.

This overlapping of responsibility goes some way to explain why the results of the Commissariat général à l'Information were so poor. But other points of weakness played a large part. It has often been said that Giraudoux was not equal to the situation, even though he had seriously discussed the position of France in Europe, in his book *Pleins pouvoirs* (written during the first half of 1939, but not published until December). His assessment was characterised by his xenophobia, as well as some questionable judgements concerning the strength and weakness of France compared to Nazi Germany.[5] Giraudoux's half-hearted and often incompetent staff faced with the confusion over authority and the lack of legal and practical power, failed to achieve anything more than incoherent improvisation. This well-known incapacity was denounced after 1940 by opponents of the regime and its policies,[6] more recently confirmed by several historians.[7] When Paul Reynaud succeeded Daladier, on 21 March 1940, he replaced the Commissariat général with a Ministry of Information, and called upon Frossard, to whom he granted additional powers and means. But little changed. Giraudoux was made Head of a High Council of Information which existed in theory only. After the ministerial reshuffle on 6 June 1940, Frossard was replaced by Jean Prouvost, industrialist and owner of the newspaper *Paris-Soir*, who hardly had time to move into his office before France fell. Prouvost remained in charge of propaganda in the first Petain government, but that does not concern the present study.

In August 1939 Giraudoux had recruited people he had known during his long stay in the Ministry of Foreign Affairs; in particular those who were to become involved with films. The Commissariat général's Service de Diffusion (service responsible for distribution) included several sections; printed matter, photography, radio and, of course, film. At the head of this section was a civil servant from the Service des Œuvres française à l'étranger, Yves Chataigneau. When he was mobilised in January 1940, he was replaced by Henry Torrès, a lawyer and cinema enthusiast. Both Chataigneau and Torrès were assisted by another ex-Foreign Affairs member of staff, Suzanne Borel, who guaranteed contact with the film press. Ludovic-Oscar Frossard and Jean Prouvost retained more or less the same teams at the Ministry of Information.[8]

The first important step of the Commissariat général had been to take charge of film censorship, until then entrusted to an *ad hoc* commission of the Ministry of Education and Fine Arts.[9] For several weeks after the opening of the war the distribution of films already in circulation was almost totally suspended, and many cinemas were temporarily closed down. Gradually they began to reopen, but many films were withdrawn by order as the Commissariat général published a list of the films banned for the duration of hostilities. Suzanne Borel explained to the press that the 60 or so French and foreign films withdrawn largely belonged to three undesirable groups – pacifist, coarse military humour (*comique troupier*) and 'depressing, morbid and immoral' films.[10] These included *La Bête humaine*, *Les Bas-fonds*, *Les Dégourdis de la 11e*, *Hôtel du Nord*, *Ignace*, *J'Accuse*, *Quai des brumes*, *The Big Parade*, *Kameradschaft* and *All Quiet on the Western Front*. Inconsistency already had begun to set in. It is hard to understand how the choice was made in each of these groups, or why some films were put back into circulation in February 1940, and others not.[11] In some cases various cuts and changes had to be made before re-release; for example the film *Le Déserteur* (*The Deserter*) which reappeared under the title *Je t' attendrai* (*I Will Be Waiting for You*). Other problems arose immediately after the cinemas began operating normally, in early November 1939. Completed films had to wait for their certificate; here again there was selection. Comedies were given priority, for example the extremely xenophobic film by Sacha Guitry, *Ils étaient Neuf Célibataires* was the first new film to appear on the screen after war began. A few nationalistic films appeared, and, even more surprisingly, a few films which were easily as depressing as those which had just been banned.[12] On the other hand, other films, either serious or comic, remained unseen for no apparent reason.

The most acute problem for the producers was continuing their work. A good many films were in the middle of shooting or preparation in September 1939. Mobilisation had deprived them of actors and technicians and unless the cinemas were to show only foreign films, it was essential to start up work again in France. During the so-called *drôle de guerre* or 'funny war',[13] films were showing to full houses, despite civil defence measures, and the major exhibitors did not want to be restricted to re-showing old films. The Cinema industry was thus united in asking Yves Chataigneau to obtain permission from the Army to complete the unfinished films.[14] These were often productions which would have fitted in extremely well in an intelligent propaganda campaign: *Tourelle 3* and *Remorques* highlighted the qualities of the French sailors; the former was never finished, the latter was not completed until June 1940. *Sidi-Brahim* depicted troops in the Alps guarding the Italian frontier, and although finished in Spring 1940, was shown only in 1945. *Macao* showed several dubious-looking Japanese characters embarking on the conquest of the Far East. The film was not finished and shown until after the Vichy government came into office. *De Mayerling à Sarajevo* was a highly critical view of Austria-Hungary before World War I, with obvious ulterior motives; Max Ophuls had considerable difficulty finishing the film, and it did not appear until May 1940. These are only a few of many examples. It seems clear that there was constant disagreement between the different ministerial departments, and that the requests from the Commissariat général à l'Information were not taken seriously, if ever they were presented.

When it came to making new films, which was obviously desirable, similar problems arose. Of course it was never considered that the State would take over private enterprise. But it could encourage it, and even, from early 1940 onwards, subsidise it; however, it did not. Production companies therefore had to take the risks and find the money and the staff without government assistance. Despite this 35 films (including three documentaries) were begun between November 1939 and May 1940.[15] The three documentaries and seven feature films, all comedies, were finished off quickly and distributed before the French collapse in June 1940. Of the remaining 25 films (five were never completed) there were 16 comedies. Entertaining people then was seen to be the main aim, with the serious side of things undoubtedly represented by the documentaries.

What was the theme for this wartime entertainment? In many cases there is no difference in either style or content between the comedies produced during the 'funny war' and those produced previously. For example between the first film begun after the declaration of war, *Le Roi des galéjeurs*, and *Un de la canebière* (1938) or between *Monsieur Hector* (the original title, *Le Nègre du Négresco*, is more revealing) and any other Fernandel film. But an even better example: *Bach en correctionnelle* goes back over earlier sketches of the same comedy actor. Of course the war comes up in these films, but is always treated lightly. Thus *Elles étaient douze femmes* only differs from the usual light theatrical entertainment or film in two ways: first the cast is exclusively female, because all the men have been mobilised, and secondly the gossiping, the arguments and reconciliations, concern a fairly unusual subject in such a fasionable circle, the creation of a 'Useless Parcels Fund for Soldiers'! In *Chantons quand même!*, a sort of musical comedy in imitation of the films of Charles Trénet, the usual roles of leading man and lady are replaced by a sergeant and a canteen woman, and the minor parts are an English soldier and a choir of Tommies. Here the war is nothing more than the setting for a few passing love affairs; it was a 1940 version of a gentleman's war, eighteenth-century style, not dissimilar from an Offenbach operetta. The same is true of *Ils étaient cinq permissionnaires*, begun in May 1940. Mobilisation even created a new dramatic situation, featured frequently in films, such as *Fausse alerte* with unexpected meetings and brief romances in air raid shelters.

Looking closely it can be even seen that in many cases the war and the mobilisation of the menfolk (husbands, fiancés, lovers) provides a chance variation on the classic vaudeville situation: the temporary absence of the husband, fiancé or lover. It is very curious however that when this absence could cause difficulties for the wife left alone, everything turns out for the best because, after all, there is nothing very serious about war. In *Faut ce qu'il faut* a woman finds herself and her child alone and with no income because the man she lived with and who was going to marry her had just left for the front. A devoted friend suggests a marriage of convenience which would make her eligible for state benefits, but fortunately an unexpected leave allows the father to return home for a few days and marry the woman he loves. At the same time, the friend finds his soul mate; and the two couples make friends with an English couple. The plot obviously reflects the times: the war is treated not as something disturbing, but just provides a convenient dramatic situation. One could even argue that in *La Fille du puisatier* (begun by Marcel Pagnol in May 1940 and only finished after the fall of the Third

Republic) everything must turn out alright because France lost the war.

Society gossip, vaudeville situations, young girls seduced and then married, illegitimate children finally acknowledged, romances on the front or back home – all this is hardly typical of cinema propaganda. It almost seems as though the Commissariat général à l'Information had no effect on cinema production. In fact its authorisation was sought and given for each of these films: the script was submitted to the censors prior to filming. In at least one case, it gave public approval. Ministers or generals often graced with their presence the premières of films considered to be of national importance. This was done for *L'Homme du Niger* in November 1939, for *Brazza, l'épopée du Congo* in January 1940, and also, at almost the same time, for *Chantons quand même!*, which was promoted implicitly as a film of great national importance.

Until now we have examined the censorship and authorisations carried out on films made by private individuals and companies. According to the government its Ministry for Information had a more important job to do than censorship of feature films and that was making or commissioning films. In this area, the military were much more efficient than civilians. Admittedly the military already possessed both the means and experience. The *Army Film Service*[16] was able either to make propaganda films, or to make available, to those companies interested, footage taken from the Army Film Service archives. In this way it was possible to make short- and medium-length films fairly quickly; for example *Alerte aux tropiques*, *Deux empires – une force*, *Front de mer*, *France, regarde ta marine* and also, on a less strictly military theme, *De la ferraille à l'acier victorieux*, to name but a few. The most important production of the Army Film Service was the weekly *Journal de guerre* begun at the end of September 1939. The idea was a highlight national activity and the action of the French forces. The editing and commentary appear clumsy in their obvious attemps to propagandise, but it was a question of fighting German propaganda, particularly in neutral countries. It was not an easy task, since the 'funny war' was providing nothing very spectacular. The *Journal de guerre* was only shown abroad and to soldiers on the front. The French civilian population, for some unknown reason, was only allowed to see it from March 1940 onwards. The most striking pictures are naturally those of the most important operations; those during the last week when the 'funny war' gave way to real war.

At the same time the Commissariat général à l'Information launched its *Magazine de la France en guerre* aimed at civilians, and especially at those in rural areas, unable to see the weekly cinema showings. The Magazine was a monthly summary of the newsreels shown each week in the cinemas, which of course first underwent civil and military censorship. Apparently there were three of these Magazines, which brought together the main propaganda themes constantly repeated in the newsreels: the responsibility of the Germans, the Anglo-French alliance, the national war effort, the success of the allies and so on. Additionally, the Commissariat général à l'Information had a major role in the making of several so-called documentaries; compilation films such as the explicitly-titled *De Lénine à Hitler* and *Eux et nous, vingt ans d'armistice*. But there were also films in which directors used professional actors to re-enact events in the history of the Third Reich: *Après 'mein Kampf', mes crimes* and *Hitler m'a dit*. The latter film was repudiated by Giraudoux, who was shocked by the ugly and brutal image given of the young Nazis; it remained unfinished.[17]

It was nothing new for documentaries to be given such government support, albeit unofficial. The same had been done for the film *La France est un empire*, selected for the Cannes Film Festival, and, slightly earlier, for the famous *Sommes-nous défendus?* It seems that the authorities did not realise that propaganda through the film could rest on anything other than authentic or reconstructed documentaries suitably edited and commentated. Pure fiction was obviously regarded as far less useful from this point of view, and the sole purpose of fiction films remained that of entertaining the public and keeping up the morale of the soldiers.

The only exception, or what seems at first glance to be an exception, is the film begun amid great publicity in Nice in 1940, *Untel père et fils*. Intended to be a hymn to eternal France, this work by Julien Duvivier was probably underwritten by the Commissariat général. It boasted a star-studded cast: Raimu, Louis Jouvet, Michèle Morgan, Suzy Prim, Fernand Ledoux, among others. Duvivier and his scriptwriters Marcel Achard and Charles Spaak had decided to depict the life of a French family over 70 years, and through them the history of France. The main events in the story of these imaginary people take place in a real historical setting, which required the reconstruction of several famous events: the Prussian siege of Paris, the construction of the Sacré-Cœur, the exploration of Equatorial Africa, the floating of the Russian loan, the air battles of 1918, the crisis of the 1930s, Munich, and finally, mobilisation. The ideological intentions are shown clearly by this choice, and underlined by various allusions, both visually and in the dialogue, to the rise of Nazism, the racial persecutions in Germany, the reception policy of France, the greatness of her achievements in the colonies, the radiance of her culture. These messages are expressed through different characters, each member of the family was chosen to embody France. Thus France's achievements in the colonies are represented by Jouvet in the last stages of alcoholism, dominated by a black housekeeper; painters of Montparnasse around 1910, dressed like characters from an operetta, represent the artistic radiance; the Sacré-Cœur, a well-known symbol of reactionary values, and the Moulin Rouge discovered by a horrified school teacher from the provinces, serve to assure the glory of Paris. At the end of the film the young doctor, who represents the fourth generation of the family, gets married before leaving for the front: he and his fiancée find themselves in the same situation as many other couples. The mayor delivers a speech in which he insists that it is time to finish off the Germans once and for all; the audience (the women dressed in white and the men in uniform) listens in silence. The next scene is in a church where the grandparents of the young doctor are praying for divine mercy on behalf of their grandson. This moving scene, coming immediately after a fervent appeal for war, neatly sums up *Untel père et fils*. The film was designed to glorify and defend France, but a France which was traditional (the very name of the family, Froment – wheat, suggests rural values), stereotyped, backward, clerical and timorous. Curious propaganda, indeed!

The message did not reach the French public in any case: as soon as the film was finished in June 1940, the negative was sent abroad in the nick of time. During the war, *Untel père et fils* was shown in English in Great Britain and the United States. It must have given a strange image of France, quite close, however, to that which Jean Renoir projected in his Hollywood film, *This Land is Mine* (RKO 1943; French title *Vivre libre*, released in 1946). When *Untel Père et fils* was released finally in France in 1945, it had lost all meaning. The production of this film aimed to illustrate the strength and durability of French values but it was a failure in every sense, and typical of the results of film propaganda during the 'funny war'.

Another interesting aspect of government cinema concerned relations with foreign countries. France had always exported a considerable number of films and continued to do so after the declaration of war. It was obviously important not to leave foreign screens the sole preserve of German propaganda, and the Army weekly, *Journal de guerre*, was designed to be, and was, shown outside France. An export licence was established in September 1939 to deal with fiction and documentary films. It was to be avoided at all costs, as Suzanne Borel pointed out, 'that we should represent our country, our traditions and our race in a false way, distorted by the prism of an individual creativity, often original, but not always healthy'.[18] Conversely, some films were shown in neutral countries (Switzerland, Belgium, Sweden), but not in France; for example Abel Gance's pacifist film *Paradis perdu* – which is understandable – but also a militarist, colonialist, moralist film of Jean-Paul Paulin, *Le Chemin de l'honneur*. Its title immediately gives away the course of the action and it would have been logical to have shown this film to the French people.

On the other hand, two films made before the war by the ACE (*Alliance Cinématographique Européene*), a subsidiary of the German firm UFA, were passed by the ministry censors. Critics protested against the showing on French screens of films made in Berlin, and in particular against *L'Entraineuse*, indisputably a 'depressing' and 'immoral' film.[19] On the other hand, films such as *Terre de feu* made in Italy (in both French and Italian versions) before or at the beginning of the war, when Italy was not yet belligerent, not were released in France, or at least not in Paris. This suggests inexplicable inconsistency, but that is not all, for at that moment the Ministry for Foreign Affairs was trying to revive co-operation with Italy in film matters in an ill-fated attempt to promote Franco-Italian friendship. It insisted that French film-makers (especially L'Herbier and Renoir) go and work in Rome, having obtained the necessary military authorisations.[20] This illustrates a singular lack of co-ordination between the government departments. Moreover this inconsistency only succeeded in worsening the contradictions which existed within Foreign Affairs itself. While some members of the Quai d'Orsay were endeavouring to revive the failing Franco-Italian friendship, other employees in the same Ministry were planning the first Cannes Festival for September 1939. The new festival was founded with the quite open intention of competing with the Venice Festival, which was accused of unjustifiably awarding prizes to films from the Axis countries and their satellite nations. In fact the Cannes Festival was never held because of the war, but the films which were to have entered were ready.[21] Among them was Feyder's *La Loi du nord*, which is supposed to be set in the frozen wastes of Canada, but in fact was filmed near Kiruna. Why, just when France and Britain were in full co-operation, was this film not shown to the French public during the 'funny war'? They were allowed, on the other hand, to see the rich and pushing English girl and the rather dumb American girl in *Ils étaient neuf célibataires*. The shooting of *Le Collier de chanvre* was permitted, an idiotic police comedy, which paints a rather unpleasant picture of English gentry. But in the same period, important roles of good guys were given to English soldiers in *Chantons quand même!* or *Ils étaient cinq permissionnaires*. Yet more contradiction.

By the summer of 1939 Daladier's government had come to the conclusion that propaganda had to be mobilised in the impending struggle with Nazi Germany. Focusing on one aspect of this official attempt, the cinematic involvement, provides one with some indication of the problems it faced both in promoting the security and unity of France and combating Nazi propaganda in the surrounding neutral countries. Ten months proved to be an insufficient period of time either to develop a clear and consistent propaganda policy of film production and censorship, or to resolve the inter-governmental conflicts. Those in charge at the Commissariat général à l'Information never got to a real understanding of the problems facing them. They were aiming at a resounding victory over Nazi Germany in the struggle for public opinion. But Giraudoux's staff had to face Dr Goebbels' propaganda machine, and it was no more efficient in its field than Gamelin's soldiers when they had to face the Panzer divisions.

Appendix 3.1

French films shown in Paris from September 1939:

1939

September	–	
October	–	
November	1	*Ils étaient neuf célibataires*
	8	*Dernière jeunesse*
	15	*Le Chasseur de chez Maxim's*
		Vision saharienne
	29	*Le Bois sacré*
December	13	*Tourbillon de Paris*
	16	*Pièges*
	27	*Vive la nation*!

1940

January	10	*Menaces*
	17	*Cavalcade d'amour*
		L'entraîneuse
	24	*De Lénine à Hitler*
		L'homme du Niger
	31	*Brazza*
February	3	*Battements de cœur*
	14	*La Charrette fantôme*
		Les Musiciens du ciel
	21	*La France est un Empire*
		Sur le plancher des vaches
	27	*Chantons quand même!*
	28	*Sérénade*
March	6	*La Famille Duraton*
	13	*Après 'mein Kampf', mes crimes*
		Nadia, femme traquée
	14	*L' Émigrante*
	20	*L'Homme qui cherche la vérité*
	22	*Sans lendemain*
	27	*Le Danube bleu*
		Grey contre X
April	3	*Narcisse*
		L'Or du Cristobal
		Tempête
	11	*Le président Haudecœur*
	17	*Paris–New York*
	24	*Elles étaient douze femmes*
May	1	*De Mayerling à Sarajevo*
		Face au destin
		Le Feu de paille
		Marseille mes amours

	8 *Eux et nous*	
	Miquette	
	Les Surprises de la radio	
	9 *Le Café du port*	
	15 *L'Héritier des Mondésir*	
	Le Roi des galéjeurs	
	23 *L'Intrigante*	
June	5 *Bach en correctionnelle*	

Appendix 3.2

Films begun in France from September 1939:

1939		
September	–	
October	–	
November	20 *Frères d'Afrique*	(unfinished)
	L'Homme qui cherche la vérité	
	27 *Le Roi des galéjeurs*	
December	1 *Chantons quand même!*	
	6 *Bach en correctionnelle*	
1939		
Exact date unknown	*Après 'mein Kampf', mes crimes*	
	De Lénine à Hitler	
1940		
January	2 *Miquette*	
	Untel père et fils	
	22 *Ceux du ciel*	
	Trois Argentins à Montmartre	
	25 *Monsieur Hector*	
February	6 *Fausse alerte*	
	22 *La Grande leçon*	(unfinished)
	– *Hitler m'a dit*	(unfinished)
March	1 *Faut ce qu'il faut*	
	4 *Le Collier de chanvre*	
	Le Diamant noir	
	6 *Elles étaient douze femmes*	
	18 *La comédie du bonheur*	(in Italy)
	26 *L'enfant dans la tourmente*	
	27 *Mariage par procuration*	
	– *L'Irrésistible rebelle*	
April	1 *Soldats sans uniforme*	(film never distributed)
	2 *Documents secrets*	

	25	*L'Acrobate*	
		Soyez les bienvenus!	
	–	*Coup de foudre*	(unfinished)
May	3	*Finance noire*	
	7	*Parade en sept nuits*	
	10	*Une Robe blanche dans la nuit*	(unfinished)
	20	*La Fille du puisatier*	
		Ils étaient cinq permissionnaires	

1940

Exact date unknown	*Eux et nous*
	Les Surprises de la radio

Appendix 3.3

List of French films mentioned in the article:

Title	Director	Date of first showing in Paris
FEATURE FILMS		
Après 'mein Kampf', mes crimes	Alexandre Ryder[a]	1940
Bach en correctionnelle	Henry Wulschleger	1940
Bas-fonds, les	Jean Renoir	1936
Bête humaine, la	Jean Renoir	1938
Brazza ou l'épopée du Congo	Léon Poirier	1940
Chantons quand même!	Pierre Caron	1940
Chemin de l'honneur, le	Jean-Paul Paulin	1945
Collier de chanvre, le	Léon Mathot	1940
De Lenine à Hitler (documentary)	Georges Rony	1940
De Mayerling à Sarajevo	Max Ophuls	1940
Degourdis de la 11e, les	Christian-Jaque	1937
Déserteur, le	Léonide Moguy	1939
Elles étaient douze femmes	Georges Lacombe	1940
Entraîneuse, l'	Albert Valentin	1940
Eux et nous, vingt ans d'armistice (documentary)	Antoine Rasimi	1940
Fausse alerte	Jacques de Baroncelli	1945[b]
Faut ce qu'il faut	René Pujol	1946
Fille du puisatier, la	Marcel Pagnol	1941[c]
France est un empire, la (documentary)	Jean d'Agraives	1940
Hitler m'a dit	Robert Alexandre	(unfinished)
Homme du Niger, l'	Jacques de Baroncelli	1940
Hôtel du nord	Marcel Carné	1938
Ignace	Pierre Colombier	1937

Ils étaient cinq permissionnaires	Pierre Caron	1945
Ils étaient neuf célibataires	Sacha Guitry	1939
J'accuse	Abel Gance	1938
Je t'attendrai see *Le Deserteur*		
Loi du nord, la	Jacques Feyder	1942
Macao	Jean Delannoy	1942
Monsieur Hector	Maurice Cammage	1940
Nègre du Négresco, le see *Monsieur Hector*		
Paradis perdu	Abel Gance	1940
Quai des brumes	Marcel Carné	1938
Remorques	Jean Grémillon	1941
Roi des galéjeurs, le	Fernand Rivers	1940
Sidi-Brahim	Marc Didier	1945
Sommes-nous defendus? (documentary)	Jean Loubignac	1938
Terre de feu	Marcel L'Herbier	1942
Tourelle 3	Christian-Jaque	(unfinished)
Un de la Canebière	René Pujol	1938
Untel père et fils	Julien Duvivier	1945

Notes: a. Under the pseudonym of Jean-Jacques Valjean.
b. Shown in non-occupied France during the war.
c. Shown in non-occupied France in 1940.

SHORT FILMS AND NEWSREELS

Alerte aux tropiques	P.A. Martineau and A. Michel	1940
De la ferraille à l'acier victorieux	Etienne Lallier	1940
Deux empires, une force	O.M. de Andria	1939
France, regarde ta marine	Pierre Chichério	1940
Front de mer	(anonymous)	1940
Journal de guerre		
Magazines de la France en guerre		

Notes

* The text was written originally in French and translated by Rachel Parsons and Norma Falcy-Evans.

1. See Paul Léglise, *Histoire de la politique du cinéma français*. Vol. I: *Le cinéma et la Troisième République*. vol. II: *Le Cinéma entre deux Républiques (1940–1946)* (Paris, 1970–77).

2. M. Pascal Ory suggests that the ministry entrusted to Frossard by Léon Blum in 1938 was likewise supposed to limit its action to propaganda outside France.

3. See Philippe Amaury, *De l'information et de la propaganda d'Etat. Les deux premières experiences d'un 'Ministère de l'Information' en France* (Paris, 1969; Bibliothèque de droit public, 89); Gilles le Béguec, 'L'évolution de la politique gouvernementale et les problèmes institutionnels', in René Rémond and Janine Bourdin (eds.), *Edouard Daladier, chef de gouvernement* (Paris, 1977), pp. 55–74.

4. See Ladislas Mysyrowicz, *Autopsie d'une défaite. Origines de l'effondrement militaire français de 1940* (Lausanne, 1973); Henri Michel, *La Défaite de la France (septembre 1939 – juin 1940)* (Paris, 1980); Henri Michel, *La drôle de guerre* (Paris, 1971).

5. Jean Giraudoux, *Pleins pouvoirs* (Paris, 1939). Two papers given at a conference on 'la perception de la puissance en Europe occidentale à la veille de la seconde guerre mondiale' (Sèvres, 14–17 April 1982) have been used: Antoine Marès, 'Les "Œuvres Françaises" de 1936 à 1939', and Fred Kupferman, '*Pleins pouvoirs*: Cassandre 1939 ou les réflexions de Jean Giraudoux sur le mal français'. Fred Kupferman dates the publication of *Pleins pouvoirs* in December 1939; Gilles Le Béguec puts it a short while before the appointment of Giraudoux as 'Commissaire général à l'Information' ('L'évolution de la politique' p. 70). During the war, Giraudoux assessed his experiences in *Sans pouvoirs*, published after his death (Monaco, 1946).

6. For example Robert Cardinne-Petit, *Les Soirées du Continental. Ce que j'ai vu à la censure 1939–1940* (Paris, 1942); Paul Allard, *La guerre du mensonge. Comment on nous a bourré le crâne* (Paris, 1940).

7. For example Guy Rossi-Landi, *La drôle de guerre. La vie politique en France (2 septembre 1939 – 10 mai 1940)* (Paris, 1971; Fondation Nationale des Sciences politiques. Travaux et recherches de science politique, 14); François Fonvieille-Alquier, *Les Français dans la drôle de guerre* (Paris, 1971).

8. Among the memoirs published by various former members of the Giraudoux staff, see Suzanne Bidault, *Souvenirs de guerre et d'occupation* (Paris, 1973); Roger Weil-Lorac, *Cinquante ans de cinéma actif* (Paris, 1977).

9. Concerning film censorship before World War II, see Jean Bancal, *La Censure cinématographique* (Paris, 1934); Neville March Hunnings, *Film Censors and the Law* (London, 1967); Rémy Pithon, 'La Censure des films en France et la crise politique de 1934', *Revue historique*, vol. 258 (1977), pp. 105–30.

10. Quoted in *La Cinématographie française*, no. 1093/1094 (14/21 October 1939), p. 2; the list of films banned by the censors appears in nos. 1098 (18 November 1939), p. 2 and 1099 (25 November 1939), p. 5. Much of the information contained in the present article has been taken from *La Cinématographie française*, *Pour Vous*, *Choisir*, *Cinémonde* and other film magazines.

11. The present study is based largely on the viewing of the majority of the films mentioned. For the fiction films, reference may be made to two valuable catalogues: *Catalogue des films français de long métrage. Films sonores de fiction 1929–1939*, compiled by Raymond Chirat (Brussels, 1981; 2nd edn); *Catalogue des films français de long métrage*. Raymond Chirat *Films de fiction 1940–1950* (Luxembourg, 1981). See also Joseph Daniel, *Guerre et cinéma. Grandes illusions et petits soldats 1895–1971* (Paris, 1972; Cahiers de la fondation nationale des Sciences politiques, 180); Rémy Pithon, 'Le Cinéma français de la drôle de guerre', *Ecran 75* [Paris], vol. 40 (1975), pp. 7–10.

12. See Appendix 3.1 For example *Dernière Jeunesse*, *Sans Lendemain*, *Tempête*, etc.

13. The period from September 1939 to May 1940 was called by the French 'la drôle de guerre', on the model of the English expression 'phoney war' which originated during the Crimean War. The usual translation 'funny war' is unfortunate; it is based on an approximate homophony, but is in fact a misinterpretation: in French, the expression 'drôle de . . .' does not mean 'funny, amusing', but 'strange, peculiar, unconventional'. The translation 'phoney war' is thus nearer to the French meaning. See Fonvieille-Alquier, *Les Français dans la drôle de guerre*, pp. 12–13.

14. See Appendix 3.1

15. See Appendix 3.2.

16. See André-Charles Darret, 'Le cinéma au service de l'armée 1915–1962' *Revue historique de l'armée* (1962), pp. 121–31.

17. Bidault, *Souvenirs de guerre*, pp. 13–15. I am very grateful to Mme Suzanne Bidault (née Borel) for the interview she was kind enough to give me on 21 October 1981.

18. Quoted in *La Cinématographie française*, no. 1093/1094 (14/21 October 1939), p. 2.

19. See for example *Pour Vous*, no. 584 (1940): the critic labels the picture as a 'depressing' one and mentions Goebbels.

20. See Rémy Pithon, 'Présences françaises dans le cinéma italien pendant les dernières années du régime mussolinien (1935–1943), *Risorgimento* [Bruxelles] vol. 2 (1981), pp. 181–95.

21. See Pierre Autré, 'Le Festival de Cannes qui n'a pas eu lieu', *L'Avant-Scène Cinéma* [Paris] vol. 174, (15 October 1976), pp. 23–8 and 41–6.

4 FILM PROPAGANDA IN THE SOVIET UNION, 1941–1945: TWO VIEWS*

Sergei Drobashenko and Peter Kenez

I

Sergei Drobashenko

The propagandistic nature of the Soviet cinema, as well as of all the other arts and mass media, was determined by the ideas generated by the October Revolution and the objectives of a socialist transformation of society. This conception of art organically included the theme of defending the socialist Motherland, identified in the public consciousness with consolidating the gains of the Revolution. As early as 1918 V.I. Lenin said: 'A revolution is worth its name only when it can defend itself'.[1] This proposition became one of the corner-stones of propaganda (and, in a wider perspective, of all policy) in the Soviet state, acquiring paramount importance at critical moments in the history of the country especially at the time of direct miliary conflicts. The greatest of such conflicts was the war that was unleashed against the Soviet Union by Nazi Germany in June 1941, the war that became for the Soviet people the Great *Patriotic* War. It is this adjective *Patriotic* that one must keep in mind looking for the essence, the political message of the propaganda carried on in the USSR by the Communist Party, government agencies and public organisations between 1941 and 1945.

An important characteristic of propaganda during this period was the use of all available media and, at the same time, a single objective to be achieved by various propagandistic means and techniques. This was unambiguously indicated in all the wartime documents of the party. For example, *Pravda*, the principal organ of the CPSU Central Committee, said in an editorial 'Art in the Service of the Red Army':

* The following articles on *Film Propaganda in the Soviet Union, 1941–45* should be considered in conjunction with Sergei Drobashenko's 'Soviet documentary film, 1917–40' and D.W. Spring, 'Soviet newsreel and the Great Patriotic War', both are found in Nicholas Pronay and D.W. Spring, *Propaganda, Politics and Film, 1918–45* (Macmillan, London, 1982).

> Let playwrights, composers, poets, novelists and artists glorify the heroic effect of the Red Army and the entire Soviet people, because, in these days of the Patriotic War, their work for the Red Army will help bring nearer our victory over the enemy.
>
> Let them inspire the people and our Red Army to continue the unrelenting struggle against the enemy, so that our warriors should go into battle with a menacing and a cheerful song, so that from every picture, from every frame in a film, from every page in a newspaper the artist, the poet, the writer should fire a well-aimed shot at the enemy.[2]

In the struggle against Hitler's Germany, a 'total war' waged by the entire Soviet nation, a significant role was played by the press, the radio and visual arts. The radio broadcast daily bulletins of news, reports from the front, and introduced a special programme for the troops in active combat. The unity of the country and its army was symbolised by yet another new programme which was based upon listeners' letters, where they told about themselves, exchanged addresses and asked for help in tracing their lost families and friends. All press and radio reports on the situation at the front, beginning with the third day of the war, were made on behalf of a newly-established state agency, the Soviet Information Bureau. The civil war traditions of visual agitation were revived in the TASS Windows with photographs and drawings. Propagandistic posters and leaflets were published in great numbers.

Having begun with registering separate incidents and facts, describing separate battles, propaganda gradually went over to exploring the philosophy of the war, to social and moral generalisations on a larger scale. The necessity to widen the scope of propaganda, to speak to the audience on a high conceptual and artistic level was clearly felt by artists themselves. Analysing the work of army newspapers, the well-known author and journalist Vsevolod Vishnevsky wrote in September 1941:

> Listen attentively to what life, the current events have to say. The war has changed the reader's heart . . . Speak seriously and intelligently: about probabilities of a hard, big, long war; about the soldier's nerves about the country's resources; about the enemy's tactics; about the coalition (USSR, Britain, USA), etc. These must be propaganda articles on a very high level.

With the beginning of hostilities the work of the Soviet film industry, too, underwent a radical change. It was necessary to develop new film forms which would meet the demands of the time, to concentrate on new themes, to make the cinema a useful instrument in the hard reality of war. The task of day-by-day information was successfully fulfilled by documentaries and newsreels – throughout the history of the Soviet state film documents have been charged with an effective political message. Over 250 cameramen worked at the front reporting on the progress of the military action. The documentary matter they shot during the war totalled 3.5 million metres of film. With this material, more than 120 documentaries and over 500 newsreels were made between 1941 and 1945. The first film reports from the battlefield appeared two weeks after the outbreak of the war.

As far as feature film making is concerned reorientation began with a revision of production plans. The shooting of the films that, in wartime conditions, were no longer considered relevant was stopped. The production of full-length pictures on the war took quite a long time, so the first such films were released only in the autumn of 1942. In the early period war-related themes were treated in so-called *boyevie kinosborniki* (collections of short films, each based on a separate story). Between August 1941 and August 1942 twelve such *Kinosborniki* (Fighting Film Collections) were produced. During the war the country's studios annually turned out about 20 full-length feature files; the most noteworthy of them were *District Party Secretary* (dir. Ivan Pyriev, 1942), *She Defends Her Motherland* (dir. Fridrikh Ermler, 1943), *Zoya* (dir. Lev Arnshtam, 1944), *Rainbow* (dir. Mark Donskoy, 1944), *Invasion* (dir. Abram Room, 1945) and *Person No. 217* (dir. Mikhail Romm 1945). A pronounced ideological message, connected with the war theme, was carried by some pictures which, although started before the war, were completed after 22 June 1941.

The following central themes or propaganda are reflected in this film material:

1. Authority. This principle consisted in the propagandistic idea being expressed through a person or a system of images that enjoyed the confidence of the audience.

First of all it could be the name of the artist, the director or the actor in the main part, that inspired this confidence. Among the film-makers who contributed to the art during the war years were oustanding masters of the Soviet cinema who were both popular and respected: film directors Sergei Gerasimov, Alexander Dovzhenko, Ivan Pyriev, Vsevolod Pudovkin, Grigory Kozintsev and Mark Donskoy; authors Leonid Leonov, Evgeny Gabrilovich and Yuri Guerman; actors Vera Maretskaya, Mikhail Zharov, Nikolai Kryuchkov, Boris Chirkov, Tamara Makarova, Maksim Shtraukh, Natalia Uzhviy, Lyubov Orlova, Marina Ladynina, Mikhail Astangov, Oleg Zhakov and others. There was a similar phenomenon in publicistic writing: from the first days of the war there appeared in the press articles by such prominent authors as Ilya Erenburg, Nikolai Tikhonov, Alexei Tolstoy, Mikhail Sholokhov and Alexander Fadeyev, poems by Alexander Tvardovsky, Konstantin Simonov, Alexei Surkov, Olga Berggolts. Of great value for enhancing the authority of reports on the situation in the country were articles by high-ranking statesmen, M.I. Kalinin, A.A. Zhdanov and A.S. Shcherbakov. The situation on the front was reviewed in the press and on the screen by Red Army commanders K.K. Rokossovsky, I.S. Konev. P.A. Belov and others.

The authority of film propaganda was mainly based on the imagery of the film, on its characters and action. History as well as pre-war historical pictures featuring the Russian revolution were the source of such images. In *kinosborniki* where this technique was especially widely employed, the action of an earlier feature film was continued into the present day, into the present war. And then Alexander Nevsky's troops, the army of Peter the Great, Suvorov's soldiers, rushed to attack the Nazi aggressors; the civil-war hero Chapayev (played, as in the original film, by Boris Babochkin) swam across the Ural River (and did not drown in it, in defiance of historical truth and the earlier film), went ashore and, turning to the audience, called on them to fight the enemy. Maxim, the hero of the popular films of the 1930s (B. Chirkov), 'stepped down' from the screen and addressed the spectator with a passionate, patriotic speech. The cavalry of the civil war hero Shchors (from A. Dovzhenko's film of the same name) joined in the struggle against the Fascists; Strelka, the never-say-die character from Grigory Alexandrov's pre-war comedy *Volga-Volga* (dir. L. Orlova), the good friends, tankmen in the Far East, from I. Pyriev's *Tractor-Drivers*. All these were not just popular and memorable film characters, they were also undoubtedly honest, truthful, simply good people who one could not help believing. Drawing on these qualities of the characters, the film-makers achieved an effective individualisation of socially important information, increasing not only the socio-political but also the moral and emotional content of propaganda.

A similar impact of the screen image could be seen in such films as *A Boy from Our Town* made by Alexander Stolper after a pre-war play by K. Simonov with N. Kryuchkov in the main part and E. Gabrilovich and Yuli Raizman's *Mashenka* with Valentina Karavayeva in the title role, to which their authors added new scenes after the outbreak of the war.

The spectator did not see anything strange or unnatural in this bringing back to life of the heroes of pre-war pictures in the face of tremendous upheavals caused by the war. On the contrary, this linking-up of different historical periods seemed most natural to the public. Devices and techniques of this kind were dictated by the necessity to find the means of effectively influencing the audience, even by a sort of shock treatment, as to the extreme situation, a situation that not long ago had appeared as practically impossible. Seeking the maximum propagandistic effect, the screen followed the realities of life itself.

2. Authenticity. Following in the wake of reality, reflecting it, creating on the screen real-life situations rather than something desired and thought-up, striving for authenticity – all this added up another characteristic feature of the Soviet film propaganda in the war years – authenticity. These tasks, as has been already mentioned, were mainly fulfilled by means of publicistic genres of film – the newsreel, the chronicle, the documentary.

Fact in those years meant a lot more to the public consciousness than its artistic interpretation, vivid and original as it may be. The real fact was the basis on which the individual could assert himself, it gave him confidence and helped him to carry out his duty. In the wartime conditions this was very important, it was all-important. That is why propaganda by means of film always took into account the authenticity effect with its powerful impact on the audience.

The authenticity and the inherent weightiness of fact in no small degree contributed to the fulfilment of the primary objectives of propaganda. One of them was to create an image of the enemy, to shatter the myth of the invincibility of the German fascist army, which was an especially urgent task in the first stage of the war. In newsreels and in Leonid Varlamov and Ilya Kopalin's *The Defeat of German-Fascist Troops near Moscow* (1942) the Soviet people for the first time could see the enemy on the retreat, German soldiers running for their lives or taken prisoner. Documentary footage was trustworthy evidence of the aggressor's vandalism and atrocities in the occupied territories: gallows with the bodies of patriots in the town of Volokolamsk near Moscow, defiled monuments of world culture, bodies of civilians and prisoners of war killed by a firing squad. And in opposition to all this was the image of the Soviet soldier, the defender of his country, the liberator, the image that emerged from facts, from on-the-spot reports, that was supported by real-life evidence. It was from reports of front-line correspondents and cameramen that the country first learned of the heroism of 28 officers and men from General Panfilov's division, of the young partisan 'Tanya' – a Moscow girl Zoya Kosmodemyanskaya who was sent on a scouting mission in the enemy rear – of the heroes who united in the underground group *Molodaya Gvardia* (*Young Guard*). The man with a camera recorded the hardships in besieged Leningrad, the defence of Sebastopol, the crushing offensive of the Soviet troops near Stalingrad, the irresistable westward movement of the Soviet Army, the liberation of occupied territories, the final collapse of Nazi Fascism. Up-to-date audio-visual information, real names, real events, real facts – all this made up the ample and convincing content of wartime propaganda, very much in the same way as in propaganda films of the Allies in Britain and the United States.

It is noteworthy that in many cases the Soviet propaganda of those days had international repercussions. Evidence of this can be seen, among other things, in the extensive press coverage in different countries received by such films as *The Defeat of German Fascist Troops near Moscow*, this picture was awarded an Oscar by the American Academy of Motion Picture Arts and Sciences in 1942 (American title: *Moscow Strikes Back*). It was from the documentary material shot by cameraman Roman Karmen in Poland in the summer of 1944 and his report to the United Press that the world first learned the truth of Hitler's concentration camps; Karmen was the first to show the world these death factories and their victims. It was more than a political sensation. The documentary footage helped to carry out a broad international campaign in defence of humanity, in the name of protecting the human values in man. Such actions had a very powerful propagandistic effect.

Authenticity, as an essential quality of film image, was not limited to documentaries. Numerous feature films were based on real facts, on authentic individual life-stories (V. Pudovkin's *For the Sake of Motherland*, L. Arnshtam's *Zoya*, M. Donskoy's *Rainbow* and others). The same result was achieved when there was an obvious resemblance between characters in pictures made before and during the war. In 1940 Vera Maretskaya portrayed Alexandra Sokolova, a peasant woman who became a member of the government, in Alexander Zarkhi and Iosif Kheifits's film *Member of the Government*; three years later, with striking emotional force she played the tragic role of Praskovya Lukyanova, a Russian woman who has lost her family, her home and becomes the leader of a partisan group, in *She Defends Her Motherland*. The fact that the same actress portrayed both these women and the obvious similarity in their social backgrounds emphasised the historic continuity in the life of the country and the realistic convincingness of the people shown on the screen.

3. Uncompromisingness. In 1942 the newspaper *Krasnaya Zvezda* (*Red Star*) published K. Simonov's poem 'Kill Him!' ('If your home is dear to you' . . .), filled with hatred for the fascist killer, the Nazi, the enemy. The final lines of the poem read as follows:

So, kill one, if not many!
So, destroy him without delay!
Every time that you see him,
Be ready to slay!
(*Krasnaya Zvezda*, 18 July 1942).

The categorical and stern 'Wherever you see an enemy – kill him, destroy him! left no room for consideration of the enemy's individual qualities, and whether or not he was a member of the Nazi party did not change anything either. Such an attitude was dictated by the situation, by the cruelty of the Germans in the occupied territories.

The war had brought forth new aesthetic standards, it had broadened the range of what was 'allowed' in art. It fused together joy and wrath in people's hearts, suffering and hope, expectations of an early victory and hard work it to gain it. 'The joy of our offensive goes across devastated land that has been tortured by the enemy, that is strewn with bodies of our compatriots', author and film director A. Dovzhenko said in those days. 'What mixed feelings one is filled with now: wrath and sorrow, and a fierce determination to take revenge on the enemy, and a thought about the future.'[4] The Soviet cinema in these conditions did not go into psychological niceties: the opposing forces were painted in black and white, with out any nuance: the Soviet soldier, the Liberator, was opposed to the German Fascist, the Murderer. The Soviet people exhibited unbreakable spirit, heroism and dedication. These qualities could be observed not only in Soviet Army soldiers, but also in a simple peasant woman who sacrificed her own life to kill the uninvited guests in her house (*A Feast in Zhirmunka*, dir. V. Pudovkin and M. Doller, *Kinosbornik* No. 6). Soviet soldiers fighting the enemy and Soviet workers at the home front deserved great respect, and the image of the nation defending its liberty incorporated not only righteous actions and attitudes but also high moral values. The image of the enemy, of the Fascist, on the other hand, could evoke no other feelings but hatred and disgust. This opposition was shown with dramatic force both in M. Romm's *Person No. 217* and in M. Donskoy's *Rainbow*.

Sometimes it would seem that in certain wartime pictures this maximisation law implying strict division in the use of film idiom was treated with a degree of laxity. For example, in *White Crow* (*Kinosbornik* No. 7) a German officer appearing in the house of a Dutch watchmaker as a polite and courteous guest and a knowledgeable lover of antiques. However, this turned out to be no more than a cunning trick: two days later the German returned and took all the valuable possessions of the Dutchman, to prevent, as he explained, their possible damage in a British air raid. The German officer in this short film was magnificently played by a veteran Soviet actor and director, Nikolai Okhlopkov.

The propagandistic effect of such unequivocal, poster-like, 'black-and-white' representation in art was, in his time, pointed out by the poet Vladimir Mayakovsky. Recalling his work in the ROSTA Windows in the years of the Civil War, Mayakovsky remarked that the number of troops for the Red Army depended on how fast you spread the news from the fronts, or how easy to understand the presentation of this news was in graphic terms. 'And this part of the general agitation campaign, too, recruited volunteers for the front.'[5] The same audience reaction mechanism was at work at the time of the Great Patriotic War. The propagandistic, mobilising mission of the cinema was stressed in party periodicals. *Pravda* said in an article on the occasion of the release of *Kinosbornik* No. 2 which showed the real face of the aggressor:

> Violence, plunder, massacre of helpless civilians, killings of children and old people, mass shooting – all that fills the pages of newspapers in Europe and America is now presented in artistic images. And they give more fuel to the fire in our hearts and build up our wrath, and our hands reach for a gun . . .[6]

At the same time, Soviet propaganda, even when the war was at its hardest, saw a Germany of the future, free from the brown-shirt plague of Nazism, and to this Germany Soviet people were ready to hold out their hands. A. Dovzhenko, a man of uncompromising views, wrote in his leaflet *A Letter to an Officer of the German Army* (*A Letter to the Enemy*): 'Will Germany as a state, as a nation, perish after its defeat? No, it will not. The great German people cannot perish . . . Hitler will perish. And with him all those who have debased the German people with a brutal slaughter. But Germany will live'.[7] It is symptomatic that these lines were written in the spring of 1942, when the situation at the front was extremely difficult, when the enemy was moving forward.

In films, however, such distinction between 'Nazism' and 'the German nation', 'a German' and 'a Fascist' was not made until the last days of the war. In this respect the cinema was more steadfast in its assessments than the press. There was no evolution of the screen image of the enemy, it was never modified through psychological analysis, or dialectics of emotions, or an historical approach. The documentary shots showing tens of thousands of German prisoners of war march through Moscow in 1944 can be seen as a kind of symbol of the cinematic representation of the enemy at that time: a grey, indiscriminate, hostile mass of people moving in an alien space of the Soviet capital. Mikhail Romm, formulating the propagandistic objective he tried to achieve with his film *Person No. 271* about the fate of 'Eastern slaves' in Germany, said that he had sought in this picture to show 'the dimensions of the abyss that divided the Soviet people and the Germans, the dimensions of their mutual inability to understand each other, the extent of their psychological differences'.[8] In those years the screen did not show that there were different Germans, two different Germanys.

4. Individualisation. The war was a great ordeal for the whole country, it brought misery to every family, and victory exacted a terrible price from the nation's resources. This is what the war was to the entire country, to all its people. And this is how the war was depicted on the screen – it was precisely for this reason that it was called *Patriotic*.

However, for the propagandistic effect of a film to be successful another aspect was also important. It was important that the story of the film would not be only a generalisation, but that it would show an individual case that the spectator could identify with. In fact, this is how it was in reality – the war that destroyed the normal way of life of millions of people also broke millions of individual lives. Besides, individualised information, as is known, is more readily and fully perceived. All this was taken into consideration by film-makers when they determined the propagandistic effect of their work.

F. Ermler's film *She Defends Her Motherland* can be used as an illustration of this principle. The war, as it is shown in this picture, is a really nationwide calamity. It has disrupted the traditional way of life. It has caused huge material damage and has turned towns villages and ploughed fields into battle-grounds: it also brought misery to every individual. The narrative of the film centres on the fate of a simple woman, a tractor driver, Praskovya Lukyanova. Scenes from her life before the war shown her happy family, her respectful, though modest, position in the community. But the war comes, and this joyful life lies in ruin. Praskovya's husband is killed in one of the first battles. Soon her child dies a tragic death: in front of the mother a Nazi throws the boy under the tracks of a tank. Stunned with grief, the mother walks through a forest. Within hours the young woman has become old . . . This is how she had earned her right to revenge. Praskovya becomes the commander of a partisan unit, in one of the engagements with the enemy she meets the German who has killed her son and crushes him with her tank.

The indisputable psychological motivation of the woman's actions in the circumstances of the film was her individual destiny – as well as a typical fate shared by many others.

Similarly individual, earthly and concrete life-stories were shown on the screen in *District Party Secretary* with Vasily Vanin in the title role; in *Zoya* where young Galina Vodyanitskaya revealed the inner world of the heroine with her restrained and precise acting, and in many others.

The significance of these films and the propagandistic idea behind them was that they displayed the source of heroism, showed the development of an individual personality. In certain cases the protagonist of the film acquired such qualities that the character could serve as an inspiring example, and the theme of an individual tragedy became one with that of the tragedy of the nation.

A big part in the life of people like Praskovya Lukyanova or another woman-partisan, Olena Kostyuk (played by Natalia Uzhviy) in the film *Rainbow* was their personal grief, the unbearable blow they had received. But, though grief had its place in the mixture of feelings that were brought about by the war, it did not exclude the others, it could live side by side with courage and the historical and social optimism in relation to the war. In this connection it is worth quoting the words of writer L. Leonov: 'In the logical chain: war – grief – suffering – hatred – revenge – victory, it is difficult to leave out suffering, a weighty word'.[9]

The feeling in wartime films had such strong propagandistic potential because the way of suffering that the people on the screen had to go was also the way to Victory.

5. *Social motivation*. The social contents of propaganda during the war years is its most important characteristic, clearly discernible in the films of the period. The theme of defending the Motherland was interpreted, through screen images, as protection and consolidation of the political, moral and material values of the Soviet people, as defence of the Socialist system. The imagery, the conflict, the collision of ideas in a film – all these were first and foremost seen in a *social context*.

To achieve this aim, film propaganda made use of a number of major themes:

(a) The unprovoked attack by the Fascist army without declaring war was a grave breach of international law and an act of treachery and vandalism that would inevitably entail punishment. This was the reaction of Soviet people in all films which showed the beginning of the war (*District Party Secretary*, *She Defends Her Motherland*, etc.). The news of the German aggression did not cause panic or despair. On the contrary, it was a call to action, to mobilisation of moral strength. District Party Secretary Kochet, for instance, believes that the fact that his district is occupied by the Fascists does not leave him any less responsible for it, on the contrary, his responsibility is now greater. And he does everything he can to fan the flames of partisan resistance and to preserve Soviet Power in the occupied territory.

(b) Historical examples had the effect of supporting the social optimism of the nation, giving it faith in ultimate victory. We have already said that these were Bolshevik characters from earlier films

popular with Soviet audiences (Maxim, Chapayev), as well as episodes of Russia's military glory used in *kinosborniki*. The theme of the revolution and the struggle for national independence often made up an important element of the content of a film, in some cases its central subject: for example, *Alexander Parkhomenko* by Leonid Lukov, *The Defence of Tsaritsin* by the Vassiliev brothers, *His Name is Sukhe-Bator* by Alexander Zarkhi and Iosif Kheifits or *Kotovsky* by Alexander Faintsimmer. The propagandistic value of these pictures, apart from direct impact of their protagonists, was that they emphasised the unity of an individual and a people, so important in time of war. The indestructible unity of the country, of the millions of people made one by the same feeling, the same action, was vividly shown through images of Soviet Army soldiers and officers of different nationalities.

(c) The unity of the various nationalities of the country, their common striving for the same goal, was an extremely important, basic subject of wartime propaganda. For Socialist culture the theme of the brotherhood and unity of different peoples, big and small, living in the USSR, is traditional, it was born with the October Revolution. As is known, Dziga Vertov paid a great deal of attention to it; it was the subject of films made by Alexander Dovzhenko, Igor Savchenko and other artists. When the war began the multi-national Soviet Union did not fall apart as the Nazi leaders had hoped it would, it became stronger in the face of common danger. And in the war years, side by side with Russians in *District Party Secretary*, *She Defends Her Motherland*, *Ivan Nikulin, a Russian Sailor*, *Two Soldiers* there on the screen were Ukrainians (*Rainbow*, *Kotovsky*), Tadjiks (*The Son of Tadjikistan*), Armenians (*David-Bek*), Byelorussians, Kazakhs, Georgians, representatives of other peoples of the country. This theme of unity and friendship in the multi-national state defending its freedom was consistently developed by means of documentary cinema as well.

(d) The struggle against Nazi ideology was much assisted by film propaganda. This was done through appraisal of the Soviet heroes, through the Germans' actions and utterances. The ideology of Fascism, like the images of its followers, German soldiers and officers, was depicted without any nuances. In this respect the screen went in the wake of the press which throughout the war published material vehemently exposing the misanthropic nature of Fascism.

It is worth remembering that even before the war there had appeared several Soviet films on the problem of racism (*The Oppenheims*, *Marsh Soldiers* and others) which had prepared the public reaction to the inhumanity and racialism inherent in Fascist ideology.

(e) The 'little man' theme on the screen: one of the historic achievements of the revolution was that it put an end to social inequality. This fact was extensively used by Soviet propaganda as an expression of the justice of the new society. Consequently, the 'little man' theme, traditional for Russian art, was somewhat transformed in the cinema as well as in other arts. The 'little man' was now a fully-fledged member of society, capable of solving complex problems, participating in the common cause, equal among equals. Thus he was portrayed in some wartime films: as an army cook Antosha Rybkin (played by B. Chirkov) who first appeared in *Kinosbornik* No. 3 and, later, in a full-length comedy *Antosha Rybkin* by Konstantin Yudin, or as the brave soldier Švejk, the Czeck writer Jaroslav Hašek's famous character, who was extremely popular with the Soviet reader (*New Adventures of Švejk* by Sergei Yutkevich).

Finally Soviet film propaganda in this period made extensive use of documentary material that informed the Soviet public about the Allied contribution to the common struggle against Fascism. For example, British reports on the fighting were included in *kinosborniki* Nos. 3, 4, 5, 6 and others, and in several issues of *Soyuzkinozhurnal* (*Soviet Film Magazine*). British documentary footage constituted the basis for Esfir Shub's montage film *Fascism Will Be Crushed* (1942), which was among the first convincing evidence that victory in the war against Fascism was possible.

Songs, originally written for the screen, were often taken up by the entire country and many of them called on people to rise up in the fight against the enemy; the most popular and most powerful of such songs was *The Sacred War* set to Alexander Alexandrov's music.

The Soviet cinema carried out its patriotic duty throughout the years of war. Along with the other arts it was an agitator, a propagandist, an organiser of the masses, in line with the demands of the time. On the screen, the struggle of the Soviet people against the Fascist aggressor was shown in keeping with historic reality, not merely as a struggle of two armies, but also as a struggle of two ideologies, of principles of justice and humanism against inhumanity and racism. The images of films on this theme quite often acquired epic dimensions. The variety of events, of real-life material, of human feeling led to the use of different genres. On the wartime screen we see a heroic drama, a tragedy, grotesque and lyrical films, a comedy and a documentary report.

With the military successes of the Soviet Army and its mighty final offensive, the propagandistic tasks of the cinema somewhat changed. But even under the new conditions, propaganda retained its primary, strategic idea: mobilisation of the nation's potential and the moral strength of every individual for an ultimate defeat of the enemy. Not defence or resistance, but victory, a complete and final victory, was the order of the day throughout the war. It is necessary to underline this once again: this strategic objective which determined the major characteristics of the Soviet propaganda in the years of the war was clearly formulated in the very first hours after the German attack. The government statement broadcast on the morning of 22 June 1941 said:

> In its time a patriotic war was our people's answer to Napoleon's invasion of Russia, and Napoleon suffered a defeat, he found his end here. The same destiny awaits the conceited Hitler who has made a new attempt to invade our country. The Red Army, the whole Soviet people will fight a new victorious patriotic war for their Motherland, for their dignity, for their freedom. Ours is a just cause. The enemy will be crushed. We shall win.

A Red Army soldier printed on a contemporary poster drove a bayonet into Hitler's rat-like face that has broken through the text of the non-aggression pact between USSR and Germany, and the slogan read: 'We shall ruthlessly crush and destroy the enemy!'

Maximisation, uncompromisingness, clear-cut political orientation – these and other characteristics of the Soviet wartime propaganda imbued it with profound patriotism and made it an effective ideological instrument in meeting the immediate demands of the day as well as in a wider historical perspective.

II

Peter Kenez

In World War II the Soviet regime used the medium of the cinema as an important means of indoctrination and film makers contributed to the victory of the Soviet people over the Nazi invaders. The subject of Soviet film propaganda is important and interesting. All belligerent countries used this instrument extensively and we can begin to put Soviet efforts in a comparative context. Such an approach gives us valuable insights into the particular genius of the regime. Also, it is enlightening to place the war years within the framework of the history of the Soviet cinema. By looking at the themes which were emphasised in those years we gain a better understanding of what the war meant for the Soviet people and for this system of government. Soviet film propaganda used the vehicles of the newsreel; the compilation-documentary (often feature-length) and, to a greater extent than either the western Allies or Nazi Germany, the feature film. Without any doubt the most significant and striking fact about the Soviet cinema world was its complete mobilisation.

The Party and the government well understood the propaganda significance of the newsreel and compilation-documentary film and did not stint on resources. In the course of the war over 250 cameramen shot approximately 3.5 million metres of film and thereby produced a remarkable chronicle of the monumental Soviet war effort.[1] When in the autumn of 1941 the film makers were evacuated to the East, the documentary studios remained in Moscow. It was here that the raw film was cut, edited and provided with accompanying material, such as maps and texts explaining the military action and exhorting the people. It goes without saying that the combat cameramen had to perform their tasks under exceptionally difficult conditions, and many of them displayed great heroism.

The first works were the least successful. It took some time for the cameramen to learn their trade. During the first months they (according to a reviewer in the *New York Times*) rarely photographed actual military action. Instead of taking pictures of front-line troops, they were restricted to filming second- and third-echelon units. They filmed manoeuvers and presented their versions as if they were actual battles; they also staged events; and contemporary audiences as a rule saw through the pretence.[2]

The main problem, however, was not inexperience, but the fact that reality was hardly suitable for being shown. Very little happened during the first four or five months of the war which could honestly be told in such a way as to increase the self-confidence of the people and to convince them that the German army was not invincible. When the Soviet people most needed such encouragement, documentaries, which, after all, were to a large extent dependent on reality, could least provide it.

The most successful and memorable from the early footage were not the battle scenes, but pictures of the homefront. A newsreel, for example, made in July 1941, showed the intent and serious faces of the listeners to Stalin's first wartime speech. The pictures of men, workers, peasants and bureaucrats, who volunteered to go to the front, well captured the mood of those dark and threatening days.[3]

In the development of wartime documentary film, as in the history of the war, the successful defence of Moscow was a turning point. The news of the first major German defeat of the campaign had an electrifying effect and the newsreels, presenting visual evidence, amplified the impact. The Russians now could see on the screen destroyed German tanks and other war material strewn on the snowy fields around Moscow. Most importantly, they saw German soldiers, as prisoners of war, led through the streets of the capital. Since the newsreels presented a victory, the cameramen could also show the sufferings of the Russians, which up to that time had to be hidden, or at least down-played. In this new context such pictures did not frighten or discourage, but deepened the hatred against the invaders. The edited collection of newsreel material *The Defeat of the German-Fascist Troops near Moscow* (1942) attracted huge audiences throughout Russia; the people obviously wanted to see what the cameramen had to show.[4] The film was also successfully exhibited in America as *Moscow Strikes Back*, receiving the award for the best 'war-fact' film from the New York film critics in 1942.[5]

Making feature-length documentary films out of combat footage became a regular feature (more than 120 were made) of Soviet cinema. The defence of Stalingrad, the Siege of Leningrad, the battle for Sebastopol, the battle of Orel, the liberation of the Ukraine and later the liberation of the countries of Eastern Europe all became subjects for full-length documentaries shown in the Soviet Union and abroad. Well-known directors, such as Iutkevich,

Raizman, Heifitz, Zakhri and Dovzhenko, among others, participated in this work. The documentaries gained from contributions of such experienced artists and, no doubt, the directors' work in the long run was enriched by their wartime experience.

To a greater extent than we perhaps realise, our image of Russia's war comes from the work of Soviet documentary makers. This is true, for example, about the battle of Stalingrad. Scenes, such as two groups of White-clad Soviet soldiers, after completing the encirclement of the Sixth German Army, meeting jubilantly (this scene was reconstructed for the cameramen), have a lasting impact. The same way we recall the emergence of Field Marshal von Paulus from his bunker. Perhaps the most memorable were the pictures of bedraggled German soldiers. The fact that the juxtaposition of German soldiers receiving iron crosses from Hitler and the crosses on their graves is much too predictable and cheap from an artistic point of view, was much less important than the inherent strength of the material.

As it was, combat footage was dominated by airplanes dropping bombs, tanks rolling across fields, anti-aircraft batteries firing and enemy planes burning in the sky and crashing. The impersonal dimension of war had a corrective, however. Soviet documentarists, as documentarists elsewhere, knew that it was more effective to concentrate on small details, on single individuals, with whom the audience could identify, rather than depict impersonal battle scenes. Dovzhenko, who spent the war years making newsreels about his native Ukraine, was a master of such details. His battle scenes lack originality, but his pictures of individuals and landscapes behind the front betray the work of an artist.

To what extent can one talk about a particular Soviet style documentary? National characteristics and objective circumstances did matter. We can take for granted that the courage of cameramen on the two sides of the battleline was equal. Further, it is clear that, in purely technical quality, Soviet documentaries were unimpressive. By contrast, it is generally recognised that the Nazis used their visual material imaginatively and with originality. The biggest difference between the early German (such as *Baptism by Fire* and *Victory in the West*) and Russian documentaries was that the Germans showed victorious, fast-moving armies and skipped over the images of human suffering, while the Russians made it clear that war is hell. The Russian attitude toward depicting suffering was different partly because of objective circumstances: since the Soviet Union had not started the war, it was not responsible for the misery. While the depiction of dreadful scenes could make a contribution to Soviet propaganda goals, such as deepening the hatred of the enemy, it could not possibly serve as a function for the Nazis. In making this juxtaposition between Germans and Russians, one must also not forget the cultural background. It is perhaps not irrelevant that the Russians always had had a fascination with human pain. Even so, such objective film reporting only came after the victory at Stalingrad at the end of 1943. Russian newsreels uniquely preserve an air of reality which is lacking in its Nazis counterparts. The propaganda value of Soviet newsreels (over 500 appeared between 1941 and 1945) came from the inherent strength of the material: these films depicted a people which suffered a great deal, which rebounded after a defeat, and was then on the way to an historic victory.

The war seriously disrupted the Soviet feature film industry. When in the summer of 1941 the Red Army withdrew from Kiev, a major studio was lost to the enemy. From the autumn of 1941 conditions in Moscow and Leningrad prohibited film making and, together with other important industries, the studios were moved to the East. During the decisive years of the war, directors made their movies in the hitherto small and not well-equipped cities of Central Asia. Tashkent, Alma-Ata, and Ashkhabad became the important cinema centres of the Republic, and the Caucasian studios of Tbilisi, Erevan and Baku acquired new importance.[6] Naturally, the technical quality of the films, never very high before, suffered. The landscape was a special problem. It required great ingenuity to depict partisans suffering in the cold and snow in scenes shot on Central Asian locations. It is hard to imagine, for example, how Mark Donskoi succeeded in portraying the beauty of the Ukrainian landscape, which is a major theme in his movie, *Rainbow*, having shot it in Turkestan.[7]

The industry suffered, along with all of Russia, tremendous difficulties, but ideologically the regime was well prepared. First of all, the leaders well understood the importance of film as a propaganda device, and therefore the directors were in a good position to compete for ever-scarce resources. It is impressive that, even in the worst period of the war, feature-film making never stopped and only barely slowed down.

Second, given the nature of the Soviet political system, the propaganda machine could easily make a 180-degree turn, without anyone's being unduly disturbed. During the first half of 1941 the studios continued to churn out anti-British and anti-Polish propaganda such as *Bogdan Khmelnitskii* and the theatres suspended the showing of anti-Nazi films. Two crudely anti-British movies appeared in Soviet cinemas in April. One pictured Iudenich, a White general in the Russian Civil War, as a tool of the English. The other was entitled *The Girl from the Other Side*.[8] In this film an Iranian girl helps Soviet authorities to unmask a British agent, who is trying to cross the border illegally in order to engage in subversion. On 22 June 1941 these and similar films disappeared. On learning about the German attack, Sergei Eisenstein must have derived some satisfaction from knowing that his *Alexander Nevskii* would be shown again to Soviet audiences.[9] The Soviet people took such turn-arounds as a matter of course. Their past had well prepared them.

It was one thing, however, to be ideologically prepared for the use of the film as a propaganda instrument and another to have a realistic view of the war. Naturally, during the terrible summer of 1941, the film makers could not have known the nature of the struggle in which their people were to be engaged for four years. They could not have depicted in their earliest work the flavour of the battle, the true face of the most brutal enemy and the magnitude of the suffering which was in store for the Russian people. It is therefore understandable that, in retrospect, the earliest products seem naïve and on occasion downright silly.

The leaders in the movie industry saw that it was essential to provide the people with propaganda films quickly. The scope of the national emergency soon became evident, and obviously there was no time to wait until full-length films could be made and shown. The sudden and sharp need for a new type of war propaganda material was answered by the development of a new medium, the film novella. It is impressive how quickly Soviet film makers appreciated the need and how quickly they found the answer. Only a few weeks after the outbreak of the war the *boyevie kinosborniki* (Fighting Film Collections) were already in production and the first collection appeared in Soviet movie houses on 2nd August, followed by two others that month. Each *kinosbornik* consisted of several short films (as few as two and as many as six); and they were not individually titled, but numbered. Numbers 1–5 made up a series entitled *Victory will be Ours*, a line from Molotov's first wartime speech. In the course of 1941 seven collections were made and in 1942 five more. After No. 12 no more appeared; by that time the industry could provide the country with full-length war-oriented feature films. Although similar film novellas continued to be produced, no more collections were put together.

The idea of making agitational film novellas came independently to film makers in Leningrad and in Moscow. Undoubtedly, the directors recalled the experience of the Civil War, when agitational films, the so-called *agitki*, played an important role in the Bolshevik propaganda arsenal. At that time, the shortage of raw material and the lack of technical equipment had forced directors to make short films, which could be used to agitate among the peasantry.[10] These *agitki* were also called 'film posters'; they conveyed a mood and an attitude and did not always even attempt to tell a story. The message was always crystal clear and extremely simple. It is striking, but not surprising that in 1941, at a time when the Bolsheviks once again felt their rule threatened, they turned to the use of a propaganda instrument which had worked well at another dangerous time.

Most of the luminaries of the Soviet cinema world participated in making these simple films. Iutkevich, Pudovkin, Gerasimov, Eisymont and Aleksandrov directed some of these shorts and such popular writers as L. Leonov and N. Erdman wrote scenarios. In genre, style and quality the films greatly varied. Four of the collections included Allied, i.e. British, war documentaries on such subjects as the British Navy, women in the navy and the Blitz. These were the first Allied documentaries available for Soviet audiences. Most of the film novellas in the collections were simple dramas. In No. 1 there appeared a short based on Leonov's scenario, entitled *Three in a Shell Hole*.[11] A wounded Soviet soldier, a wounded German and a Russian nurse find themselves after a battle in the same shell hole. The nurse, as a true Soviet humanist, provides help even to the German. The vicious German none the less is about to kill the young woman, when the alert Soviet soldier prevents him by a well-aimed and well-timed bullet. Another Leonov story, *A Feast in Zhirmunka*, appeared in No. 6 in November 1941. By general agreement this simple drama was far more successful than Leonov's previous attempt. Praskovia, a Soviet *kolkhoz* woman, invites the occupying Germans for a meal in her house and poisons the food. She then eats it herself in order to encourage the guests to eat also. When the partisans arrive they find everyone dead.[12] In No. 2 there is a short, titled *Meeting*, about a White Russian who had almost been killed by the Germans in 1939, when they occupied Poland. At that time the man was to be executed because he had been saving a bottle of milk for a sick child, but he managed to escape into the Soviet Union. Two years later, on the first day of the war he meets on the field of battle – but now with weapon in hand – the very same German officer who had been about to kill him.[13]

Perhaps more effective, and certainly in perspective less absurd, were those short sketches which did not pretend to be realistic. The second collection, for example, contained a vignette entitled *Incident at the Telegraph Office*, made by Arnshtam and Kozintsev. We see Napoleon at a telegraph office sending Hitler this message: 'I have attempted it. I do not recommend it.'[14] A most successful semi-comic short film, *Antosha Rybkin*, was about a cook who wanted to be a hero. Against his wishes, in the army he also had to work as a cook; however occasion soon arose for him to show his courage and help his country not only by cooking for soldiers but also by killing Germans.[15]

In a discussion of Soviet wartime film propaganda the genre of the *Fighting Film Collection* deserves special attention because it was a peculiarly Soviet form. It is easy to see why the Soviets, and only the Soviets, used this method of agitation. No European or American audience, including German would have put up in 1941 with such crude, transparent and boring propaganda. In Goebbels' opinion, and he was obviously correct as far as German audiences were concerned, propaganda had to be camouflaged in order to be effective.[16] The Communists were in a better position. Their long-term monopoly over all forms of media had prepared the Soviet people to accept whatever was given to them. Of all the warring nations only the Soviet Union did not fear and could afford to label propaganda films for what they were.

From mid 1942 the Soviet film industry settled down to the wartime conditions and began to produce full-length war films. *Mashenka*, the *Guy from our Town* and *The District Party Secretary* were the first important products. Understandably, as the war went on the character of the films changed somewhat. The tone of films made when Russian armies were withdrawing was different from those made at a time when the ultimate victory was only a question of time. At the beginning of the war directors knew little about the nature of specific Nazi brutality and about the true horrors of the war. Consequently, indeed, inevitably, the dramas they presented were schematic and abstract and had little to do with reality. The Nazis were simply mean, cowardly and stupid, while the representatives of the Soviet people were the opposite. The theme of vigilance was relatively more pronounced in the early films. Of course, all belligerent nations made films about spies, but in the Soviet case the preoccupation with this subject carried a residue from the terrible 1930s. In the early shorts everyone, including children and old women, unmasks spies. A particularly amusing example of the spy genre was first shown in November 1941. This short, *In the Sentry-Box*, is amusing because it is an unconscious self-caricature. Red Army soldiers uncover a German spy, dressed in a Red Army uniform and speaking flawless Russian, when the spy does not recognise on the wall the baby picture of Stalin.[17] True enough, no adult who had survived the 1930s could possibly fail such a test. Stalin protected his people even in the form of a picture, even as an icon.

Although the style and quality of Soviet films obviously varied, in their basic conceptions and attitudes they shared enough for us to make generalisations about them. Between 1942 and 1945 directors made 70 full-length feature films. (This number does not include a few films made especially for children and filmed versions of concerts.) Of these 49 dealt with the present and these, with a single exception (a musical, which took place on a collective farm and which is described by the annotated catalogue of Soviet films as 'vaudeville') could be characterised as war films. The 21 'historical' films made up a heterogeneous category, which included filmed versions of nineteenth-century classics, spectaculars based on the history and folklore of national minorities and, most frequently, films whose topic had a transparent relevance to the present. One of the 21 films, amazingly enough, however, was an operetta, *Silva*, based on a Kalman libretto.

How did Soviet artists depict the war, their own people and the Nazi enemy? The heroism of the people was most effectively conveyed through partisan stories, particularly about women partisans. Three important films chose such heroines. The earliest of the three, *She defends her Motherland* (in America shown under the title *No Greater Love*) was first shown in May 1943. The director, F. Ermler, first shows us the happy life of the central figure, Praskovya Lukyanova, before the war. But, on the first day of the war her husband is killed by the Germans. Soon they also kill her young son. She is determined to take revenge and escapes into the forest in order to organise a partisan detachment. She returns to the village when she hears the rumour that Moscow has fallen to the enemy. She wants to shore up the courage of her compatriots by telling them the truth. The Nazis capture her and are about to execute her, when her fellow partisans appear to liberate her and the village.[18] Although foreign critics judged the film to be crude and stagey,[19] it unquestionably moved Russian audiences.

Rainbow, directed by Mark Donskoy and released in January 1944, was judged to be much better. Indeed, it may have been the most powerful and effective of the patriotic films. In it the heroine, the partisan Olena Kostyuk, returns to her Ukranian village because she is about to give birth and wants this event to take place at home. Terrible suffering is in store for her. The Germans capture and torture her and kill her infant before her eyes in order to make her betray her comrades. But Olena resists all tortures. At the end of the film the Red Army liberates the villages then saves her.[20]

Based on the exploits of the 18-year-old partisan heroine, Zoya Kosmodemyanskaya, *Zoya* appeared on the screens in September 1944. In the film, Zoya endures terrible torture but gives no information to the enemy and dies a martyr's death. It is significant that of the three heroines only Zoya dies at the end.[21] By September 1944 the Soviet people were sure enough of victory that they did not need the false consolation of a phoney rescue.

The three films have much in common. Directors chose heroines for their stories because by depicting the courage of women they conveyed the message that men could do no less. Further, by making the Germans torture and abuse women, they could best arouse the audiences' hatred against the brutal enemy. The killing of children in *Rainbow* and in *She Defends Her Motherland* has special significance. In the eyes of Russians, no crime could be greater than the murder of innocent children. Each of the three films contrasts the happy and serene life of the Soviet people before 22 June 1941 with the terrible present. From a dramatic point of view such a contrast had obvious benefits, but it also had a political message: the people had much to fight for. The three central figures are all flawless heroines; they are meant to personify the patriotism and courage of the Soviet people. But of the three, it is Zoya who is the most self-conscious. As a school girl she admired the historical figure of Ivan Susanin who had saved the Tsar. The director this way blends Russian and Soviet patriotism. At the time of her torture Zoya says: 'All through our lives we have thought about what is happiness? Now I know. Happiness is to be a fearless fighter for our country, for our fatherland, for Stalin.'[22]

Several Soviet films celebrated the home front. These made the correct point that in a modern war every citizen who performs his task well makes a contribution to victory. Significantly, the majority of these films also chose women as central figures. Gerasimov's film *Great Land* first shown in August 1944, was about the growth and development of Anna, who after her husband's departure to the front goes to work in a factory and becomes an excellent worker.[23] By contrast, *Actress*, made in 1943 was a rather silly semi-comedy, full of the most fantastic coincidences. The point of this movie was that those who sing in musicals are also important for the war effort, because they keep up the morale of the fighters.[24]

Interestingly, unlike British and American films at the time, few Soviet productions dealt with actual military exploits. Perhaps the war was too serious an affair for the Soviet people to be depicted as a series of adventures. *Malakhov Kurgan* (first shown in December 1944) was one of the few war action films to be made and it was severely criticised by *Pravda* for not showing the scale of the struggle – in this instance the defence of Sebastopol. The review, amusingly, also objected to the sailors' using jargon.[25] In any case, none of the military action films was as memorable or made such an impact on Soviet audiences as those dealing with the struggle of partisans and the home front.

Patriotism, of course, was the central theme of all war films. As far as expression of Russian patriotism was concerned, the director could not overdo it. The Russians, prepared for such expressions, considered nothing excessive. The Humphrey Bogart *persona*, so much favoured by American audiences, which showed a man's commitment to decency and to his country's cause in spite of himself, so to speak surreptitiously, would have been unthinkable in a Russian film. The Soviet Union, however, was a multi-national Empire. Friend and foe well understood that the relationship among the peoples of the Union might be a source of weakness. The Nazis attempted to take advantage of the existing national hostilities and jealousies. Soviet propagandists tried to parry the danger by making films about the 'friendship of peoples'. The audience would see, for example, a Georgian and a Russian soldier going together on a dangerous mission and the success of the mission would depend on their co-operation. At the end, either the Russian would save the life of the Georgian, or *vice versa*; as always in Soviet propaganda films the message was crystal clear. (Interestingly enough, Hollywood war films invariably had carefully chosen ethnic representatives in the characters seeking to promote in American society the same sort of 'friendship of peoples' as their Soviet counterparts.)

In order to harness the histories of the minorities for the Soviet cause, the film studios during the war produced one major epic for each important nationality: there was a Ukrainian (*Bogdan Khmelnitskii*; finished in April 1941 it was bitterly anti-Polish), a Georgian (*Georgii Saakadze*, a two-part film), an Armenian (*David-Bek*), an Azerbaijdzhanian (*Arshin-Mal-Alan*) and several Central-Asian films. Some of the best of these, from a propagandist's point of view, would also show that the 'friendship of peoples' could be projected into the past, and the well-being and happiness of, let us say, Armenians, always depended on their alliance with the great Russian people. There was one nationality which was conspicuous by its absence from Soviet films after the summer of 1939 and the Molotov-Ribbentrop Pact; nowhere was it mentioned that the Nazis had a murderous policy towards Jews (Hollywood, on the other hand, ignored Negroes). The Soviet Union used prominent Jews for attracting help abroad, but the opinion makers well understood that denouncing anti-Semitism was not good propaganda material. Soviet newsreels, for example, reporting liberation of concentration camps, did not point out the nationality or race of the victims. In encouraging the nationalism of minority peoples, the policy makers had to draw a fine line. On the one hand patriotism was essential in order to encourage resistance to foreign invaders; on the other such patriotism in excess, in the opinion of the leaders of the party, could harm the interests of the Soviet Union. These people regarded the Ukraine as a country which required particular caution. Dovzhenko, the 'film-poet' of his native Ukraine, wrote a scenario which was neither realised as a film nor published as a scenario, because Stalin personally decided to ban it for its excessive Ukrainian patriotism. During the war Dovzhenko never made a feature film, but poured his love for his native land into his impressive and highly individualistic documentaries.[26]

Who should be the allies of the Soviet Union in the great struggle? Not, as one might have expected, the 'workers of the world'. The internationalism of the past was long forgotten. German, Japanese and Italian workers were enemies. Instead, during the war the theme of Slavic solidarity came to play a major role. Never have Soviet film makers paid as much attention to Czechs, Yugoslavs and Poles as in these years. The Russians made a large number of films about the underground struggle of oppressed Slavs against the Germans. In a second-rate film about the Czech underground, *Elusive Jan*, the secret radio station announced clearly the theme of Soviet propaganda: 'The hour has come when the entire Slav people should unite for the quickest and final defeat of German fascism.'[27]

Unlike Czechs and Yugoslavs, the Poles posed a special problem. Poland, while an ally, also claimed territories which the Soviet Union was determined to retain. The making of *Dream* was begun by director Romm in 1941 before the invasion. This film showed the miserable lives of the people in the Western Ukraine under Polish rule and how their dream was realised in 1939 when they became 'free citizens in a free country', i.e. when their land was annexed by the Soviet Union. Once the war started it was inappropriate to exhibit such a film. The film's première was postponed until September 1943.[28] That it was released at that time was an indication that Stalin had decided to insist on retaining the 1939 borders at the end of the hostilities.

By and large Soviet films were more successful in depicting the Russian people and its allies in the struggle than in portraying the enemy. Especially in the earliest films, the Nazis are not only bestially cruel, which, of course, they were, but also silly and cowardly. In one short sketch, for example, *Elixir of Courage* (1941), the Germans dare to go on the attack only under the effect of alcohol.[29] In another, *Spiders* (1942), doctors in a German hospital murder severely wounded German soldiers.[30] The film, *Person No. 217*, first shown in April 1945, takes place in Nazi Germany. A 'typical' German family is exploiting, abusing and torturing Russian slaves. In the process they show themselves to be inhumanly cruel, stupid, degenerate and money grubbing.[31] Neither here nor elsewhere did Soviet artists succeed in depicting the particular viciousness of Nazism. Perhaps expecting such an understanding would have been asking too much from a people engaged in a life-and-death struggle. After all, British and American films on this subject do not create a much more believable Nazi figure. Significantly, Soviet propaganda shapers made a conscious decision not to allow the presentation of 'good' Germans. Pudovkin in 1942 (on the basis of Brecht's play) made a film, *Murderers go out on the Road*, in which he showed fear among ordinary citizens of the Third Reich, and native victims of the regime. This film never appeared in movie houses, for it was contrary to the propaganda notion that everything German was hateful.[32] When the films projected the wickedness of Nazis into the past and when they attacked Russian citizens of German background, they became racist. One particularly reprehensible movie, *The Golden Path* (1945), depicts German colonists in 1918 as smugglers of Russian gold.[33] This movie implicitly justified the mass deportation of the Volga Germans during World War II.

Historical films, as all others, reflected Soviet reality at the same time as serving immediate propaganda interests. It is striking that most of the historical films derived their title from a central figure: Ivan the Terrible, Alexander Parkhomenko, Kutuzov, Kotovsky, Georgii Saakadze, David-Bek, etc. These movies were aptly named for they were made to celebrate a hero. Gone were the days when directors, such as Eisenstein in *October* or in *Battleship Potemkin*, made the masses the hero. In the age of Stalin such a portrayal would have been an anachronism. Movies made at this time conveyed the message that it was leadership that mattered. Now, as in the past, the fearless and all-wise hero would lead his people to victory. This principle led to a sharp contrast in the film depiction of General Kutuzov who had been immortalised by Tolstoy as the nemesis of Napoleon precisely because he did not try to lead his troops, but to follow, in a sense, their lead. In *Kutuzov* (1944) he is shown as a brilliant strategist and his army almost disappears as an active agent.[34] No one would have expected from the Soviet directors an accurate and dispassionate portrayal of the past. Nevertheless, it is still striking how brazenly the movies rearranged history and with what ease the scenarist rewrote literature. Perhaps the most remarkable example of the liberties which movie makers took with literature was Donskoi's film, *How the Steel was Tempered*. In Ostrovskii's novel, Pavka Korchagin's adventures in 1918 in the German-occupied Ukraine take up only a few pages. The film version, by contrast, concentrated entirely on this period. The scenarist in order to fill the gap had to rearrange some incidents and make up others.[35] To turn Korchagin into a nationalist freedom fighter was all the more remarkable because Ostrovskii's book was perhaps the best-known Soviet novel. Almost everyone in the audience knew that, to put it mildly, the director had not been faithful to the original.

Historical accuracy as well as literature fell victim to the directors' need to produce propaganda. At times the reference to the present was merely a wink from the director to the audience. In *Ivan the Terrible* Eisenstein, long returned from the political wilderness, played up the Tsar's alliance with Elizabeth of England, something which would not have been possible either a little earlier of a little later. He depicted the Russian campaign against Kazan to show the invincibility of Russian forces – even in the sixteenth century. Other directors went much further. *Alexander Parkhomenko* (Leonid Lukov) for example, depicts battles between the Red Army and the Germans in 1918, which in fact never happened.[36] In *The Defence of Tsaritsin* (dir. Vassiliev) Voroshilov fights the Germans at Likhaia in 1918, another imaginary encounter.[37] As one might expect, in Soviet films the Germans of World War I behave with the same brutality as they did in World War II. Who could point out the contradictions, the untruths, the distortions?

How effective was Soviet propaganda? This is a difficult question to answer, for propaganda cannot easily be separated from the system which produced it. Given the character of the Soviet regime between 1941 and 1945, it could hardly have produced very different films, but the movies which were made were essential for the functioning of the system. The methods of influencing public opinion through films were as essential features of the regime as its particular ways of organising industry. If we measure the strength of the regime by its ability to survive a terrible modern war, then, naturally, it was strong.

Soviet cinema was a mirror of Soviet society: the Soviet people were thoroughly mobilised; the leaders had a profound understanding of the significance of boosting morale, of influencing public opinion, of keeping out 'harmful' ideas; the Party had an unparalleled control over the spread and distribution of ideas; Soviet-communist ideology unlike the Hitlerite one, claimed a relevance to all aspects of human existence and the Party jealously guarded its monopoly.

Aside from the character of the regime, directors were influenced by the objective conditions. Since the Soviet Union did not choose to go to war, but hostilities were forced on it, Soviet movies, unlike German ones, could show that 'war is hell' and at the same time not undermine morale. The war was a popular one in the sense that at least a majority of the Russian people understood that there was no choice, only an inhuman enemy to be fought at all cost until final victory. Russian audiences, unlike German ones, did not seem to tire of the subject of the war.

Furthermore, film makers operated not only in a political, but also in a particularly Russian cultural context. When the most successful Soviet war films were shown in the West, they on occasion seemed silly, exotic and, because of their bombast, counterproductive. An American critic reviewing *No Greater Love* found the scene farcical in which a mother, whose child had just been murdered chases a German tank.[38] For Russians this was an intensely moving moment.[39] The films, of course, were made for domestic audiences.

Propaganda films, by definition, distort reality. Allied and Nazi war films alike depicted the enemy as stupid, vicious and cowardly, and their own people as clever and heroic. Soviet movies, in particular, made little effort to preserve verisimilitude and gave the most biased and one-sided presentation of events and characters.

Yet, and this is an irony of the history of the Soviet cinema, wartime products were more realistic than what were made before or after. From the early thirties until the late fifties movies could not even touch on any genuine problem of Soviet society. Directors either turned to the past for subject matter, or depicted a never-never land of always-smiling collective-farm peasants and workers cheerfully competing against one another in fulfilling the plan. Eisenstein, to his sorrow, found out in 1937 that even he could not make a film about a genuine issue. His work, *Bezhin's Meadow*, was to be about Pavlik Morozov, the martyr-hero boy who had denounced his father as an enemy of the regime and therefore was killed by his relatives. Needless to say, Eisenstein's political point of view was absolutely 'correct', but nevertheless he was not allowed to complete this work.[40] It is not an exaggeration to say that in these decades not a single film was made in the Soviet Union which commented on any genuine issue facing Soviet society, even from a 'correct' point of view.

In this context the war, in spite of the boundless suffering it inflicted on the Soviet people, was a liberating experience. Now, on the most fundamental issues of the day there was no reason to lie; the leaders and the people, for once, were in the same boat. The call for sacrifice found an echo; and the depiction of the endurance and heroism of the Soviet people on a most basic level was truthful. The products of war propaganda were the most realistic films made in the Soviet Union between the time of collectivisation and Khrushchev's liberalisation.

Notes

I. Drobashenko

1. V.I. Lenin, *Complete Works*, vol. 37, p. 122. Delivered on 22 October 1918.
2. *Pravda*, 14 February 1942; The leading article: 'Art-in the Service of the Red Army'.
3. Vsevolod Vishnevsky, *Collected Articles, Diaries, Letters* (Moscow, 1961), p. 596.
4. 'Dovzhenko Speaks to us', *Iskusstvo Kino* No. 9, (1969), p. 21.
5. Vladimir Mayakovsky, *Selected Works* (2 vols., Moscow, 1953), vol. 1, p. 90.
6. *Pravda*, 11 August 1941.
7. A. Dovzhenko 'A Letter to the Enemy' in *Collected Works*, 4 vols (Moscow 1967), vol. 2, p. 421.
8. Mikhail Romm, *Feature Film in the Days of the Great Patriotic War* (Moscow, 1944), p. 10.
9. Leonid Leonov, 'Voice of the Motherland', *Literatura i Iskusstvo* (Literature and Art) 5 June 1943.

II. Kenez

1. V. Zhdan, *Kratkaia istoriia sovetskogo kino* (Moscow, 1969), p. 305. The Soviet Union had a significant documentary film tradition going back to Esfer Shub's *Fall of the Romanov Dynasty* and *The Great Way* made in the mid-1920s.
2. *The New York Times*, 6 June 1942. The newspaper reviewed a documentary collection entitled *Red Tanks* (p. 9).
3. There is an important Soviet documentary film collection in the Axelbank Collection of the Hoover Archives, Stanford, California.
4. Institut istorii iskusstv. Ministerstva Kul'tury SSSR, *Istoriia Sovetskogo kino*, 4 vols (Moscow, 1975), vol. 3, p. 21.
5. *The New York Times*, 17 August 1942, p. 19. According to *Istoriia Sovetskogo kino* (v. 3, p. 21) this film was chosen by the American Academy of Film as best film of 1942; the Soviet author somewhat exaggerates.
6. Jay Leyda, *Kino. A History of the Russian and Soviet Film* (New York, 1960), pp. 369–70.
7. *Ogonek* (February, 1944), nos. 5–6.
8. My knowledge of the content of these films, as indeed of most of the others described in this article, comes from *Sovetskie khudozhestvennye fil'my (S. kh. f.) Annotirovannyi katalog* (Moscow, 1961), vol. 2, pp. 252–361; *The Girl From the Other Side* is described on page 265.
9. Leyda, *Kino* pp. 365–6.
10. Richard Taylor, *The Politics of the Soviet Cinema, 1917–1929* (Cambridge, 1979) pp. 48–51; also Taylor's *Film Proganada*: *Soviet Russia and Nazi Germany* (London, 1979) especially Part Two: 'Soviet Russia.'

11. *S. kh. f.*, pp. 254–5.
12. Ibid., p. 259.
13. Ibid., p. 255.
14. Ibid., p. 258.
15. Ibid., p. 256.
16. Roger Manvell and Heinrich Fraenkel, *The German Cinema* (New York and Washington, 1979), pp. 68–9.
17. *S. kh. f.*, p. 262.
18. Ibid., p. 321.
19. *The New York Times*, 25 February 1944, p. 23.
20. *S. kh. f.*, p. 323.
21. Ibid., p. 331.
22. *Pravda*, 22 September 1944.
23. *Pravda*, 19 August 1944; *S. kh. f.*, p. 327.
24. Ibid., p. 311. V. Kuznetsova, 'Sud'ba razvlekatel'nykh zhanrov v gody Velikoi Otechestvennoi Voiny' in *Ministerstvo Kul'tury RSFSR. Leningradskii Gosudarstvennyi Institut Teatra, Muziki i Kinematografii*: *Voprosy istorii i teorii kino*, pp. 128–30; and R. Iurenev, 'Ogon' i smekh' in *Mosfilm* (Moscow 1961), pp. 275–6.
25. *Pravda*, 10 December 1944.
26. Marco Carynnyk (ed.), *Alexander Dovzhenko. The Poet as Filmmaker. Selected Writings* (Cambridge, Mass, 1973), pp. 30–1.
27. *S. kh. f.*, p. 305; *Ogonek* (1943), No. 27, p. 14.
28. *S. kh. f.*, pp. 271–2.
29. Ibid., p. 260.
30. Ibid., p. 294.
31. Ibid., p. 341.
32. *Istoriia sovetskogo kino*, vol. 3, pp. 56–7.
33. *S. kh. f.*, p. 352.
34. See Academician Tarle's review of this film in *Pravda*, 15 March 1944.
35. *S. kh. f.*, p. 301.
36. Ibid., p. 289.
37. Ibid., p. 305.
38. *The New York times*, 25 February 1944, (p. 23).
39. *Pravda*, 24 and 25 May 1943 and *Ogonek* (1943), No. 14.
40. For Eisenstein's work on this film see *Istoriia sovetskogo kino*, vol. 2, pp. 165–71; Leyda, *Kino*, pp. 327–34; Marie Seton, *Sergei M. Eisenstein*, (revised edn, London, 1978), pp. 351–78.

5 RACIAL AMBIGUITIES IN AMERICAN PROPAGANDA MOVIES

Thomas Cripps

During World War II for the first time since post-Civil War 'reconstruction' the question of racial justice for America's black minority became a political issue. In large measure, this wartime nationalising of what had been a traditionally local matter came about because of the Roosevelt government's need to present a unified front to its foreign enemies. That is to say, even though Afro-Americans and their liberal white allies looked to the war as an opportunity to enhance their political advantage, many government officials treated racial issues as purely 'necessitarian' – a series of manipulative tactics that might give blacks a reason to fight in a war characterised by some blacks as 'a white man's war'.

Reduced to its most often-invoked catchwords, the government called on Americans to display a sense of 'unity' across racial lines while racial liberals asked for a deeper commitment to 'brotherhood'. The resulting dual stream of propaganda, the one government-sponsored, the other produced in Hollywood, brought forth two distinct metaphors that expressed the two poles of American opinion. The government films invited blacks and whites into harmonious alliance against foreign enemies, while avoiding any hint of eventual change in traditional patterns of racial segregation. The Hollywood-based liberals, on the other hand, matured from mere 'conscience-liberals' with their hearts in the right place to genuine activists whose films promised blacks an improved lot in life in exchange for their participation in the war.

In show business circles, *Variety* gave it a bannerline: 'GEAR SHOW BIZ VS. RACE BIAS'. The historian, James T. Shotwell, predicted an era of the 'thinking motion picture' for American audiences tempered by the experience of war.[1] The new black magazine, *Ebony*, agreed, reporting that 'it was the thing to do' to hear Josh White at the Village Vanguard singing 'The Free and Equal Blues', or to join Paul Robeson in singing the liberal anthem, 'Ballad for Americans' in dozens of concerts around the country.[2]

Other indexes of a drift away from traditional racial attitudes were revealed in the reformist tone of Harry S. Truman's civil rights committee report of 1947, *To Secure These Rights*; a nationwide boom in memberships in the National Association for the Advancement of Colored People; tentative waverings from custom reported in the polls of the American Institute for Public Opinion; and in the growing political consciousness of critics in metropolitan dailies and in national magazines. Typical of the new mood was Bosley Crowther's *New York Times* review of Walt Disney's *Song of the South*. He wrote: 'You've committed a peculiarly gauche offense in putting out such a story in such a troubled day and age, . . . Put down your mint julep, Mr. Disney.'[3]

At first light of the dawning of peace, the crop of wartime movies, both government and Hollywood, seemed to serve the cause of postwar conscience-liberalism in that they all celebrated the best of black life.[4]

Unfortunately for blacks and their liberal allies, the official propaganda emphasised unity by side-stepping the depiction of the social conditions under which blacks lived, thereby presenting them with no clear investment in the outcome of the war. This meant that at the end of the war, the trade unions, churches and social activists on the left who might have made use of aggressively argued documentary movies found themselves with access to a corpus of films that presented racism only as a wartime aberration induced into an innocent America by foreign agents. At the same time, Hollywood liberals, although recalling the war as a seed-time of a liberal revival, felt constrained by a general feeling on the studio lots that war movies and social themes no longer attracted moviegoers.

This is not to argue that American propagandists fell into two inflexible and mutually antagonistic camps. In fact, one of the central themes of the war emerged from the co-operation of black activists, Hollywood liberals and government officials in the Office of War Information in the production of movies that contributed to making racism into a national issue. But at the same time, it must be seen that the films of most political use to blacks, the Hollywood war movies, passed most quickly from view in the months of euphoria following the war, thereby leaving the field to the relatively more conservative movies produced by the government. Thus the movies that had helped bring racism to national attention during the war inadvertently served as a conservative brake on racial liberalism after the war – at least until Hollywood resumed production of social themes in the late 1940s in the form of a cycle of films known as 'message movies'.

The anomaly, not to say riddle, of how motion pictures intended to preach a kind of interracial civility, mutual respect, and ethnic unity against a common foreign enemy, served, after their military usefulness had come to an end, as a momentary baffle to liberals, forms the central theme of this essay. Both the movies made by the government, or commissioned by it, and the movies made by Hollywood, shared a common propaganda goal – the creation of an emotionally satisfying metaphor for national unity that avoided any hint of postwar changes in customary racial arrangements. But black activists and their conscience-liberal allies had been moving toward a bolder re-ordering of American society based upon more equitable access to education, opportunity and public accommodations of all sorts. To them the government movies seemed at first 'progressive' in that they nominally included blacks in various activities that contributed to the prosecution of the war. At the same time, these films foreshadowed little postwar change in the racial *status quo*. That is, they took up race as a national issue for the duration of the war, but seemed to replace it exactly where they had found it. It took Hollywood liberals, many of them intimidated by political blacklisting, fully four years after the end of the war to re-invent the wartime cinematic metaphors and turn them to peacetime social uses in the fleeting age of the 'message movie'.

The liberal drift had begun at the opening guns of the war with OWI's halting efforts to weld together Allied war aims and the vague ideals set forth in documents such as President Roosevelt's 'Four Freedoms' speech into an effective call for national unity. By the end of the war it had become, in the words of Claude Nolen, 'a great assault on white supremacy' that enlisted a broad range of Americans.

In show business circles, *Variety* gave it a bannerline: 'GEAR SHOW BIZ VS. RACE BIAS'. The historian, James T. Shotwell, predicted an era of the 'thinking motion picture' for American audiences tempered by the experience of war.[1] The new black magazine, *Ebony*, agreed, reporting that 'it was the thing to do' to hear Josh White at the Village Vanguard singing 'The Free and Equal Blues', or to join Paul Robeson in singing the liberal anthem, 'Ballad for Americans' in dozens of concerts around the country.[2]

Other indexes of a drift away from traditional racial attitudes were revealed in the reformist tone of Harry S. Truman's civil rights committee report of 1947, *To Secure These Rights*; a nationwide boom in memberships in the National Association for the Advancement of Colored People; tentative waverings from custom reported in the polls of the American Institute for Public Opinion; and in the growing political consciousness of critics in metropolitan dailies and in national magazines. Typical of the new mood was Bosley Crowther's *New York Times* review of Walt Disney's *Song of the South*. He wrote: 'You've committed a peculiarly gauche offense in putting out such a story in such a troubled day and age . . . Put down your mint julep, Mr. Disney.'[3]

At first light of the dawning of peace, the crop of wartime movies, both government and Hollywood, seemed to serve the cause of post-war conscience-liberalism in that they all celebrated the best of black life.[4] For example, *Henry Browne, Farmer*, a Department of Agriculture film, which made no reference to life after victory, urged black civilians to contribute, in this case by growing oil-bearing crops such as peanuts and by enlisting in flight-training at the all-black Tuskegee Air Force Base.[5] The widely used indoctrination film, *The Negro Soldier*, played to both civilian and military audiences with its message that the historically segregated black army deserved both commendation and perpetuation.[6] Those films that admitted American racial antipathies blamed them not on racial discrimination but on foreign agents and their ideologies that momentarily duped otherwise admirable Americans. This theme was the line taken by *Teamwork* and *Don't Be a Sucker*, two of the last films commissioned by the Army.[7]

In contrast to these conservative government films (that, it must be said, were well received by blacks who were grateful for the small favours), Hollywood movies were given direction by two integrationist metaphors derived from actual combat adventures. The first occurred at Pearl Harbor when Dorie Miller, a messman in the segregated Navy, emerged from below decks of the crippled battleship *West Virginia*, then being 'constantly shaken by bomb hits', took up a machine gun, and became a legend in the pages of the black press. A few days later, over the South China Sea an American patrol bomber engaged a Japanese ship that was erroneously reported as *Haruna*, the largest warship in the Imperial Navy. Aerial bombs set the ship afire and it ran aground under a pall of smoke that made identification impossible. Fragmentary reports drifted into command posts hungry for a victory and grew into a beautiful legend in which the plane was manned by a harmonious, ethnically diverse crew led by pilot Colin P. Kelly, Jr, and bombardier Meyer Levin – a scenario that might have been drafted at OWI. Thenceforward the two stories merged into the formula that provided the foundation for a solid genre of war movies about lost patrols (*Bataan* and *Sahara*), bomber crews (*Air Force*), ships' companies (*Crash Dive*) and eventually, in the age of Sidney Poitier, rosters of dinner guests.[8] The metaphor of the ethnically representative platoon gave visual reinforcement to the, till then, entirely rhetorical message that, for example, Bing Crosby crooned in *Star Spangled Rhythm*: 'We need all the Washingtons: George, Martha, and Booker T'.

Across the nation in cities and farms, Afro-Americans devoured the movies as they debated with each other in search of reasons to fight in what some regarded as a white man's war. In general, the movies provided support for a nationwide black decision in favour of patriotism. Some blacks harboured indelible resentments of Hitler's snubbing of Jesse Owens during the 'Nazi Olympics' of 1936; others bitterly recalled the humbling of the black boxing champion, Joe Louis, by the German champion, Max Schmeling, and Louis's avenging of the defeat. The more political among them took the line put forth by the *Pittsburgh Courier* and other black newspapers that mounted a 'double V' campaign that insisted on a linkage between black enlistment in the war and postwar changes in black social status – in effect, a war simultaneously against domestic racism and foreign fascism.[9] Even in the Army, where a secret report on black grievances revealed reluctance to fight 'wholeheartedly' and soldiers who felt 'bitter' and 'impaired' by the racism that confronted them in and around Army posts, the chaplains were known to be preaching the line taken by the black editors – 'the Double V' that would lead to 'the day when all the races would be equal'.[10] The OWI did what it could, including several empty gestures such as segregated newsreels and a 'Negro Good Will Caravan', as it sought to develop a 'blueprint of a program for strengthening Negro morale in the war effort'.[11] The debate raged throughout the war, but with a distinct bias toward anti-fascism, supported by the government's propaganda directed at blacks. Indeed, not only did the Army's observers notice a black political decision to refuse accommodation 'to a discriminatory system at home while preparing to fight for the four freedoms overseas', in the spirit of the 'Double V' campaign, but they also reported white suspicions that blacks 'were trying to use the war as a wedge to pry open the doors of social equality'.[12]

In civilian life, black activists, especially in the National Association for the Advancement of Colored People (NAACP), pressed government officials and Hollywood film studios for substantive changes in the depiction of blacks in propaganda. Led by its executive secretary, Walter White, the NAACP held its 1942 annual convention in Los Angeles, close to the heart of filmmaking, exacted promises from the Hollywood 'moguls', pressed the Army to release its propaganda films to civilian audiences, filed *amicus curiae* briefs in courts in efforts to block distribution of films made for segregated audiences, and mended relations with the political left. In the case of the Army's film, *The Negro Soldier*, for example, White touted the film to the leftist UCLA Writers' Congress of 1943 as 'an outstanding contribution to the morale of Negro troops and civilians'; the more leftist National Negro Congress praised the film as 'the best ever done'; and the new magazine, *Negro*, headlined its story on the film as 'Army Shows Hollywood the Way'.[13]

The work of the NAACP in Hollywood coincided with, and contributed to, a growing sympathy among conscience-liberals for the plight of blacks. White's calls for the studios to depict the Negro 'so that he occupies his rightful place in . . . normal wholesome American life' not only enlisted some of the moguls in his cause, but helped cultivate a responsive liberal audience. A typical correspondent wrote of an MGM B-movie that had neglected to include a black doctor in an international medical team: 'Don't they see how they can pioneer a new, free world by employing such touches?'[14]

The alliance of black activists and white liberals touched movies in many small ways through advice, direct pressure, and the panning of each regression to old habits. Walter White complained to MGM about *Bataan* and thereafter, according to a black actor, 'they immediately put the colored boy's role back in'. The Communist writer, John Howard Lawson, needed no prodding at all on *Sahara*, a Columbia film into which he inserted a black soldier as part of a poly-ethnic platoon. When good intentions failed, as in Alfred Hitchcock's *Lifeboat*, studios received mail, in this case complaining of Canada Lee's portrayal of a black stoker that seemed no more than 'a strikingly non-essential . . . sop'. Sometimes activists influenced films as early as the scriptwriting stage. Together, OWI, the NAACP and Hollywood liberals succeeded in reworking, albeit to the satisfaction of no one, the filmed biography of President Andrew Johnson which the NAACP had predicted would 'militate against the achievement of complete national unity . . . [and] do enormous injury to morale by feeding a divisive sectionalism'.[15] In a similar case, *The Adventures of Mark Twain*, White queried the studio on the use of black extras; the liberal scenarist, Jesse L. Lasky, Jr, inserted a line that gave Twain a slight Abolitionist bias; and the Breen office, the censorship arm of the Motion Picture Association of America, cautioned that '"nigger" should be omitted, as offensive to the colored race'.[16]

The combined operations of black activists, conscience-liberals in OWI, and Hollywood liberals, helped nationalise racism as a political issue. Although a glance at the modest volume of mail in the NAACP records suggests only an incremental following among audiences, the press readily joined in the cause. Typical of metropolitan critics was John T. McManus on the leftist newspaper *PM*, who plugged the Army's film, *Teamwork*, as a step beyond mere 'equality' toward a dramatisation of blacks and whites, 'fighting, working and living together in mixed units' – an image that would become an article of liberal faith.[17]

As though to cover their ideological flanks, the NAACP also attacked vestigial remains of 'race movies', a genre of B-movies made on low budgets for the consumption of segregated audiences. When two of these films went into release in the middle of the war, the NAACP challenged one of them, *We've Come a Long, Long Way* (1944),[18] a documentary by Elder Solomon Lightfoot Michaux and Jack Goldberg. The NAACP argued not only that 'the picture is lousy', but also that it undercut the 'enormous potentialities for good in stimulating the morale of American Negroes and in educating white Americans'.[19] In opposing the release of the film, which was a variation on the theme of *The Negro Soldier*, the NAACP directly confronted the notion that there was any room in the realm of American popular culture for advocacy of racial segregation.

Unfortunately the government's propaganda films, however eagerly they invited blacks to enlist in the war, never admitted that racial bias had been a pervasive stain on the American social fabric. At the same time, by blaming the Germans for racism, the government films implicitly deferred reform to some distant future. Carlton Moss's *The Negro Soldier*, the most widely distributed of all, set the tone for those that followed by focusing on a black preacher (Moss himself) who reads from *Mein Kampf* a passage in which blacks are depicted as ineducable 'half-apes'. In an important set-piece in the film Joe Louis and Max Schmeling appear as icons of the values of their respective cultures, the former as a quietly resolute soldier of democracy, the latter as a parachutist in an army that 'makes men into machines'.[20]

Moss's second movie, *Teamwork*, despite its more explicit foreshadowing of integration as a national goal, extended the image of Germans as the source of American racism. Dramatised sequences depicted smirking, black-uniformed officers in an ornate chamber identified by a voiceover as the centre of German propaganda. 'Divide and conquer!' chants the narrator, as on a broken record. One of the Germans (Martin Kosleck) picks up the idea. 'A powerful weapon', he says with a B-movie leer. 'In the American Army one out of every ten soldiers is a Negro. We are working constantly, through our agents in America, to divide these black men from the whites.'

The government's hoped for black response is immediately made clear. 'The mongrel American army' is described with barbed irony that is belied by a lengthy montage in which blacks engage America's enemies. They take hostile fire without flinching, advance through the Low Countries and the Po Valley, drive the trucks of the celebrated 'Red Ball Express', lay communications wire while under fire, clear paths through minefields, construct airstrips almost overnight, and fly fighter-cover for bombers over Germany – each staunch image underscored by an arch reference to a traditional stereotypical black trait – laziness, stupidity, and so on. These are the men who will, says the narrator, 'blast the crazy notion of a Master Race'. 'These are the men who couldn't work together', he says, hammering home the point that racism has a foreign origin, 'They don't agree with you, Dr. Goebbels'. To depict the idea visually, the Germans fire leaflets into the midst of an improbably integrated American unit, but the Americans after a few hesitant glances at each other in closeup, rise as one and advance against the Germans. The sequence closes on a closeup of an artillery shell on which is chalked: 'From Harlem to Hitler'.

In an ending tacked on as though to acknowledge the end of the war, the narrator reaffirmed the point that foreigners, not Americans, were the sources of racism. Americans 'hammered out a monument to the idea of unity [an early catchword for 'integration']', he says. 'And they fashioned a tomb for the idea of a Master Race.' Joe Louis himself supplies the coda. 'There's nothing wrong with America that Hitler can fix', he is quoted, and 'there's nothing wrong with America that Americans can't fix'.[21]

The last Signal Corps film of the war, *Don't Be a Sucker*, provided an ideological bridge between war and peace, when Paramount released it to civilians 'without profit'. Not only did it reassert the thesis that located the roots of racism in foreign soil, but set its message in a timely civilian milieu. It opens on a slice of American life, a card game on a train where 'Mike', the hero, seems casually content with life. But an ominous voiceover warns us that 'there are guys who stay up nights figuring how to take it away from him'. Later he hears a street orator and pamphleteer who claims to be 'an average American' and who resents 'people with foreign accents making all the money'. Momentarily Mike accepts this 'truth' about foreigners until he finds himself lumped together with these 'others' because of his membership in the Freemasons.

Finally in the last reel, just before Mike is tempted to act upon his worst instincts, the audience sees racism as a symptom of a foreign virus. A Hungarian-American professor explains it to his class. 'I saw it in Berlin', he says of Hans, a typical German who 'pumped up his ego' with doses of Nazi anti-Semitism which provided him with a convenient theory of Jewish inferiority and a licence to confiscate Jewish property. The sequence ends with stormtroopers barging into the classroom and dragging the professor away, thus confirming the German origin of racism.[22]

Hollywood studios undertook at least three short films that followed variations on this government line, each of which dramatised a moment of decision in which the loyalty of a American is affirmed in a way that emphasised German enemies rather than hoped for reforms in the lot of Afro-Americans. As the historian, Lewis Jacobs, then on the lot at MGM, recalled: 'They could not refuse to do this kind of film for fear of appearing slack in "doing their bit".'[23]

The protagonists in each case were blacks who, in the words of one of the scripts, were intended to prove 'to American white people . . . that the Negro is foremost in patriotism and loyalty'. This script – for MGM's *Liberty Ship* – begins with German agents who cozen a black stevedore into their service. He is an easy mark because he is demoralised by his squalid neighbourhood in the shadow of the national capital and his failure to break the racial covenants that keep him there. But along the way a black GI sets him aright by putting his anger in historical perspective. 'I ain't fighting for what's bad', says the soldier. 'I'm fighting for what's good now, and what'll maybe get better.' Unlike other such films, a brighter future was at least a 'maybe'. In an upbeat ending, Paul Robeson and the Fisk Jubilee Singers perform on the mall before the Lincoln Memorial – or would have, had the project survived.[24]

At Warner Brothers, Jack Warner prodded the chief of his 'shorts' unit, Gordon Hollingshead, to undertake a similar film, *The Launching of the Booker T. Washington*, a project that Hollingshead attributed to direct pressure from OWI. It too combined a story of wavering black loyalty with an account of the activities of German agents, and also probably never went into wide release.[25]

Of all these short films inspired by the changing social mood of World War II, only one went into release in time to pass its message onto wartime audiences – MGM's *Shoe Shine Boy* (1943). In this one, a black kid, hurriedly recruited from the custodial staff, played a shoeshine boy who yearns to play the trumpet. When war comes, he volunteers as a bugler. 'You're a real American', says Sam Levene, one of his regular customers. 'Blow one in Hitler's eye for me'. 'Sho' will', says the kid, just before a montage of troops in combat. The message lacked only a foreign agent whispering sedition in the bugler's ear.[26]

At the end of the war such films spoke to black activists and their conscience-liberal friends with paralysing ambiguity. On the one hand they provided vehicles for maintaining racial issues on a national scale, while on the other they exposed none of the evocative detail of black life to public view. Moreover, they never set forth a political agenda that might have meshed with and helped define the NAACP's still-forming goal of racial integration. Even at their best, they put a most strict construction on OWI guidelines, depicting America as a 'melting pot' of ethnics who made 'contributions' to a unified nation. In this way, American propaganda called for 'genuine understanding of alien and minority groups' and an end to 'the stereotyped pattern which has long existed in Hollywood films', but without engaging its audience in the issues raised by the black 'Double V' campaign.[27]

Thus at the first peacetime moment when government agencies gave away their surplus films to trade unions, schools, churches and political activists, the wartime propaganda rang hollowly because of its avoidance of depicting American social conditions. These politically conscious agencies therefore faced their constituencies with keen and aroused political sensibilities but with a body of film that seemed to hold that racism had been no more than a fleeting fever induced by foreign agents. In fact, some black critics agreed with George Norford's essay in the National Urban League journal, *Opportunity*, in which he argued that blacks should look to the Hollywood poly-ethnic platoon movies as the most politically promising source of peacetime propaganda. Hitchcock's *Lifeboat*, he said, 'did wonders for the morale of the Negro GIs who talked about it for days. To them it was the symbol of changing times, of acceptance, of integration into the pattern of American life.' It was to this genre, and not to government films, that he looked to 'spotlight the discrepancies between democracy as practised and democracy as promised'.[28]

But until Hollywood rediscovered its liberal metaphor that it had invented in the heat of battle – the multi-ethnic platoon – political activists on the left could only make do with the half measures imbedded in government films such as *The Negro Soldier* and *Teamwork*. So they demanded the release of the films to post-war civilian audiences as 'reflections of national unity' that would 'promote racial unity now and for the future'.[29]

By 1947, more than 50 such activists, hungry for films to express their racial politics, formed a 'permanent front to act as a corrective democratic force'. The NAACP and professional groups such as the Educational Film Library Association began to distribute lists of 'audiovisual aids' that included the government films to be used, as EFLA put it, 'to spearhead drives to broaden the place of film in the present social scene'. A few activists began to promote and sponsor their own films.[30]

And yet during the immediate postwar years, no filmmaker successfully translated the wartime need for ethnic 'unity' into the post-war liberal catchword, 'integration'. That is, they had not yet found a moral equivalent of Nazi heavies. The award-winning documentary, *The Quiet One*, despite taking up the matter of juvenile deliquency from the point of view of an angry black boy, avoided making delinquency a racial issue. Robert Rossen's and Abraham Polonsky's independently produced *Body and Soul* used the boxing arena, complete with a black fighter as victim, but mainly as an anti-capitalist rather than anti-racist metaphor.[31]

In Hollywood, in the short term, the issue was compounded by the need to keep an eye on the marketplace. For example, General Lyman Munson, known to blacks as 'the power behind *The Negro*

Soldier', in 1945 retired to a vice presidency at Twentieth Century-Fox where his duties included unaccustomed attention to the box office. Of a recently purchased property he warned production chief Darryl F. Zanuck: 'The situation of the Negro doctor would get Joe Breen's axe. I think, too, the South would resent the Jew-baiting label.' Down in Culver City at MGM, Dore Schary gave his maiden speech to the salesmen, optimistically telling them 'don't be afraid of that term – social background', even as he fretted over the trouble he would have selling them *Intruder in the Dust*.[32] And at RKO, art imitated life when the studio bought Niven Busch's novella about the problems encountered by red Indians and blacks upon their return from the war. At the same time, two of their young actors, Guy Madison and Robert Mitchum, became favourites of the teenaged audience, so as the book grew into the movie, *Till the End of Time*, the Indian and black roles gradually became white to accommodate to the realities of starmaking. All that remained of the racial angle was a single episode in which the two heroes avenge a racial insult to a fellow soldier by joining a barroom brawl.[33]

Only once did a major studio set out to translate the wartime metaphor into civilian terms – and then only in a one-reel short that lacked the thrust to carry its politics beyond the limits set by the wartime formula. *The House I Live In* grew out of a meeting of Hollywood liberals – Albert Maltz, a radical writer; Frank Ross, a producer; and Frank Sinatra, a popular singer – at the home of Mervyn LeRoy, a director possessed of his own liberal credentials. Liberal Hollywood loved their idea – 'a short film on racial tolerance', as Maltz called it – and joined in promoting it. RKO, probably through its liberal production boss, Dore Schary, gave them a sound stage and donated the profits to combatting juvenile delinquency; the government contributed still scarce raw film stock; and the Academy of Motion Picture Arts and Sciences gave it an Oscar.[34]

Unfortunately, their hope for a flowering of peacetime liberalism failed to grow beyond its roots in propaganda movies. *The House I Live In*, from script to screen missed its mark, preferring the relatively safe ground of religious bigotry rather than the emerging national issue of racism, and recycling the metaphor of the poly-ethnic platoon into a juvenile gang.

The House I Live In opens with Sinatra taking a break from a recording session. As he steps into an alley for a cigarette, he finds a gang of urchins bullying a swarthy boy in their midst because, as their leader says: 'We don't like his religion, see Mista'. Sinatra, as though reading from a dog-eared OWI script, warns them of the sinister forces who feed their bigotry and smear America's reputation for religous and ethnic diversity. 'Somebody's been making suckers out of you', he says. He even retells the parable of the legendary sinking of the *Haruna*.[35] Clearly, Hollywood's conscience-liberals had marshalled their finest forces at the height of their powers, and still could not move off the ideological centre established by wartime propagandists.

In order to study this struggle against formerly useful, but politically dated, cinematic imagery, it will be useful to follow one of the films from script to eventual release. because its production records survive, Warner Brothers' *It Happened in Springfield* (1946) most conveniently allows the historian to observe building on obsolescent propaganda while struggling to overcome its limits. Late in the summer of 1944 the task seemed clear. Gordon Hollingshead and his bosses at Warner Brothers, eager to apply their journalistic style to the problem of racism, much as they had to the Great Depression, engaged a consultant from Columbia University Teachers' College and assigned the script to Crane Wilbur, a journeyman writer-director.[36]

Unfortunately for the originality of the project, each member of the unit brought in his baggage a predisposition to follow the line of government propaganda, even as the coming of peace rendered it pointless. Hollingshead had matured in the Warner Brothers tradition of solving American social dysfunctions by means of a happy ending. Wilbur grew up in racially integrated schools that left him feeling, as his widow recalled, that racism was to be expunged with 'no pushing, no making over people because of their color' – that is, with neither social agitation nor structural change. His assignments ran to tabloid fictions in the Warners' style that neatly solved problems in the last reel – *Crime School*, *Hell's Kitchen* and later *He Walked by Night*, *The Phenix City Story* and *Girls on Probation*. At the top was Jack Warner who had spent a lifetime making 'problem films' and during the war had found the famous Warner formula easy to graft onto propaganda movies.

From the beginning, Warner saw no other means of taking up the matter of American racism than to place it in the brain of a foreigner. As he told Hollingshead, the heavy of the plot should be seen reading a pamphlet 'which praises the Nazi system to indicate the enemy origin of [racist] thinking'. At the same time, as though distrusting the good instincts of his audience, he suggested softening the ethnic traits of the victim by depicting him 'not as a foreigner but as an American with his foreign extraction indicated by dialogue'.[37]

In their ways the members of the Warner unit were not evading hard questions, as much as they were fictionalising the biographies of Warner and many other Hollywood executives; the approach was easy assimilation into American life without resorting to collective demands for reforms. For this reason, the Warners imagined their movie to be on the cutting edge of liberal ideology. Indeed, one executive described Harry Warner as '100 per cent sold [on] a great picture, a monument, if you will, to the Company and to the principles for which it stands'.[38]

With a script based on an actual incident, a small town that had responded to a race riot by introducing into the public school curriculum materials that modified racial attitudes, the unit moved to its location in Springfield, Massachusetts, where for the first time they began to encounter the pressures of the marketplace and the box office. The script had begun by calling for 'dignified colored youngsters' who were 'respected' by white children, and for a solidly professional black teacher who suffered from no racial 'inferiority complex'. But in trying to borrow out-takes from a similar *March of Time* sequence with 'scenes in which Negroes are shown mixing with whites', they learned that the film had faced boycotts in 'the greater part of the Southern territory'. Already constrained by the strings that linked them to wartime formulas, they grew more cautious at the threat of eventual financial loss.[39]

Soon the black roles and extras began to disappear, replaced in the script by Chinese kids who took up their lines. They moved from a public school to a parochial one as an added check on the numbers of visible black kids. And in a telephoned peptalk, Hollingshead confirmed for Wilbur the growing timidity in the Burbank studios. 'Don't put any beards on people', he snapped, 'And don't be too heavy on [the] colored angle.'[40]

As the film neared its final cut, their fear of turning out a pious statement with an 'OWI flavour' that might chill theatrical bookers drew them toward further compromises. At last they saved face and perhaps their modest investment by making a blandly neutral theatrical print while preserving their ideals in a rental version that would finds its way into churches, schools and union halls. As they told their cutter: 'In 35mm use children without Negroes in group. Use Negroes in 16mm.' Hollingshead, daunted and drained by the project, reported to his masters in the front office that 'all of the objectionable scenes you speak of are out of it', but to a friend he confided, 'this is the strangest two reels we have ever made.[41]

In its final form the soundtrack of *It Happened in Springfield* affirmed its makers' liberalism, but visually it left the message in the cutting room. In stark Warner Brothers style, the story opens on an ominous encounter between stonefaced bigots and a harmless immigrant shopkeeper whom they try to intimidate. A riot flares into life when they bomb his shop. The good citizens of the town quickly form a committee that drafts a school curriculum designed to teach ethnic pluralism by embedding liberal sentiments in the daily experiences of the pupils. The classroom activities are packed with social exercises in which the children express their ethnicity in a warm mixture of group-pride and dutiful respect for other nationalities. Flags of all the United Nations seem to fill the rooms; map lessons become pretexts for pupils to tell stories about their ethnic heritages; and the audience is left to conclude that only in America is this possible. But more importantly, the viewer sees that a few well-managed pedagogical strategies can innoculate future generations against the alien virus of racism while requiring not a single structural or social change in American life.[42] As they had cheered the apparent progressivism of Army propaganda movies, the tradepapers and *Ebony* pronounced the film a 'magnificent' and 'not too preachy' merger of 'good citizenship with good picture making'.[43]

But in the first months of peace, black activists, their conscience-liberal allies, and their government which had begun to accept racial issues as the matter of national concern that it had become during the war, had already begun to make *It Happened in Springfield* seem old-fashioned. The NAACP had won judicial challenges to segregation statutes; the ruling Democratic Party struggled with itself to strengthen its stand against racism, knowing that the price would include the loss of its Southern wing; and President Truman's committee on civil rights was in the midst of its investigation which would result in a call for a nationwide end to racial discrimination.

Audiovisual catalogues and reviews preserved in the files of Warner Brothers reveals the inadequacy of *It Happened in Springfield* in a time described by Walter White as 'a rising wind', the time that *Variety* had signalled with a bannerline. The catalogues touted the film as 'a natural for your school teachers', precisely because by depicting racism as a foreign infection it offered classes a 'neat story which offers information and neatly sidesteps a controversial issue'. Mildred Fleming, a reviewer, guessed the source of the film's diffidence: the fear that 'Southern exhibitors would refuse to show the film'. The predictable result, according to her, was a film that went 'astray' from the actual events leading up to the riot that had rocked the city of Springfield, thereby softening its message, shifting attention to the external trivia of ethnicity, and placing at the centre of the drama easily-assimilable groups whose social status 'obviously has no bearing on the Jewish or Negro problem'. Unavoidably, a movie that should have challenged its audiences to deal with the shifting politics of race ended by adopting, in Fleming's words, 'a smug "America-is-better-than-any-other-land" attitude'.[44]

The brief career of *It Happened in Springfield* ended thus, a critical and commercial irrelevance that Warners eventually played off to an audience far below their original expectations. This is not to brand the government films and their Hollywood descendants political failures. During the war they had performed a vital service for conscience-liberals by giving visual substance to the black presence in American life as the left-centre of American politics began to bring racism to the status of a national issue. But in their zeal to make movies that gave blacks a reason to fight, they had settled on defining racism as an ephemeral symptom of a passing infection, an overnight fever that did not affect the next day's plans.

It remained for Hollywood conscience-liberals to reinvent the metaphor of the integrated platoon that had formed the central meaning of the legends of Colin Kelly, Meyer Levin and Dorie Miller, and to draw a moral equivalent of Nazi heavies from the ranks of America's own domestic racists. In other words, Hollywood movie-makers who invented the isolated small group, aircrew and lost patrol each with its lone black warrior, as metaphors for an American society that needed its black members, would necessarily turn their attention to depicting blacks in peacetime, honorably discharged, with jobs, schools and housing – 'just like white folks'. It took almost five years, much of it under NAACP pressure in the form of *amicus curiae* briefs in Southern censorship cases, lobbying in Hollywood studios, and in the case of *Pinky* (1949) and other films, actually rewriting fragments of scripts.

Such movies eventually grew into 'the message movie' era to which almost every major studio contributed. *Pinky*, *No Way Out*, *Lost Boundaries*, *Intruder in the Dust* and other movies recast the metaphor of the poly-ethnic platoon into civilian terms, reintroduced the lone black figure into American movies and created a genre of conscience-liberal movies that lasted almost a quarter of a century and which persists in the serial drama, daytime 'soap operas' and situation comedies of American television. One actor, Sidney Poitier, built a durable career upon this social, artistic and commercial model, topped by his Oscar in 1963 for *Lilies of the Field*, a sweetly comic film of William Barrett's novella that could have been shot from the scripts of *Sahara*, *No Way Out*, or almost any other message movie. That the genre and Poitier suffered the derision of the next generation of black critics testified to the continuing rapidity of changes in American racial arrangements.

Notes

1. *Variety* (10 January 1945), p. 1; Claude H. Nolen, *The Negro's Image in the South: The Anatomy of White Supremacy* (Lexington, SC, 1967), p. 204; Shotwell quoted in *Amsterdam News*, New York (25 August 1945).

2. The liberal mood reached chic circles when *The Negro Soldier* appeared as an item in the 'People Are Talking About' column of *Vogue* (clipping in Carlton Moss Papers, loaned through courtesy of Moss). 'Josh White', *Ebony*, vol. II (March 1946), pp. 3–7; on 'Ballad for Americans', see James Agee, 'Folk Art', *Partisan Review* (Spring 1944), *Nation* (28 December 1946), both in *Agee on Film*, vol. I (1964), pp. 235, 404–10.

3. George H. Gallup, *The Gallup Poll: Public Opinion, 1935–1971*, vol. I (New York, 1972, 3 vols.), pp. 142, 396, 528, 658, 722, 748, 782, 810; an excerpt from the president's committee report is in Robert D. Marcus and David Burner (eds.), *America Since 1945* (New York, 1972), pp. 22–3; Crowther in *New York Times*, 8 December 1946.

4. Clayton R. Koppes and Gregory D. Black, in their 'What to Show the World: The Office of War Information and Hollywood, 1942–1945', *Journal of American History, vol. LXIV* (June 1977), p. 103 and in their recent paper, 'OWI, The Movies, and Race' (American Historical Association, Los Angeles, 1981), find a lack of desire for racial reform on the part of OWI which preferred, it seemed, to leave well enough alone. But it must also be seen that individual staff members acted in sympathy and concert with black activists and Hollywood liberals to promote the cause of racial reform as a logical expectation in the postwar scene.

5. A print of the film is in the National Archives, as are *The Negro Sailor*, *Wings for This Man*, *Easy to Get* and *Negro Colleges in Wartime*.

6. Thomas Cripps and David Culbert, '*The Negro Soldier* (1944): Propaganda in Black and White', *American Quarterly*, vol. XXXI (Winter 1979), pp. 616–40.

7. A print of *Teamwork* is in National Archives; a treatment of *Don't Be a Sucker* and other documents are in the records of Paramount Pictures, Academy of

Motion Picture Arts and Sciences, Beverly Hills, California. The script of *Teamwork* is to be published in a multi-volume (including microfiche) series edited by David Culbert with Richard Wood and William Murphy, *Film and Propaganda in America: A Documentary History* (Greenwood Press, Westport, Conn., forthcoming).

8. Dorie Miller's story is told in Walter Karig and Welbourne Kelley, *Battle Report: Pearl Harbor to Coral Sea*(New York, 1944), p. 73; and John Toland, *Not in Shame: The First Six Months of World War II* (New York, 1961), pp. 86–8. Miller did not live to enjoy being a legend in his own time. Shortly after receiving the Navy Cross on the deck of his ship on 27 May 1942, he shipped out on a small auxiliary aircraft carrier that was subsequently lost in the battle of the Coral Sea. The *Haruna* story became a legend not only in adult media but in a new children's art form, the four-colour lithographed 'comic book', *True Comics*, and later in Frank Sinatra's and Mervyn LeRoy's short film, *The House I Live In* (1946). The feature films are all in the rental catalogues. See Phyllis Ranch Klotman, *Frame by Frame: A Black Bibliography* (Bloomington, Ind., 1977).

9. The Joe Louis angle is taken up in Bill Libby, *Joe Louis: The Brown Bomber* (New York, 1980); Joe Louis, with Art Rust, *Joe Louis: My Life* (New York, 1978); and especially, Gerald Astor, *'And a Credit to His Race': The Hard Life and Times of Joseph Louis Barrow* (New York, 1974). On the 1936 games, see Richard Mandell, *The Nazi Olympics* (New York, 1971), *passim*. Quotation from Harvard Sitkoff, *A New Deal for Blacks: The Emergence of Civil Rights as a National Issue: The Depression Decade* (New York, 1978), p. 299. The 'Double V' campaign reached a peak in the pages of the *Courier* early in 1942 where it had taken the form of both cartoon and editorial copy.

10. First Lieutenant Cyrus J. Colter to Colonel Carl L. Ristine, 13 June 1944, in Major Bell I. Wiley, *The Training of Negro Troops, Study No. 36* (Historical Section, Army Ground Forces, 1946), pp. 31, 35, 38, 53–5 loaned by Tanya Hall, Morgan State University.

11. Memorandum for Mr Bell (on which find in holograph, 'copy went to Henry Pringle Saturday'), n.d., 'suggestions for some basic governmental action which will encourage negro morale'; Richard Wright to Archibald MacLeish, Office of Facts and Figures (a precursor of OWI), 21 December 1941, in which Wright volunteered for service; Ulric Bell, assistant director, to Carlton Duffus, Department of the Treasury, 2 June 1942, proposing the use of radio as a black morale builder; 'A Proposal for Negro Good Will Caravan', n.d.; 'Tokyo Radio: In English to North America', excerpts labelled 'file negro', in which the government's halting and belated actions toward ameliorating racial nettles are branded as 'showy gestures'; T.M. Berry, 'Blue Print of Program for Strengthening Negro Morale in War Effort', dated 15 March all in Box 40, entry 5; and T.M. Berry to George Barnes, Office for Emergency Management, 18 March 1942, 14 pp, in Office of Facts and Figures folder labelled 'Negro', in Box 65, entry 3, Record Group 208, Washington National Record Center, Suitland, Maryland [*WNRC*].

12. Wiley, *The Training of Negro Troops*, pp. 7, 53–5.

13. A file on the case against *We've Come a Long, Long Way*, including correspondence of the NAACP counsel, Thurgood Marshall, and press releases, is in Judge William Hastie file, Box 224, RG 208, *WNRC*; copies of the briefs are in NAACP Records. White's speech is in Hollywood Writers' Mobilization, *Proceedings* . . . (Berkeley, LA, 1943). Mabel R. Staupers to General A.D. Surles, 25 February 1944 and National Negro Congress to Surles, 19 February 1944, RG 107, Modern Military Records National Archives, Washington, DC; *Negro*, vol. II (September 1944), p. 94, in James Weldon Johnson Memorial Collection, Beineke Library, Yale University; see also Cripps and Culbert, '*The*

Negro Soldier', pp. 633–4.

14. Walter White, 'Race – A Basic Issue of This War' and Lola Kovner to Walter White, 28 November 1942, in NAACP Records.

15. Arch Reeve, MPAA, to Walter White, 24 July 1942; Lola L. Kovner to Walter White, 28 November 1942; Roy Wilkins, NAACP, to William Goetz, 20th Century-Fox, copy, 17 February 1944; Caleb Peterson to Walter White, 7 January 1943, in NAACP Records. On voluntary changes agreed to under OWI pressure, see Manuel Quezon, President of the Philippines, to Lowell Mellett, OWI, 17 August 1942, in Box 1439, entry 264, RG 208, *WNRC* in which he takes up *The Real Glory*, a Goldwyn film of 1939 (scheduled for wartime re-release) which featured a fratricidal war between Christian and Moro (Islamic) Filipinos. On *Tennessee Johnson* see Thomas Cripps, 'Movies, Race, and World War II: *Tennessee Johnson* as an Anticipation of the Strategies of the Civil Rights Movement', *Prologue: The Journal of the National Archives*, vol. XIV (Summer 1982), pp. 49–67. On *Sahara* see John Howard Lawson, *Film: The Creative Process* (1964), pp. 140–2, an account corroborated in correspondence between Sue Lawson and Thomas Cripps. See also, *Amsterdam News* (New York), 29 January 1944.

16. Joseph Breen to Jack Warner, 17 June 1942; Nelson Poynter to 'Dear Jack', 21 January 1942; and drafts of the script of *The Adventures of Mark Twain*, in file 2703, Warner Brothers Records, Doheny Library, University of Southern California [*Warners USC*].

17. John T. McManus, 'Movie Pledge of New Deal for Negroes is 6 Months Old', n.d.; McManus on *Teamwork*, n.d.; Joseph Foster, 'Hollywood and the Negro, *New Masses* (24 October 1944), p. 28, all in 'Black Films' file, Central Files, Museum of Modern Art.

18. A print of one of them, *Marching On*, is in the University of Illinois film library, Champaign-Urbana, Il. The legal aspects of the case are cited in note 13. See also, Roy Wilkins to Truman Gibson, April 1944; Michaux to Milton Eisenhower, 3 February 1943; Jack Goldberg press release, 17 January 1944, in Box 224, Hastie file, RG 107, *WNRC*. George Norford, 'On Stage', *Opportunity*, vol. XXV (Summer 1947), pp. 74–5.

19. All of the films cited are in National Archives, save for the Goldberg-Michaux and Spencer Williams films.

20. A print of *The Negro Soldier* is in National Archives and several other repositories. See also Cripps and Culbert, 'The Negro Soldier', *passim*.

21. A print of *Teamwork* is in National Archives. I have been loaned a script and other documents in the National Archives through the generosity of Tanya Hall, Baltimore, MD.

22. A copy of a 'release dialogue script', dated 1 May 1946, is in a thin file in the Paramount Pictures Records, Academy of Motion Picture Arts and Sciences, Beverly Hills, CA.

23. Telephone interview between Lewis Jacobs and Thomas Cripps, summer 1977.

24. *Liberty Ship* was uncompleted, unreleased, or given only a limited distribution. No print appears to have survived. A script is in the MGM legal file, seen courtesy of Herbert Nusbaum, Culver City, CA. The ending was grafted onto another Army film, *Easy to Get* – an anti-venereal-disease film. Print in National Archive.

25. *The Launching of the Booker T. Washington* may never have been completed. Indeed, neither its author, Lillian Hellman, nor its director, Vincent Sherman, recall working on it. A file of correspondence is in Warners USC.

26. A print of *Shoe Shine Boy* (1943) is in the Library of Congress.

27. On the view that the 'melting pot' metaphor provided a central theme for

American propaganda, see Harry Albert Sauberli, 'Hollywood and World War II: A Survey of Themes of Hollywood Films About the War, 1940–1945' (Master's Thesis, University of Southern California, 1967), especially the appendix which quotes *Variety* on the need to place 'colored' soldiers in crowds and in the ranks of officers, and the Government Information Manual for the Motion Picture Industry, 8 June 1942 which is quoted. The last quote is from an interview with Dorothy B. Jones, author of *The Portrayal of China and India on the American Screen, 1896–1955* (Cambridge Mass., 1955), p. 321.

28. George Norford, 'On Stage', *Opportunity*, vol. XXVI (Summer 1948), pp. 108–9.

29. Quotations from Virginia Warner, *People's Voice*, 16 March 1944; and Roy Wilkins to General A.D. Surles, copy, 22 August 1945, in NAACP Records. The NAACP Records and the papers of Carlton Moss contain almost identical sets of clippings from the black and liberal press, reinforcing omens of a rising tide of liberal consciousness toward making postwar use of Army films.

30. The lead quotation is from *Variety*, 19 February 1947, a clipping in the 'Hollywood Bureau' file of the NAACP Records. For evidence of professional film-users' attraction to government film, see Leonard Bloom in *California Eagle*, 16 March 1944; Esther L. Berg, 'Film to Better Human Relations', *High Points*, a pamphlet of the Brooklyn Jewish Community Council (n.d.); and several bound volumes of minutes of the Educational Film Library Association, in possession of, and loaned through courtesy of Audio-Visual Department, Enoch Pratt Free Library, Baltimore, Helen Cyr, Director, from which the last quotation is taken.

31. Bari Lynn Gillard and Helen Levitt, '*The Quiet One: A Conversation*', *Film Culture* (1976), pp. 63–4 and 127–39; *New York Times*, 21 March 1949; John Garfield and Canada Lee, 'Our Part in *Body and Soul*', *Opportunity*, vol. XXVI (Winter 1948), pp. 20–1; interview between Abraham Polonsky and Cripps, 20 July 1977.

32. Lyman Munson to Julian Johnson, 11 September 1946; Munson to Darryl Zanuck, 13 November 1945; Zanuck to Fred Metzler, *et al.*, 12 May 1947, in Munson Papers, American Heritage Center, University of Wyoming, Laramie, Wyoming; Dore Schary, 'Sales Meeting', speech, dated 8 February 1949, Box 107, Schary Papers, Wisconsin Center for Film and Theatre Research, Wisconsin State Historical Society, Madison.

33. Correspondence and script drafts in *Till the End of Time* file, RKO Records, Los Angeles; interview between Niven Busch and Cripps, June 1981.

34. *The House I Live In* script-treatment in Twentieth Century Collection, Mugar Library, Boston University; Mervyn LeRoy, *Take One* (as told to Dick Kleiner) (New York, 1974), pp. 129, 155; *Variety* (5 December 1945), p. 2; and *Daily Worker*, 3 June 1945, clipping in Schomburg Collection, New York Public Library.

35. *The House I Live In* (1945), print in Library of Congress.

36. Ray Graham, 'Report of Progress of Americans All – Immigrants All, 1943–1944', mimeo; course outline given to teacher trainees, Springfield College, on which is inscribed 'Mr. Warner: This may interest you'; signed C.R.W. (Clyde R. Miller, Associate Professor, Teachers College, Columbia University); 'Facts About the Springfield Plan', pamphlet; Clyde R. Miller to Crane Wilbur, 8 August 1945; Gordon Hollingshead to Ray Obringer, copy, 23 August 1944; *New York Times*, 8 September 1944; and Jack Warner to Hollingshead, memo, 1 September 1944, all in file 1469, *It Happened in Springfield*; *Warners USC*.

37. Warner to Hollingshead, 1 September 1944, in file 1469, *Warners USC*; interview between Mrs. Crane Wilbur and Thomas Cripps, August 1977.

38. Harry Warner's approval in Norman Moray to Hollingshead, 4 October 1945, in file 1469, Warner Records.

39. Dialogue Transcript, *c.* 1945, reel 1–B; Joseph Breen to Jack Warner, 10 October 1944; Wilbur to Hollingshead, 16 September 1944 (first draft finished); Hollingshead to 'Charlie' Einfield, 12 September 1944 (on *March of Time*); 'Cast for "It Happened in Springfield" – As They Appear', n.d., all in file 1469, *Warners USC.*

40. 'Cast for "It Happened in Springfield"'; transcript of telephone conversation between Wilbur and Hollingshead, n.d., both in file 1469, *Warners USC.*

41. Hollingshead to Jack Warner, copy, 19 December 1944; 'Sweet Land of Liberty' – cutter's notes, 20 November 1944; and Hollingshead to Norman Moray, 16 December 1944, in 1469, *Warners USC.*

42. A print of *It Happened in Springfield* is in the Library of Congress, albeit presently unavailable to researchers.

43. *Showman's Trade Review*, 7 April 1945; *Hollywood Reporter*, 4 April 1945; and other clippings and letters; Mildred Fleming's review, clipping, n.d., quotes from Helena Huntington Smith's article in *Woman's Home Companion* (June 1944), which first brought to a national readership the story of Springfield's attempt to use its schools to teach right thinking on the subject of race and ethnicity.

This sort of story reflected a strong vein running through America's popular culture. A good example of how children were taught the new social values may be found in Hilah Paulmier and Robert Haven Schauffler (compilers and eds.), *Good Will Days: Poems, Plays, Prose Selections, Essay Material, Anecdotes and Stories, Speeches and Sayings, for the Promotion of Racial Good Will* (New York, 1947, 1956), a book used in urban school systems. On the title page Lincoln is quoted as asking Americans to 'dwell together in the bonds of fraternal feeling', and Franklin D. Roosevelt as reminding Americans of their 'duty to make sure that, big as this country is, there is no room in it for racial or religious intolerance'.

44. Ephemera in file 1469, *Warners USC.*

6 HOLLYWOOD FIGHTS ANTI-SEMITISM, 1940–1945

K.R.M. Short

Hitler's persecution of the Jews of Europe posed a profound problem for the Allied propagandists, whether they represented the official opinion of the governments of the United States and Great Britain or the private efforts of individuals (not always Jewish) of how to bring the appalling enormity of virulent anti-Semitism into focus for the citizens of the Western democracies. Part of the problem was that it was easy to criticise Nazi Germany for anti-Semitism but difficult to reconcile that criticism with the anti-Jewish prejudice that prevailed throughout almost every section of the United States or with the British 1937 White Paper limiting Jewish immigration into its mandate territory of Palestine, a policy, in the face of Hitler's intensive campaign against the Jews, that looked in part to be anti-Semitic itself. Between 1933 and the outbreak of war roughly half of the Jewish population of Germany emigrated to the United States, Great Britain and Palestine; a total of about 250,000 people. This migration to safety only partially solved Hitler's Jewish problem, as with the *Anschluss* (13 March 1938) he added another 180,000 Jews to the 250,000 remaining in Germany; it was with the launching of the Blitzkreig against Poland that the majority of Europe's Jews came within his murderous reach, partially as the result of Russia's volte face of that August; Russia's Jewish population was 3,000,000 and Poland's was 3,275,000. *Lebensraum*, or rather the need for it, created the Jewish problem in the East for which Hitler's solution was genocide.

The Soviet fear of the Nazi eastward movement, a movement as old as the Teutonic Knights themselves, the defeat of which was so marvellously dramatised by Eisenstein's *Alexander Nevsky* (1938), had brought Stalin into European politics, first with the League of Nations in 1934 and a year later with the introduction of Popular Fronts in the nations of Western Europe. Soviet propaganda, especially in feature films, prominently featured Nazi anti-Semitism in such justly famous films as *Professor Mamlock* (1938) and *The Oppenheim Family* (1939). *Mamlock* was widely shown in the United States during late 1938, as it was in France with equal popularity. The film, sponsored by the London Film Society, was banned however in Great Britain in the late spring of the following year. The rules of the British Board of Film Censors would keep overt criticism of any aspect of the Nazi policy towards Jews off the screen until the barriers went down with the declaration of war and even then the movie industry continued the silence until almost the very end of the war itself when Two Cities released *Mr Emmanuel* in 1944.[1] There had not been a total silence in Britain on anti-Semitism, however.

After several unsuccessful efforts to get anti-Nazi scripts past the British Board of Film Censors, Gaumont-British, whose board of directors included the well-known Jewish financier Isidor Osterer, managed to get permission to film Lion Feuchtwanger's historical novel *Jew Süss*. Released in October 1934, starring the famous German actor Conrad Veidt (who never returned to Germany, his wife being Jewish), the film provided the gory record of anti-Semitism in eighteenth-century Württemberg, a city with its own proto-Nazi population oppressing the ghettoed Jews of the time. While predicting from the safety of history that Jews could be burned in 1930, Gaumont British offered the fervent prayer in the film's conclusion that 'Perhaps one day the walls will crumble like the walls of Jericho and all the world will be one people.' The Osterers had at least made their passionate statement upon the behalf of the Jewish people.

Similiar personal statements were to emerge in France through the films of Jean Renoir, in particular, *La Grande Illusion* (1937), *La Règle du Jeu* (1939) and *La Marseillaise* (1938), while the other references to Jews in the French cinema of the 1930s were hardly complementary. Whereas a few Jews made appearances in French films, Jewish characters are largely absent from the infinitely larger 1930s Hollywood output.[2]

There are significant exceptions to this statement, one of which was the George Arliss vehicle, *The House of Rothschild* (dir. A. Werker), released in March 1934. Produced by Twentieth Century Studios headed by the Jewish Joseph Schenck and the non-Jewish Darryl F. Zanuck, the film was a statement against Nazi anti-Semitism thinly disguised as an historical film. As one reviewer plainly put it, the film was thinking 'more about Hitler and Goering and Goebbels than it is about the kingdom of Prussia on the eve of Waterloo . . . the idealistic Rothschilds become modern protagonists of their race, struggling against German oppression –

as represented by the sinister Mr. Boris Karloff (Prince Ledrantz) as sort of a Hitler ogre . . .'.[3] Two quite positive Jewish images had earlier emerged in films based on plays by Elmer Rice, *Street Scene* (1931, United Artists, dir. King Vidor) and *Counsellor-at-Law* (1933, Universal, dir. William Wyler). The first film concerned a Jewish family with an ineffectual Communist father on the way up from East-Side poverty, while the second featured a highly successful Jewish lawyer overcoming WASP prejeduce by maintaining contact with his immigrant roots.[4]

There was something of a British equivalent to the two Elmer Rice stories, the delightfully warm and sympathetic comedy made by British Warner Brothers at Teddington – *Mr. Cohen Takes a Walk*. Released in mid-December 1935, the film was about Jake Cohen (played by Paul Graetz), a totally lovable character who had started as a peddlar and ended up owning a department store, now run by his son who lacked the sense to care for his employees. Jake, the humanitarian, helps everyone that he meets and then returns to take over the store in time to end a strike by re-establishing his personal relationships with the employees of the Empire Department store; an interesting comment in the midst of the depression on the need for good employer-employee relations. Warner Brothers also took up the story of Emile Zola's championing of the Jewish Artillery Captain on the French Army's General Staff convicted of spying for the Germans, Alfred Dreyfus. The story had been filmed in 1898 (George Mélies) 1899, 1908, 1930 and most recently British International's *The Dreyfus Case* (1931) starring Cedric Hardwick. Jack Warner's decision to turn the Geza Herczeg/Heinz Herald story into a new *biografilm* was partly dictated by the studio's need for a new starring vehicle for Paul Muni who had just won an Oscar for his portrayal of Louis Pasteur. The Jewish Muni played the Catholic Zola to the Jewish Dreyfus acted by the Jewish Joseph Schildkraut, son of Rudolph Schildkraut. The story was primarily the Zola story with Muni dominating the famous set-piece courtroom scene in which he sought to awaken the conscience of the French nation. The film made it absolutely clear that Dreyfus was chosen the scapegoat for the failures of the French Army solely because he was a Jew. *Zola* contains a full frame shot of the General Staff list which stops over the entry:

Dreyfus, Alfred
Captain in the 14th Regiment Artillery
Born: Mulhouse, Alsace
Religion: Jew

Then a hand appears in the frame with the finger pointing at the word Jew, 'That's our man!' says the voice. Warner Brothers through *Mr Cohen Talks a Walk* (released in the USA in February 1936 as *Father Takes a Walk*) and *The Life of Emile Zola* (directed by William Dieterle, it won Oscars for the best film and best script of 1937) established that its social and political consciousness extended to the deepest reaches of prejudice, racial prejudice, as it turned against Jews.[5]

As the German panzer columns rolled across the plains of Western Poland and the Red Army waited with engines running for their own penetration from the east, the caution of Hollywood slowly eased. MGM producer Sidney Franklin (best known for his pro-English films) decided to film *The Mortal Storm* by the Anglo-American authoress Phyllis Bottome. The novel had hit the best seller lists shortly after it appeared in April 1938. Directed by Frank Borzage and written by Claudine West, Andersen Ellis (the German émigré, Hans Paul Rameau) and the Austrian Jewish refugee George Froeschel, the film was released in the summer of 1940 as the panzer columns turned westwards into the Low Countries and France.[6] Miss Bottome (*New York Times*, 16 June 1940, cable from London) found the transformation of her book to the screen a 'miracle' comparing it, as only an authoress might, with *Gone with the Wind*, *Wuthering Heights* and *The Grapes of Wrath*. Although the film did show what it was like to be a Nazi with 'unequivocal sincerity and life-likeness', she was very critical of the scene where the Jewish professor inadequately explained to his son, ten-year-old Rudi, what it meant to be a Jew. This watering down of courage was unfortunate but not unexpected for it merely reflected the Hollywood urge to hide Jewishness. Nowhere in the film is the word Jew used – only 'non-Aryan'. The only suggestion of Jew is the letter *J* on the shirt-cuff bands worn by the professor in a concentration camp. When the camera focused on his file card in the hands of the concentration-camp officer it contained only name, birth date, profession and a stamped notion that 'Dept. is not interested in the release of this prisoner'. MGM lacked the courage of Warner Brothers' *Zola* in rejecting the opportunity to have the word JEW on the card. This may be less important than it seems for although non-Aryan was the term it is inconceivable that the average American moviegoer did not know that the film was about the Nazi persecution of Jews, even if they are called non-Aryans. And yet when compared with Charlie Chaplin's *The Great Dictator*, which opened four months later (*Mortal Storm* opened on 20 June 1940) calling a Jew a Jew and pogroms anti-Semitism, MGM's reticence is apparent. That was June when Great Britain evacuated the remnants of its expeditionary force, along with some French troops, from the French port of Dunkerque.

The story of *The Mortal Storm* documented the changes forced upon a family in an obviously southern German university town ('somewhere in Europe' was how the film put it) by the rise of Hitler to power; the family was that of an internationally famous professor of physiology, Viktor Roth (Frank Morgan). The 'non-Aryan' Roth, celebrated his sixtieth birthday on 30 January 1933. His family consisted of an Aryan wife (Irene Rich), and her two sons by a previous marriage, as well as two children of their own Freya (Margaret Sullavan) and Rudi. Two university students, Fritz (Robert Young) and Martin (James Stewart) were in love with Freya and she initially chose the heel-clicking Fritz. Roth was an extraordinarily popular absent-minded professor honoured by all for his scholarship and humanity, personally proud of his family and its gracious living, tolerance and sense of humour. His stepsons and Fritz join the SA and Roth finds himself confronted in his classroom by belligerent Brown shirts demanding that he conform to the Nazi ideology of racial purity and change his teaching that there was no difference in the blood of the races. Unlike Professor Mamlock's public humiliation, Roth's agony initially comprised of seeing his students desert him and watching, from the safety of his window, the burning of books written by Einstein and Heine. Devoting his energy to research having been deprived of his professorship, he is arrested on the eve of attending a conference in Vienna. He is murdered by the Gestapo shortly after his wife visits him in the concentration camp. In the end Freya is killed as she and Martin escape to Austria, murdered by a Nazi patrol led by Fritz; only Mrs Roth and her half-Aryan son, Rudi, escape.

Critical reaction agreed that such a film was long overdue estimates ranging from three to five years. Yet, most reviews agreed with Bosley Crowther's assessment (*New York Times*, 23 June 1940) that *The Mortal Storm* did not tell anyone anything that they did not already know, chastising Hollywood for being irresponsible: Crowther had entitled his review 'Lost Opportunity, or where was Hollywood when the Lights in Germany went out?' Unfavourable comparisons with the 'grimly realistic' presentation of *Professor Mamlock* were also made, but the overall emphasis of the reviews was not on informing Americans of the terrors of anti-Semitism, but rather Hollywood's responsibility in taking the lead in informing the American nation as to how to preserve the American heritage against the Nazi menace at all cost (William Boehnel, *New York World Telegram*, 21 June 1940). Archer Winsten, in conclusion (*New York Post*, 21 June 1940) was happy to 'welcome it as a serious picture defending the highest ideals of freedom and tolerance. They need defence nowadays.'

Mayer's MGM could be accused of tentativeness in approaching the problem of anti-Semitism in *The Mortal Storm*, yet the studio also released that year another film which dealt with anti-Nazis and concentration camps, *Escape* (dir. Mervyn LeRoy). Norma Shearer played the American-born German Countess von Treck, mistress of General Kurt von Kolb, played by the ubiquitous Conrad Veidt. Robert Taylor, still at the peak of his popularity, was the young German-American, Mark Preysing, who returns to Nazi Germany in search of his actress-mother, Emmy Ritter (Nazimova). Preysing finds his mother in a concentration camp for her anti-Nazi stand, and about to be exterminated. He arranges for the camp doctor (Philip Dorn) to inject her with a coma-inducing drug so that the 'dead' body could be released and subsequently smuggled out to freedom. All of this was made possible by Countess von Treck out of her love for Mark Preysing; she is left in Germany to meet her fate. According to Lester Friedmann, although 'not specifically dealing with Jews' it provided some early recognition of the existence of concentration camps.[7]

American moviegoers had not been entirely insulated from the reality of anti-Semitism, at least not those who attended theatres where *The March of Time* was shown. On 18 October 1935 an issue (Vol. 1, No. 7) featured the problems of resettlement of Jewish immigrants in Palestine; and then *Inside Nazi Germany – 1938* (21 January 1938) reported that Goebbels's propaganda machine continued to bear down upon the Jews and Christian churches.[8] If in American movie theatres, entertainment was king and ruled alone, that did not mean that the newspapers, magazines, journals, radio, novels and plays did not contain ample documentation as to the development of anti-Semitism, short, of course, of genocide which was beyond the imagination of the civilised populations of the liberal West.

The newsreels may have been bland in their commentaries and naïve in their understanding of what was happening in Europe, but they did bring before their audiences the apparently comic antics of the two strong men of western Europe; the fat, strutting, lip-thrusting Mussolini and the equally comical Austrian Hitler in a German uniform sporting a toothbrush moustache, looking anything but the ideal representative of the Master Race of Teutonic purity. It was the moustache that caught the eye of British movie producer Alexander Korda; he had seen it before and it belonged to Charlie Chaplin's little tramp. Sometime in 1937, Korda suggested to Chaplin (they were business associates in United Artists) that he do a Hitler movie based on mistaken identity, with Chaplin playing both parts. Although not immediately interested in the idea, within a year Chaplin took it up seriously saying: 'As Hitler I could harangue the crowds in jargon and talk all I wanted to. And as the tramp I could remain more or less silent. A Hitler story was an opportunity for burleque and pantomime.' The film took two years from inception to finish and about half-way through (sometime in 1939) United Artists was advised by the Hays Office that the film would face censorship in its projected form, an assessment possibly based on a reading of the script begun in January 1939 by Chaplin. United Artists' London office was apparently advised by the British Board of Film Censors that there was an excellent chance that *The Great Dictator* could not be shown in Great Britain since it lampooned the heads of 'friendly' states. Shooting did not begin until 9 September 1939 and before he had finished the film in March 1940 the world seemed to be on fire. Chaplin recalled 'the news was growing gloomier, England was fighting with her back to the wall. Now our New York office was wiring frantically; "Hurry up with your film, everyone is waiting for it".' Despite the threats of censorship and crank letters promising stink bombs, riots and shooting up the screen, Chaplin's $2,000,000 film opened at both the Astor and Capitol theatres in New York on 15 October 1940. And despite Harry Hopkins's personal opinion that although a very worthwhile film, it would lose money, *The Great Dictator* ran for 15 weeks in New York alone and ended up as Chaplin's biggest grosser.

Chaplin opened the film with a prologue: 'This is a story of a period between two World Wars – an interim in which Insanity cut loose, Liberty took a nose dive and Humanity was kicked around somewhat.' The opening scene is on a battlefield in France at the end of World War I. Chaplin's tramp, a little Jewish barber, is a Tomanian artilleryman (the national symbol was the double-cross ‡) who fires a gigantic cannon destroying only an outdoor toilet and whose second shot finds the shell dropping out of the barrel. Ordered to defuse it, the shell points at him no matter which way he turns. Later the barber saves Schultz (Reginald Gardiner) a Tomanian pilot, but himself becomes the victim of amnesia. Twenty years pass with the little barber hospitalised. Changes in time through the 1920s are marked by newspaper headlines which end with 'Hynkel seizes power in Tomania'. Memory regained, the barber returns home unaware that the Hitler-like Adenoid Hynkel is his 'twin' in appearance. The puzzled barber finds his shop filled with the dust and spiders of 20 years but he cleans up and reopens for business.

Schultz, now one of the dictator's advisors, looks for his rescuer who by now was facing the threat of the storm-trooper attacks on the ghetto where Tomanian Jews had to live. JEW is painted on his barbershop but the barber ignorant of this new world simply cleans the word off to find himself attacked. At this moment the Jewish girl Hannah (Paulette Goddard) comes to the rescue but more storm troopers arrive and it is the appearance of Schultz that prevents the barber from being hung from the lamp-post.

Hynkel, the great dictator, prepares to invade Austerlich by cancelling the current pogroms in anticipation of securing a large loan from the Jewish financier, Epstein. Hynkel's fantastic ballet, danced to Wagner's music with the globe, is one of the most memorable scenes in the history of the cinema. In the end the globe bursts and Hynkel weeps hysterically. The loan is refused and the anti-Jewish pogroms are resumed despite the arguments by Schultz. Arrested for attempting to protect the Jews, Schultz escapes to the ghetto to join the barber and Hannah in hiding. The barbershop is destroyed, the people panic as the storm troopers hunt out the hiding population. All the while, the incomprehensible babblings of Hynkel are broadcast over the city's loudspeakers. Schultz then involves the barber in a plot to blow up Hynkel but their disguise as golf-playing tourists fails. Arrested, they are sent to a concentration camp while Hannah escapes to Austerlich.

Hynkel then combines forces with his rival, Benzino Napaloni,

Dictator of Bacteria, played with tremendous style by Jack Oakie. To calm the suspicions of the threatened Austerlich, Hynkel dons Tyrolean garb and goes duck shooting near the frontier. Schultz and the barber steal uniforms and escape from the nearby concentration camp while Hynkel capsizes, swims ashore and is arrested as the escaped barber! The barber, assumed to be the dictator, is driven into Austerlich by the invasion force while along the road posters announce that the ghetto has fallen and all Jewish property has been confiscated. Hannah and other Jewish refugees are facing assault by the invading Tomanian storm troopers. In the capital of the conquered nation, Tomanian foreign minister Garbitsch denounces liberty, equality and democracy to be immediately followed by the barber's plea for those very virtues which dictatorship sought to destroy. Chaplin's long sermon at the conclusion of the film (for which he was criticised) is best summarised in the opening paragraph.

> I'm sorry, but I don't want to be an emperor. That's not my business. I don't want to rule or conquer anyone. I should like to help everyone – if possible – Jew, Gentile, black men – white. We all want to help one another. Human beings are like that. We want to live by each other's happiness – not by each other's misery. We don't want to hate and despise one another. In this world there is room for everyone. And the good earth is rich and can provide for everyone.

Although Chaplin later admitted that he could not have made the picture burlesquing the dictators had he known the horrors against humanity which were being perpetrated, that did not change the message which was contained in his six-minute concluding speech – it was undoubtibly a unique example of an intensely personal statement on Europe's genocidal dictators.[9]

Warner Brothers had continued its interest in the European decline into barbarity and the potential effect upon the United States with its graphic, if not melodramatic, *Confessions of a Nazi Spy* (dir. Anatole Litvak) released in April 1939 which starred Edward G. Robinson as the G-man, Leon G. Turrou, Francis Lederer as the spy Schneider, and Paul Lukas as the German American Bund leader, Dr Kassel. Based on the sensational trials of 1937 in New York and the Canal Zone which followed the FBI's smashing of German espionage rings, the film vividly painted the

Nazi menace to American freedom by both spies and the German American Bund. The magnitude of the German propaganda effort was illustrated by an animated map of Europe featuring a revolving globe, swastica flags and German speakers in a style reflecting the influence of the *March of Time* and prefiguring its further development in the US Army's *Why We Fight* series, directed by Frank Capra. The film warned America of the Nazi menace but made no comment on Jewish persecution in Europe.

A positive Jewish statement was to be made in a muted way by Edward G. Robinson's next film for Warner Brothers *Dr Ehrlich's Magic Bullet* (dir. William Dieterle) released in February 1940. Although Robinson remembered only playing one specifically Anglo-Saxon role in his long and illustrious career, this superb characterisation of the discoverer of a cure for syphilis may have been his only specific Jewish role and he remembered it as his favourite film. The problem for the Hays' experts was not the Jewishness of its central character but the word syphilis; it was eventually to be spoken in the film for the first time in a legitimate Hollywood product but only after another twelve uses of it had been deleted. The Jewishness of Ehrlich was muted but quietly underlined by fine supporting performances by well-known Jewish character actors : Montague Love as Professor Hartmann and 73-year-old Albert Basserman in his first Hollywood film, after escaping from Germany as Robert Koch, the discoverer of anthrax bacillus. It was a film which lacked Chaplin-style preaching but in order to make a fine statement about the contribution to humanity by a Jewish scientist and doctor Warner Brothers took on the Hays Committee and its taboo on venereal disease.

The next Hollywood film to appear dealing with Nazi anti-Semitism was *So Ends Our Night* in 1941 (David L. Loew-Albert Lewin Production, United Artists dist.) directed by John Cromwell. The film follows the escape of an anti-Nazi German army captain from a concentration camp to the comparative safety of pre-Anschluss Vienna and, after its fall, on to Prague. Separated from his wife and without a passport, Josef Steiner (Frederic March) is but one of the thousands of refugees of post–1937 Europe, the central theme of Eric Remarque's novel *Flotsam* upon which the film was based. Paralleling the story of Steiner and his wife is that of two young Jewish refugees whom he has befriended, Ludwig Kern (Glenn Ford) and Ruth Holland (Margaret Sullavan). Steiner finally returns to Nazi Germany to be with his dying wife, later he commits suicide while in Gestapo custody. Quite remarkably for a Hollywood film, the young Jewish couple, having escaped across Switzerland to France and Paris, are the central love story and survivors of the plot, thus the characters with which the audience would have tended to identify. Although, as in the case of *The Mortal Storm*, Jews were non-Aryans, this stylish film was an important contribution to Hollywood's 'documentation' of the Nazi-directed barbarity against the Jewish people in Europe.[10] Four major films had been released within a period of twelve months that had a Jewish 'message' which had not been sent by Western Union!: *Dr Ehrlich's Magic Bullet* (February 1940), *The Mortal Storm* (June 1940), *The Great Dictator* (October 1940) and *So Ends Our Night* (January 1941). There were more messages to come.

Between 1941 and 1945 non-Aryans became Jews. Most of the Jews that were now to be seen in Hollywood movies were, not unexpectedly, heroes, particularly in films coming from Warner Brothers and Twentieth Century-Fox. *Action in the North Atlantic* (Warner Brothers, 1943, dir. Lloyd Bacon) is a good example of identifying Jewish characters by name, as well as casting Jewish actors in the roles. In this instance it was Sam Levene who played the important and heroic role of a merchant marine seaman, 'Chips' Abraham, fighting the weather and the U–boats. Warner Brothers followed this up in the same year with *Air Force* (dir. Howard Hawks) which had George Tobias as Corporal Weinberg; in 1944 the now notorious *Objective Burma* (dir. Raul Walsh) which had Errol Flynn defeating the Japanese without reference to the British army had a Jewish character, played by William Prince, promoted to Lieutenant Jacobs. (George Tobias played one of the paratroopers – non ethnic, however.) Twentieth Century-Fox, having in an earlier corporate form made *The House of Rothschild* (1934) took its social conscience gently in hand and publicised the existence of American Jews in the film version of Moss Harts' *Winged Victory* (1944, dir. George Cukor) which dealt with pilot training. The cast included such leading Jewish players as Judy Holliday, Lee J. Cobb and Red Buttons. Other films of this genre which recognised the Jewish contribution to the American war effort, included Fox's *A Walk in the Sun* (1945, dir. Lewis Milestone) and *Guadalcanal Diary* (1943, dir. Lewis Seiler). The laurels for the most unusual Jewish portrayal of Jewish servicemen had to go to *Bataan* (1943, dir, Tay Garnett, MGM) in which

Thomas Mitchell played his usual Irish iron-man role but this time with the name of Corporal Jake Feingold. Although there are other examples of the insertion of Jewish characters into the all-American fighting team featured in movie after movie, the most significant 'Jewish-contribution-to-the-American-way-of-life' role was that of Lieutenant Wayne Greenbaum in Darryl F. Zanuck's *The Purple Heart*, released in March 1944.

Based on the trail of eight captured American airmen who had been part of James Doolittle's famous B–25 raid on Tokyo, 18 April 1942, Greenbaum was part of an all-American crew which represented White Anglo-Saxon America, as well as the immigrant communities of the Irish, Italians and Poles, and the religious beliefs of Protestantism, Roman Catholicism, as well as Greenbaum's Judaism. Navigator for one of the aircraft, Greenbaum (Sam Levene) was a law graduate of City College of New York, that city's subway university for its aspiring masses of second-generation hypenate Americans like George Simon, the Jewish lawyer in Elmer Rice's *Counsellor-at-Law* (1933). Greenbaum was given the responsibility for defending the American sense of law and justice before the Japanese court, whose legality he challenged quoting from memory the entire prisoner-of-war clause from the Geneva Convention.[11]

This survey of Jewish war heroes makes it quite clear that of the major studios, Warner Brothers was most concerned, with Twentieth Century-Fox coming on very strong at the end of the war, with presenting a positive portrayal of the American Jew to the 40,000,000 or so movie-goers across the nation and in the theatres of war where these films were shown free of charge to servicemen through the auspices of the War Activities Committee of the Motion Picture Industry. In 1943 Jack Warner had put out a press statement after an extensive trip through the South, to New York, Chicago and Washington. As the release put it, after talking at length with high Government officials he came away from Washington 'with the conviction that motion pictures, while they cannot write the shape of the peace, can at least dip the pen in the ink . . . they can help interpret it and they must interpret it with the wisdom and power they apply to telling the story of the war'. Warner, the executive producer of Warner Brothers' Studios, along with his brothers was proud that they had dedicated their studios in 1943 to the 'production of pictures which will help the people to understand the peace and the victory'. He went on to list

Casablanca, *Yankee Doodle Dandy*, *Air Force*, *Watch on the Rhine*, *Action in the North Atlantic*, *Edge of Darkness* and *Mission to Moscow*. Jack Warner had also apparently committed himself to promoting a positive view of the Jewish contribution to America as part of his self-appointed task of helping 'the people to understand the peace and victory' in Warner Brothers' movies.[12] There were four possibilities. First, there was the Nazi-persecution context which MGM's *The Mortal Storm* and *Escape* utilised, as did the Loew-Lewin production of *So Ends the Night*. The second possibility was much favoured by Warners, being the presentation of the Jewish war hero in the on-going battle against the dictators; an approach favoured not only by Warner Brothers but by Twentieth Century-Fox. The third possibility harkened back to Warners' decision to look at anti-Semitism outside of the Nazi context by presenting the story of Captain Dreyfus in *Zola*, but of course that was French and historical anti-Semitism and thus distancing and less useful. A fourth possibility was the presentation of the positive Jewish contribution to civilisation, in one instance medical science, through *Dr Ehrlich's Magic Bullet* or simple humanitarianism in Warner Brothers British's production of *Father Takes a Walk*. Warner Brothers was apparently not totally opposed to making reference to anti-Semitism but preferred the more positive statements of humanitarian contribution and support of the war effort. The situation had, however, drastically changed and other voices were now fervently demanding the rescue of European Jewry using every means at their disposal to achieve their goal, including Hollywood.

Details of Hitler's 'final solution' had come finally from Gerhart Riegner, a representative of the World Jewish Congress, who had escaped from Germany to Switzerland and had communicated with Rabbi Stephen S. Wise, leader of America's Reformed Jewry and president of the American Jewish Congress. Wise, President Roosevelt's principal New York Jewish political manager, requested from the State Department confirmation, which it secured through an enquiry to the US legation at Bern. Wise published the horrifying information of genocide without any appreciable effect on American government policy. On 7 October 1942 the government promised that Nazi war criminals would be punished at the war's conclusion and on 17 December condemned the policy of Jewish extermination but Roosevelt's policy that victory would bring rescue prevailed. In January 1943 the Bern legation transmitted a second cable from Riegner (addressed to Dr Wise) reporting that the Nazis were killing 6,000 Polish Jews a day. Victory was too far off to offer rescue at that rate; the American Jewish Congress mounted a campaign to rescue their co-religionists, which included mass meetings (including Madison Square Garden), deputations to Washington, press releases and every form of political pressure and public persuasion that could be used was used. This included a direct approach to leaders of the Motion Picture industry with the plea that some studio should produce a film dramatising the genocide raging in Europe.[13]

The American Jewish Congress, apparently having been rebuffed by its Hollywood Jewish contacts, wrote to Lowell Mellett, Chief of the Bureau of Motion Pictures, Office of War Information,[14] requesting that he make representations to the studios as to the importance of making feature films depicting the enormity of the Nazi crime against the Jewish people of Europe. Mellett, a close advisor of President Roosevelt and long-time member of the Executive Branch, wrote to the American Jewish Congress of 5 February 1943 advising that the Hollywood office of the bureau had taken soundings amongst the various studio heads and had found that the reaction was that 'it might be unwise from the standpoint of the Jews themselves to have a picture dealing solely with Hitler's treatment of their people, but interest has been indicated in the possibility of a picture covering various groups that have been subject to the Nazi treatment. This of course would take in the Jews.'

The reaction to this advice was one of disbelief as it was expressed in a letter of 13 February to Mellett. The American Jewish Congress knew that the treatment of the Jews was 'unique in its horror' and that since 'our last meeting new and most harrowing information has come to us indicating that the extermination program has been so far accelerated as to have taken new toll of hundreds of thousands and possibly a million Jews'. (This would have been Riegner's second cable from Bern.) The AJC was prepared to provide the Office of War Information with explicit information; it was essential to provide the American people with the knowledge of these horrors through a major Hollywood movie. Such a film would be able to communicate the news that 'a whole people is being destroyed and . . . that the destruction of these people is an index of Hitler's intentions with respect to other innocent civilians'. The suggestion that Hollywood could meet the need by a general film treating persecution was sharply rejected with the comment that such a film had already been done on the Czechoslovakian town of Lidice. It did not fill the need, yet AJC was prepared to accept any feature film which could be made dramatising the Nazi campaign against 'all civilian populations' so long as the 'particular tragedy visited upon the Jews' was not neglected.[15]

Mellett and his Hollywood bureau headed by fellow New Dealer Nelson Poynter was not keen for any movie to be made that had anti-Semitism at its core; in fact, unknown to the American Jewish Congress, Mellett and Poynter were actively trying to stop production of a major film from Warner Brothers that, although making reference to Jews in Nazi concentration camps, was about anti-Semitism in the 'land of the free and the home of the brave' – the United States itself.

After the comparative success of *Dr Ehrlich's Magic Bullet*, Warner Brothers decided to move on from the Jewish humanitarian, while fostering the image of the Jewish war hero, into the serious waters of interpreting Jack Warners' 'shape of the peace' to come; that demanded that the American people face their own anti-Semitism. Adopting the tried and true Book-of-the-Month Club approach, Warner Brothers had settled on the novel *Mr Skeffington* by 'Elizabeth'. A modernised version of Job's sufferings, it featured the hard life of a completely devoted and admirable Jewish stockbroker married to a vain and totally self-centered debutante who refused to grow up. Julius and Philip Epstein were chosen (volunteered?) to produce the film and write the screenplay. The brothers had been initially responsible for *Casablanca's* script but had left it to Howard Koch (the three shared the Oscar), when they joined Frank Capra's newly established *Why We Fight* team in Washington in January-February 1942. They then returned to Hollywood to make *Mr Skeffington*, a film which would not explain war but would illustrate the manifestations of WASP prejudice towards Jews. The Revised Temporary Script of 26 September 1942 (178 pages) does not reach the Hollywood Office of the Bureau of Motion Pictures, OWI, until mid-February 1943, just at the moment that the news of the European genocide had been reconfirmed and the American Jewish Congress was unsuccessfully applying pressure for a major Hollywood film on the extermination of the Jews.

The Epsteins chose for their director the Georgia-born Vincent

Sherman, a highly competent technician with a flair for melodrama which fitted well into the standard Warner Brothers requirement. As an actor, he had most effectively played the part of the young Communist, Harry Becker, in the film version of Elmer Rice's *Counsellor-at-Law* (Universal, 1933) which had starred John Barrymore as the second-generation New York Jewish lawyer, George Simon. The most impressive scene in that film was the confrontation between Simon and the young Communist Jew, Becker (who later died from injuries received from a police beating), over how to deal with America's problems, by revolution or by assimilation, the latter being Simon's approach, as well as Job Skeffington's.

Job Skeffington had been born on New York's lower East Side in the same immigrant poverty as George Simon with his Jewish parents eking out a bare living with his father peddling chocolate with almonds from a pushcart. The name Skeffington was given by an immigration official who could not spell Skaviinskia. Job goes to work on Wall Street as a messenger, studies in night school and by 1910 or so is a major New York stockbroker with a mansion and racing stable. A young WASP ne'er-do-well, Trippy Trellis, defrauds Skeffington's firm of $24,000 which he squanders, as he had the family fortunes, on high living and betting on Job's horses. All seems lost when Trippy's beautiful sister Fanny decides to solve the family's problems by marry Job; he does not resist. Trippy is furious with his sister's marriage to a Jew and goes off to France to fly in the Lafayette Esquadrille against the Hun. Fanny continues her self-centred life, despite having given birth, reluctantly, to a daughter also called Fanny. Job silently suffers through all of this giving his love to the daughter and finding 'consolation' with a series of 'secretaries'. When Fanny learns the truth (she was in the company of a notorious gangster) she divorces Job, who not only relieves her financial anxiety by an overly generous settlement but takes the responsibility of raising the daughter. To escape the love he still holds for Fanny he moves his business to Berlin, only sending the daughter, a dark-haired beauty, back to the United States ten years later in the face of the Nazi threat. The beautiful blond-haired Fanny faces her daughter, a measure of her own fading youth, and a serious case of diphtheria which destroys her remaining beauty and almost herself. At this point Job reappears blind and destitute, the victim of a Nazi concentration camp. Fanny has lost her beauty but Job can only see her as she was. He still loves her totally. She takes him in and thus the happy ending.

OWI Hollywood could just see Bette Davis as Fanny and Claude Rains as Job – the film, which would be a major Warner Bros production, had to be stopped in the interests of the war effort.[16]

> 'Confidential'
> This script, in its present form, is gravely detrimental to the War Information Program. The most acute problem is the introduction of the anti-Semitic problem.

More specifically it dealt with the anti-Semitism faced by the four-and-a-half million Jewish American citizens.

> From the standpoint of the [OWI] Overseas Branch, the Jewish question is presented in such a way as to give credence to the Nazi contention that the discrimination for which American [sic] condemn the fascists, is an integral part of American democracy. Furthermore, the characterization of Skeffington, a Jew, as the richest and most powerful man in Wall Street, lends colour to the Nazi propaganda that Jews control the money interests in all countries. Americans and the values of the American way are misrepresented. The characterization of them as chiefly concerned with money is a further confirmation of Nazi world propaganda about America. And the only Congressman in the story is shown to be completely unfit for his job.
>
> From the domestic standpoint, minority problems in this country are a social evil and should be treated as such. Nothing is gained by a presentation which states a problem yet fails to examine it and offers no solution. Skeffington's characterization as a Jew is not essential to the development of the story and it is strongly recommended that the studios be urged to eliminate entirely any connotation of a minority question, which, unless presented as a social document, offers a major problem from the standpoint of OWI.

There was also an objection to talking about 'Socialists on streetcorners' which reflected badly on one of America's allies, Russia. The assessment of Hollywood OWI (done by P. Fenwick and Dorothy Jones, with Poynter's concurrence) was echoed by Ulrich Bell of the Overseas Branch and his boss, formerly Hollywood's highest paid screenwriter, Robert Riskin.

Riskin was (letter of 1 March) especially worried about the Skeffington project 'not only because it is more objectionable than the others, but because it is bound to emerge as a very important film, and therefore, receive wide distribution'. He was less worried about the relatively unimportant cheap films, as he put it, in the pipeline, possibly referring to two films at Columbia Studios (which might have been a response to the American Jewish Congress plea for films on the genocide of Jews): *None Shall Escape* (released in 1943, 85 minutes in length) and *Address Unknown* (1944, 72 minutes).[17]

Warner Brothers ignored both the Office of War Information's criticism and its veiled threats and pressed on with the film as it had been originally conceived and presented to OWI in the revised script. It was not enough to show the Jewish fighting hero; it was also necessary to show the discrimination that he suffered in peacetime as an unjustified aspect of his American citizenship. There was a difference between American prejudice which Job Skeffington suffered and Nazi racism which blinded and almost killed him. The Epsteins obviously had faith in the American audience understanding the qualitative difference between the two forms of anti-Semitism and ameliorating its attitude towards its American Jewish fellow citizens.

The film was not oblivious to its reponsibilities towards propaganda and the war effort, as is clearly evidenced by an after-dinner scene in the Skeffington home after America had entered World War I. Job, now Captain in the US Army, settles down at home with his family to watch newsreels from the western front. One scene showing the King of England provokes from Fanny the comment 'He looks like a very nice man' to which Job replies 'He is'. Contrast the pro-British assessment (by the projectionist of the hand-cranked machine) with the following sequence of Field Marshall Hindenberg reviewing German troops: 'They all look the same . . . They start goose-stepping at 2 years old.' Trippy, the brother, flying with the Lafayette Equadrille (also seen in the newsreel) at the beginning of the war, later joins the Army Air corps on the US entry only to be killed in action.

There was some sensitivity to the OWI criticism about painting anti-Semitism too strongly and the script's reference to hotels which would no longer welcome Fanny with a Jewish husband was dropped. The main scene where Jewishness (as opposed to the ongoing discrimination faced by Job) was discussed was in the restaurant where Job tried to help young Fanny (Gigi Perreau) understand the future now that her parents were divorced. Job's daughter desperately wanted to stay with her father, despite the court's awarding of custody to her mother, who had never shown the child any affection. Job explains that being half Jewish would make her very different in Europe, as if, by implication, no such prejudice existed in America; an implication totally rejected by his own experience. References to Nazi censorship and persecution are made after the daughter returns to the United States, but all of this is prior to the opening of the war in 1939. The message of American anti-Semitism was clear and yet the film, when it was released in August of 1944 proved a resounding success. Drawing rave notices, the 146-minute film earned Academy Award nominations for both Bette Davis and Claude Rains and took another step in forcing the nation to look critically at its own unwarranted prejudice. This was not illusory prejudice but a very real prejudice which was measured each time the Office of War Information surveyed public opinion. A typical example is the opening paragraph from a report of 27 July 1942 entitled 'Group Attitudes and prejudices in the War Effort – Anti-Semitism'. That report found widespread anti-Semitic sentiment in half of the 42-states survey with an 'extreme concentration in the populous States east of the Mississippi and north of the Ohio River'. Criticism included the contention that Jews had taken over the Government, were war profiteers, avoiding the draft and seeking noncombatant commissions in the military. An OWI Field Representative report from Pennsylvania claimed: 'There is definite antagonism against the Jews. This unreasonable hate, voiced at the bridge tables and at dinner parties in the homes of the middle class, convinces us that all is not going too well in our effort to make this war meaningful.' The anti-Semitism explicit in these charges prevailed throughout the war despite the efforts of some Hollywood studios, such as Warner Brothers, to re-educate the American people.[18]

Members of the American Jewish Congress might well have been pleased when they learned that their pleas for movies on the specific persecution of Jews had been answered, albeit by 'cheap' rather than prestige films, such as *Mr Skeffington*. The first of them was Columbia's *None Shall Escape* which, when it had been released in Boston and New York in January 1943, produced 'disturbances in the theatres, in most cases deliberately planned and carried out by anti-Semitic elements . . . When the Jews were being mowed down, they cheered!' This film was a war-crime trial film in which Wilhelm Grimm's (a former German schoolteacher in the Polish town of Litzbark) fanatical Nazi past is recalled. The most horrifying scene took place when Grimm (Alexander Knox – soon to play Woodrow Wilson) ordered the Jews of Litzbark into trains bound for the concentration camps. When the Jews respond to their Rabbi's call to fight, they are machined gunned to death. Another film to draw strong public reaction of a pro-Nazi variety was Paramount's *The Hitler Gang* (1943) made by Buddy DeSylva who wanted to made a film as effective as *Ohm Kruger* which he had seen earlier that year. He did not succeed and *The Hitler Gang* was not widely distributed. A third film in this persecution genre appeared, also from Paramount, entitled *Address Unknown* from a story by Kressman Taylor. The horrifying conclusion of this tale was the bloodstained handprint of a Jewish American actress hunted by dog-led Gestapo across Germany where she hoped to find sanctuary with her father's former partner and her father-in-law-to-be. She is rejected and dies.[19] Finally MGM committed itself to a prestige production of *The Seventh Cross* (1944, dir. Fred Zinnemann) which starred Spencer Tracy as George Heisler, one of seven men to escape from a Nazi concentration camp. Only one of the seven, who were crucified by the camp commandant as they were captured, was Jewish but with the story set in 1936 it would not have been an unreasonable number and reflected the OWI concern to keep the Jewish persecution in the overall context of the Nazi general crimes against humanity. In one important scene, however, producer Pandros Berman dramatically presents the Jew as hero and humanitarian, an achievement in cinemagraphic terms which Jack Warner could appreciate. In the escape Heisler seriously injures his hand and goes to a doctor for treatment. Dr Lowenstein tells Heisler that by law he must notify all prospective patients, 'I am a Jew'. Heisler accepts the treatment and Lowenstein, well aware that Heisler is wanted by the Gestapo, risks his life by not reporting the incident.

Warner Brothers continued to project positive Jewish values into every film that could handle the message without seeming too obvious. The story of *The Grand Hotel* (1932) was resurrected and retitled *Hotel Berlin*, while working into the plot two Jewish-related stories. Since the film was released in early 1945, the American columnist Walter Winchell took delight in announcing that Warner Brothers had beaten the Russians to Berlin! The film is perhaps more interesting from the point of view of the criticism it received for being too kind to the Germans as they watched the remains of the Third Reich collapsing about them. One film which must be taken into consideration was quite unlike any of the others mentioned thus far in what we might call the Hollywood 'Jewish output'. It was not a persecution, nor war hero, nor humanitarian film quite in the sense of the others mentioned. *Tomorrow the World* (1944, dir. Leslie Fenton, dis. United Artists) was scripted by Ring Lardner Jr and Leopold Atlas from the play of the same name by Arnaud D'Usseau and James Gow. The Jewish heroine with the incredible name of Leona Richards was played by Betty Field. The central figure of the film is a Nazi youth whose anti-Nazi father has died in a concentration camp and is being raised by his uncle, an American college professor (Frederic March). The twelve-year-old boy wreaks havoc at school with his racism and hatred and has his democratic 'conversion experience' only on the verge of being committed to a reformatory for the attempted murder of the professor's teenage daughter. The problem was set clearly by one character when she asked: 'If we cannot solve the problem of one Nazi child now heaven help the twelve million of them after the war'. By 1944 Jewish references could be made with less concern, at least so it would seem. The film was selected by the Hollywood Writers Mobilization for a premiere and town meeting on 30 January 1945 giving *Tomorrow the World* its first (and last?) Writers Award for Distinguished Motion Picture Achievement.

Meanwhile Warner Brothers producer Jerry Wald had adopted another perpective for the post-war problem of anti-Semitism in America. Whereas blind Job Skeffington had been a wealthy stockbroker World War I Army officer, Wald would update the story on a working-class level with *Pride of the Marines*, showing both the heroism of a Jewish Marine in the South Pacific and his own fears that the peace he had been fighting to win would be clouded with the anti-Semitism he had faced in his youth. *Pride of the Marines* was taken from a book by Roger Butterfield, with the adaptation by Marvin Borfield and the script by the Communist screenwriter Albert Maltz. Starring the Jewish actor John Garfield as working-class Al Schmidt, the love interest was supplied by Eleanor Parker. When Pearl Harbor is attacked, Al decides that it would be 'more fun shooting Japs than bears'. Schmidt joins the Marines and finds himself with the rest of his machine-gun crew on Guadacanal where intercut newsreel material adds a marginal note of authenticity in a film generally short on realism. Symbolically the 30-calibre machine gun has a Shamrock, the word 'Chief', and the Star of David painted on the side of the breech. The Jewish crew member, Lee Diamond (Dane Clark) is wounded and Schmidt blinded by an exploding grenade is forced to fire the gun alone against a Japanese counterattack. Schmidt and Diamond are sent to a Navy Hospital in California. Here Virginia (Rosemary De Camp), a Red Cross worker, tries to wrench Schmidt out of his self pity and face probable permanent blindness. Director Delmar Davies anticipated the central theme of William Wyler's *The Best Years of Our Lives* (1946) with a sensitive set piece of a dart game where the recuperating Marines expressed their doubts as to their ability to return to their wives and to society. It is Lee Diamond who breaks in: 'Ah, come on, climb out of your foxholes, what's a matter you guys, don't you think anybody learned anything since 1930? Think everybody's had their eyes shut and brains in cold storage?' The GI Bill of Rights was cited as evidence that they were going to have a shot at a new life and a college education as well as the guarantee of their old jobs. One man bitterly said his old boss was in a new business and his old job 'just ain't'. Another says that when he gets back to El Centro he will find a Mexican has got his job. The racial jibe is caught by a wheelchair-bound Mexican-American Marine, Juan. It is Diamond who calls down the racist remark saying that Juan has spent more time in combat than the other man in the Marine corps. Diamond continues by saying that just because they fought the war they could not expect a free ride: 'I fought for me, for the right to live in the USA. And when I get back into civilian life if I don't like the way things are going, OK its my country; I'll stand on my own two legs and holler! If there's enough of us hollering we'll go places – Check?' After establishing the need for political involvement to prevent another war, Diamond proceeds to 'wrap it up' with the background music of 'America the beautiful' slowly coming up: 'One happy afternoon when God was feeling good, he sat down and thought of a rich beautiful country and he named it the USA. All of it – Al, the hills, the rivers, the lands, the whole – works. Don't tell me we can't make it work in peace like we do in war. Don't tell me we can't pull together. Don't you see it guys, can't you see it?'

Schmidt tries to break with Ruth because of his blindness, but he is ordered to the Philadelphia Naval Hospital. As the train approaches Al's home town of Philadelphia, Diamond compares

Al's physical disabilities with those he suffered as a Jew. He accuses Al of being 'a hopped up kid looking for excitement' – not a hero. Diamond says that some had to die and others be maimed but they were not 'suckers' but 'had lost some chips in the winning'. Al replies that Lee has no problems. He answers: 'That's what you think. Sure there will be guys who won't hire you even when they know you could handle the job. But there's guys who won't hire me because my name is Diamond instead of Jones; because I celebrate Passover instead of Easter. Do you see what I mean? You and me, we need the same kind of world, a country to live in where nobody gets booted around for any reason.' It is Lee who arranges with Ruth for the reconciliation, completing the pivotal role he plays in the film. Al eventually accepts his blindness, although the realistic edge is considerably blunted by a partial return of his sight, unlike Job Skeffington, at the end of the film. The German-American Al Schmidt was a hero in the foxhole but the post-war strength and optimism is that of Diamond, who is both an American Marine hero and a Jew; a man who has known prejudice but alone of the wounded Marines in the hospital holds out the promises of the American dream against the pessimism of his comrades. The parting worlds of the two Navy Cross winners, Schmidt and Diamond, was the Hebrew phase *Shalom Aleichem* – Peace be with you.[20] It would be another two years before such an articulate Jewish war hero would again appear, and then it would be John Garfield in *Gentlemen's Agreement* (1947).

It was perhaps fitting that the most active of the pro-Jewish studios, Warner Brothers, should see the war out with an entirely different sort of film. For five years it had been injecting pro-Jewish themes into relevant pictures stressing the humanitarian contribution, the military contribution, and finally the domestic implications for anti-Semitism in the new America adawning. While Jerry Wald was producing *Pride of the Marines* with the Jewish Al Diamond reminding his war-shattered comrades of the reality of the American dream as well as the anti-Semitism which severely limited his share of it, Howard Koch and Elliot Paul were writing *Rapsody in Blue*, loosely based on the life of the Jewish composer George Gershwin. The Jewishness of Gershwin's family made 'vaguely evident by fearfully playing an occasional Jewish melody in the background and by using for comedy purposes a limited number of Jewish attitudes, some of which are pretty funny (*New Republic*, 23 July 1945)'. As a whole the film provided a highly sympathetic portrait of Gershwin, his Jewish family and friends (Oscar Levant played his usual self-deprecating Jewish self).

This study of Hollywood films that recognised the existence of the Jewish people in terms of their suffering[21] as well as their contributions to America and the world, has inadequately illustrated the dilemma felt by those wholly sympathetic to all Four Freedoms, especially Freedom of Religion. There was a tradition that in America said: Anti-Semitism here is not so bad. If we complain about it, it will get worse. Others, led, it would seem, by Jack Warner[22] argued that you could not build a new tomorrow for all Americans if the problem were not faced squarely and overcome. To that noble end Warner Brothers Studios worked throughout the war years, continuing a committment which went back to *The Life of Emile Zola*. MGM and Twentieth Century-Fox made their contributions, as did Harry Cohn's Columbia Studios. These films are, however, but a handful when seen in the context of Hollywood's output of 2,000-plus films in the war period, although a significant handful considering the general silence before 1940. These wartime Jewish-component films fall into the three general categories: (1) Jewish war heroes, (2) Jewish persecution and (3) Jewish humanitarian contributions. Whereas the Office of War Information happily supported the presence of Jewish members in each and every all-American fighting team on land, sea or in the air the persecution pictures fall largely into the period at the end of the war when OWI Domestic influence was fading due to budgetary cutbacks, but Hollywood's independence from such political pressure was evident throughout 1940–5. *Mr Skeffington*, as a humanitarian suffering WASP bigotry, emerges as the most significant statement on American prejudice which OWI wanted to ignore temporarily. Al Diamond's Chaplin-like sermon at the end of *Pride of the Marines* put the sum total of Job Skeffington's experience of American anti-Semitism: The dictators were dead but racism lived on; could post-war America defeat that enemy as well?

Notes

1. *Mr Emmanuel* (Two Cities, dir. Harold French) had a screenplay by Louis Golding (who wrote the novel upon which it was based) and Gorden Wellesley. Finished in 1944, it was not released by United Artists in the United States until

January 1945. Felix Aylmer played the title role of Mr Emmanuel, which in Hebrew means 'God with us'.

2. Cf. Pierre Sorlin, 'Jewish Images in the French Cinema of the 1930s', *Historical Journal of Film, Radio and Television*, vol. I, no. 2 (1981) and Elizabeth Strebel, 'Jean Renoir and the Popular Front' in K.R.M. Short (ed.), *Feature Films as History* (London, 1981), p. 89.

3. Based on a play by George Hembert Westley, Nunnally Johnson wrote the screen play. The film premiered in New York at the Astor Theatre in mid-March 1934 and on 23 April a report from Paris stated that the French censors had banned the film, despite United Artists' appeal. Whether it was the reference to Napoleon as the 'blasted little Corsican' or its blatant anti-Nazi, and thus anti-neighbour, theme that was the basis of the rejection is not clear; it might have been both. The quotation is from Richard Watts Jr, *New York Herald Tribune*, 18 March 1934. *The House of Rothschild*, Watts also noted, with its emphasis upon the world-wide power of this Jewish family had the effect of reinforcing one of the central anti-Semitic themes prevalent in America and Europe. Dr Goebbels apparently considered sub-titling or dubbing the sound track to his own anti-Semitic purpose but eventually settled for using the long section of the Rothschild patriarch hiding everything of value (including the roast) from the extortionist tax collector and then pleading poverty in *Der Ewige Jude* (1940). Goebbels cut the scene at the point where the tax collector takes a bribe rather than exact the full demands of the Jew-oppressing state.

4. For a detailed discussion of these two films and others of the period see K.R.M. Short, 'The Experience of Eastern Jewry in America as Portrayed in the Cinema of the 1920s and 30s' in K.R.M. Short and K. Fledelius, *History & Film: Methodology, Research and Education* (Eventus, Copenhagen 1980). For further discussion of these films and others featured in this article, see Lester D. Friedman, *Hollywood's Image of the Jew* (Ungar, New York, 1982) an extremely well-written and stimulating survey of the subject from the early silents to 1980.

5. Friedman (ibid.) in his chapter 'The Timid thirties' (pp 55–85) unfortunately perpetuates the statement (to be found in discussions of this film) that '"Jew" is never heard in the movie' (p. 78). Technically correct, it totally ignores the visual impact of the scene described which has the word 'Jew' covering a very large part of the movie screen. Friedman takes only a brief notice of *Father Takes a Walk* (also Warner Brothers), but a detailed look at *Confessions of a Nazi Spy* (Warner Brothers). Jack Warner in his book *My First Hundred Years in Hollywood* (New York, 1964) provided one clue to Warner Brothers' marked antagonism towards the Nazi regime with his recounting of the 1936 murder by Nazi thugs in Berlin of Warner Brothers' chief salesman in Germany, Joe Kaufman. Warner Brothers may have been prompted finally to close down their German operation by this event, but the causal relationship is far from clear.

6. Victor Saville claims to have produced and directed most of *The Mortal Storm* because Sidney Franklin was tied up with *Waterloo Bridge* and Borzage had trouble 'dealing with the Jewish business'. I am grateful to Jan-Christopher Horak for pointing this out and for several other most helpful comments on an early draft of this article.

7. Friedman, *Hollywood's Image of the Jew*, p. 103.

8. Warner Brothers' theatre circuit of two hundred theatres refused to show the *March of Time's Inside Nazi Germany* (Vol. 4, issue 6) because it was considered to be pro-Nazi propaganda; Warner Brothers had exclusive contractual rights for MoT. It also rejected the *Nazi Conquest – No. 1* (Vol. 4, issue 9) later that year, but without comment. For a detailed discussion see Raymond Fielding, *The March of Time, 1935–1951* (New York, 1978), Ch. 8, pp. 229ff. Until there is a comprehensive study of the contents of the American newsreels, there is no way of

estimating the extent to which they informed audiences as to the Nazi menace or the anti-Semitic persecution.

9. Charles Chaplin, *My Autobiography* (Harmondsworth, 1976), pp. 393ff. The entire text of the concluding speech is reproduced here.

10. Erich von Stroheim played the Gestapo agent who died handcuffed to Steiner when he leapt to his death from Gestapo headquarters. The film also contained memorable comic relief scenes by Leonid Kinskey – 'The Chicken'.

11. A detailed description of *The Purple Heart* is found in K.R.M. Short, 'Hollywood Fights Anti-Semitism, 1945–1947' in K.R.M. Short (ed.), *Feature Films as History* (London, 1981) pp. 158ff.

12. Press release, unheaded, no date; Box 1433, entry 264, Office of War Information, Record Group [RG] 208, Washington National Records Center, Suitland, Maryland [*WNRC*].

13. See particularly H.L. Feingold, *The Politics of Rescue: The Roosevelt Adminstration and the Holocaust, 1938–1945* (New Brunswick, NJ, 1970). The Assistant Secretary of State, Breckinridge Long, forbade further use of the Bern-Wise link, actively suppressed further information on the Final Solution and used delaying tactics to prevent rescue efforts. As a result the Americans, at least a great majority of them, remained ignorant of what Hitler was doing to the Jews. The situation was overcome partically with the establishment of the War Refugee Board in early 1944. Typical of the US government's reaction to the news of Jewish genocide is the statement made by Secretary of State Cordell Hull on 30 October 1942 in connection with the twenty-fifth anniversary of the Balfour Declaration of 2 November 1917: 'This country was shocked and outraged when tyranny and barbarity again commenced their march, at the brutality which was inflicted on certain races, and particularly on the Jewish populations of Europe. Apparently, no form of abuse has been too great, and no form of torture or oppression too vile, to be meted out to these populations by the Nazi despots. And, in taking this attitude toward the Jewish race, they have made it plain by concrete acts that a like attitude would be taken toward any other race against whom they might invent a grievance.

The Jews have long sought a refuge. I believe that we must have an even wider objective; we must have a world in which Jews, like every other race, are free to abide in peace and in honor.' (In Box 1832, Office of Government Reports RG44, *WNRC*).

14. The development and activities of the OWI are summarised in A.M. Winkler's *The Politics of Propaganda, The Office of War Information, 1942–1945* (New Haven, Conn. 1978).

15. Correspondence in Box 1440, entry 264, RG 208, *WNRC*. There were, in fact, two films made and released in 1943 dealing with the murder of Heydrich and the extermination of the town and population of Lidice; *Hitler's Madman* (MGM, dir. Douglas Sirk) and *Hangmen Also Die* which was directed and produced by Fritz Lang with Berthold Brecht.collaborating with Lang on the script. There was also the fascinating British Ministry of Information production by Humphrey Jennings which was shot in documentary style. Entitled *The Silent Village* (1943) it featured the inhabitants of a Welsh mining village playing the parts of their martyred Czech counterparts.

16. Bette Davis had won two Academy Awards for Best Actress playing just such roles while Rains had recently been nominated for Academy Awards for roles in *Mr Smith Goes to Washington* (1939) and *Casablanca* (1943).

17. Boxes 3510, 1434, entry 566, RG 208, *WNRC*.

18. Box 1842, entry 144, RG 44, *WNRC*.

19. Before the war Paul Muni almost did *Address Unknown* for the CBS programme Mercury Theater radio series (produced by Orson Welles) but the

sponsor, Campbell's Soups, vetoed it on the grounds that it was too controversial. See Jerome Lawrence, *Actor: The Life and Times of Paul Muni* (London, 1975) p. 248.

20. *Pride of the Marines* did not figure in the major Academy Award nominations that year, which were dominated by Billy Wilder's *The Lost Weekend* (Paramount), winning best picture, best direction and best actor. While *Pride* was making a straightforward statement on the American Jew, in *The Lost Weekend* the writer Don Birnam (Ray Milland) staggers down New York's Third Avenue clutching his typewriter looking for a pawn shop. In the novel he found out from two Jews in their 'Sunday best' that all Jewish owned pawnshops were closed for Yom Kippur and that was all. In the screen version Birnam cries: 'What about Kelly's and Gallagher's [other pawnshops]?' They explain 'They keep closed on Yom Kippur and we don't open on St Patrick's', which was to say that the Jews at least were no more peculiar than the Irish. At best it was an apologetic approach to the role of the Jew as a despised pawnbroker.

21. Two 'black comedies' are relevant to the discussion but have not been dealt with in this article, *Once Upon a Honeymoon* (RKO, dir. Leo McCarey, 1942) and Ernst Lubitsch's *To Be Or Not To Be* (United Artists, 1942); a third comedy worth study is *Margin for Error* (Twentieth Century-Fox, dir. Otto Preminger, 1943). These films had not been viewed by the author and thus have been excluded from the study; they are, however, discussed in Lester Friedman's *Hollywood's Image of the Jew* (pp. 109–15). Another film that has been excluded, which might surprise readers, is Jean Renoir's *This Land is Mine* (RKO, 1943). Several film historians have listed this as dealing with anti-Semitism but Renoir, perhaps under studio restraint, did not make his usual statement on Jews in French (the setting is 'European') society. Also *Three Faces West* (Republic, dir. B. Vorhaus, 1940) starred Charles Coburn as a post-Anschluss Viennese refugee 'Dr Braun' but no effort was made to establish why he was a refugee.

22. The conjecture that Jack Warner was largely behind the conscious pro-Jewish productions of his studio will remain only that until the corporate records of the studio deposited at the University of Wisconsin, the University of Southern California, and Princeton University are carefully sifted. Even then the answer may not be available. Harry Warner seems to have been involved in the efforts to block the making of *Gentleman's Agreement* in 1947. See Russell Campbell, 'The Ideology of the Social Consciousness Movie: Three Films of Darryl F. Zanuck', *Quarterly Review of Film Studies*, vol. 3, no. 1 (Winter 1978).

7 'WHY WE FIGHT': SOCIAL ENGINEERING FOR A DEMOCRATIC SOCIETY AT WAR

David Culbert

The past decade has seen an important shift in emphasis by historians interested in World War II, from battles and strategy to transportation of supplies, secret codes and morale – what might be termed the 'soft' side of military history.[1] We look to the war's indirect effects on the home front for which industrial productivity and military manpower requirements are responsible. Geoffrey Perrett is correct in describing a social revolution which occurred within the United States between 1941 and 1945, the actuality which New Deal slogans had been unable to bring about.[2] The key to that revolution is economic prosperity combined with technological innovation, in a society whose distinctive contribution is often a triumph of scale. Within the American Army, acceptance of social science research techniques and heavy reliance on media technology suggests that generals can sometimes be True Believers. Total war proved the right time to give innovation a massive degree of support.[3]

Military enthusiasm for social science research and media technology relates to the concept of Social Engineering, an outgrowth of behavioural psychology arguing that human behaviour can be manipulated towards socially desirable goals.[4] Critics of industrial societies had long complained that as technology spread its benefits, it also eroded traditional values. Optimistic social scientists believed that a 'humane' or 'liberal' use of film could reaffirm the values of a democratic society. In practice the relation between film and social science proved to be symbiotic: each used the other to gain popular acceptance.

There is another way of defining social engineering: the need to offer a reason *why* to an educated citizenry. 'Give me the man who knows that for which he fights', Oliver Cromwell declared, 'and loves that which he knows.' Mass education made it harder to avoid factual explanations; if the Light Brigade really charged into battle without knowing 'the reason why'; few citizens could be found in Depression America so willing to follow authority blindly. In 1916, 1.7 million Americans were in high school; in 1940, 7.1 million. In

1916, 400,000 attended college; in 1940, 1.4 million.[5] Franklin Roosevelt's 'fireside chats' assumed educated Americans who wanted explanations for citizen obligations. Acceptance of state policy, everyone seemed to agree, demanded some reason why. Not necessarily the whole truth, mind you, but at least plausible justification.

As a result the Army found new responsibilities in the area of morale, long a matter of interest to field commanders, but now allied with the 'science' of public relations and behavioural psychology. Within the Army the Morale Branch, or the Information and Education Division or I&E as it was finally called, became the centre for dramatic experimentation, an entire division which might have been called the Center for Social Engineering. Dedicated to offering reasons why, its seven orientation films, the *Why We Fight* series, must be considered one of its greatest achievements. The title suggests a fascination with reason, and the propagandist's understanding of combining patriotism with selected facts. The medium showed a sturdy faith in technology's ability to wed the educated citizen to his soldier's calling.

Brigadier General Frederick H. Osborn headed I&E.[6] A wealthy New Yorker without prior military service, Osborn had impeccable family connections and a genius for administration. His father was one of Secretary of War Henry Stimson's close friends; an uncle, Henry Fairfield Osborn, had been largely responsible for the rise to international prominence of New York's Museum of Natural History. Osborn, also a board member of the Social Science Research Council, with a scholarly study of eugenics to his credit, came to the Army persuaded that morale could be determined by scientific means, and that traditional morale boosters – sports, camp songfests, 'decks of cards and dice and tonettes' – belonged to a bygone era. Osborn also had a physical presence of immense value when selling new ideas to possibly resistant career types; he was, as Alfred Kazin remembers him, 'spectacularly tall'. When Osborn needed to, he could also be a tough fighter amidst the empire-builders who saw wartime as just the right moment for any number of elaborate ideas.

The most important reason for Osborn's success was not his ability to keep immensely-gifted people working in some sort of harmony, but the backing of Secretary of War Stimson, and, in particular, General George C. Marshall, Army Chief of Staff. Osborn's greatest interest lay in social science research and the group headed by Samuel Stouffer which introduced *What the Soldier Thinks*. For General Marshall, a more important I&E priority was film. As a Civilian Conservation Corps Commander in the Pacific northwest during the 1930s, he had seen how effective feature films shown off the back of trucks could be for morale.[7] Since President Roosevelt never put much stock in a civilian propaganda agency, really elaborate film programmes required the backing of the military and the protection 'wartime defence' afforded.

What really turned Marshall into a zealous proponent of educational film was his intense dissatisfaction with existing methods of troop indoctrination – mandatory orientation talks. Few human beings are inspiring public speakers; the Army's canned lectures made it less likely that individual delivery could be effectively related to the subject – especially in 'recreation halls' where the talks were given. The Bureau of Public Relations prepared 15 lectures in the autumn of 1941 to explain foreign affairs, 1919–39, to all new troops. The results were disastrous; most commanders considered orientation a waste of time or a mandatory rest hour. Few could see how the past could be made vivid and interesting enough to make some uninformed eighteen-year-old see why he was being inducted.[8]

Although these talks failed completely, the idea of using film for orientation was not Marshall's alone; it was an idea whose time had come. A single film, Leni Riefenstahl's *Triumph of the Will* (1935) did more to make all of World War II's belligerents rely on film for morale purposes than anything else. *Triumph of the Will* showed military leaders and filmmakers the world over how compelling a device film could be for the propagandist. Also effective distribution of the film to remote parts of Germany suggested that film could unify an entire population.

There are extraordinary similarities between the concept and practice of information, orientation, and propaganda but the *Why We Fight* series is propaganda, no doubt about it. Facts were selected with an eye to offering emotional reasons for supporting one's own war effort, the cause of one's allies, and for fearing and hating one's enemies. The specific content of the seven completed films (the final film was originally in two parts) cannot be discussed here, but the series justified American participation as unavoidable. *Prelude to War* conveniently simplified things by dividing the world into free and slave; *The Nazis Strike* showed the *blitzkrieg* in the Low Countries and Poland, and made the enemy appear suitably threatening; *Divide and Conquer* attributed the collapse of France to fifth columnists – it seemed at times to lecture more about internal subversion than the reality of France's collapse. *The Battle of Britain* pulled out all the stops to make the heroism of the British admirable enough to paper over memories of Chamberlain; *The Battle of Russia* used Soviet and German footage to depict Soviet heroism, especially at Stalingrad. Not only was the film effective, but its official origin made it one of the most persuasive attempts at quieting persistent anti-Soviet sentiment inside the United States. *The Battle of China* was a fairy tale, or flatfooted propaganda which relied on too much Hollywood feature footage. The film was formally withdrawn from circulation but later reissued. *War Comes to America* went over the same ground as *Prelude to War*, but was more concerned with visualising the American people and tracing the growth of pro-war sentiment than in defining the universal threat of Fascism. Especially interesting was the use of Gallup poll data to document graphically changes in public opinion.[9]

To term the *Why We Fight* films propaganda is not to dismiss them as a tissue of lies. They were truthful in the way Emily Dickinson sensed all effective propaganda must be:

> Tell all the truth, but tell it slant –
> Success in circuit lies.
> . . .
> The truth must dazzle gradually,
> Or every man be blind.

A technological society depends on propaganda to persuade its citizens that its actions are legitimate. It becomes an enterprise, Jacques Ellul argues, 'for perverting the significance of events and of insinuating false intentions'. Michael Balfour distinguishes between the method of science and art of propaganda, 'inducing people to leap to conclusions without adequate examination of the evidence'.[10] Ellul struggles to relieve propaganda of its negative or pejorative connotations, for he feels that propaganda is necessary to modern decision-making, that in practice it cannot be separated from information, education, or public relations, and that with more education we become even more susceptible to the allure of propaganda. The reason, Ellul believes, is obvious:

> Modern man worships 'facts' – that is, he accepts 'facts' as the ultimate reality . . . Facts in themselves provide evidence and proof, and he willingly subordinates values to them; he obeys what he believes to be necessity, which he somehow connects with the idea of progress.

In spite of Ellul, the cynical definition of propaganda offered by F.M. Cornford finds continued acceptance: 'that branch of the art of lying which consists in very nearly deceiving your friends without quite deceiving your enemies'.[11]

The more thought one gives to the struggle between ends and means the more slippery the concept of objective truth becomes; the less easy to say with certainty what the contextual significance of any fact is. Education assumes the rational man as an attainable ideal; given sufficient facts or sufficient perception of objective reality, so one is taught to believe, it is possible to know the truth about public issues of the day. But propaganda lies behind every opinion we hold on public issues. No moral or religious code arms the citizen sufficiently in the quest for separating what is true from what is not. 'Arguments can easily cancel one another out', Balfour concludes, 'and the upshot of discussion may be that all possible courses of action seem open to objection, so that Mr Valiant-for-Truth ends up as Mr Facing-both-Ways.'

Such concerns have the greatest importance to an understanding of the *Why We Fight* films, whose technical expertise is extraordinary, but whose overall purpose is a mixture of twisted fact, deceit, simplification and emotion of what, in World War II, was proclaimed the 'strategy of truth', or the 'propaganda of fact'.[12] A *New Yorker* cartoon which appeared a few years ago makes the same point. We see a room of filing cabinets variously labelled 'our facts', 'their facts', 'semi-facts', 'good facts', and 'bad facts'. The original purpose of the films was to define war aims in an exciting but truthful fashion; in the end truth took a back seat to emotional patriotism. Or, as Peter Kenez argues, one really distinguishes issue-propaganda from a nation's *Weltanschauung*-propaganda. The former allows for cynical decisions about gradations of truth; the latter may not be apparent except to those outside the culture.[13]

The series became mandatory viewing for all military personnel in 1942; eventually three found commercial distribution in movie theatres within the United States. Worldwide distribution followed the addition of foreign-language soundtracks in French, Spanish,

Russian and Chinese. In England Churchill wanted to see the series widely distributed but the Ministry of Information's Film Division generally disliked the series and did what it could to restrict circulation.[14]

The Army proved a hotbed of intrigue, for career men deeply resented I&E civilians given high rank just after Pearl Harbor. Osborn spent much of his time protecting I&E activities from diehard opposition of officers in the field, and rivals in the Signal Corps and Office of War Information, whose activities were termed 'an amazing cloud of double talk, recrimination . . . and no small amount of chicanery'.[15] Osborn wanted morale film but sensed that the proposal of the Signal Corps, for 'John Doughboy, an inspirational poem set to music and picturized', was not what the doctor ordered.[16]

Even among those of good will, problems of distribution and proper utilisation proved further hindrances. One base might have 50 prints of the same film (49 unneeded) while another had none. The 16mm projector was too fragile for the demands placed upon it in the field. Murphy's Law was also in evidence when it came to spare parts – the various projectors all used different parts and many turned to cannibalisation.

Some commanders thought that film taught as if by magic, or knowingly sabotaged orders that troops see particular films. They would march their troops for six hours, feed them a big meal, place them in an over-heated room and proceed to screen several hours of detailed instructional material. In such a regimen technological innovation was reduced to the subliminal. I&E found that enthusiasts for the potential of audiovisual instruction needed all of their charisma in selling techniques to career officers certain that push-ups were the key to discipline and close-order drill the zenith of creative soldiering.

Hollywood's Frank Capra received the assignment to make the *Why We Fight* films. A Sicilian-born immigrant who studied chemical engineering at the Californian Institute of Technology, Capra had enjoyed a string of commercial hits including *It Happened One Night* (1934), *Mr. Deeds Goes to Town* (1936) and *Mr. Smith Goes to Washington* (1939). Under five feet tall, and up from the bottom, Capra identified with the little guy; to him the American Dream was real and wonderful.[17] A sense of the comic tempered the faith of the zealot. Capra had worked as an editor ('cutter') for comedies in the 1920s; he understood that straight preaching could empty any commercial theatre in the land. The *Why We Fight* films represent Capra's personal values and beliefs. There is humour and plenty of patriotic emotion; the world divides neatly into places where the little guy ('John Q. Public') has a chance against the regimented world of Fascism. The people, we are told in all seven films in the series, will surely triumph over the tyranny of Fascism.

In 1940 Capra accepted a reserve commission in the Army Signal Corps which meant he had made himself available well before Pearl Harbor. Many in Hollywood did the same (someone said they were 'acting like a bunch of kids') though few were directors of Capra's stature.[18] In November 1942 Capra testified under oath about how he got the *Why We Fight* assignment. Because of the distortions in Capra's *Autobiography*, his earlier testimony is worth quoting in full:

> Q: What were the circumstances?
> A: Of my commissioning? [11 February 1942]
> Q: Yes.
> A: About a year or two prior to that . . . Colonel Schlossberg of the Signal Corps and Colonel Wright had come out in connection with the training film program. At that time I expressed to Colonel Schlossberg my desire to be of any use that I could in the war program, and that if I could be of any use to call upon me. On December 8 . . . 1941, I was called upon by Colonel Schlossberg and Captain Si Walters, both of the Signal Corps, who were visiting at Warner Brothers where I was shooting a picture on the set. They came to me and asked me if I was still willing to join the service and I said I was. So I signed an application which they brought out to me then. Subsequently to that, before being commissioned they asked me to come to Washington on an interview with General Osborn who was then head of the Morale Branch. I did, and I met General Osborn and we talked and he told me of his program and what he was trying to do, for which I had great sympathy, and I agreed to help him in any way that I could. He asked that I come into the Army just as soon as I could . . . The first job I was assigned to was the putting into film of a series of 15 lectures that were to be delivered to the armed forces by the Bureau of Public Relations.[19]

Work began with a group of Hollywood scriptwriters all

temporarily located at the Library of Congress in Washington. In March an optimistic press release announced that the films would be issued 'twice a month', though the final film in the series was not actually released until June 1945.[20] Capra set to work lining up talent and scrounging film from newsreel companies. The importance of his project, and his knowledge of men in the industry enabled him to get many of the best cutters, screenwriters and directors in Hollywood.[21]

Capra was supposed to make documentary films but, he claims, had never seen one. Records from the Central Files of the Museum of Modern Art Film Library (MOMA) tell a good deal Capra fails to mention in his unreliable autobiography. MOMA Curator Iris Barry secured a print of *Triumph of the Will* on a visit to Germany in 1936.[22] She sent this and other film material to Washington since editing equipment was located in the cooling tower of the Department of the Interior (where Capra's friend Edgar Peterson had made a couple of educational films). Capra and his staff first saw Riefenstahl's film in the splendid new fifth-floor auditorium of National Archives in March 1942.[23]

Nazi footage had already been translated and analysed at MOMA under a grant arranged by Nelson Rockefeller; Siegfried Kracauer is the best known of those who worked on the project.[24] MOMA learned of additional German footage seized by the Treasury Department and arranged to have it transferred to New York, first telling Capra about this new source. Capra took the footage himself, then refused to let MOMA analysts come to the cooling tower except late at night. In the meantime Richard Griffith, a MOMA employee, formally joined the Capra unit as an expert on compilation footage.[25] MOMA's crucial role (the provision of *Triumph of the Will* alone entitles the Film Library to such recognition) has never been documented since those who planned to tell the story never got around to publishing what they knew.

Editing techniques in *March of Time* obviously influenced Capra. The extensive narration and the recreation of historic events within what purported to be a factual presentation encouraged Capra to find his own style of filmmaking in which many of the distinctions between documentary and fiction film were blurred. Especially influential was *The Ramparts We Watch*, which traced shifts in American attitudes from isolationism to interventionism (the very theme of *War Comes to America* and, less fully, *Prelude to*

War). The use of footage from *Feldzug in Polen* not only suggested exactly how to cut enemy footage into one's own propaganda film, but the exact source. Only someone with a poor memory, or the instincts of a showman would, as Capra has, neglect to note the obvious connections with the *Why We Fight* series.[26]

In April Eric Knight joined the Capra unit. Now there was someone well informed about British documentary films who could influence Capra's thinking. Born in England, Knight had been film critic for the Philadelphia *Public Ledger*, and contributor to journals seen by British documentary film-makers. Knight captured the interest of Paul Rotha, who lectured at MOMA in 1937. Rotha and Knight exchanged thousands of pages of single-spaced letters, only a few of which have appeared in print. Knight saw all of the important British documentaries, either in New York, or on his own trips back to Britain, the last of which took place in autumn 1941. Rotha of course was greatly influenced by John Grierson, chief spokesman for the British documentary movement, who in turn as a young man studied at the University of Chicago where he was specifically introduced to the concept of Social Engineering by political scientist Charles Merriam.[27]

Eric Knight was an extraordinary catalyst in the planning of the *Why We Fight* scripts during the spring and summer of 1942. In May he prepared a detailed analysis of the philosophical bases of propaganda which helped outline basic possibilities just as I&E was setting up shop. Knight argued that 'positive assertion of your beliefs and aims' was more effective than 'refutation of enemy assertions'; he claimed that film is possibly the best means of propaganda for the home front. Film, he added, 'is peculiarly adept at expressing most glibly one of the subtlest tricks of the propagandists: to state a well-known truth, and bracket it with a new truth or a half-truth or a patent lie'.[28] The *Why We Fight* series, from the outset, was created by people immensely intrigued by the way combination of image and narration can be used to make viewers conclude something based as much on emotion as documented fact. Knight knew about filmmaking and scriptwriting, in fact it was he who wrote the scripts for the first four films in the series and not, as Capra remembers, Anthony Veiller. Knight's almost daily letters to his wife during the summer of 1942 provide a fascinating glimpse of how the films were conceived. Knight wrote the Army *Pocket Guide to Britain* in the summer of 1942; the exact wording from the Guide is found in *Battle of Britain*. And Knight had spent time at Fort Sill, Oklahoma, in 1934, seeing how the Army made official training films. Thus Knight could understand, for example, the need for careful explanation of military tactics which might otherwise seem inexplicable to a modern viewer of *Divide and Conquer*. Finally, Knight had long been interested in animation. He was assigned to work at the Disney studio in July 1942 to work out the extraordinary animated inserts for the first four films.[29] The Disney staff considered what they did all in a day's work, but the *Why We Fight* series has the most brilliant animated maps ever to appear in official films; the poor inserts in such war documentary classics as *Desert Victory* (1943) or *San Pietro* (1945) suggest why Disney was indeed the best in the business.

The achievement of the series owes much to others besides Knight and Capra. Anatole Litvak, who directed the *Battle of Russia*, and Veiller were important to the success of each film. Walter Huston and Veiller did the narration (Veiller was the voice of the little guy, or the sceptic). Dimitri Tiomkin, uncharitably termed the 'world's loudest composer', did the scoring. William Hornbeck, one of Hollywood's most experienced cutters, did the editing. And Capra had a hand in the contents of each film, here insisting on an emotional touch; there, a bit of humour; here, faster pacing; there, music up. Above all, Capra was Mr Film to the Army; he guarded his troops from educational filmmakers in other branches of the service.[30]

A chronology of the making of the series is as follows. In the autumn of 1941 the Army's Bureau of Public Relations prepared 15 orientation lectures on foreign affairs. Right after Pearl Harbor a group of screenwriters met at the Library of Congress to begin putting these lectures into film form. Capra saw some of the available compilation footage in March. In May Knight began revising draft scripts in light of what he knew about documentary films and the compilation footage at hand. During the summer of 1942 Capra, Knight, Litvak and Veiller argued round-the-clock in Hollywood about the wording of the scripts. The conception of the series was fixed by September 1942, some of the scripts in pretty complete form, much of the compilation footage chosen thanks to the work of Richard Griffith. After the spring of 1943, an administrative shakeup put Capra's independent 834th Signal Service Photographic Detachment under the Army Pictorial Service, the latter soon headed by Lyman Munson, Jr, Capra's West Point supervisor at I&E. Now Capra had a hand in every sort of film project that sounded important, and was often out of the country, which meant that the final two *Why We Fight* films were subject to all sorts of delays.[31]

The technical perfection of each film, the time necessary for completion and the expensive production shots were not originally intended. Like Topsy, the series just grew and grew. Knight found what was happening, the arguments and the resulting delays, terribly frustrating, but Capra and Litvak were perfectionists, insisting that their orientation films be the very best possible.[32] In selling the concept of film as a medium for orientation, there is much to recommend Capra's insistence on perfection, but as a result the first in the series, *Prelude to War*, was released only in November 1942. This meant that millions went through basic training without seeing any of the series, though most later saw them at military theatres. It is important to remember that the impact of the series was much greater in quality 35mm prints shown in post theatres, instead of the ancient 16mm copies which are generally available today. As a general proposition, for American soldiers, audiovisual instruction existed mostly on paper until the autumn of 1943. Not only were films not ready, but distribution and effective utilisation remained acute problem areas until that time.

Prelude to War was a big hit. Capra says it was his favourite in the series since after that his favoured position as military filmmaker was assured. Henry Stimson noted in his diary that it was a 'most powerful picture . . . when we came out we felt very somber'. Marshall, Stimson, and the other most significant military leaders in Washington felt that now they had a weapon to win the hearts and minds of their troops. They had no qualms about special pleading; in total war, here was total success. They knew what they were getting because the factual content of the script was subject to endless official supervision. In July 1942 Colonel Herman Beukema, who had supervised the 15 orientation lectures, was sent to the Capra unit to work out details on battle tactics in the scripts.[33] In the Pentagon and other Washington civilian agencies as many as 50 offices checked the contents of each script. Rough cuts were screened in the Pentagon theatre by Stimson, Marshall, and other high-ranking officers.

Such minute attention from those directing the war is particularly significant.[34] Such concern suggests the need to place film in a prominent place in any overall appraisal of war aims. Such official concern enables us to accept one of Capra's most extreme claims: the *Why We Fight* series really does define American official war aims. Not Capra but official Washington deserves the credit (or blame) for factual omissions, for a varnishing of the truth, for what is conveniently passed over. The films represent a classic example of the strategy of truth so much talked of at the time. Only *The Battle of China* strained everyone's credulity too far. The recall of General Joseph Stillwell made it public knowledge that something was seriously wrong with a film that ignored the existence of the Chinese Communists and pretended that a united China was throwing out the Japanese invader. The film, released in the fall of 1944, was withdrawn briefly, then used anyway. At least 3.75 million people had seen it by 1 July 1945.[35]

Ironically, the research techniques of social science undermined the value of the Capra series. No scientific sample could show that a will to win had been instilled solely through these films.[36] How could one be sure that soldiers had not learned about the nature of the enemy from a thousand other sources of information? All one could prove was a marginal improvement, in those tested, in specific factual details. Was such a little mouse all that emerged from the vast mountain of expenditure? Nobody could say for sure. Nevertheless, 'Why Korea?' and 'Why Vietnam?' films were made, with lower budgets and little evidence of success.[37]

There are two ways of responding to a question about proof that the series increased the patriotic zeal of the viewer (a variant of the immensely-complex problem of relating mass media to political decision-making). One is the brilliant appendix of Ellul's *Propaganda*, where he demolishes the methodology of the scientific sample, asserting that film's effects are much more widespread than any questionnaire can discover and that film's impact relates to group participation in a way that defies sampling.[38]

Some never saw the films; some slept through them; some film enthusiasts worried about theatrical touches; others, perhaps looking for an emotional reason to support official war aims, found the films remarkable. Alfred Kazin, son of Russian immigrants, recalls, some 35 years later, the impact of *The Battle of Russia* on him:

> Everything came to a head one glowering winter day [1944] at a great army camp and hospital in southern Illinois. . . . Sitting in the dark post theater, we were all of us at ease; we were at the movies. On the screen, the dear exciting movie screen, best

friend many an American ever had, jagged arrows leaped across the map to show the Nazis poised against France in 1940, against England, finally against Russia on June 22, 1941. Loud thunderclaps of music burst against my brain as I sat with hundreds of soldiers in the theater. In the excitement and terror of seeing the large swastika map move across England, I felt together with these men, knew that with the trustworthy old American movie magic working on us like a liberating storm, our political souls were being cleansed and invigorated. We would come out of the theater knowing what was agreed on all sides – that it was our privilege to erase the evil in the world that was Hitler.

Now *The Battle of Russia* comes on, and there it is, the real thing. This is not the visual Walt Disney diagrams. . . . On the sound track, abysmal mourning, low Slavic chords, muttering thunder. On the screen, a dead muddy winter scene as old men and women from a village in the Ukraine stoop over the muddy blood-soaked ravines where their people have been left after being shot by the Nazis. The Russian sky behind them is dark and soggy, rain is coming on, and the villagers bend in agony over their dead. Now they are playing broken chords from the *Pathétique*. Nothing I was to see after the war in Russia and East Berlin, with its vast sarcophagi of Russian soldiers, was to bring out the torment of the Russians in the Hitler war as did those scattered shots from captured Nazi newsreels and Soviet sources which I saw on a snow-soaked day at a camp in Illinois. Sitting in the post theater, embracing Russia as my parents had not been allowed to embrace it, I see coming together the divided forces of the Red Army encircling the Germans at Stalingrad. Two long lines of Russian soldiers are running to each other in the snow, hugging each other, bussing each other man to man in the hearty Russian fashion. Stalingrad! Long lines of anti-aircraft guns are lined up in this 'beautiful' ballet of war, the katusha rockets whiz brilliantly through the air, soldiers are slithering through the snow toward a ruined apartment house. Doughty, cheeky, round Red Army men, all bundled up in their winter greatcoats, are striding toward victory. The movie makes it easy to sit in southern Illinois and to accept that lovely Russian sacrifice in my behalf. I lose all separateness, feel absolutely at one with the soldiers in that dark theater.

It was a physical shock, walking out of the theater in the gray

> dripping twilight, watching the men plodding back to their barracks in the last slant of light, to realize how drained I was, how much I had been worked over, appealed to. In the end, as so often happened to us after a terrific American movie, we were stupefied. There was no magic bridge between a snowed-on American soldier and the movie he was forced to see about the sufferings of the Old World.[39]

How, as well, can we hope to know the precise impact of this film on Russian audiences – Stalin approved the distribution of this film to commercial theatres throughout the Soviet Union in 1944?

There is a second way of responding to the effectiveness of these films, a way social scientists did not choose to explore. We must, as historians, be satisfied with certain kinds to data, none by itself conclusive, relating to distribution, and focus our attention primarily on conception and filmic realisation, for here proper documentation survives, and here we can see the significance of the entire series. The *Why We Fight* series represented a pioneering attempt at standardising orientation; they did a better job of instilling morale than canned lectures – which is not to say that they were superior to an individual commander able to speak brilliantly to his troops. The problem is the inability of any army to find enough such commanders to handle millions of men. In such a situation standardised instruction involving audiovisual techniques is literally the only alternative. And since the series soon was intended to explain war aims to a world audience, it took on obligations far beyond the confines of basic training. Those who have argued that America lacked an emotional involvement in World War II as compared with World War I have surely overlooked the ardent emotionalism of those who sponsored and those who made the *Why We Fight* series.

The worldwide impact of the Capra series suggests how varied the lessons of the past become when one looks from outside one's own culture. Karsten Fledelius says that the Capra series influenced an entire generation of Danish documentary film-makers, and to this day in Denmark is considered a model for effective films of *persuasion. In 1947, the Soviet director Pudovkin predicted that Why We Fight*-style films would become a permanent feature of international communications. Montage, based on actuality footage, would break down international barriers. 'I am convinced', he wrote,

> that this form of the documentary feature film will gain ever-increasing significance in the post-war period, first, because we need no longer doubt that it can be understood by all the peoples of the world, and second, because, thanks to this advantage, it can be widely used for fully and profoundly acquainting peoples with one another and can serve to a very considerable degree in expressing universal ideas in a graphic and striking way.[40]

Such an optimistic prediction, though incorrect, suggests two reasons why tough-minded American scholars who find the emotional patriotism of the series too much to take, are guilty of varying degrees of ethnocentrism. First, the person outside American society sees the *Why We Fight* films as important collective statements of an American mythology to the rest of the world. The films are seen as documents of New Deal ideology, with their exaggerated notions of populist democratic concepts. Secondly, the series suggests a technical means for amplifying leadership; it seems a successful Roosevelt-era device for using technology to lead a mass society. The British documentary film movement favoured cadre propaganda – the vanguard as target, not the masses. Roosevelt and Capra hoped to communicate with the masses of the world, and succeeded.[41]

World War II destroyed Capra as an effective filmmaker. In a recent interview, he offered a convincing explanation for what happened:

> The war was a terrible shock to me. I hated the unnecessary brutality. Women and children being killed, terrified, huddling in fear. Going around dropping bombs on women and children. *What the hell is wrong with us*? I thought that perhaps I had put too much faith in the human race – you know, in the pictures I made. Maybe they were too much as things should be.[42]

The *Why We Fight* series also says something important about technological innovation and the military. We can perceive a central goal of leaders in twentieth-century society – the necessity of providing an educated citizenry a reason why – from these seven films. Film was the chosen tool of enthusiasts for Social Engineering. The Army way, veterans say, is to send ten times as much of everything in hopes that one-tenth will arrive where it can do some good. Those who consider the series tendentious ignore the reality of the need to give citizens an emotional feeling of patriotic community in total war. In Britain, *In Which We Serve* had a demonstrably greater impact than *A Diary for Timothy*, in spite of the latter's subtle artistry.

Each nation in World War II had the major problem of spelling out war aims so as to instil sufficient civilian zeal for sacrifice. Churchill may have been correct in his insistence that nobody ever won a war with his mouth, but World War II was a moment when everyone looked to film in hopes that propaganda might have the desired effect.[43] The *Why We Fight* films defined American war objectives to military and civilian audiences throughout the world in a way Roosevelt's Four Freedoms never could. It is the medium of film which provides the most comprehensive statement of war aims produced in America between 1941 and 1945.

Notes

1. See, for example, James MacGregor Burns, *Roosevelt: The Soldier of Freedom* (New York, 1970); Richard R. Lingeman, *Don't You Know There's a War On? The American Home Front, 1941–1945* (New York, 1970); Richard Polenberg, *War and Society: The United States, 1941–1945* (New York, 1972); John Morton Blum, *V Was for Victory: Politics and American Culture During World War II* (New York, 1976); and Allan M. Winkler, *The Politics of Propaganda: The Office of War Information, 1942–1945* (New Haven, 1977).

2. Geoffrey Perrett, *Days of Sadness, Years of Triumph: The American People 1939–1945* (Baltimore, 1974), pp. 9–12.

3. For the relation between social science and film see Thomas Cripps and David Culbert, '*The Negro Soldier* (1944): Film Propaganda in Black and White', *American Quarterly*, vol. XXXI (Winter, 1979), pp. 616–40; Thomas Cripps, 'Movies, Race, and World War II: *Tennessee Johnson* as an Anticipation of the Strategies of the Civil Rights Movement', *Prologue*, vol. XIV (Summer, 1982), pp. 49–67; and David Culbert, 'Walt Disney's Private Snafu: The Use of Humor in World War II Army Film', *Prospects*, vol. I (December, 1975), pp. 80–96.

4. For a good analysis of social engineering see Chapter XVI, 'Science and Democratic Social Structure', in Robert K. Merton, *Social Theory and Social Structure* (rev. edn, Glencoe, Ill., 1957); see also Alvin M. Weinberg, 'Can Technology Replace Social Engineering', in Albert H. Teich (ed.), *Technology and Man's Future* (New York, 1972), pp. 27–35. For the origin of the term see H.S. Person, 'Engineering', in Edwin R.A. Seligman *et al.* (eds.), *Encyclopaedia of the Social Sciences*, vols. V–VI (New York, 1931), p. 542.

5. Samuel A. Stouffer *et al.*, *Studies in Social Psychology in World War II: Vol. I The American Soldier: Adjustment During Army Life*; *Vol. II Combat and Its Aftermath*; *Vol. III Experiments in Mass Communication*; *Vol. IV Measurement and Prediction* (Princeton, N.J., 1949–50), vol. I, pp. 65, 57 [hereafter *SSP*].

6. There is a vast literature about morale and its importance. See Wesley Frank Craven and James Lea Cate (eds.), *Services Around the World*, vol. VII of *The Army Air Forces in World War II* (Washington, DC, 1958), pp. 431–76, for a

good introduction to the problem. The scientific study of morale was an outgrowth of World War I. See Edward L. Munson, *The Management of Men: A Handbook on the Systematic Development of Morale and the Control of Human Behaviour* (New York, 1921); Munson's son was in I&E and had much to do with the film programme; he too wrote a widely-used guide to morale: Colonel Edward Lyman Munson, Jr, *Leadership for American Army Leaders*, *The Fighting Forces Series* (rev. edn, Washington, DC, 1944). Alfred Kazin, *New York Jew* (New York, 1979), p. 115.

7. After 1945, Marshall was attacked for being a New Deal liberal because of his involvement with CCC camps. See Senator Joe McCarthy, *The Story of General George Marshall* (n.p., n.d. [Milwaukee, 1952]), pp. 10–11.

8. Report, Osborn to Marshall, 6 August 1945, 9, 319.1 cos, Box 371, Records of the Chief of Staff, Troop Information & Education, RG 319, Modern Military Records, National Archives, Washington, DC; Osborn and A.D. Surles to Chief Signal Officer, 10 December 1941, 062.2 ocsigo, Box 750, A43–B–28, Washington National Records Center, Suitland, Maryland [hereafter *MMR–NA*; *WNRC*]. On Marshall's intense commitment to the welfare of the average soldier see Forrest C. Pogue, *George C. Marshall: Organizer of Victory, 1943–1945* (New York, 1973), in particular pp. 80–114. For a practical guide to government records relating to film production, see David Culbert, 'Note on Government Paper Records', pp. 235–43, in Bonnie G. Rowan (ed.), *Scholars' Guide to Washington, D.C. Film and Video Collections* (Washington, DC, 1980).

9. For information about the series see William Murphy, 'The Method of *Why We Fight*', *Journal of Popular Film*, vol. I (1972), pp. 185–96; also helpful is Karsten Fledelius, *et al.*, '*Why We Fight*: An Example of Wartime Orientation' (Copenhagen, 1974); and Thomas William Bohn, *An Historical and Descriptive Analysis of the Why We Fight Series* (New York, 1977); Richard W. Steele, 'The Greatest Gangster Movie Ever Filmed: *Prelude to War*, *Prologue*, vol. XI (Winter, 1979), pp. 221–36.

10. Jacques Ellul, *Propaganda: The Formation of Men's Attitudes* (New York, 1973), p. 58. For the relation between film and propaganda see David Culbert (ed.), *Mission to Moscow* (Madison, 1980). Michael Choukas, *Propaganda Comes of Age* (Washington, DC, 1965), p. 37, provides a reasonable definition of propaganda: 'the controlled dissemination of deliberately distorted notions in an effort to induce action favorable to predetermined ends of special interest groups.' Michael Balfour, *Propaganda in War 1939–1945: Organisations, Policies and Publics in Britain and Germany* (London, 1979), p. 421.

11. Ellul, *Propaganda*, pp. xv 137; Cornford, *Microcosmographia Academica: Being A Guide for the Young Academic Politician* (London, 1966), p. 5.

12. Balfour, *Propaganda in War*, p. 422. For a good discussion of the problem see Paul F. Lazarsfeld and Robert K. Merton, 'The Psychological Analysis of Propaganda', in Writers' Congress, *The Proceedings of the Conference Held in October 1943 Under the Sponsorship of the Hollywood Writers' Mobilization and the University of California* (Berkeley, California, 1944), pp. 362–80.

13. Peter Kenez argued with me about propaganda every waking hour during the Bellagio Conference, to my vast intellectual profit.

14. Mandatory viewing announced in War Department Circular 368, 1942. The War Activities Committee agreed to commercial release of *Prelude to War* on 27 May 1943; *Battle of Russia*, 11 November 1943; *War Comes to America*, 14 June 1945; War Activities Committee, *Movies at War 1945* (New York, 1945). For overseas theatrical distribution of the first five in the series in 'Australia, New Zealand, Tasmania, Egypt and the Middle East, Africa (south of the Equator) and India' see Overseas Motion Picture Bureau Report, 16 November–15 December, 1943, Box 19, entry 6, Records of the Office of War Information, RG 208, *WNRC*;

Frances Thorpe and Nicholas Pronay, *British Official Films in the Second World War: A Descriptive Catalogue* (Oxford, 1980), p. 237. Pronay told me at the Bellagio Conference that *War Comes to America* was withheld from British cinemas because of its pronouncements regarding isolationism and the United Nations.

15. Munson to Capra, 17 December 1943, 062.2 ocsigo, Box 49, A45–196; concerning OWI opposition see Nelson Poynter to Lowell Mellett, 10 November 1942, Box 1438, entry 264, RG 208, both in *WNRC*; and Secret Minutes, Meeting of General Council, 10 May 1943, 8, 334 ocs, Box 30, Records of the Office of Chief of Staff, RG 165, *MMR–MA*.

16. Osborn and A.D. Surles to Chief Signal Officer, 10 December 1941, 062.2 ocsigo, Box 750, A43–B28, *WNRC*.

17. Frank Capra, *The Name Above the Title: An Autobiography* (New York, 1971), pp. xi–xii, 3–16; Robert Sklar, *Movie-Made America: A Cultural History of American Movies* (New York, 1976), pp. 205–14. The newly-opened Frank Capra Archive, Wesleyan University, Middletown, CT, should offer important information about Capra's wartime work. The war years files may be opened to scholars in 1983; Jeanine Basinger, Curator, to author, 22 August 1982.

18. Sol Levinson to Richard Schlossberg, 8 December 1941, 333.9 ig, Box 1161, Records of the Inspector General, RG 159, *WNRC*.

19. Capra verbatim transcript, 25 November 1942, 318, 333.9 ig, Box 1165, RG 159, *WNRC*. Osborn's call on 8 December is corroborated in Army Pictorial Service, *Summary Report on Photographic Activities of the Signal Corps Since August 4, 1941 in the Fields of Motion Pictures and Visual Aids* (typescript, Washington, DC, 26 February 1943, 412, copy in US Army Center for Military History Library, Washington, DC [hereafter *APS Summary Report*].

20. Press Release, 2 March 1942, 'BPR-War Dept' folder, Box 3, Lowell Mellett Papers, Franklin D. Roosevelt Library, Hyde Park, NY. In Osborn to Chief Signal Officer, 2 March 1942, 062.2 ocsigo, Box 750, A43–B28, *WNRC*, he speaks of 'six 30-minute pictures to emphasize, to supplement, or to substitute for the present fifteen one-hour lectures'. On 1 March Marshall, Capra, and Osborn talked for an hour about the projected films, *APS Summary Report*, 434. The group at the Library of Congress consisted of Jerome Chodorov, John Sanford, Julius and Philip Epstein, Ted Paramore, S.K. Lauren, Leonard Spigelgass, and Capra. Munson to Robert Cutler, 18 August 1945, 062.2 ocsigo, Box 49, A45–196, *WNRC*.

21. Those who wrote drafts of the scripts included John Gunther, William Shirer, Leonard Spigelgass, Anthony Veiller, and Eric Knight. Editors and directors included Merrill White, William Hornbeck, Anatole Litvak and, of course, Capra himself.

22. Details, including the legal contract, are found in 'German folder-UFA', Central Files, Museum of Modern Art Film Library, New York, NY [hereafter *CF–MOMA*]. I am grateful to Eileen Bowser for opening these records to me.

23. For instance, March 1942: 'Projected 30 reels of German propaganda films from our archive for Capra . . . sent him English transcripts of the commentary and visuals.' April 1942: 'Duped our print of *Triumph des Willens* and provided Major Capra with a print, at cost.' [Iris Barry], 'Special Activities for Government Offices from Jan 42 to Jan 43', 'OSS' folder, *CF–MOMA*.

24. On 9 March 1942, Richard Griffith sent Capra rough transcriptions of visuals and commentry for *Triumph des Willens*, *Feldzug in Polen*, and *Flieger, Funker, Kanoniere*. 'They're rather curiously phrased', he added, 'because Dr. Kracauer wrote them when he was just beginning to learn English.' On 15 March Griffith sent Capra a list of all the stock footage and foreign films he could locate which would be appropriate to each of the 15 orientation lectures. Both in 'War

Dept' folder, *CF–MOMA*.

25. [Barry], 'Brief Report of Work by MOMA on Contract OEMcr–112 as of 4 January 1943', in 'CIAA' folder, *CF–MOMA*.

26. Raymond Fielding, *The March of Time, 1935–1951* (New York, 1978), in particular pp. 243–72.

27. P. Rotha, *Documentary Diary: An Informal History of the British Documentary Film, 1928–1939* (London, 1973), pp. 19–21, 171–212; Rotha (ed.), *Portrait of a Flying Yorkshireman: Letters from Eric Knight in the United States to Paul Rotha in England* (London, 1952); Rachael Low, *Films of Comment and Persuasion of the 1930s* (London, 1979), p. 178. Erik Barnouw helped me gain access to Eric Knight's widow, who has an important collection of Eric Knight Papers in her possession. Bary Karl, *Charles E. Merriam and the Study of Politics* (Chicago, 1975).

28. Munson to Col. Watrous, 26 May 1942, Box 2, Lyman Munson Papers, Manuscript Division, University of Wyoming, Laramie, WY.

29. David Culbert, '"A Quick, Delightful Gink": Eric Knight at the Walt Disney Studio', *Funnyworld* (No. 19, Fall, 1978), pp. 13–17.

30. The fervour with which Capra viewed his assignment is suggested in a memorandum he sent his unit on 22 August 1942, ending: 'THE GREATEST GLORY THAT CAN COME TO ANY MAN IS TO JOIN THE SERVICE WHEN HIS COUNTRY IS IN DANGER.' 062.2 ocsigo, Box 3, A46–484, *WNRC*; telephone interview with Capra, 18 January 1977. It was only in August 1942 that the series was named *Why We Fight*.

31. 'General Surles . . . "borrowed" Colonel Capra and some of his best men to organize and direct the making of pictures of American troops in combat.' Osborn to Marshall, 12 February 1944, 062.2 ocs, Box 133, RG 165, *MMR–NA*.

32. Knight to Eric Knight, 24 August 1942, Eric Knight Papers, Quakertown, PA [hereafter Knight MSS].

33. Stimson Diary, Yale University, 23 October 1942; telephone interview with Capra, 18 January 1977; Knight to Jere Knight, 21 July 1942, Knight MSS; Munson to Robert Cutler, 18 August 1945.

34. Telephone interviews with General Osborn, 4 November, 5 November 1976; Pogue, *Marshall, Organizer of Victory*, pp. 91–2; Capra, *Name Above the Title*, pp. 325–67.

35. Figures from F.H. Osborn, *Information and Education Division* (privately printed, October 1945), p. 7, copy kindly sent me by General Osborn; telephone interview with Osborn, 10 November 1976; Surles (with concurrence of Osborn) to Munson, 4 January 1945, 062.2 ocsigo, Box 749, A43–B28, *WNRC*.

36. *SSP*, III; interview with Irving Janis (who worked for I&E's Research Branch and helped write *SSP*), New Haven, Connecticut, 7 February 1978.

37. Many films on such subjects are briefly described in DA PAM 108–1, *Index of Army Motion Pictures and Related Audio-Visual Aids* (Washington, DC, January 1977), in particular pp. 154–6, 184–91.

38. Ellul, *Propaganda*, Appendix I, pp. 259–302.

39. Kazin, *New York Jew*, pp. 129–31.

40. Comment at Bellagio Conference session devoted to American film propaganda; Vsevolod Pudovkin, 'The Global Film', *Hollywood Quarterly*, vol. II (July, 1947), p. 330, quoted in William J. Blakefield, 'A History and Analysis of "Know Your Enemy – Japan"', Master's thesis, University of Maryland, 1981.

41. Comments by Fledelius, Pronay at Bellagio Conference.

42. Quoted (without Karp's interpolations) in Walter Karp, 'The Patriotism of Frank Capra', *Esquire*, vol. XCV (February 1981), p. 35.

43. Balfour, *Propaganda in War*, p. 437.

8 PROPAGANDA AT RADIO LUXEMBOURG: 1944–1945

Erik Barnouw

Radio Luxembourg was an extraordinary phenomenon. Serving a tiny nation, it had one of the continent's most powerful transmitters, able to penetrate a large part of Europe. Capable of broadcasting with 150,000 watts, it was more potent than any American domestic station, the most powerful of which were at that time limited to 50,000 watts. During the 1930s much of the Radio Luxembourg programming had been beamed to Britain in English in the interests of mainly American commercial sponsors: British broadcasting was still entirely non-commercial. American manufacturers of toiletries, household products and packaged foods, eager to duplicate their American radio-advertising successes in Europe, especially in the British Isles, had found Radio Luxembourg ready to take their money and sell their products. The station had some competition in this from Radio Normandy, but was far more powerful and successful, and had built a large British following with programming that included American jazz and soap operas.[1]

In the spring of 1940 the German armies, sweeping westward, took possession of the station and proceeded to use it over the next four years for their own propaganda needs. In 1944, as the Allied troops drove in the opposite direction, Allied psychological warfare units were following closely behind, seizing and using any radio facilities they found intact or repairable. They especially wanted the facilities of Radio Luxembourg, but scarcely expected to find it in usable shape. At the station the retreating Germans set dynamite charges but inexplicably failed to detonate them. It is said that Radio Luxembourg's head engineer (who had served the Germans throughout their occupation and use of the station) encouraged them at the time of their departure to destroy the transmitter tubes; his idea was to divert the Germans from more catastrophic destruction. When the Americans arrived, he dug up from the garden a complete duplicate set of tubes he had buried four years earlier for such a day.[2] This enabled the station to resume broadcasting twelve days after the Allied entry into Luxembourg.[3] On 22 September 1944, the psychological warfare unit of the 12th

US Army group put Radio Free Luxembourg back on the air.

Radio Free Luxembourg now launched a variety of programming. The activities came under the executive supervision – generally exercised from Paris – of such luminaries as William S. Paley and Davidson Taylor of CBS and Allied counterparts, all seasoned radio veterans who had gone into uniform for psychological warfare duty. The station's administrator was William Harlan Hale, but the propaganda strategy was the work of the remarkable Hans Habe.

Hans Habe, born János Békessy in Hungary in 1911, was a prominent journalist and newspaper editor in pre-war Vienna; he claimed credit for the discovery that Hitler's name was Schicklgruber. Békessy fled Austria in 1939, enlisted in the French army, was captured by the Germans, managed a romantic escape through concealment in a brothel, made his way to Vichy and thence to the United States. Then he enlisted in the American army and after special training was involved in psychological warfare both in North Africa and Italy. With the steady advance towards Germany, he became the key strategist at Radio Luxembourg. Because the name Békessy was on a Nazi execution list, he lived under the name Hans Habe. At Radio Luxembourg he directed both its 'white' and 'black' – acknowledged and unacknowledged – broadcasting activities.[4]

During daytime and evening hours, with its full power and established frequency, Radio Free Luxembourg addressed Germans in the German language, as an avowedly American voice. It offered frequent news programmes called 'Frontpost', a title also used on millions of leaflets showered on Germany during the allied advance towards the Rhine river. A potent Frontpost feature was a daily segment called *Briefe Die Sie Nicht Erreichten* (Letters That Didn't Reach Them). It consisted of excerpts from the huge quantities of undelivered German mail seized during the Allied drive through France. The selections were very simply read aloud by a Luxembourg girl with a warm, appealing voice. The personal nature of this material was probably a powerful factor in winning attention for the station. American staff members were among those who found the letters deeply moving, mirroring as they did the total disruption of lives everywhere. Another feature, designed as a spur to desertions from the German forces, was a carefully selected procession of prisoners brought to the Radio Free Luxembourg microphones, who said in effect 'Hello Mother! I'm safe! I'm a prisoner of the Americans!' The selection of prisoners for these on-the-air appearances was supervised with great care by Habe.

There were also grimmer features. Two Germans in civilian clothes had been captured nearby on an espionage mission. Radio Free Luxembourg broadcast their trial, and then interviewed the convicted prisoners *en route* to the prison courtyard. Asked if they realised that the penalty for what they had done was death, the prisoners said no, their officers had not told them that. Shortly afterwards the radio audience was allowed to hear the click of the rifle bolts, the shouted command, the volley and the echo of the rifle fire. *Yank*, the serviceman's magazine, thought this was probably the first on-the-air execution.[6]

In contrast, the station also made successful use of humour. This revolved around a figure presented as 'Corporal Tom Jones', from Green Bay, Wisconsin. He was actually a fictious character, whose creation was masterminded by Hans Habe.

Though *Yank* referred to 'Corporal Tom Jones' as 'a sort of Central European Bob Hope', Jones was never brash. Rather, he spoke in a guileless, unassuming manner. The voice was that of Richard Hanser, former city editor of the New York newspaper *PM*. He had never been to Green Bay, Wisconsin; he had been born in Buffalo, NY, in 1909. It was Hans Habe who decided that 'Tom Jones' should be from Green Bay; it sounded so American to him. Hanser had once studied for the ministry at Concordia Lutheran Institute of Bronxville, NY, which required every student to learn enough German to deliver a sermon in that language. Thus Hanser had some fluency in German, along with a quaint accent which Germans tended to find utterly charming, and which won him the role of Jones. Hanser, a civilian on the OWI staff, was then put into uniform and assigned to the 12th US Army group with 'assimilated' rank as a major, though his on-the-air role was that of a corporal.

The 'Corporal Tom Jones' segments, inserted each evening into the 8–8.15 Frontpost programme, were never argumentative or hortatory. They included matters seemingly unrelated to the war – a key part of Habe's strategy. 'Jones' would reminisce about things he did as a boy in his spare time in Green Bay. The aim was to suggest an extreme personal freedom, devoid of obligatory youth groups. It probably conveyed a Huck Finn aura, of much appeal in the turmoil of war. One element in the humour did relate to the war. 'Corporal Jones' would relay underground jokes he said he had heard from German prisoners – anti-Nazi jokes, known as *Flüsterwitze*, or whisper-jokes. Here was forbidden matter suddenly emerging on the public airwaves. Hundreds of such jokes were collected via interviews with prisoners, and they became a regular 'Corporal Tom Jones' sign-off feature and a smash hit. Some were *Galgenhumor*, gallows humour, but Jones relayed them ingenuously, as though not quite understanding their devastating significance. Hanser remembered the following examples.

> They used to say, 'No enemy aircraft over the Reich!' They still say it, but differently. Now they say, 'No Reich under the enemy aircraft!'
>
> In the old days, it used to be that you'd go to the railway station, and the train was gone. Now you go for a train, and the station is gone.
>
> A man told a Gestapo agent, 'I'd rather work for the Nazis than anyone else!' The pleased Gestapo agent asked, 'What sort of work do you do?' 'I'm a gravedigger.'[7]

Word of 'Corporal Tom Jones's' fame eventually spread to Green Bay, his alleged home town. As a result, the Associated Press received a request from a Green Bay newspaper editor for information about its famous son. The AP actually despatched someone to Luxembourg to interview Jones, but the Corporal's true identity was kept secret.[8]

The programmes mentioned so far were part of Radio Free Luxembourg's daytime and evening offerings as an acknowledged American voice, heard over Radio Luxembourg's regular place on the dial, with its full available power. But the psychological warfare group also used the transmitter for an entirely different activity, which occupied the middle of the night, from 2 a.m. to 6 a.m.

Using lower power, 30,000 watts, the station now purported to be an underground German station operating behind German lines. It used a different frequency – 1,212 kilocycles – and called itself 'Twelve Twelve'. It went on the air with: 'Hello, this is Twelve Twelve calling'. It was not overtly anti-Nazi but suggested that the German authorities were fallible and making mistakes. On every programme Twelve Twelve carried detailed, scrupulously accurate reports about the military situation within Germany. Its task, at this stage, was to establish total credibility and trust. Only a few German voices, of a regional quality to suggest a location in the Rhine valley, were used on Twelve Twelve. The idea was to convey the image of a compact underground group.

Much of its strategy had been planned in advance. Music was never used – only talk. The Twelve Twelve team was made to live in isolation, to avoid any hint of interaction with other Radio Luxembourg programming. The group was housed in a fine villa in Luxembourg's Rue Brasseur, once the property of a German coalmine manager. Military police guarded the premises day and night.[9]

That the group's programmes were soon winning trust was reflected in the fact that German prisoners, when interrogated about the situation within Germany, began to quote Twelve Twelve. But the winning of trust was only the first step. The trust had a purpose: it was a weapon, potentially devastating. During the Moselle assault and breakthrough by Allied troops, Twelve Twelve suddenly began to create chaos with disinformation. Among other bulletins, it reported Allied tanks near Nuremberg and Friedrichshafen, causing panic in those cities. This confusion was its ultimate task. Immediately afterwards, its job done and credibility shattered, Twelve Twelve vanished as abruptly as it had appeared. It had been on the air just 127 nights.[10]

Of all Radio Luxembourg's activities under the psychological warfare group, the Twelve Twelve caper was perhaps the most innovative, and an extraordinary success. At a time when people were just beginning to talk about 'black radio', this was the most telling example of what it could do.

Notes

1. Burton Paulu, *British Broadcasting: radio and television in the United Kingdom* (Minneapolis, 1956), pp. 26–31, 360–1.

2. *Yank*, 11 May 1945. Also D. Taylor in Columbia University Oral History interview (New York, 1956), p. 43.

3. Richard Hanser, in Columbia University Oral History interview with the author (New York, 1967), pp. 5–6. Miraculously, a large collection of undamaged Guy Lombardo, Benny Goodman, Dorsey Brothers, Glenn Miller and other phonograph records – mostly from pre-war days but used by the Germans for their own radio blandishments – was found available, and was put to work for Allied purposes.

4. Hans Habe, *All My Sins: an autobiography* (London, 1957), pp. 340–50.
5. Hanser, Columbia University Oral History, pp. 7–10.
6. *Yank*, 11 May 1945.
7. Broadcast on *Frontpost* 11 December 1944; 6 and 15 April 1945.
8. Hanser, Columbia University Oral History, pp. 7–14.
9. Habe, *All My Sins*, p. 347.
10. *Publicity and Psychological Warfare, 12th Army Group: history, January 1943–August 1945* (ETO, undated), pp. 197–200.

Hans Habe, chief Luxembourg broadcasting strategist during this period, was awarded the Bronze Star with Oak Leaf Cluster, and the Luxembourg *Croix de Guerre*. Under the Allied occupation of Germany, he was for a time in charge of all German newspapers, but seems to have fallen out with the Occupation and resumed his peripatetic, often flamboyant, career. He wrote a number of novels based on his war exploits, some of which were translated into English – including *Walk in Darkness*, *Off Limits*, and *The Mission*. He had brief Hollywood sojourns and wrote an autobiography, *All My Sins*. His five marriages in five different countries included one to the daughter of the legendarily wealthy Majorie Merryweather Post, Post Toasties heiress who had married Ambassador Joseph E. Davies. Habe eventually settled in Switzerland.

Richard Hanser served a post-war stint as writer for RKO-Pathe on the *This Is America* series of film shorts, then had a distinguished television career as chief writer for NBC's 'Project Twenty' documentaries and co-author with Henry Salomon of the *Victory At Sea* series. He published books that included *Putsch! how Hitler made revolution* and *A Noble Treason: the revolt of the Munich students against Hitler*. He was the translater of *Walk in Darkness*, one of the novels of his former mentor, Hans Habe.

PART THREE: PROPAGANDA IN FASCIST EUROPE

9 NAZI WARTIME NEWSREEL PROPAGANDA

David Welch

> The rank and file are usually more primitive than we imagine. Propaganda must therefore always be essentially simple and repetitive.
>
> Joseph Goebbels (January 1942)

War was an important aspect of National Socialist ideology and as such Goebbels, as Minister for Popular Enlightenment and Propaganda, experienced little difficulty in shifting his operations to a wartime footing. As Jay Baird noted 'the movement had a dialectic and teleology of its own which was expressed in the symbols of combat'.[1] However both Goebbels and Hitler appreciated the burden that a war would place on the Nazi propaganda machine, particularly as the unexpected announcement of war in September 1939 did not arouse the same kind of war hysteria which had seized the masses in August 1914. The dejected mood among large sections of the German population and the conspicuous lack of enthusiasm and flag-waving for the war were observed by Albert Speer:

> From the start the populace took a far more serious view of the situation than did Hitler and his entourage . . . The atmosphere was notably depressed; the people were full of fear about the future. None of the regiments marched off to war decorated with flowers as they had done at the beginning of the First World War . . . The streets remained empty.[2]

For a totalitarian police state, where the illusion at least of monolithic unity between leadership and people had to be preserved at all costs, the war presented considerable strains on the political system. The manner in which it responded to these tensions would depend on the Propaganda Ministry's efficiency in forging an effective link with the regime's leadership and on the credibility of propaganda itself. Not only did propaganda have to convince the German people of their own cause and invincibility but abroad it need to win over neutral nations and at the same time undermine the enemy's spirit of resistance.[3]

Very soon after the outbreak of war and with it the alarming slump in public morale, Goebbels began to realise that propaganda could not remain entirely untouched by reality. He would have to temper the constant repetition of well-worn clichés and slogans with a more down-to-earth approach which reflected the everyday experiences of wartime life. Thus throughout the war years the propaganda machine would constantly be forced to scale its operations down and organise aid programmes ranging from free cinema tickets for war victims to the re-allocation of rationed goods like fruit and vegetables. However, the war was still a military fact and the main task of propaganda was to instil in the German people an absolute obedience, a willingness to die, and an unshakeable belief in final victory. Of all the means of communication at Goebbels' disposal film was particularly suited to this type of 'appeal *with* emotion'. The whole concept of 'self-sacrifice' inevitably evokes emotional rather than intellectual responses. It is prompted by emotional extremes that range from universal despair to a blind faith in the rightness of a particular cause. What it invariably lacks is a middle ground of rational thought. Thus, whether by means of direct political instructions or by covert use of entertainment genres to create a false sense of security or normality, Nazi feature films constantly attempted to counteract the negative opinions held by the population during the war.[4]

In this respect the effort of the feature film was greatly enhanced by the accompanying newsreels and documentaries. Both the newsreel and full-scale documentaries that were made from newsreel material were an excellent vehicle for portraying the invincible might of the armed forces, and in the first crucial years of the war in particular they served to reinforce a feeling of security and reassurance on the part of a reluctant German audience. Compare for example this SD- (Sicherheitdienst – Security Service) Report shortly after the outbreak of war on how the audience responded to a newsreel (*Wochenschau*) dealing with military operations in Denmark and Norway:

> Great applause.
> The *Wochenschau* undoubtedly increased confidence in victory.
> From *Breslau*: 'by means of this *Wochenschau* it was thrillingly paraded before the people's eyes how strikingly powerful and

quick as lightning our armed forces are . . .' Total silence in the cinemas – people had to pull themselves together afterwards. From *Dresden*: reports that *Wochenschauen* are awakening an understanding of the geographical difficulties the military are experiencing in Norway and it was suggested that for propaganda purposes, more use should be made of maps in the newsreels to highlight the distances that the Luftwaffe travel and the scale of their achievement in occupying Norway.[5]

Until the outbreak of war there were four newsreels operating in Germany, *Ufa-Tonwoche*, *Deulig-Woche*, *Tobis Wochenschau* (which developed in 1938 out of *Bavaria-Tonwoche* which in turn developed from *Emelka-Woche*) and *Fox tönende Wochenschau* which was American-owned. A fifth newsreel, *Ufa-Auslandswoche*, distributed German home news abroad. It was the Propaganda Ministry's task to co-ordinate these newsreels into a powerfully controlled and stringently organised propaganda weapon. Initially this was achieved by establishing a German 'news-bureau' (*Wochenschaureferat*) under the chairmanship of Hans Weidemann of the RMVP (Reichsministerium für Volksaufklärung und Propaganda) in an attempt to combine all newsreel reports into one 'official' version of contemporary Germany.[6]

As the political ideas and authoritarian claims to the film industry became more pervasive so the newsreels became less and less the product of journalistic enquiry. Even before 1933, Alfred Hugenberg, who owned the largest and most prestigious film company Ufa (*Universum-Film-Aktiengesellschaft*), had used Ufa newsreels to gain support for the National Socialists. After 1933 the aim of the newsreel was to create mass intoxication and to obtain mass approval for the projected deeds of the regime in both domestic and foreign affairs. As a result of this a special style appeared in both structure and documentary sequences which had little connection with objective reporting. Increasingly, then, German newsreels became a formalistic, carefully planned artistic transformation of reality in an attempt to achieve the propaganda intentions of the Nazi regime. An American correspondent, John McCutcheon Raleigh noted an excellent example of this practice:

One day, returning from the Rundfunkhaus after a broadcast, I saw a group of Hitler Youth posing with shovels and picks for an

> official cameraman. They shovelled industriously while the camera whirred. When the cameraman had sufficient material the group formed into squads and marched off, singing in unison. Later in the week I saw the same pictures released for propaganda in the current newsreels. The commentator proudly announced that the Hitler Youth was bending its back to clear away the snow. All winter this was the only time I saw youths in Hitler-Jugend uniforms wielding shovels.[7]

In order to achieve the most effective final results, newsreel cameramen were given special facilities for effective filming together with the most detailed instructions on the staging of a particular event.[8] They were assisted in this by legislation, notably the so-called 'Newsreel Law' – *Gesetz zur Erleichterung der Filmerichterstattung* ('*Wochenschaugesetz*'), which was introduced on 30 April 1936 in order to ease the problems of distribution and copyright.[9] Two years later, in October 1938, further legislation reduced the number of editions (including regional variations) from 15 to 8 and made the showing of a newsreel compulsory at every film programme.[10] Under the new law hire charges were also simplified so that in future cinema owners paid the newsreel distributors 3 per cent of the box office takings.[11] This meant that it was no longer cheaper to hire old newsreels. These reforms ensured not only that film audiences would see the very latest newsreels (which was not the case before 1938), but also that propaganda material could be dispersed as widely as possible.

Nazi authorities increasingly began to take the newsreel more seriously even as the propaganda aims of the RMVP became well defined. These trends were clearly reflected in the content of pre-war newsreels for politics represented almost 50 per cent of the content of Ufa newsreels in the season 1935–6.[12] Writing in 1937, Fritz Hippler, later President of the Reich Film Chamber, outlined the importance of the newsreel and hinted at the new instructional use that was being made of the medium: 'The newsreel must not only hold a mirror up to contemporary society, but it must facilitate a recognition of our present needs and the tasks that still have to be achieved in the future.'[13] Not surprisingly, a propaganda weapon as important as the newsreel was subject to control before being distributed. Censorship was exercised by the *Wochenschauzentrale* (having replaced the Wochenschaureferat in 1938) which was directly subordinate to Goebbels. By 1939 when Hippler had taken over control of the Wochenschauzentrale (from Weidemann), its responsibilities included not only routine matters of liasing between the four newsreel companies but more importantly, 'the arrangement of film reports according to the political and cultural points of view of the State'.[14] Furthermore, Hippler's responsibilities extended to the supervision and production of much longer documentary propaganda films. Thus in August 1939 Hippler directed *Der Westwall*, a 45-minute documentary on the building of the Siegfried Line. Newsreels were removed from cinema programmes to accommodate this film which stressed Germany's military preparations against an attack from the West. The commentary claimed that the 'Westwall' made war less likely as it would act as a deterent: '1914 encirclement but undefended boundaries – today? – encirclement but invincible boundaries!' In this respect the film echoed the sentiment of the time that was expressed in the propaganda slogan, 'He who wants peace must also prepare for war'.

Throughout 1939 the newsreels had continued in this vein, attempting to prepare the nation psychologically for the coming war by increasing their emphasis on military subjects. In the spring of 1939 they reported on the war in Spain and took great delight in recording the exploits of the Condor Legion. A few months later the newsreels already were giving the impression of a Germany at war, provoked as it were, by Polish atrocities. On 29 August Ulrich von Hassell noted in his diary: 'Last night I saw in the cinema a disgusting example of how human misery is exploited for purposes of propaganda. Weeping women and children are shown and in voices choked with tears as they describe their sufferings in Poland.'[15] The *Film-Kurier* reporting on the same newsreel prior to the invasion of Poland commented: 'This newsreel on the sad fate of German refugees fleeing from Polish barbarities had a profound effect on German audiences.'[16]

After the outbreak of war the RMVP merged the existing four newsreels into a single war newsreel. This was achieved with a minimum of disruption due largely to the legislative measures taken by the Ministry of Propaganda since 1936. On 21 November 1940 the *Deutsche Wochenschau GmbH* was founded and all other other newsreel companies were dissolved.[17] Goebbels ordered that in future the war newsreel should simply be referred to as *Deutsche Wochenschau*. Until this time the public were largely unaware that the newsreels were state controlled as very little was known about the Wochenschauzentrale. From Goebbels' point of view such a revelation would have reduced their effectiveness and therefore no hint had been given of his Ministry's role in this field. But this reticence was to change after 1940, so much so that a Propaganda Ministry spokesman could later assert:

> The *Deutsche Wochenschau* bears little resemblence to the newsreels of the past. It is now totally different both in terms of its structure and contents. As a result of the personal supervision of the Propaganda Minister this new cinematic creation consistently captures stirring images of the war.[18]

War reporting was the responsibility of the *Propaganda Kompanie Einheiten* which was established in 1938. PK units were appointed by the RMVP but at the front they operated under the command of the OKW (*Oberkommando der Wehrmacht*).[19] However, all film shot was at the exclusive disposal of the Propaganda Ministry. The PK man was a soldier, he was trained as a soldier after initial technical instruction at the *Landesbildstelle* in Berlin, and he was expected to be at the heart of the battle. Referring to these 'soldier-cameramen' in a speech given to the *Filmwelt* in 1941, Goebbels claimed that they heralded a new era in reporting and presentation and he left the audience with the impression that they were *his* idea:

> In past wars it was the fashion for a few civilians to follow on behind the fighting troops and describe the events of war out of the mouths of general staff-officers. These civilians had no real immediate contact with the experiences of battle. We have done away with this situation. With our battle-reporters and propaganda units, we have assembled an organisation which is right in the heart of the events of war. Instead of working with machine-guns, pistols or rifles, they are working with cameras and pens . . . And with what success! This was shown in the first weeks of the Polish campaign. Suddenly the whole nation experienced war in its totality. What I had anticipated and predicted in fact happened. The people were more satisfied with this realistic portrayal than with any kind of poetic transfiguration.[20]

The material shot by the PK Units was further used in the

prestigious 'Blitzkrieg' documentaries: *Feldzug in Polen* (*Campaign in Poland*), *Feuertaufe* (*Baptism of Fire*), *Sieg im Westen* (*Victory in the West*). In fact only a small percentage of newsreel footage was used in the Deutsche Wochenschau, the rest was stored in the National Film Archive and preserved as historical documents to be revealed after the war. The guiding principle behind the production of newsreels at this early stage of the war was a desire to influence contemporary German audiences combined with the intention to produce 'historical documentaries which would impress later generations'.[21]

But Goebbels was also aware of the potential psychological effects that these newsreels and documentaries could achieve when they were shown by German embassies to audiences in neutral countries. Film rarely allows itself to threaten its audience, however, as the film historians Furhammar and Isaksson noted, 'this rule has a single exception in the way the Nazi Government used newsreels of its army offensives at the beginning of World War II'.[22] In this respect early war newsreels (and documentaries) were deliberately compiled to illustrate the lightning speed and devastating power of the German armed forces. Such films could be exploited as a psychological weapon against those countries that were due to be attacked (or thought they were) next. E.K. Bramsted succinctly stated how the Nazis hoped this intimidation would be achieved: 'they [newsreel material] illustrated that resistance to the mighty German armies, up to date in their weapons, was equivalent to committing suicide'.[23]

The importance of the newsreel war that it offered the propagandist all the advantage of a modern communication medium, in that it was topical, periodical and universal. Its success, particularly during the early stages of the war, depended on the ability of the cameramen to capture topical and exciting events allied to the skill of the editor in selecting and manipulating an intensive linkage of moving pictures and creating what was believed to be a 'factual' reportage of reality. And of course this was reinforced by its conscious placement in the film programme and the manner in which it was contrasted by preceding the more 'theatrical' experience of the feature film.

The war newsreel undoubtedly contributed to the increase in cinema audiences. The SD stressed in particular the 'force and intensity' of the war newsreel which they claimed has 'substantially heightened an already existing interest in contemporary subjects in films.'[24] By 1940 cinema attendances had almost doubled within two years. The newsreels proved especially popular in the rural areas where the peasants were not regular cinema-goers.[25] Goebbels responded by providing 1,000 mobile cinemas continually travelling around the country ensuring that all Germans had the chance of seeing a film show (with a newsreel) at least once a month.[26] Public fascination with these reports in the war led Goebbels, in the spring of 1940, to set up special newsreel shows. Initially these were Saturday screenings of past and present newsreels and were shown continuously. Admission charges were 30–40pf, soldiers and children paying half price with the theatre owners expected to contribute 20 per cent of the costs.[27] After 1940, newsreels were also incorporated into the schools and Hitler Youth programmes with considerable success.[28] On 20 June 1940, the SD reported on the reception of the fifth issue of the wartime Wochenschau. The report reiterated the undoubted success of the newsreel at this time in presenting military victories and it also mentioned how the promotion of the *Führerprinzip* had been received:

> *Allenstein*, *Münster*, *Halle*, *Breslau*, *Stuttgart*, *Lüneburg* – just some of the areas that have confirmed an enormous success. Many reports state that this is the best *Wochenschau* yet – a peak has been reached with cinemas reporting overflowing auditoriums . . . The taking of Dunkirk made an overpowering impression and was followed breathlessly by spectators . . . Reports from *Brunswick*; spectators want to wreak destruction above all on England in order to gain revenge for the crimes she has committed against Germany. Shots of the Führer . . . according to reports from all over the Reich, spectators applauded and there were shouts of 'Heil'. Applause however turned to a pregnant silence when these shots were followed by pictures of Hitler moving to the map-table with his Generals. Every move of the Führer's was followed with rapt attention. The people discussed, above all, the tired and serious features of his face. Reports from *Aachen* speak of relief in the auditorium when 'Adolf' laughed – the people are very concerned for his health and safety . . .[29]

The increased length and improved circulation of the newsreel was another important factor contributing to its early success. In May

1940 it was announced that all German newsreels would last for 40 minutes and that the number of copies of each newsreel would be doubled to 2,000,[30] the latter having the effect of reducing circulation time from eight weeks to four weeks. Moreover, by 1942 the *RMVP* were producing nearly 1,500 copies a week of the *Auslandswochenschau* and distributing them abroad in over 30 languages.[31] These measures enabled the Propaganda Ministry by means of a continuous and uniform repetition to illustrate the German fighting qualities abroad and also to reinforce firmly held prejudices at home. Goebbels believed that a propaganda theme must be repeated, but not beyond some point of diminishing effectiveness. This posed various technical and artistic problems for the newsreel editors: how, for example, were they to accommodate the enlarged format and still make it interesting and exciting? While German armed forces were still registering victories this did not pose too great an obstacle – a skilled editor need only compose subsequent scenes by stressing similar 'facts' (i.e. the invincibility of German military might) to ensure the desired interest and response. SD Reports were showing that this was still proving a successful formula well into the summer of 1941:

> Reports from all over the Reich reveal the insatiable interest of the population for newsreels dealing with the Eastern front. Numerous reports speak of overflowing cinemas at the special newsreel performances. It is often commented that the new kind of newsreel has achieved the almost impossible by reaching the same standards as its predecessor. It is emphasised that the film sequences, despite their length, are not at all tiring, but extremely varied and exciting. According to some reports, people consider the extended format to be more successful in that it allows for greater flexibility.[32]

In the midst of such euphoria German audiences would certainly not question domestic policies and thus under the pretext of 'historical truth' and 'factual reportage' the newsreels could openly and effectively reinforce nationalist and Nazi prejudices. Witness the following response, reported in the same SD Report, to the anti-Semitic campaign being whipped up by Goebbels at this time:

> The pictures showing the arrest of Jews involved in murder were enthusiastically received, and people commented that they were

> still being treated too leniently. The film sequences showing Jews being forced to do clearing-up work were greatly appreciated. The 'lynch justice' meted out by the people of [the Baltic city of] Riga to their 'tormentors' was greeted with shouts of encouragement![33]

In fact, as early as August 1940, *Gaupropagandaleiter* were informing the SD that shots of coloured prisoners of war shown in the newsreels were 'effectively supporting the nation's teaching on heritage and race – particularly in Catholic regions where the doctrine of the master race is not always positively received'.[34] They urged the RMVP to exploit the Wochenschau more fully as a means of reinforcing Nazi racial theory.

According to Siegfried Kracauer these early war newsreels were distinguishable from their British and American counterparts by their much greater length, their use of sophisticated editing, the utilisation of music for emotional effect, and a preference for visual images at the expense of the spoken commentary. In Kracauer's view these pointed to a greater understanding of the film medium and an awareness of the importance of newsreels as an effective instrument of war propaganda:

> A work of art comes closest to perfection when it complies with the specific conditions under which it is achieved, and this is exactly what the Nazi newsreel set out to do. In so far as they play off the picture against the word, they expand within a dimension which belongs entirely to the film.[35]

Goebbels certainly believed in the supreme importance of the Wochenschau and, like Hitler, had been receiving a personal copy of the latest newsreel since 1938. Explaining why he immediately provided the Wochenschauzentrale with emergency headquarters after a particularly heavy air-raid towards the end of 1943, he said: 'It costs much trouble to assemble the newsreel correctly each week and to make it into an effective propaganda weapon, but the work is worthwhile; millions of people draw from the newsreel their best insight into the war, its causes, and its effects.'[36] And in an earlier speech to the Reich Film Chamber (*Reichsfilmkammer*) the Propaganda Minister lamented that feature films had failed to match the power of the Wochenschauen:

> the most striking evidence of the deficiences of the old type of films was that the cinemas were filled, not because of the feature films, but because of the newsreels. [Loud applause]. On numerous occasions it was noted that people left the cinema after the newsreels because they knew that the films which followed could not bear comparison with the broad sweep of the *Wochenschau*.[37]

There can be little doubt that stylistically the Deutsche Wochenschauen are impressive examples of film propaganda. But as the war dragged on they suffered, as did all Nazi propaganda, through their close association with German military success. Indeed, their effectiveness depended on their ability to report the victories that German leaders promised. While confidence in the Führer was high, the contradictions of Nazi propaganda mattered little. Attitudes could easily be altered as long as the regime exuded strength. However, this was all to change towards the end of 1941. The time of blitzkreig and easy victories was over and therefore the enemies of the Reich (and what they said) had to be taken more seriously. The newsreels also had to adapt to the changed circumstances, there were no more sensational marches into enemy territory and German audiences had to be content with the more mundane activity of warfare. In the knowledge that there would be no speedy end to the war, Nazi propaganda increasingly depended on irrational themes at the expense of factual war reporting. One can detect the deliberate evasion in Nazi propaganda at this time concerning material problems such as food shortages, labour difficulties and air raids. By prescribing what could and could not be shown or mentioned in the mass media, the Nazis betrayed how little they were concerned with reality. In July 1941, the RMVP received a message from the *Führerhauptquartier* that:

> The Führer wants shots of Russian cruelty towards German prisoners to be incorporated in the *Wochenschauen*, so that Germans know exactly what the enemy is like. He specifically requests that such atrocities should include genitals being cut off and the placing of hand-grenades in the trousers of the prisoners.[38]

However in June 1940, Goebbels had already issued a directive to the effect that, while the severity, magnitude and sacrifice of war may be shown, any excessively realistic representation likely to arouse a horror of the war must be avoided at all costs.[39] A month before this directive, the *OKW* instructed cameramen and editors that pictures should not be used which 'are apt to produce fear, horror or revulsion' of the war, 'unless they acquire documentary value for this reason'.[40] Despite Hitler's demand that German film audience should occasionally be shocked by the horror of war, these principles were followed to the end of the war with the result that newsreel never showed the fighting in its true frightfulness and murderous intent. The early Wochenschauen, in particular, give the impression of an invincible military machine sweeping forward against the enemy without the loss of a single life or machine. This abolition of death from all newsreels was a peculiarity of Nazi propaganda.[41]

It would appear that even before the first major set-back of Stalingrad, disillusionment had set in and audiences had started to question previous assumptions and the banality and lies they were witnessing in the weekly newsreels. Only a month after the propaganda Minister addressed the Reichsfilmkammer in February 1941 and proclaimed the supreme importance of the Wochenschau, the SD reported that Germans were lingering outside the cinemas until the newsreels which came first on the programme were over.[42] Goebbels responded by closing all cinema box offices during the showing of the newsreel, so that if patrons wanted to see the feature attraction they were forced to sit through the newsreel as well![43]

By 1943 this disillusionment was clearly reflected in the reception given to the war newsreels. No longer were Germans willing to comment spontaneously on the content of the Wochenschau as the following SD Report illustrates:

> Reliable reports have commented that the newsreels have been unable to regain their former popularity. It has been confirmed from wide sections of the population that people no longer want to go to the cinema just to see the newsreel. It is only seldom now that people make spontaneous comments about newsreels. Observation of this kind are confirmed constantly and, as a result, wide sections of the community are not allowing themselves to be influenced by the newsreel.[44]

The armed forces on the other hand were complaining that the *Waffen SS* was appearing too frequently in the Wochenschau.[45]

However the RMVP was finding it increasingly difficult to secure enough documentary footage and was therefore only too willing to use the excellent material available on the SS.

After the defeat of Stalingrad, German propaganda had shed all agitational pretentions; instead, it limited itself to strengthening the community spirit in the struggle for 'total war'. Goebbels was one of the few Nazi leaders to realise that final victory could only be achieved by a full mobilisation of German resources which would incorporate every citizen. The Propaganda Minister envisaged a radical departure from the measure that other leaders like Martin Bormann, Hitler's powerful secretary, had established for civilian defence. For Goebbels, success could only be achieved by the complete mobilisation of the home front in order that Germany should become one fighting unit, united under a powerful leader. He informed a group of journalists in March 1943 that 'To applaud a blitz campaign needs no toughness. But I have the feeling that this war will not come to an end quickly. So we must prepare our minds and hearts for bitter experiences.'[46] This meant a change of policy from the buoyant, arrogant claims of the previous three years. In particular, Goebbels attempted to create toughness in the civilian population by resorting to one of the oldest techniques of persuasion – the indoctrination by fear. Fear of the sub-human Bolshevik 'beast-man' endangering Western civilisation became the leitmotiv of his propaganda programme in the winter of 1943. In his 'Total War' speech of 18 February 1943 (which formed the basis of a single newsreel) total sacrifices and hardship were put forward by Goebbels as the only alternatives to the type of destruction that the *Wehrmacht* was preventing.[47] If the Secret Police Reports are to be believed, then Goebbels would appear to have enjoyed some success with this campaign. The SD noted that 'this newsreel made a deep impression and subsequently dissipated any feelings of scepticism which have prevailed up until now.'[48] Writing in 1943, H. Herma shrewdly observed:

> The concept of propaganda had been redefined by National Socialism. It has been closely linked to the totalitarian organisation of society and may more aptly be called 'psychological management' than propaganda. It does not want to persuade or convince. It introduces the element of fear, and aims at the elimination of rationality.[49]

From 1943 onwards, Nazi propaganda continued to insist that final victory was assured however great the difficulties of the moment may seem. The development of the Deutsche Wochenschauen detailed the gradual retreat of National Socialist propaganda into myth from 1939 to 1945. By invoking the *Untergangsmotif* and declaring that war was an ideological struggle, a 'fight to the death', Goebbels was once again appealing to German fears of the barbaric Bolshevik that he had employed so successfully in 1933. In the last phase of the war fear and terror became a dominant theme of Nazi newsreel propaganda. The contents of the newsreel Deutsche Wochenschau No. 45/46, released towards the end of 1944, illustrates how the fear tactic was employed even as the Russian troops advanced on Berlin:[50]

Deutsche Wochenschau No. 45/46, 1944

Introduction: Trumpet fanfare, bells ringing, and the Nazi version of the German eagle (designed by Albert Speer)

1. *Food substitutes*: ash berries when harvested and pressed produce a floury substance which can be refined and bottled. It is claimed that 2 cupfuls of these berries are the equivalent of 7 lemons in Vitamin C.

2. *Volkssturm*: 'The hour of battle has arrived for us all. Men and women between the ages of 16 and 60, regardless of class or occupation, enrol to save the nation.' 18 October: it is the 131st Anniversary of the Battle of Leipzig. Himmler reads the Führer's instructions for the Volkssturm: 'Our enemies must be shown that an invasion of Germany – were that possible – would cost them dearly and that the national spirit would be aroused to the utmost resistance.'

Service of dedication at the Annaberg Memorial. A mass Volkssturm rally is held at Leipzig: 'Hundreds of thousands have volunteered from the eastern regions and are ready to defend the Fatherland with their blood.' A local Gauleiter is seen addressing the rally and the Volkssturm recruits receive rifles and anti-tank weapons. The Hitler Youth march behind: 'They also are ready to fulfil their oath to their Führer.'

3. *The Stone Lion at Belfort*: Metz Cathedral, the Moselle Valley and Triers have all been under air attack 'but the people of these regions have learned to accept this with courage and stoicism'.

4. *West Front*: German reserve divisions move up to the front, 'the enemy have severely extended themselves through their mistaken belief in Germany's impending collapse!' At Geilenkirchen, pupils of the Officers' School in Julich take over the defence of the city and demonstrate the effectiveness of their anti-tank missile in repelling an American attack. The commentator refers to the American prisoners (whose battle-soiled faces are shown in close-ups and include a number of negroes) as 'these gum-chewing liberators of Europe who only prove that they spring from the same stock as Stalin's hordes from the Steppes!'

5. *East Front*: The battle regions in East Prussia – naval detachments provide support for the army in the Baltic near Memel and defence positions are formed near Goldap and Gumbinnen.

Nemmersdorf: the Wehrmacht have discovered evidence of Bolshevik atrocities 'no restraint is placed upon Bolshevik soldiers and this has resulted once again in women being raped, old men beaten to death, and children murdered. The whole countryside is ravaged by death. This testimony of brutal bestiality may be the last warning to Europe.'

6. *Final Sequence*: Air and tank battles on the Eastern Front. The commentator claims that the Russians have lost a good deal of their equipment in just a few days and that the German people have a 'fervent determination to save their country from Stalin's hordes!'

In the final year of the war 'heroism' and 'sacrifice' often appeared in the newsreels; there was no mention or suggestion of surrender. As the Wochenschau No. 45/46 demonstrates, when other methods of persuasion failed, terror was employed as the antidote to cowardice. And of course linked to this was a need for endurance on the part of the population. Goebbels also made a major effort to intensify personal commitment to the cult of the Führer. An example of this new emphasis can be found in the Deutsche Wochenschau (No. 712) released in April 1944 to celebrate Hitler's fifty-fifth birthday.[51] It was to be one of the last appearances that Hitler made in the German newsreels. At an *NSDAP* concert on the eve of his birthday (where Beethoven's 'Eroica' was played), Goebbels offered the Party's congratulations to Hitler and reaffirmed the nation's faith in him:

> On our Führer's birthday we wish to express our hopes for his continued health and strength. We want to assure him that he is able to rely on his people absolutely in this great struggle: that he is today as he always was – our Führer!

The scene in the concert hall is followed by shots of a bomb-damaged Berlin recovering from an Allied sortie. In the background, barely visible, slogans can be seen daubed on the ruins and on banners hanging from windows. As the commentator says that this is the German people's gift to Hitler, the camera tracks in to a ruined wall upon which was painted a slogan demonstrating the nation's unbending will: 'Our walls may break but our hearts do not – as long as the Führer lives!'

Goebbels once remarked that, 'the essence of propaganda consists in winning people over to an idea so sincerely, so vitally, that in the end they succumb to it utterly and can never again escape from it'.[52] By this criterion, the war newsreels undoubtedly failed, for in the final analysis they were unable to instil into the German population what Coleridge termed a 'willing suspension of disbelief'. As the war continued the Deutsche Wochenschauen suffered through their close association with German military success, until in the end they had almost totally substituted myth for reality. Myth need not necessarily be reconcilable with truth, but if such propaganda is to prove successful it must survive the battlefield. Furthermore, as Jay Baird has observed: 'When at the end of their rope, Hitler and Goebbels made one final, frantic effect to survive – they blurred the distinction between Party and nation in an attempt to convince the people that the demise of one guaranteed the destruction of the other.'[53] In other words, Germans were no longer fighting an ideological battle for National Socialism, but for the survival of Germany. Although the German people's response to this may suggest that Goebbels enjoyed a limited success in 1945, this was due less to the 'power' of the Nazi war newsreels than to a traditional German patriotism and a people intuitively defending their country.

Notes

1. J.W. Baird, *The Mythical World of Nazi War Propaganda* (Minneapolis, 1974), p. 8.

2. A. Speer, *Inside the Third Reich* (London, 1971), pp. 240–1.

3. An extremely succinct discussion of these problems can be found in W.A. Boelcke, *The Secret Conferences of Dr Goebbels: The Nazi Propaganda War 1939–43* (New York, 1970), pp. x–xxi.

4. See, D. Welch, *Propaganda and the German Cinema, 1933–45*, (OUP, 1983).

5. Bundesarchive Koblenz (hereafter BA), *R58 (Akten des Reichssicherheitshauptamtes), 150/2*, 29 April 1940. There is some disagreement over the value of the SD Reports as an indicator of public opinion. However, they remain the best source available and I have included their assessment of audience reaction to the newsreels where they are relevant. Moreover, all the newsreels discussed in this article are available for either private viewing or hire from the Imperial War Museum, and have been chosen with this in mind.

6. BA, *R109I (Akten der Ufa-Film GmbH), 1030b, 1079*, 14 May 1935.

7. J. McCutcheon Raleigh, *Behind the Nazi Front* (London, 1941), pp. 247.8.

8. For an interesting example of just how detailed these instructions were see, F. Terveen, *Die Entwicklung der Wochenschau in Deutschland: Ufa Tonwoche No. 451/1939 – Hitlers 50. Geburtstag* (Göttingen, 1960).

9. H. Tackmann, *Filmbandbuch als ergänzbare Sammlung herausgegeben von der Reichsfilmkammer* (Berlin, 1938), RGB1. I, 1936, p. 404. See also 'Warum Wochenschaugesetz?', *Der deutsche Film*, vol. 1, (1936), p. 89.

10. Tackmann, 31 October 1938.

11. Ibid., 28 August 1938.

12. *Film-Kurier*, 18 September 1936, reproduced in J. Wulf, *Theater und Film im Dritten Reich* (Gütersloh, 1964), p. 362.

13. *Der deutsche Film* (August 1937), p. 52, quoted in K.W. Wippermann, *Die Entwicklung der Wochenschau in Deutschland: Ufa-Tonwoche No. 410/1938* (Göttingen, 1970), p. 18.

14. H.J. Geise, 'Die Film-Wochenschau im Dienste der Politik' (Diss., Leipzig, 1941), p. 59; reproduced in Wippermann, *Die Entwicklwng der Wochenschau*, p. 19. Further information can be found in BA, *R55 (Akten des Reichsministeriums für Volksaufklärung und Propaganda)*, folders 175 and 486.

15. U. Von Hassell, *The von Hassell Diaries 1938–44* (London, 1948), p. 64.

16. *Film-Kurier*, 25 August 1939. The last newsreel released prior to the war (*Ufa Tonwoche 469*, 30 August 1939) showed German troop movements and lampooned Allied politicians.

17. BA, *R55/504, (Gründung bei Deutsche Wochenschau GmbH: 1940–42)*. The new company was made a subsidiary of Ufa for financial reasons with Deulig holding 25 per cent of the capital and Ufa 75 per cent. *R2 (Akten des Reichsfinanzministeriums), 4809*, 3 December 1940.

18. H. Traub, *Die Ufa. Ein Beitrag zur Entwicklungsgeschichte des deutschen Filmschaffens* (Berlin, 1943), p. 110. See also Traub (ed.), *25 Jahre Wochenschau der Ufa* (Berlin, 1939).

19. In fact the Luftwaffe and the navy also had their own film units.

20. *Speech by Reich Minister Dr Goebbels on the Occasion of the War Conference of the Reichsfilmkammer*, 15 February 1941. The full speech is reproduced in G. Albrecht, *Nationalsozialistische Filmpolitik. Eine soziologische Untersuchung über die Spielfilme des Dritten Reichs* (Stuttgart, 1969), pp. 465–79.

21. F. Terveen, 'Das Filmdokument der Nazis und sein Wahrheitsgehalt', *Das Parlament Bonn*, Nos. 21–5 (May 1955), p. 8.

22. L. Furhammer and F. Isaksson, *Politics and Film* (London, 1971), p. 188.
23. E.K. Bramsted, *Goebbels and National Socialist Propaganda 1925–45* (Michigan State University Press, 1965), p. 67.
24. BA, *R58/155*, 24 October 1940.
25. H. Boberach, *Meldungen aus dem Reich. Auswahl aus den geheimen Lagerberichten des Sicherheitsdienstes der SS 1939–44* (Neuwid and Berlin, 1965), p. 116.
26. BA, *Sammlung Sänger (Aus der Kulturpolitischen Presskonferenz) Zsg. 102/63*, 13 June 1941.
27. BA, *R109I/1034a, 1412*, 16 June 1940.
28. BA, *R58/155*, 24 October 1940.
29. BA, *R58/151*, 20 June 1940.
30. *Licht-Bild-Bühne*, 23 May 1940.
31. A point stressed by Goebbels in his speech to the Reichsfilmkammer on 15 February 1941. See above, no. 20.
32. Wippermann claims that they regularly reached an audience of 30 million *Die Entwicklung der Wochenschau in Deutschland: 'Die Deutsche Wochenschau' No. 10/651 February 1943* (Göttingen, 1970), p. 45. They were still being distributed abroad in the Spring of 1944. BA, *R55/665*, 13 May 1944.
33. BA, *R58/161*, 24 July 1941.
34. BA, *R58/153*, 12 August 1940.
35. S. Kracauer, 'The Conquest of Europe on the Screen. The Nazi Newsreel, 1939–40', *Social Research*, vol. 10, no. 3 (September 1943), p. 340.
36. Quoted in L.W. Doob, 'Goebbels' Principles of Propaganda', in D. Katz *et al.* (eds.), *Public Opinion and Propaganda* (New York, 1954), p. 513.
37. Goebbels' speech of 15 February 1941. Hitler is reported to have remarked in 1941: 'I've been thrilled by our contemporary newsreels. We are experiencing a heroic epic, without precedent in history.' H. Trevor-Roper, *Hitler's Table Talk* (London, 1973), entry for 25/6 September 1941, p. 43.
38. BA, *NS18 (Reichspropagandaleitung der NSDAP/Gruppe Filmwesen), 282*, 10 July 1941.
39. Boelcke, *The Secret Conference of Dr Goebbels*, p. 51. Also Boelcke (ed.), *Kriegspropaganda 1939–41, Geheime Ministerkonferenzen im Reichspropagandaministerium* (Stuttgart, 1966), 10 June 1940, p. 132.
40. Ibid., 24 May 1940, p. 129.
41. This effect was achieved by carefully editing. William Shirer recounts viewing uncensored newsreels in the Propaganda Ministry which showed quite clearly death and destruction. *Berlin Biary, 1934–41* (London, 1970), p. 267.
42. BA, *R58/158*, 27 March 1941. One explanation supplied by various Gauleiter to the RMVP was that Hitler was not appearing frequently enough in these newsreels. From Munich it was claimed that when the Führer was not shown 'morale sank – but when he appeared a new desire and will for victory emerged'. BA, *NS18/341*. 6 August 1942.
43. Boelcke, *Kriegspropaganda* p. 652. In fact cinema owners had been instructed to keep their doors closed during the showing of the war newsreel from as early as July 1940. By 1943 Gauleiter were ignoring these instructions. Goebbels was forced to remind them of this directive and the need to impose it rigorously. BA *NS18/341*, 9 July 1943.
44. BA, *R58/1148*, 4 March 1943.
45. BA, *NS18/341*, 24 September 1943.
46. R. Semmler, *Goebbels – The Man Next to Hitler* (London, 1947), entry for 3 April 1943, p. 73.
47. For a detailed analysis of this newsreel see Wippermann, *Die Entwicklung der Wochenschau*.

48. BA, *R58/1148*, 4 March 1943.

49. H. Herma, 'Goebbels' Conception of Propaganda', *Social Research*, vol. 10, no. 2 (1943), p. 217.

50. I have checked the contents of this newsreel against the print held with the Imperial War Museum. They also provide a brief translation.

51. *Deutsche Wochenschau No. 712* – also avalaible for hire from the Imperial War Museum. The *DW* numbering is confusing because it did not follow chronologically.

52. Speech on the 'Tasks of the German Theatre', 8 May 1933. Quoted in J. Fest, *The Face of the Third Reich* (London, 1972), p. 151.

53. Baird, *The Mythical World of Nazi War Propaganda*, p. 11.

10 ITALY: THE REGIME, THE NATION AND THE FILM INDUSTRY: AN INTRODUCTION

David Ellwood

When Mussolini decided to enter the war at Hitler's side in June 1940, Fascism had been in power for almost 20 years. Just how solid the regime was politically and economically at the time is still a much-debated question. Certainly there was no sight whatsoever of any credible alternative to Fascism, and from the outside (where in fact very little was known of how Italy really worked) the system continued to impress. Churchill's conviction that Mussolini had made only one big mistake – becoming an enemy of Great Britain – is well known. Fascism in Italy was, after a fashion, consolidated by 1940, and a generation had grown up – the generation which would fight the war – knowing nothing else, hardly able to imagine even what an alternative system might be like. Here was a significant difference in experience between Mussolini's nation and that of his Axis partner, Nazi Germany.[1] Mussolini's regime's relationship with the Italian people, always ambiguous, had changed, and this had its effect on the rhetoric which was so much of the Fascist way. The frenzy, the deliberate, hammering vulgarity and the high-pitched sloganeering of the early years were by now much toned down and Mussolini's personal rapport with his famous mass audience had also evolved: the balcony speeches now played down the role of the Fascist Party as such and played up the nation; they tended to be concentrated around single episodes of key importance rather than generically extolling visions of the future, and they became less numerous as other media were developed. When the war came they disappeared altogether from the newsreels.[2]

Above all Fascism in 1940 had to take account of how contradictory and arbitrary its relation with Italian reality really was. The Fascist 'revolution' was nowhere near as total as the Fascists pretended, or as the other great 'revolutionaries' of the time, Hitler and Stalin, achieved. Towards the end of Mussolini's career Dr Goebbels commented disparagingly on how the Italian dictator had been far too strongly rooted 'in the earth of his own people' to become a true revolutionary; the Duce's regime reflected this contradiction. Large areas of Italian life remained relatively untouched by it; these included the State apparatus, much of industry, the aristocracy and the large southern landowners. Geographically the depth of Fascist penetration was extremely uneven; some areas, such as Emilia Romagna, were known as Fascist strongholds, while others, such as Piedmont, were only superficially involved. There was nothing like the attempt at systematic restructuring of German social life, with all the traditional layers of association of churches, political parties, trade unions, voluntary networks separating the masses from the ruling groups removed. Rather, in Italy the regime had struck up various forms of cohabitation with traditional institutions: where it could neither take over completely or simply ignore, arrangements had sprung up or been established by which appearances were maintained and some of the regime's needs met, but without compromising seriously the autonomy of the partner. The Vatican Concordat was the most dignified of these accords. Relations with very large industrial firms, such as Fiat, also come under this heading, but there were many other lesser, often curiously contradictory, examples and among them, as we shall see, was the film industry.

It was on the plane of values that Fascism made its most telling compromises with Italian tradition. Exploiting to the full its credit with the Church and the Monarchy, the regime exalted the triad of God-Fatherland-Family to the highest place in its rhetoric, increasingly insisting on it and, as time went on, less on Fascism itself as a value. This was especially true after the war adventure began in 1940. It was these older values which tied the language of late Fascism together with the rituals of the Monarchy and the symbolism of the Church, and helped conserve the regime's legitimacy and authority in the eyes of a population deeply conservative in much of its outlook. Despite the Fascist rhetoric of achieving modernisation and industrialisation, its love of everything technical and potent, fast and futuristic, Italy remained an overwhelmingly agrarian nation. Outside Turin, and to a lesser extent Milan and Genoa, the presence of a working class was negligible: the vast majority of the lower-class population was peasant, as Mussolini well knew from his own background. The regime was forced to come to terms with this reality in its politics and its propaganda, in its modernising effort and in its rhetoric. Hence the symbolism of grain and the concerted efforts to increase its production, using new methods, new land won by reclamation, a great deal of exhortation via films, radio, mass projects and of course the Duce's personal example in 'the battle of grain'. 'Grain and glory': the language of a populism based on fecundity, plenty, self-reliance and Fascism's presumed mobilising capacities, the language of many an *Istituto Luce* newsreel, especially after the formal establishment of autarcky in 1936.

The pre-war cinema had its own pact with Italian social reality. As a form of mass culture (Fascism's achievement in developing Italy's first mass culture is not doubted) it was officially called upon by the regime to play a distinctive part in 'organising the consensus'. But when Italian film production began in a substantial way in the 1930s the overwhelming majority of successful features produced were found to be not epics exalting Fascist heroes or ideals but light comedies, adventure stories or fables. In 1934 the State equipped itself with a *Direzione generale per la Cinematografia*, headed by the propaganda expert Luigi Freddi, to put political and financial pressure on the industry and so obtain a more committed, recognisably Fascist, film product. The realisation gradually emerged that this was practically impossible, that *there was no such thing as a Fascist cinema*.[3] The reasons for this conspicuous failure of the regime have been listed as follows by the Italian film historian G.P. Brunetta:

> – the presence in important positions from the beginning of antifascist film technicians and directors such as Barbaro, Solaroli and Aldo Vergano, whose professional and critical skills made them indispensable;
> – the lack of a coherent group of writers and artists willing or able to develop appropriate forms of film propaganda technique;
> – the unwillingess of the public to accept anything other than light entertainment;
> – the difficulty of transmitting explicit political messages in comparison with other media such as press or radio;
> – the problems involved in changing the regime's image away from the early stereotypes of the blackshirt squads, the cod liver oil, the assaults etc.[4]

What the regime settled for was a sustained effect to impose on film production of all types the standard of being *edifying*, to use the word of the film critic Giorgio Cremonini.[5] Contrasting the worst aspects of society allegedly seen in French films of the time, the then director of the *Direzione generale per la Cinematografia*, Pavolini, asserted in his annual report for 1941:

> Ours is a society in which the decline of the birth rate has been stopped, in which crime is rapidly declining, in which morality is upheld not only by the State but in the lives of every family and individual. Are we demanding then a cinema in which everything is rose-coloured, in which everyone behaves perfectly, without any of the drama which rises up when good meets evil? Certainly not. Our censorship has demonstrated that it is anything but narrow-minded. But the fundamental demand remains: that Italian life be reflected as it is – not without its imperfections, but for by far the greater part noble and commendable.[6]

Censorship had been called upon to play its part in this effort from the beginning of the Direzione generale's work. In the words of its first director, Freddi, its role was not 'a coldly repressive vigilance, but a form of positive, energetic encouragement aiming to encourage the spiritual and cultural growth of the Nation as a civilisation'.[7] Hence in addition to the pre-existing (pre-Fascist) codes of censorship, the Direzione generale added a ban on any reference to class conflicts or class hatred, and the rules became so comprehensive that almost all the major films produced outside Italy in the 1930s, including Lewis Milestone's *All Quiet on the Western Front* (1930), *Scarface* (1932) and *A Farewell to Arms* (1933), were excluded from the Italian market.

What Freddi and Pavolini looked forward to was the exaltation of good and morality, of order and respect: images of white-shirted, obedient shop assistants and clerks, of trains running on time, of numbers of clean-washed children in tranquil, provincial families. What the regime got was the 'white telephone' genre, as satirised (not without nostalgia) in *Amarcord*: 'on the one hand cancellation of all reference to real-life Italy (writes the film historian Francesco Savio), on the other the adoption of a totally improbable and incongruous view of life – hence the outrageously opulent furnishings, the huge internal staircases, the oriental rugs, and on the little marble or glass table a telephone, not always white . . .'[8] The director, Camerini, castigated as the 'confessor figure, the spiritual father of the Italian petit bourgeoisie' by his contemporary Lizzani, explained that the whole purpose was 'to send the cinemagoer home satisfied, so that he goes to bed undisturbed and unsurprised, but with a pleasant vision of life to close the day'.[9] The edifying desires of the regime soon fell behind the success of these films, so much so that by 1938 a system of cash-incentives had been installed to reward success at the box-office. The production company Cinecitta reached record rates of production by making 'the most outrageous and absurd forms of low farce', to use the words of a later critic, Umberto Barbaro.[10] Inevitably much has since been made of the unlikely fate of Mussolini's cinematographic ambitions, ending as they did in the world of the white telephones. Against those who interpret the public's preference for this genre as a form of anti-fascism, are critics who simply denounce the tone and content, the 'sugariness and simple-mindedness', perfectly adapted for a petit-bourgeois silent majority, 'superficial, ignorant, anti-working-class and closed to any forms of existence outside its own horizon'.[11]

The onset of the war in the summer of 1940 brought little change as the light comedies, adventure stories and romances continued to form by far the largest part of domestic film production.[12] There had to be some response to the war and, with the stimlus of the Nazi example, the regime awkwardly set out to gird up its loins and face the new propaganda challenge. Finally in mid-1941 Pavolini of the Direzione generale launched a programme for the film industry with the special slogan 'Discipline, Imagination, Intelligence'.

> Companions, . . . I must appeal to your discipline, intelligence and imagination, the three forces which must direct the destiny of the Italian cinema . . . In seven days a year will have passed since Italy entered the war . . . Quietly, with the calm resolution of a people of strong character, Italy took her place of honour at the shoulder of her Ally, took up her position of fate and glory against the enemy . . . We people of the cinema must make a solemn commitment . . . a commitment to reach those ends already mentioned which were always bright in our souls. Only in this way shall we be able to say that during the war the Italian cinema represented for our people a weapon of faith, resistance and serenity, just as in the world of tomorrow, under victory's renewed justice, it will be an arm of Fascism's diffusion and of Italy's prestige.[13]

In this effort the regime was immensely aided by the experience acquired during the Abyssinian invasion and the Spanish Civil War. Here comprehensive newsreel coverage, followed up by epic docu-dramas such as *Genina* and *L'Assedio Dell' Alcazar* (*The Siege of Alcazar*), had contributed materially to the all-time high point reached at that moment in Fascism's popular appeal and political solidarity. Of the two experiences, it was the conquest of Empire which held the greatest allure and the film industry, the writers and the critics did their best to exalt the 'overwhelming hum of the turbine which catches in its vortex every single Italian', the 'new-lit horizons', the 'spiritual reality' which the conquest of Ethiopia and Somalia supposedly brought in their wake. With the Italian participation in Hitler's war, much of the film material of this earlier period made a second round of the Italian cinemas, especially those post-Spanish Civil War feature films which were thought appropriate to inure people to the risks and glories of modern combat (with civilians caught in the middle whether they like it or not). The two somewhat dubious historical epics made explicitly to connect classical Rome's warlike past to contemporary Rome's warlike postures, *Scipione L'Africano* (*Scipio the African*, 1937) and *The Condottieri* (1936), were also given a second outing.[14] The newsreels, however, were in serious difficulty when war came and those directly responsible, the Luce and Incom organisations, were hard put to face the challenge. In 1939 the Istituto Luce had produced its own tribute to the twentieth anniversary of Fascism's birth, 'Ventennale del Fascismo', and had received nothing but brickbats from on high: 'an arid photographic catalogue of events', wrote Alfieri, the Minister for Popular Culture, 'boring and insipid without passion or feeling . . . a complete failure'.[15] In reply the President of the Istituto complained of his lack of resources, of the need always for a political interpretation, of the endless pressure from personages of the regime anxious to be seen on film.

There were other, deeper, problems facing direct propaganda by film. Apart from the obvious superiority of the German material already circulating in Italian cinemas and the general boredom of the public with newsreels, there was widespread unease within the regime and outside it as to what the war would mean for the country. The Duce had hesitated long before taking the plunge and he and his cohorts at the very top knew that there could be no question of prolonged campaigns far from home, at least not with any prospect of success. Amongst the general public it was difficult to arouse any enthusiasm for Nazi Germany's absorption of

Austria, or for Nazi anti-Semitism and love of war, or for the totalising impact of the Nazi revolutionary order. Thus the overall strategy for Italian psychological mobilisation had to use very different rhetorical codes from those developed by Goebbels and his Propaganda Ministry. Outside the material specifically dedicated to the war, in which radio and the Press played by far the largest role, there was, says G.P. Brunetta, 'a general turning-away from triumphalistic rhetoric and celebrations of the country's power', a development perhaps attributable to 'the perception, even if unconscious, of the tragic error into which Fascism had thrown the country with its war adventure'.[16] So instead of the heroic we have the human; instead of the glory of war we see the intimate, sentimental side of military life. Even the newsreels were involved:

> The purpose of the Luce newsreels (wrote an official commentator in 1941) was to bring the public nearer to the fighting men by looking at the details of their everyday lives, with its effort and dangers certainly, but also with its moments of light relief and those little human gestures that come out even in the face of the enemy . . . We see and feel for the soldiers marching over the endless sand and for the flyers who protect them from above. They seem to be saying, 'the war is hard and gives us little satisfaction, and it's we who are bearing the brunt. But for our country – staunchness and courage! Better times will come'[17]

This emphasis on the human element, first traceable in the features of the post-Abyssinia mood but fully developed in the docu-dramas and epics of the war period, according to Brunetta, constituted the key screening and distracting mechanism used to disguise the reality of war while at the same time perpetuating in a war context the edifying emphasis on petit bourgeois values familiar from pre-war times. In Alessandrini's *Aldebaran*, for example, 'we have a commander who goes, like a mother, to look at his soldiers as they sleep, who weeps over the cross of a dead officer. We see soldiers listening to the news from home on the radio, and who then go off singing towards the battle'.[18]

In the newsreels themselves the war is presented in a 'business as usual' fashion right up to the autumn of 1942. So alongside news of military progress, one sees fashion shows, the races, the beaches and the sporting events of the summer, or else the 'beau monde' circulating in the foyer of the Palace of the Cinema in Venice for the opening of the Cinema festival.[19] The war itself, at least the invasion of France, is made to look easy: we see applauding peasantry, girls kissing troops, much mountain scenery and hiking, very little fighting or blood (not that a great deal occurred). Mussolini has shed his politician's uniform and even his athletic image and appears smiling and comradely, sympathising and talking with his generals: the expert colleague conversing as an equal at the battlefront. His uniform is the imperial military version and Fascist symbols are rarely to be seen; the flags, pomp and trinketry of the House of Savoy are preferred. The contrast with the machinery, technical prowess and sheer fury of the Blitzkrieg could hardly be more striking, but the implication is clear: Mussolini is 'intelligent' in the special Italian way, cleverly choosing just the right moment to strike with the minimum of effort.[20]

The themes highlighted by the newsreels were only partially ideological in the first months. Each of the armed forces was given special treatment, with the Navy symbol of tradition, the Airforce as the wave of the future and the Army as the people in arms. There was also a great emphasis on the virtues of autarchy as applied to social life, agriculture and industry. Youth remained a potent Fascist symbol as always, a visual code for strength in population growth, Italianate energy and beauty, the glow of the future opposed to the worn-out past. As time passed and victory became less and less certain, the thrust of the newsreels changed. Rather than exalting Italian virtues, it is the vile features of the enemy which become the favourite target, particularly the 'demoplutosocialmasonic' British, bloodsuckers of half the world's peoples. As the jealousy and frustration of the regime grow, the tone of its propaganda steadily declines with racist elements becoming more common and sentimentality coarser. There was no concealing the fundamental difference in situation between 1941–2 and 1943, as the newsreel stories from the Russian front demonstrated. In the early days, the campaign was portrayed as a replay of the invasion of France: light-hearted, easy, reflecting Fascist pride and hatred of the Bolsheviks. After Stalingrad, the fatigue and anxiety on the faces of the retreating troops was plain for all to see. The regime improvised, concentrating once again on the human, emotional side, attempting to reassure those at home that his or her husband or son was alive, cheerful and cared for by the regime even though so far away. Audiences at home saw scenes of soldiers eating (which in reality they rarely did during the retreat), reading their mail and singing the folk-songs of their villages.[21]

It is this special form of populism which remains the constant of the film propaganda, according to the historian G. Quazza. This was a populism aimed at wrapping the hard facts in a light-hearted, fabulous story beyond history, a populism codified in the Fascist slogans and rituals which were inculcated into the young from their very earliest years at school, a populism where Destiny reigns through the medium of the Duce (though with far less fervour than in Hitler's case). Beyond the propaganda however is the far more complex reality of the feature films, products of an industry where the forces of the future were already at work and capable of bringing forth Visconti's *Ossessione*, which as early as 1942 was considered a milestone in the development of contemporary Italian cinema. The Italian cinema was never fully integrated into the Fascist regime's political project, in spite of the many compromises, the nationalism and the populism of edifying sentiments.

Notes

1. See the comments by the veteran director Renzo Renzi in the presentation pamphlet accompanying the recent conference and film exhibition on the early 1940s (organised by the Cineteca of the City of Bologna and the Cineteca nazionale, Bologna, May 1982) entitled *Quegli ambigui anni '40*, (Bologna, 1982).
2. G.P. Bernagozzi, 'La propaganda del regime' in *Vincere Vinceremo, La guerra fascista, 1940–1943* (a cura dell'Istituto Luce e dell'Archivio nazionale cinematografico della Resistenza, Bologna, 1975), p. 55.
3. G.P. Brunetta, *Il cinema italiano tra le due guerre. Fascismo e politica cinematografica* (Milan, 1975), p. 74. A possible exception to this rule is the case of A. Blasetti; cf G.P. Bernagozzi, 'Il cinema del ventennio fascista' in *Storia del cinema, Dall'affermazione del sonoro al neorealismo*, a cura di Adelio Ferrari (Venice, 1978), pp. 60–2.
4. Brunetta, *Il cinema italiano tra le due guerre*, p. 75.
5. G. Cremonini, 'Il profumo di un 'epoca' in *Quegli ambigui anni'40*, p. 18.
6. Bernagozzi, 'La propaganda del regime', p. 20.
7. Ibid., p. 18.
8. Ibid., p. 64.
9. Ibid., p. 65.
10. Ibid., p. 64.
11. G.P. Brunetta, *Il cinema italiano tra le due guerre*, p. 74.
12. Full figures are given in Cremonini, 'Il profumo di un 'epoca'; further details are provided by G. Rondelino 'Italian Propaganda Films: 1940–1943', below.
13. Cited in Bernagozzi, 'La propaganda del regime', p. 33.
14. Brunetta, *Il cinema italianao tra le due guerre*, pp. 76–9.

15. Bernagozzi, 'Il cinema del ventennio fascista', p. 72.
16. Brunetta, *Il cinema italiano tra le due guerre*, p. 78.
17. Ibid., p. 79.
18. Ibid., p. 81.
19. Bernagozzi, 'Il cinema del ventennio fascista', p. 93.
20. Cf. G. Quazza, 'La politica del consenso nei cinegiornali Luce' in *Vincere, Vinceremo, La guerra fascista, 1940–1943*, pp. 5–6.
21. Ibid., pp. 5–6.

11 ITALIAN PROPAGANDA FILMS: 1940–1943

Gianni Rondolino

When Italy declared war on Britain and France in June 1940 the film departments of the Italian armed forces prepared to document the nation's historical venture.[1] Fernando Cerchio, film editor and director at the *Istituto Luce*, said:

> At the beginning of June, on the brink of our declaration of war, the film departments of the Royal Army, Navy and Airforce and also the Istituto Luce (where the first cameramen in uniform with military-coloured vehicles were to be seen) were mobilised, so to speak; or rather, they were ready with their skilled staff and technical resources to begin the accurate documentation of our war . . . These film departments have a double aim: on the one hand historical and technical-military documentation and on the other propaganda. Except in the case of top secret material, which can be used for the first aim only, films of both kinds can be made with the same material.[2]

Thus began the production of documentary-style war films with an explicit propaganda function of presenting the war in a politically attractive and ideologically exciting way. The documentary material became propaganda material in a form notably more effective and detailed than had been the case in most of the Luce newsreels produced in the previous 15-year period.[3] Documentary material could also serve to make fiction films in which the war was presented as a dramatic situation against the background of which the characters and actions of the story were set. How significant were these Italian propaganda films made between 1940 and 1943 (before 8 September, Armistice day)? These films, which vary in type and merit, some being broadly documentary, others fictional in content, bear witness both to the commitment of the Italian cinema to the making of propaganda films and, sometimes, to the direct participation of the armed forces film departments in the planning and production of feature films.

Although the 'Ufficio Addestramento-Cinemateca' of the general staff of the Royal Army, under the directorship of

Lieutenant Colonel Guido Bagnani (documentary film director and production manager), does not seem to have provided direct help in the making of war films, the situation is notably different for the film departments of the navy and the airforce. The first film department had been created at the Naval Ministry and was directed by Lieutenant Commanders Francesco De Conciliis, Cesare Girosi (assistant director and production manager) and Francesco De Robertis (director and script-writer). It also availed itself of the services of skilled camermen, such as Carlo Bellero, Angelo Baistrocchi, Mirko Bisogni and others. A second military film unit was the result of the transformation and broadening of the old film division which had been established at the Airforce Ministry in 1923, the year of its foundation. *Centro Fotocinematografico* was staffed by Captains Vittorio Mussolini and Ardito Cristiani, Lieutenants Luciano Agosti, Rosario Leone, Romolo Marcellini, Giovanni Merli, Domenico Musti De Gennaro, Silvano Radius and Second Lieutenant Mario Craveri.[4]

Besides producing a large-scale documentary film on behalf of the Istituto Luce in 1940 (*Mine in Vista* dir. Francesco De Robertis), the Navy's film department made three feature films, in co-operation with Scalera Film. These films, which incorporated documentary elements in a fictious plot were *Uomini Sul Fondo* (1940) by De Robertis, *La Nave Bianca* (1941) by Roberto Rossellini and *Alfa Tau!* (1942) also by De Robertis. It is interesting to quote the opening credits of each of these three films in relation to the propaganda purposes which influenced their planning and production:

> *Uomini Sul Fondo* was produced by Scalera Film and conceived and directed by the Film Department of the Ministry of the Navy. Officers, non-commissioned officers and crew of our submarines took part in the action.[5]

> *La Nave Bianca* was produced by Scalera Film and conceived and directed by the Film Department of the Ministry of the Navy. In this naval story, just as in *Uomini Sul Fondo*, all the characters were filmed in their normal environment and in the course of their everyday life. Their expressions and the simple humanity of their feelings, which constitute the ideological world of every man, are presented in terms of spontaneous realism.[6]

> Following *Uomini Sul Fondo* and *La Nave Bianca*, Scalera Film presents *Alfa Tau!* the third film produced by Scalera Film in collaboration with the Film Department of the Ministry of the Navy. In this story all the details of history and environment are accurately presented. The humble sailor, who plays the lead, really lived through the event which he relives in the story. In the same way, the roles which all the other characters have in the plot correspond to the roles which each one of them has in real life. The civilians involved, who belong to various social classes, offered their services out of devotion to the naval combatants. The military personnel involved did their utmost in the short breaks between the war missions . . . Some characters in this story offered their lives in the performance of their duty. This work is dedicated to their memory.[7]

The Centro Fotocinematografico of the Airforce Ministry gave its technical and artistic supervision to the films *Un Pilota Ritorna* (1942) by Roberto Rossellini, *I Tre Aquilotti* (1942) by Mario Mattoli and *Gente Dell'Aria* (1943) by Esodo Pratelli. Tito Silvio Mursino (the anagrammatic pseudonym of Vittorio Mussolini) wrote the stories upon which the first two films were based, and Bruno Mussolini wrote the third (the credits mention: 'Subject conceived by gold medallist pilot Captain Bruno Mussolini').[8] Lieutenant Rosario Leone was one of the script-writers of *Un Pilota Ritorna* and 'officers and non-commissioned officers of the Italian Airforce'[9] were among the actors. Colonel Gentile was the aeronautic consultant on *I Tre Aquilotti*. Finally the credits of *Gente Dell'Aria* mention: 'The film was made with the assistance of the Centro Fotocinematografico of the Royal Airforce. Aeronautic consultant: Lieutenant Colonel Pio Tambornino'.[10] The *Almanacco del Cinema Italiano (1943–XXI)* reported: 'Today the centre is actively at work preparing four feature films which will exalt the deeds of Italian pilots and will be released on the occasion of the twentieth anniversary of the foundation of the Airforce.'[11]

The film departments of the Italian Airforce and Navy also collaborated, to varying degrees, in making feature films, some of which achieved public and critical acclaim, which were released through the normal commercial film channels. The Istituto Luce, whose most important activity in those war years was the making of newsreels and numerous war documentaries, also took part in the production of feature films, even if incidentally. In 1942 the Istituto

Luce, spurred on by the commercial success of *La Nave Bianca* and the fictional documentaries directed by Captain Francesco De Robertis, crossed the boundaries of its usual production to finance, together with Nettunia, the feature film *I Trecento Della Settima*, in which the actors were officers and soldiers of the I and II Alpine regiments, back from the Greek-Albanian front.[12] The film was directed by Mario Baffico from a story and script by Cesare Vico Ludovici, Mario Corsi and Mario Baffico himself. Colonel M. Bellani was the military consultant.

Fictional documentaries tried, sometimes with favourable artistic results, to combine documentary and spectacle, reality and fiction, in a cinematographic context which involved the audience on the duel levels of intellect and feeling, chronicle and history. The 'true' events, which were reinforced by the newsreel-like authenticity of the documentary shots, were combined with the 'reconstructed' events to create a gripping production which, in some aspects, anticipated the style of Neorealism. Propaganda and nationalist and Fascist ideology were conveyed through the obvious reality, sometimes surreptitiously. They arose from the apparent 'objectivity' of the events described and the emotional involvement of the audience. It was a new film genre which the critics, for the most part, greeted favourably. It was also welcomed by political leaders, who recognised its potential as a propaganda vehicle, a vehicle probably more effective than either the newsreels and documentaries produced by Luce or the dramatic feature films, such as *Giarabub* by Goffredo Alessandrini or *Bengasi* by Augusto Genina, to mention just two of the best-known war films produced in Italy during those years.

The magazine *Cinema* (edited by Vittorio Mussolini) had supported the battle for a 'realistic' and 'documentary' style of cinema on several occasions and now welcomed some of these films emphasising that their artistic value lay in their very lack of fictionalisation and their sustained and accurate sense of reality. Giuseppe Isani wrote of *Uomini Sul Fondo*: 'The direction, which is of a very natural style, is, perhaps for this very reason, extraordinarily effective. Both the direction and the acting (if you'll forgive this word) of all the performers, who, as often happens in these cases, surpass their professional counterparts, seem perfect.'[13] Isani also referred to *La Nave Bianca* as 'the most beautiful film of the naval war produced in Italy until now and that, above all, in which pure and noble propaganda purposes are combined, or rather sublimated, into the forms of beauty and art.' He added: 'To say that *La Nave Bianca* causes us to live through moments on board our warships and hospital vessels in action is to understate the case. The film lies outside the downright documentary becoming something more: a truly living human event in which one participates with the heights and depths of the soul, with the most attentive involvement and the most lively interest.'[14]

This new film genre of 'fictional documentary' gave *Cinema* the opportunity to resume and extend its examination of the subject of propaganda, realism, the relationships between reality and fiction and the characteristic of a possible and hoped-for 'new' Italian cinema (which during the war years must perforce be a cinema dealing with the subject of war) in which daily reality was presented in terms of absolute authenticity. As has been said, in order to be credible and effective, propaganda had to be conveyed through the 'credibility' and 'effectiveness' of the images and the dialogue: somehow the fiction film had to lose itself in the dramatic evidence of the 'document'.

Giuseppe De Santis lucidly revealed the mistake of the 'fictional documentary' in an acute review of *Un Pilota Ritorna*. Referring to the aesthetic-ideological precedents, which he and others had voiced in *Cinema* on several occasions, he wrote:

> On the other hand, one must attribute to *Un Pilota Ritorna* a 'documentarism' which does not succeed, except in the occasional frames, in transforming itself into essential poetry. Further the 'documented' reality in some of our Luce films, which report pieces of real war, raises itself to epic expression through a perfect, and certainly spontaneous, balance between subject and object, form and content. Rossellini could have obtained a very different result if he had been positively inspired by that source, if, in short, he had been able to recreate that balance by means of his imagination.[15]

In the same magazine the anonymous reviewer of *Alfa Tau!* echoed De Santis's views:

> In fact, certain films which fall between documentary and fiction, which have their beginnings in the newsreel and the fictional film at one and the same time, have created that compromise. But when they approach the form of the latter, the propaganda

> purpose becomes more manifest and glaring, and when they approach the form of the newsreel they become cold, schematic and essentially rigid. And, because of this compromise, the genre is not easily definable and the realization of such films seems very difficult. The director moves on a razor's edge. Two frightful ravines are on both sides: on one the most pompous form of vain rhetoric, on the other the cold reportage of the Luce newsreels which, even if well photographed, is clumsy and useless.[16]

The documentary-style war films, blending fiction and reality, were attractive and apparently effective from the point of view of propaganda (*Uomini Sul Fondo* being the forerunner of a series of interesting contributions to this genre) and thus attracted more and more critical interest as time passed; the results however began to appear less and less valid and more and more artificial in style. In fact De Santis wrote in *Cinema* in May 1943 (just before the fall of Fascism):

> Not many war or propaganda films are made in Italy and this is just as well, because these films, more than any others, require careful attention and painstaking preparation. This is for two reasons: firstly, because it is a delicate subject, secondly, because the actors in these films do not, for the most part, wear a grey-green uniform just for their hours 'on-stage' as specified in the contract, but for the fulfilment of their real duties. In short, they are ordinary men, and, therefore, a film which relies on their collaboration required a style of direction which, if it takes advantage of the contribution of such material for an effect of sincerity, is troubled by unusual pressures during the making (unusual in particular for an Italian director).[17]

Between 1940 and 1943 Italian war propaganda cinema moved in other directions as well. In addition to the newsreels and documentaries produced by the Istituto Luce and the Army, Navy and Airforce film departments' 'fictional documentaries' some commercial studies made a number of purely fictional films in which the propaganda element was even more evident. These films were made with well-known actors and reconstructed settings, although often with stories and characters based on present-day reality. Perhaps it was this kind of film which some Fascist leaders thought of when they advocated a form of propaganda cinema that might rouse the conscience of the people and promote a nationalistic and bellicose ideology.

The usefulness of a fictional propaganda cinema had often been discussed in the 1930s, but its consideration became keener and more urgent with the declaration of the war in 1940. A propaganda film, *L'Assedio Dell'Alcazar* directed by Augusto Genina, won the *Coppa Mussolini* for the best Italian film at the Venice Film Festival in September of that year. The critics wrote about it in very positive terms and it was greeted as a great success by the public; it had the longest run of the year both in Rome and Milan (20 days at the Supercinema and 16 days at the Corso in Rome; 18 days at the Odeon in Milan).[18] Michelangelo Antonioni wrote of this film:

> It's a concise film: a war film, vigorous and not at all elegant, which has its roots scrupulously sunk in history, and in recent history too. Rhetoric and emphasis stand on the threshold of the evocation of heroic deeds, deeds which, just like a bell, when scarcely touched on, will resound aloud. But Genina showed a lot of tact in not neglecting the bourgeois side (if I may use this word) of the story.[19]

The question of the simplicity, 'anti-rhetoric', authenticity and naturalness of the film arose again. Attention was returned to the problem of a 'realistic' cinema which could serve as a propaganda vehicle. Luigi Freddi, the first director of the Direzione generale per la cinematografia, was particularly aware of this. After reading the script of *L'Assedio Dell'Alcazar*, he wrote to its producer, Renato Bassoli, telling him, amongst other things:

> The first impression you receive from reading the script, the first thing that comes to mind, is this: it's a fictional documentary. And immediately one asks oneself if the relationship between the evocation and reconstruction of the historical elements (i.e. the environmental, psychological, episodic and dialectic reconstruction) and the elements created by the imagination (i.e. plot, pattern of events, action, human and romantic relationships etc.) is perfectly in harmony with the aesthetic and spectacular effects. I have very strong doubts about this point. While it is certain that the part which we have defined as 'documentary' (that is, the real events recreated by technical and

> artistic means) attains a very high emotional content (from which, however, arises a serious defect, as I will explain later), the imaginative part, that is the dramatic part in the sense of the spectacle, the part created expressly to connect the evocation of historic events with the unrelated human events, seems to me to be very weak.[20]

But *L'Assedio Dell'Alcazar*, as has been said, worked, both as an attractive film and one that was effective from a propaganda point of view. Indeed in some aspects it constituted a possible model in content and style for the Italian cinema of ideological-political and war propaganda which Fascism was pressing for; it was also compatible with the new genre of fictional documentaries pioneered by De Robertis and Rossellini with *Uomini Sul Fondo* and *La Nave Bianca*. So much so, that the Fascist Minister of Education, Alessandro Pavolini (later Freddi's successor at the Direzione Generale), wrote a letter to Augusto Genina on 15 August 1940, saying:

> I wish to tell you that you have done an excellent piece of work from both the artistic and the political point of view. You and the producer, together with all your collaborators, have rendered a service to the country. Technically [*L'Assedio Dell'Alcazar*] is in no way inferior to the best made in the world (California included) in terms of the reconstruction of battles and the staging of large-scale, animated crowd scenes. It is decidedly superior in its respect for historical accuracy, elegant sobriety and human emotion. Now that you have achieved this level you must maintain it and possibly carry our production to even higher peaks. Why don't you try to make a great film of our war? Don't you have some ideas on this subject? I would be very glad to help you.[21]

The film on the war that Genina was to direct was *Bengasi*. Its production was rather difficult, but the results were almost certainly inferior to those which Pavolini expected. In fact, the objective of the Fascist regime was to step up the production of war films, in the fields of both documentary and fictional films. In the introduction to the new edition of the *Almanacco del Cinema Italiano* (1943) Pavolini wrote: 'At this time when the noble destiny of Mussolini's Italy is about to be fulfilled, our cinema must, more than ever, support and reflect the march of the people who fight and work, in their desire to be worthy of the name given to them by *Il Duce*: "the strongest arm"'.[22] Pavolini had earlier written with pride in his 'Rapporto della Cinematografia Italiana' for 1942:

> The directive for political and war films was also widely followed. The Italian cinema showed its sensitivity and fidelity to the present historical situation. The special ministerial committee studied seventy stories and approved twenty-two. Three war films and three political propaganda films were released. Another six war films and five political propaganda films have been completed or are in the course of production; six films and many propaganda films are in preparation, three of which are being made with the cooperation of the Rumanian cinema.[23]

Moreover, the obligation of including war and propaganda films in cinema programmes (aimed predominantly, but by no means exclusively, at documentary and newsreel productions) had been established at the beginning of the war. The decree of 24 July 1940, published in the *Gazzetta Ufficiale* on 26 September 1940 and passed as Law No. 168 on 23 January 1940, stated that: 'The film trade has the duty to include in its programmes the war and propaganda films – here the final text of the law added "of particular political and national interest" – released by the Ministry of Education and the Istituto Nazionale Luce.'[24]

It is, however, true that in terms of numbers, war and political propaganda films were but a small part of the total Italian film production; there were only about 25 such films out of nearly four hundred films produced between 1940 and 1943. Gian Piero Brunetta has suggested that:

> In the widespread decision to reject triumphant rhetoric and the celebration of the efficiency (of the state) – with which the radio, the press and that part of [Istituto Nazionale] Luce dedicated to the achievements of the regime were very much concerned – there is, in my opinion, an indication of the perception, albeit still often unconscious, of the tragic error of the war venture into which Fascism had plunged the country.[25]

That is to say, the few propaganda films often 'apolitical' and 'anti-rhetorical' in nature, reflected the Fascist regime's uncertainty or even fear of mentioning an unpopular war. But is it not more likely that this phenomenon is a simple continuation of the previous attitude towards the cinema in peacetime, in which ideological and political propaganda was, to a large extent, absent. In other words, Fascism preferred to hide behind the petit-bourgeois mentality evinced in most Italian films of the thirties (a mentality which was wholly identifiable with the Fascist ideology) rather than appear 'itself' in films of an obvious propaganda nature (the Luce films were reserved for just such a purpose). So the existence of such an attitude towards the cinema on the part of the Fascist regime in peacetime (amply documented by Luigi Freddi and supported by recent historical research) would seem to noticeably weaken, or even contradict, Brunetta's hypothesis. Particularly since, although those 25 films produced between 1940 and 1943 are small in number in relation to the entire national film production of this period, they constitute a considerable and substantially unified group in relation to the entire production of political and propaganda films in Italy during the Fascist era.

Moreover it should be noted that it was the feature war films or those films with a more-or-less obvious propaganda content that met with the greatest public and often critical success. The phenomenal success of *L'Assedio Dell'Alcazar* (record box-office hit of 1940) has already been mentioned but there were other successes such as *Uomini Sul Fondo* which played for 20 days in Rome in February 1941, and 15 days in Milan in March where it topped the ratings. In October of the same year *La Nave Bianca* headed the ratings in Rome (20 days) and took second place in Milan (15 days). In April 1942 *Un Pilota Ritorna* was rated first in Rome (14 days) and second in Milan (13 days). In May *Giarabub* held top ratings in both Rome and Milan (20 and 18 days respectively). In October and November *Alfa Tau!*, *I Tre Aquilotti*, *Bengasi* and the two-part film *Noi Vivi* and *Addio Kira* by Goffredo Alessandrini dominated the Italian film market.[26] These and a few others are the key feature films of nationalistic and (directly or indirectly) Fascist propaganda content; films often of a high level of craftsmanship, of great technical merit (in relation to the average standard of the national film output). These films were made by Italy's best-known and respected directors, such as Alessandrini, Genina, Campogalliani (*Il Cavaliere di Kruja* 1940), Gallone (*Odessa In Fiamme* 1942), Righelli (*Orizzonte Di Sangue* 1942), Vergano (*Quelli Della Montagna* 1943) and Rossellini (*L'Uomo*

Dalla Croce 1943) and featured such famous actors and actresses as Maria Denis, Fosco Giachetti, Amedeo Nazzari, Vivi Gioi, Doris Duranti, Antonio Centa, Leda Gloria, Carlo Ninchi, Mario Ferrari, Alida Valli, Rossano Brazzi, Luisa Ferida, Osvaldo Valenti, Valentina Cortese and Mariella Lotti.

To what extent were the military and political institutions involved directly in the planning or making of the films? A second important question is how far the ideological propaganda resulted through the fictionalisation of the historical reality, and thirdly, what message (which we can define as nationalistic as opposed to Fascist in nature) was deliberately conveyed. To what extent did the war films' nationalistic feeling, combined with a humanitarian Catholicism, deprive the dramatic contents of any clear or precise political direction in order to appeal to a general sense of patriotism? Such films obviously could serve as an excellent vehicle for Fascist propaganda, while differing little in appearance from ordinary nationalism which, even without the pressures exerted by propaganda, is certainly more evident and explicit in time of war.

L'Uomo Dalla Croce by Roberto Rossellini, the most fictionalised and least documentary of the three films based on the theme of war directed by him during those years is a useful case study. It did not have the direct involvement of either the Navy or Airforce film departments. There was, however, a military consultant, Lieutenant-Colonel Leonardi, and above all there was the close collaboration of the Fascist journalist, Asvero Gravelli, as story and script-writer and supervisor (he was also story and script-writer on *Giarabub*). However, apart from a certain feeling of anti-Communism (which is more ideological and moral than political in nature) the contents of the film are basically religious and ethical. The film's nationalism has its roots sunk in the popular Italian culture of which Catholicism is so much a part. If it can be called a Fascist film, it is in spite of itself.

A second example is *Quelli Della Montagna* by Vergano, supervised by Alessandro Blasetti. The credits read:

> Dedicated to the memory of the director Gino Betrone, a Lieutenant of the Alpine troops, who fell at the Greek-Albanian front. This film was made under the patronage of the War Ministry with the technical assistance in the mountaineering sequences of the Inspectorate of the Alpine Troops and the

> Scuola Militare Centrale Alpinismo. The military advisor was Captain Andrea Brazzola.[27]

In short, just as in the films by De Robertis and Rossellini, there was direct participation on the part of the Ministry. But in this case we are beyond the more-or-less fictional documentary; we are in full film drama with fictional characters, settings, situations and dialogue (even if these are inspired by the reality of the moment). And it is to the sensitivity of the audience, to its level of emotion and involvement in the story that the film appeals; an appeal which includes a general propaganda purpose, but which is characteristic of any popular film. Vergano and Blasetti, like Alessandrini in *Giarabub*, and Genina in *Bengasi*, made their film following the well-tried rules of the fiction film; the audience participates emotionally because it is moved. The propaganda is conveyed through the intrinsic dramatic force of the situation presented.

The same could be said of *Giarabub* and *Bengasi* which can be considered the models of the Fascist Italian war cinema because of the success they enjoyed. These films, which are more rhetorical and bombastic in style than *Quelli Della Montagna*, owed more to the formal schemes of the propaganda cinema resulting in an obvious strain on the dramatic contents, strong characterisation, schematised situations and conflicts and a certain underlying Manicheism ('good' on one side, 'bad' on the other). In fact these films were severely criticised by members of the editorial staff of *Cinema* which, as we have seen, supported an anti-rhetorical Italian cinema, true to the reality of daily life, and which was at that very time (1942) carrying out a courageous experiment with *Ossessione*, the film-manifesto of the magazine's left-wing group (Giuseppe De Santis, Mario Alicata, Gianni Puccini and others, together with Luchino Visconti). However, the two films by Alessandrini and Genina for the most part struck the right note with the audience (even if their propaganda purpose was obvious) for the very reason that the propaganda was conveyed through the representation of two military actions – the bitter resistance at the fort of Giarabub, besieged by the English and daily life in the town of Bengasi during the long days of its siege – which the Italians had lived through with anxiety and were now able to relive under the formal guidance of a well-made and moving film.

In 1973 Alessandrini had occasion to explain his ideological position with regard to *Giarabub*. It seems that he told Asvero Gravelli, the script-writer on the film:

> Look, Gravelli, I'll take this film on, on the condition that its premier, whenever it is, is held simultaneously, so to speak, at the Barberini in Rome and at the Plaza in London, even if we are at war. In other words, I won't take anyone's side . . . Listen, if you like this idea, I won't produce a one-sided piece of work, but naturally I will praise the human virtues of our poor boys . . .[28]

In reality, the film is obviously partisan, however well the statement by Alessandrini (even if it was made many years later) reflects an attitude which we can consider common to many other directors and script-writers at that time. To extol the human virtues of the soldiers at the front – outside the constraints of rhetoric or propaganda if possible – was a way of expressing their own feeling of nationalism and patriotism. But it was to these common and widely held sentiments that Fascism made its appeal at a time in which the nation's greatest efforts were obviously directed towards the defence of its borders and victory against the enemy.

The history of *Bengasi* is very similar. As Betty Ferraris Genina, Genina's widow, recalled, the director 'was carefully searching for a subject, a subject for a war film if possible, given the success of *Alcazar*. At that moment in time Bengasi was the epic situation for the Italians, so to speak'.[29] It was an epic film, like *Giarabub*, which extolled the virtues of patriotism: the patriotism of civilians and soldiers alike. On the screen these epic deeds were tinged with the colour of rhetoric but this formed part of the general tradition of spectacle and literature which is not solely Italian.

A separate examination is required for the two-part film *Noi Vivi* and *Addio Kira* by Alessandrini (taken from the famous novel by Ayn Rand which, in its Italian translation, was enjoying great success at that time). Its anti-Communism was interpreted, for certain aspects, as a sort of masked anti-Fascism, an explanation which is, perhaps, rather forced. To the Italian public at the end of 1942, the 'menacing' communists of the film could also be interpreted as the Fascists whose presence was beginning to be less well tolerated. The nightmare atmosphere of doubt and fear which hovers in the film, set against the background of post-revolutionary Russia, differed little from the atmosphere in which the Italians lived during those years. I do not know how far this interpretation, supported by Alessandrini himself, is correct, but it is certain that *Noi Vivi* and *Addio Kira*, like most of the war and propaganda films mentioned above, fitted perfectly into the genre of romantic and adventure film.

In conclusion, it can be said that, considering the situation of the Italian cinema between 1940 and 1943 in relation to the demands of Fascist and war propaganda, and with reference to the 'strategy of consent' which Fascism widely carried out for 20 years, the films produced and put on the film market (with the exception of newsreels and documentaries) followed two main paths. On the one hand, a great number of films of very different genres, entirely unrelated in terms of theme and content to the war situation, continued to be made. On the other hand, a small but sufficiently homogeneous group of propaganda fiction films, which had a strong impact on the public, were produced. This group can be subdivided into two smaller groups, one of which includes the so-called 'fictional documentaries' and the other the fiction films, both of which were, however, clearly inspired by facts and situations contingent on the war.

An area which should be subject to further detailed investigation is that of the relationship between documentary and fiction films, 'escapist' films and war films, feature films and newsreels. Careful study of the primary sources, including film material, documentary evidence, contemporary reviews, statistical data, may or may not yield evidence of a homogeneous direction. Such research would provide a clearer view of Fascist film policy during the war years, in relation to that of the previous ten-year period; also it could encourage useful comparisons between the Italian Fascist cinema, the Nazi cinema and the cinema of other belligerent countries.

During the war years Italian Fascism occupied itself only marginally with the fiction cinema – with some significant exceptions – concentrating its major efforts on the field of the documentary and newsreel. However, it can also be said that these exceptions were extremely significant and indicate the course which the Fascist cinema could have taken also in peacetime. A course which, by stressing nationalistic tradition and the rhetoric of patriotism but sinking it in the heart of daily reality (unlike the 'imperial' grandiloquent project of *Scipione L'Africano* 1937), could establish an appealing rapport with the public, creating an excellent propaganda vehicle.

Notes

1. Italian cinema audiences were familiar with the opening months of the war through German newsreels and documentary films.
2. F. Cerchio, 'Servizio di guerra', *Cinema*, no. 97 (1940), pp. 12f.
3. M. Argentieri, *L'Occhio Del Regime. Informazione E Propaganda Nel Cinema Del Fascismo* (Florence, 1979). It has not been possible thus far to carry out a detailed study of the military film departments in the manner with which Mino Argentieri has studied Luce. This military documentation may, in fact, be buried in the Luce's film archives.
4. Cf. *Almanacco Del Cinema Italiano 1943–XXI* (Roma, 1943), pp. 45–7.
5. F. Savio, *Ma L'Amore No. Realismo, Formalismo, Propaganda E Telefoni Bianchi Nel Cinema Italiano Di Regime (1930–1943)* (Milano, 1975), p. 379.
6. Ibid., p. 227.
7. Ibid., p. 11.
8. Ibid., p. 155.
9. Ibid., p. 269.
10. Ibid., p. 155.
11. *Almanacco Del Cinema Italiano*, p. 47.
12. Argentieri, *L'Occhio Del Regime*, p. 168.
13. G. Isani, '*Uomini Sul Fondo*', *Cinema*, no. 112 (1941), p. 139.
14. G. Isani, '*La Nave Bianca*', *Cinema*, no. 127 (1941), p. 236.
15. G. De Santis, '*Un Pilota Ritorna*', *Cinema*, no. 140 (1942), p. 226.
16. Vice, *Alfa Tau!*, *Cinema*, no. 151 (1942), p. 590.
17. G. De Santis, 'I Trecento Della Settima', *Cinema*, no. 166 (1943), p. 313.
18. Cf. *Almanacco Del Cinema Italiano*, pp. 336–7.
19. M. Antonioni, 'La Sorpresa Veneziana', *Cinema*, no. 102 (1940), p. 221.
20. L. Freddi, *Il Cinema* (Roma, 1949), pp. 209–210.
21. Cited in F. Savio, *Cinecittà Anni Trenta. Parlano 116 Protagonisti Del Secondo Cinema Italiano (1930–1943)*, ed. by T. Kezich (Roma, 1979), II, pp. 524.
22. *Almanacco Del Cinema Italiano*, p. 11.
23. A. Pavolini, 'Il Rapporto Della Cinematografia Italiana', *Bianco E Nero*, no. 8 (1942), quoted in: M. Mida and L. Quaglietti, *Dai Telefoni Bianchi Al Neorealismo* (Bari, 1980), p. 36.
24. *Gazzetta Ufficiale Del Regno D'Italia*, no. 226 (1940).
25. G.P. Brunetta, *Cinema Italiano Tra Le Due Guerre. Fascismo E Politica Cinematografica* (Milano, 1979), p. 78.
26. Cf. *Annuario Del Cinema Italiano*, pp. 338–49.
27. F. Savio, *Ma L'Amore No*, p. 288.
28. F. Savio, *Cinecittà Anni Trenta*, p. 45.
29. Ibid., II, pp. 525.
30. Ibid., p. 50.

12 THE STRUGGLE FOR CONTROL OF FRENCH MINDS, 1940–1944

Pierre Sorlin

Although France played only a limited role in World War II, a great many historians have studied its social and political evolution between 1940 and 1944 (see Bibliography: General). The French case is, to a certain extent, an experimental one: what kind of independence could be maintained in an occupied country which was indirectly involved in total war? The question is especially relevant as far as propaganda is concerned. The French saw their goods, their money and their young men transported to Germany; they had few possibilities to resist the German demands. At the same time they were told by their collaborationist government that they still enjoyed independence, they were being exhorted by the Resistance to oppose the German exactions. In other countries the instruments of propaganda, controlled by the government or by the leading party, expressed one idea: we must win, we are winning. In France, people could hear three different accounts of the events. Historians dealing with Germany or the Allied nations may wonder whether propaganda was effective or not; historians dealing with France have the additional requirement of assessing the results of the continual struggle between propaganda and counter-propaganda.

Competent studies have appeared dealing with various aspects of propaganda in France during the war (see Bibliography: Public Opinion and Propaganda). Ten historians have worked upon the cinema (see Bibliography: Cinema), particularly upon its stereotypes and its relationship to the atmosphere of the time; books and articles have been devoted to broadcasting and excellent studies have been carried out on public opinion either in small districts or in departments. However, we still lack a general view of the question. Is it possible that this is due to the fact that the historians' attention has been focused more on written sources than on broadcasting and the movies? Perhaps, because the newspapers provided the French with the best source for daily information until the beginning of the TV era, research workers tend to forget that, in an exceptional period, when papers and magazines were reduced drastically by the shortage of printing-paper and by the censorship, the wireless audience grew very fast and that, by the middle of 1944, the majority of the French were regular radio listeners. Another difficulty is linked to the characteristics of wartime by which I mean the evolution of events. It is almost impossible to adequately describe a situation which never stops changing; sometimes, for instance at the end of 1942, or during the summer of 1944, it would be necessary to follow the alteration of propaganda day by day, which would put many difficulties in the historian's way and would be hardly likely to interest the reader. Additionally it does not make sense to study broadcasting or the movies without taking into account their respective influence on the public.

This exploratory essay begins with a look at the situation before the armistice; it then describes the organisation of the three main forces involved in a competitive attempt to 'capture' the French audience. The themes of propaganda are discussed as well as the extent to which cinema and radio were able to influence large audiences, perhaps the most difficult aspect for the historian to judge.

On the eve of the war, there were about 4,000 cinemas operating in France; some 250,000 spectators attended these cinemas every year which, for a population of 40,000,000 people, represented a little less than six visits a year for every person over ten years old. This figure is of course misleading, for the majority of the 20,000,000 people living in small towns or in the countryside rarely went to the movies. Cinema programmes normally consisted of a short documentary, a newsreel and a feature film or a newsreel and two full-length feature films. American companies like Fox, MGM and Paramount sometimes distributed their own newsreels but the majority of theatre-owners preferred to rent the French newsreels produced by Eclair, Gaumont and Pathe. Between 420 and 450 new feature films were offered to the cinemagoers every year. A good half of these pictures were American, a quarter were French, while at the same time the impact of German feature films was steadily declining from a maximum of 60 in 1935 to 26 in 1938. Feature films were censored to ensure the moral value of the movies and to ban attacks against the French national traditions. In the 1920s a few Soviet films were banned; in the late 1930s it was the turn of a few Nazi films. The actual effects of censorship on film exhibitions was very limited.

The influence of Germany over the French cinema was strong,

particularly at the beginning of the talkies when many French films were shot and edited in the Berlin studios. At that time, one of the most important producers in France was a subsidiary of Tobis which made five films in 1933. For reasons that have not as yet been explained German influence had declined sharply by the end of the 1930s. There were fewer and fewer French films shot in Berlin and French Tobis Company produced nothing in 1939 and only one film in 1938 (1935: 16; 1936: 11; 1937: 5). Dr Joseph Goebbels and the leaders of the Nazi-dominated film industry certainly were aware of the fact that Germany was losing the battle for French screens to Hollywood.

During the 1930s the number of radio licence holders was about 5,000,000 but this figure does not tell us what the size of the actual listening public was. A quarter of the licences were registered in Paris and its immediate neighbourhood. Roughly speaking we can distinguish the listening France of Paris, Normandy, the North and the most important towns, from the non-listening ones of mainly the rural areas where wireless sets were virtually unknown. National Broadcasting, the responsibility of the Post Office, consisted of a central transmitting station, *Radio-Paris*, with 20 relay stations. Thus Radio-Paris could be heard everywhere in France and its news bulletins gave the government's point of view. Unlike Germany and Great Britain there were also commercial stations (mainly the *Poste-Parisien* and local stations in other towns) whose sources of revenue were derived from advertising. They were more 'popular' in the sense that they attracted larger audiences and that the urban working class was probably more fond of them than of Radio-Paris. Radio listeners could also tune into foreign broadcasts in French, particularly from Stuttgart and London. The German station, which used only pro-Nazis Frenchmen as its speakers, emphasised the efforts made by Hitler to keep peace and protect the world from war. At the same time it criticised, in a quite vague way, all those who tried to lead the French into another war. The BBC, which began its French broadcasting after Munich, described selected aspects of British life, while stressing the importance of British war preparation. It is impossible to assess the influence of radio upon the French audiences at this time other than to note that after the Munich crisis the French, like the Americans, became avid listeners of new broadcasts.

It has often been said that France entered World War II

unprepared for war. The situation of the audiovisual media supports this opinion. Before 1939 radio and cinema had scarcely been used to propagate political ideas. During the 1936 national elections (the last before the war) the leaders of the Popular Front and their opponents organised meetings throughout France but they only occasionally spoke on the radio. French politicians were convinced that liberty and competition guaranteed extensive and reliable information. They supported such preliminary censorship as prevented journalists from giving essential information to the enemy and from disturbing audiences with bad news, but they could not imagine that it was possible to mobilise and control public opinion. Impressed though they were by Hitler's propaganda machine, they neither sought to emulate Hitler nor to endeavour to inform the French nation. It was not until 29 July 1939 (a month before the declaration of war) that Prime Minister Daladier began co-ordinating all the media controlled by the government (chiefly the broadcasting) and organising propaganda through a Department, later Ministry, for Information. From the beginning of the war, on 1 September 1939, until 10 May 1940, when the Germans finally attacked France, the Ministry of War produced a weekly magazine which from March 1940 was shown in the cinemas after the newsreels. Audiences were bored with endless shots of Anglo–French military ceremonies and with photographs of healthy, happy soldiers. Who could have believed that the Germans were about to attack? On the wireless, writers, artists, politicians daily delivered lectures on French traditions and civilisation. Programmes were silent on Nazism (the only criticism was directed personally against Hitler who was portrayed as a 'bloody madman') on German military organisation, and on the countries already overwhelmed by the German war machine. Significantly, a good half of the people working for National Broadcasting (387 of 694) were called up by the French military. (NB For an extended discussion of the Department/Ministry for Information see Rémy Pithon's 'French Film Propaganda, July 1939–June 1940', above, Ch. 3.)

Two weeks after the German offensive began the French nation was divided into separate districts which had no information about the other parts of France. Adequate information could have prevented civilians from leaving zones already under German control and from clogging the already overcrowded roads. It could also have given the French the feeling that the authorities still controlled the situation. But, instead of being kept near the front line, the few surviving members of National Broadcasting were withdrawn further and further south. It may be assumed that the lack of information played an important part in the panic of May–June 1940 and that Pétain's messages were welcomed partly because they provided people with news, however bad it was.

The advancing Germans had cleverly used broadcasting to increase confusion. From 19 May to 19 June mobile transmitters were set up behind the German front line and French Nazi sympathisers set about destroying what remained of French morale. Ostensibly supporting the defence of the country, they broadcast that the German army was exceptionally strong and well trained, that the British, who forced France into war, were now re-embarking and that the government was unable to master the situation. Here is an example of a talk (broadcast on the evening of 6 June, eleven days before the armistice, on a German mobile station calling itself 'Awakening of France'): 'Frenchman, in order to supply the deficiency of our government, in order to prevent the attempts made to still shed French blood, oppose this war organised by the Jews, led by the Jews'. Britain, the Jews, the bad politicians; these slogans would not change until the end of the war.

Even if it was possible to roughly assess the consequences of the silence of National Broadcasting, we unfortunately know nothing about the influence of these German broadcasts. Karl Drechster (see Bibliography: Radio), who has published the records of these underground stations offers no documentation regarding their impact. We can easily surmise that those who were influenced by the German talks of 1940 did not boast about it after the armistice. We shall probably remain ignorant of the overall effects of one of the first of World War II's 'mental intoxication' operations.

As a result of the armistice, France was divided into two parts in which the north and west of the country were occupied by the Germans, while the south remained theoretically independent. The Vichy government endeavoured to maintain the fiction of a unified country. As a matter of fact, no Vichy law could operate in the occupied zone without German permission.

Two distinct areas of information, cinema and broadcasting, must clearly be distinguished. Obviously the competition was reduced to only the Germans and the French, as far as the movies were concerned. During the first months after the armistice the French filmmakers believed that they would be able to develop an independent cinema by using the existing studios in Nice. They were soon faced with two difficulties: (1) the majority of those involved in production (directors, actors, technicians) did not want to leave Paris and preferred to work for German Companies rather than 'exile' themselves to Nice; (2) the Southern market was a narrow one (because of its small population). If France had a 'free' Vichy-sponsored cinema, as well as a German controlled one, the German occupation government would very soon rid itself of the French competition. The Vichy government negotiated an agreement with the German occupation authorities which was signed in February 1941. Films produced in the south could be shown in the north provided they were accepted by the German censorship; in exchange German films could be freely distributed everywhere in France. In effect, France became an open market for the German movie industry. In 1941, 41 per cent of the films distributed in France came from Germany, although the proportion tended to decrease somewhat during 1942–3. French cinema had become, not unexpectedly, entirely dependent upon Nazi censorship, and largely dependent on German produced films.

The Vichy French government's attitude towards the cinema reveals its political ambition, as well as its inability to actually control the situation. The Vichy-men were moralists who intended to rebuild a healthy France, thus they banned some 200 French and foreign films for licentiousness or lack of national pride. One of their primary goals was to reorganise and strengthen the country and its economy. They had created Organising Committees in every branch of trade and industry. These were small committees of professionals entrusted with issuing directions likely to increase the production and put an end to trade disputes. The Organizing Committee of the Cinematic Industries, established in Paris in December 1940, took a few decisions which were so obviously useful that they would not be abolished after the war (for instance it forbade block-booking and the projection of double-features and it subjected, for the first time, the number of admissions to a close inspection) but it was unable to go further and influence the actual production of the movies. The Vichy-men were liberals, even if they dreamt about a renewed liberalism. The French cinematographers were hampered by severe restraints for they had to comply with directions issued by the German occupying forces, the Vichy government and the Organising Committee; then they had to cope with the censors. However the industry received no preproduction instructions; it was submitted to negative rules which prevented the films from becoming vehicles of anti-Nazi or anti-Vichy propaganda.

Dr Goebbels' fragmented diaries partially document the Nazi attitude towards the French cinema. Goebbels wanted France to produce poor films for only domestic customers and to buy more and more German films. It was not a matter of propaganda but a purely commercial operation from the German point of view. The 17.5mm projectors and films, a peculiarity of the French exhibition system, were strictly forbidden and replaced by the German 16mm material. German companies effectively competed with the French companies for raw material, cameras, distribution and exhibition. The German company Continental, a subsidiary of UFA, became the most important production company in France, well ahead of Pathe-Cinema. The figures for the years 1941–3 are shown in Table 12.1.

Table 12.1: Production Figures, 1941–3

	French total production	Pathe	Continental	Ratio continental to total production (%)
1941	60	6	11	18
1942	77	7	7	9
1943	60	3	11	18

The Continental films, mainly sentimental comedies and detective stories, were generally well filmed; some of them, notably *The Raven* (*Le Corbeau*, 1943, dir. G.H. Clouzot), are among the best of the period, but none of them has anything to do with propaganda (see the critical assessment by Elizabeth Strebel, in 'Vichy Cinema and Propaganda', below, Ch. 13).

Immediately after the armistice, the German distributing company set up the distribution of a French version of the German newsreel *Deutsche Wochenschau* which exhibitors were compelled to show in the occupied zone; the Germans also tried to conclude agreements with the exhibitors of the southern zone. In order to prevent them from encroaching upon the south, the Vichy government forced the three French newsreels companies to create a unified Company and issue the weekly French Newsreels. The newsreel distribution monopoly in the Southern zone was entrusted to this company, which eliminated both the American newsreels and the French Deutsche Wochenschau/World Newsreels. In France therefore audiences were faced with two distinct newsreels, screening two different versions of reality. There was no competition between them since the spectators, according to the zone where they lived, saw only French Newsreels or Deutsche Wochenschau/World Newsreels; once again the Vichy-men thought that they were the losers since there were more people in the occupied zone. Their obsession of unity led them to a convention with their German masters in which Deutsche Wochenschau/World Newsreels and French Newsreels were merged into a new firm, France Newsreels, whose shares were 40 per cent German, 60 per cent French. The German-censored unified newsreels were projected in all the cinemas from August 1942 to the Liberation. It must be underlined that Vichy applied to the Germans for the convention and that the agreement was signed long before Germany, using the pretext of the allied invasion of North Africa, occupied the south of France. Vichy willingly abdicated its independence and complied with German censorship over information films. Part of the reason for this was simply that the Vichy-men could not conceive of either feature or news films as effective propaganda tools. For them the most important propaganda medium was the radio and it is over its control that the real battle took place. Significantly, the Vichy-Nazi competition, which did not exist on fiction films and was limited on newsreels, became extremely sharp where radio broadcasting was concerned.

The military organisation of occupied France is well known thanks to Hans Humbreit's book, *Der Melitarbefehlshaber in Frankreich* (1968) and thus it is not necessary to describe it in detail. Suffice it to say that a central office, the German Army's *Propaganda Abteilung* was set up in Paris in June 1940, whilst four regional offices, the *Propaganda Staffeln*, were located in Paris and in three provincial towns. These offices were subordinated to Goebbels' Ministry of Propaganda and thus were not concerned with the occupying forces; their only task was to propagandise the French population. At the same time the German embassy, which was of course supervised by the Foreign Ministry (*Wilhelmstrasse*) was entrusted with 'politically guiding press, radio and propaganda in the occupied zone and influencing the agents which fix the opinion in the non-occupied zone' (instructions issued in October 1940). The unavoidable conflict between the *Wehrmacht* and the Wilhelmstrasse was complicated by a secondary competition inside the army itself. Roughly speaking the Propaganda Staffel of Paris (settled in Paris on 26 June 1940), traditionally linked with the Nazi party, attempted to develop a political propaganda, whilst the Propaganda Abteilung (which was settled on 18 July 1940) aimed primarily at helping the Wehrmacht by first dissuading the French from resisting the Germans and secondly by persuading them to work for the Reich. Nobody in these two propaganda offices thought that France could play an important part in Europe during or after the war. On the contrary, the German ambassador believed that France could usefully support the German policy in post-war Europe and did his best to gain Frenchmen's good will. It was the Propaganda Staffel of Paris which restarted the radio broadcasts with French musicians and German language news bulletins, broadcast from Berlin, in September 1940. A French team was entrusted with organising, for the occupied zone, a French-speaking radio, under the control of the Germans. The German broadcasts ended on 13 October 1940 but the men of the Propaganda Staffel continued to supervise the radio broadcasting. Hence the initial clash which led to the elimination of the Propaganda Staffel and its substitution by the Propaganda Abteilung for broadcasting (January 1941). The rivalry between the two offices persisted until the Propaganda Staffel was eventually suppressed by Berlin in November 1942. The second conflict between the embassy and the Propaganda Abteilung led to an agreement (July 1942) according to which the first was charged with 'cultural' relationship with France, while the second was charged with censorship.

Meanwhile in the southern zone the Vichy government was anxious to restart broadcasting, be it only to give practical advice to the two million refugees, who did not know how to go back home. The first broadcasts were made on 6 July and, five days later, Pétain delivered his first wireless talk. As Vice-Prime Minister Laval was inclined to collaborate with Germany, pro-Nazi journalists and politicians penetrated the radio staff where they were very soon at odds with those who wished to preserve France's 'neutrality'. The struggle for the control of radio played an important part in the contest between Laval and other ministers which culminated in

Laval's eviction from the government on 13 December 1940. The pro-Nazis were obliged to leave Vichy; many of them went to Paris where they entered the German-oriented broadcasting. Meanwhile the victors over Laval strengthened their control upon Vichy's free radio, restricting it almost entirely to commentary on local events in the southern zone.

From December 1940 until Laval's return to power in April 1942, these two radio networks were in direct competition. The broadcasting system of the occupied zone Radio-Paris, closely supervised by a German staff, used five transmitting stations which enabled it to cover all of the North and West of France but not penetrate into the remote parts of the southern zone. Vichy radio, called *National Broadcasting*, was unable to broadcast over the whole German occupied zone but, thanks to an agreement with the Germans (one of the few advantages gained by Vichy), two Vichy news bulletins were broadcast every day on Radio-Paris. The competing systems were very different in programme style. Programmes of National Broadcasting were filled until 7 p.m. with local chronicles and parlour games, then some members of the government described what had been done by the Maréchal and his fellow ministers and the evening programming ended with a concert or a play. Vichy radio was a small, monolithic organisation where innovation was not encouraged. On the contrary there were constant comings and goings in Radio-Paris where young, inventive, intolerant men were asked to join the staff and try dynamic formulas. Provided they supported the German policy, the speakers were allowed to develop the most provocative views and the German authorities even encouraged them to criticise Vichy's neutrality. Radio-Paris drew upon the services of the extensive pool of Parisian singers, musicians, actors and a great many contemporary popular songs were popularised by radio programmes. Instead of relaying boring speeches from politicians or writers, the staff of Radio-Paris interviewed people in the street. A new conception of programming, a mixture of music, variety shows and running commentaries, emerged during these years. It has often been said that the Germans conceived their task as the provision of radio entertainment in order to distract the French from the temptation of resistance, but there is no positive evidence of such a policy. What can be asserted is that many aspects of the French post-war radio were anticipated by Radio-Paris whose programmes were vastly more attractive than the Vichy ones.

When, as the result of German pressure, Laval returned to power, he sought to concentrate the means of propaganda under his authority. The staff of National Broadcasting was strong enough to resist such attempts for more than 18 months and only then did Laval's appointees succeed in supervising the political orientation of the Vichy radio. In November 1943 a well-known collaborationist, Marcel Déat, speaking on Radio-Paris was still denouncing Vichy as a government of bankruptcy which had managed to complete the defeat of France. In January 1944, one of the fiercest collaborationists, Philippe Henriot, who had been delivering a daily talk on National Broadcasting for nearly two years, was named to the Ministry of Information and Propaganda. Henriot was an excellent propagandist, a good, convincing speaker and, under his direction, National Broadcasting for the first time seemed to be in concert with Radio-Paris. Although they had some programmes in common, the two radio networks remained independent.

The French men and women who listened to the programmes of both networks could not fail to recognise that there were many dissonances between Radio-Paris and National Broadcasting. The conflict was less perceptible and probably less serious in London. On 13 July 1940 the BBC started the broadcasting of a daily news bulletin in French. The time allowed to the broadcasts towards France increased little by little, but in 1944, with five and a half hours a day, it had become the most important BBC foreign language programme. This programme was of course strictly supervised by the British Political Warfare Executive (PWE). Every week a conference was held between the PWE and the British members of the French section of the BBC; the decisions were then transmitted to the French members of the BBC's French section. The news bulletins were written by the British and translated and read by the French. There were many reasons for that implicit lack of confidence, the most important being that the British government often disagreed with de Gaulle, nor could the French fully agree amongst themselves on policy. De Gaulle wanted to be recognised as the leader of the French Resistance and successor to French legitimism, whereas the British wanted to co-operate with the other Resistance leaders and, at least until November 1942, dealt tactfully with Vichy. Even then the Gaullists were only granted a daily five-minute talk and de Gaulle himself seldom spoke on the BBC. After North Africa had been liberated, de Gaulle opened a broadcasting station in Algiers but its broadcasts could not be heard in France, except in some districts of the south. Eventually, on the eve of the Normandy invasion, the Gaullists were fully integrated in the team which managed the France broadcasts.

It is always a mistake to conceive of propaganda as a well-defined set of ideas and this is particularly true for occupied France during World War II. Between 1940 and 1943, attention cannot be restricted to the three main stations, London, Paris and Vichy, for in each of these stations there were policy conflicts which contributed to inconsistent programming. A most important question is then: 'to what extent did the French use that confusion to infer what was really happening from the information which was delivered to them?'

The structure of propaganda organisations in defeated France produced ample opportunity for competition and confusion as Nazi-oriented media contrasted with Vichy-controlled media. What of the content of these propagandas in terms of their main themes and evolution? First, what of the content of the feature films about which there has been much historical discussion? Were they simply intended to distract French audiences from the problems of the day; were they more or less the same sort of romance and comedy so characteristic of the 1930s? (For another possibility-subtle propaganda, see Elizabeth Strebel, 'Vichy Cinema and Propaganda', below, pp. 271–88.) In the most recent study on the Vichy cinema, François Garçon does not recognise significant differences between the pre-war and the occupation-period movies. Paternalism, moralism, deference to family, authority, law and order, so typical of the Vichy era had featured largely in the films produced between 1936 and 1940; the plots, the characters, the shooting and editing processes are consistently the same until the middle of the 1950s. Only four films (out of more than 220) go beyond what was typical of the pre-war cinema. These are: *Mermoz* (PFC, 1942, dir. Louis Cuny), *Home-Port* (Pathé-Cinéma, 1942, dir. Jean Choux), *The Cross-roads of the Lost Children* (MAIC, 1943, dir. Léo Joannon), *Impulsive Act* (Harispuru, 1943, dir. René Le Hénaff). Unlike Garçon (who does not mention *Home-Port*) I am not inclined to detect a Fascist temptation in these films. All of them describe demobilised soldiers or young boys who, at the end of World War I or after the recent defeat, cannot settle down; the governing bourgeois does not help them and they are nearly reduced to destitution. Then a strong man makes them face their destiny and, united behind their leader, the now brave outcasts defeat their enemies (the fights staged in these films are among the best filmed battles of the period). The role of the leader, the male predominance, this sort of 'triumph of the will' could be labelled Fascist. However, the outcasts do not fight to renovate the society. On the contrary, their task is to make the dominant bourgeoisie acknowledge and accept their traditional attitudes. Arguing about the influence of these pictures would be irrelevant for they convey the same values as the majority of contemporary films.

Before the war the movies were less popular in France than in many other European countries, but they became increasingly an important form of wartime entertainment. From a late 1930s average of 250,000,000, the number of cinema admissions rose to 281,000,000 in 1942 and 304,000,000 in 1943. Lacking documentation on film distribution, we do not know who saw what. There is evidence that many people attended free exhibitions of *Hitler Youth Quex* (1933), *Uncle Kruger* (1941), *The Eternal Jew* (1940), sponsored by the pro-Nazis in the occupied zone. We know also that, owing to the protests raised by the spectators, the collaborationists were obliged to stop the projection of *Jew Süss* in the southern zone.

Fiction films are not, in my opinion, likely to produce direct, short-term effects; they have an indirect, long-term influence by shaping the values and facilitating certain ways of thought. A few German films which were shown at most to ten thousand people did not trigger violence against the Jews or increase anti-democratic prejudice. On the contrary, the main thrust of propaganda in French wartime cinema was the weekly newsreels; they were designed consciously to help to create a pro-Nazi or pro-Vichy consensus of opinion. For an understanding of how these competing Fascisms sought to develop a consensus, a close study of the manner in which the newsreels and radio presented information and opinion is essential. The four years that run from the defeat to the Liberation are filled with so many important events that it is necessary to follow closely the chronological order.

During the Summer and Autumn 1940 the Germans tried to impress the French favourably. Neither Radio-Paris nor the Deutsche Wochenschau-based World Newsreels insisted upon the occupation of two-thirds of the country. German soldiers were mentioned when they came to the assistance of French children or women. In the Summer the railways were still partially inoperative and it was difficult to travel. Both Nazi-dominated Radio-Paris and the Vichy National Broadcasting offered information to the refugees attempting to return home. The main difference between the two radios (at least regarding the reorganisation of the country) was that Radio-Paris seldom spoke of the French soldiers held prisoner in Germany, whereas National Broadcasting constantly recalled them to French minds. The opposition between the two radios is clear; Vichy emphasised the fact that France was no longer involved in the war, had to rebuild its economy and that the first task was the repatriation of the prisoners. For the German inspired propaganda the war was still in progress and the subordinate problem of the prisoners would not be solved before the achievement of the final German victory.

Both Paris and Vichy violently attacked the corrupters who were the politicians of the late Republic: Jews and Freemasons. Vichy's *French Newsreels* drew its audiences' attention to the prosecution started against some leaders of the Third Republic while National Broadcasting criticised the Jews in such a violent, hostile manner that many listeners protested by writing to Pétain demanding that he reprimand the speakers! Although Vichy was about to publish a law which defined the Jews as the members of a different race and prohibited them from a great many public or private jobs, the attacks against the Jewish citizens became less frequent. Here again we note an opposition between the two capitals: long lists of Freemasons were read on Radio-Paris with hostile commentaries but few, if any, surnames were mentiond by National Broadcasting. Vichy-men were afraid of any sort of excitement and they found it sufficient to inform the population without expanding upon or explaining their decisions. The Paris-men, on the other hand, believed they would particularly please the Nazi occupiers if they were sharply critical of Jews and Freemasons. The Germans clearly appreciated programmes which were likely to make the French forget the increasing problems of their daily life.

Radio-Paris dwelt on the British responsibility in the war while the World Newsreels showed the port of Mers el Kebir after the British raid and interviewed French soldiers who, having been transferred from Britain to France shortly after Dunkirk, were extremely critical of English policy. Radio-Paris daily spoke of the Battle of Britain, describing at length the bombings of London and Coventry. On the other hand, National Broadcasting gave southern

Frenchmen less information on the war. During the Summer of 1940, it often charged Britain with responsibility for the French defeat but by the end of that year it scarcely mentioned London. National Broadcasting was, however, extremely critical of Communists and the Soviet Bolshevik government; Radio-Paris, on the other hand, was more cautious with news of the Soviet Union.

During these months the BBC's French language programmes from London were severely reduced. Daily talks centred upon continued British resistance and the RAF bombings of German cities; the Vichy government was rarely criticised and the BBC's major theme was: 'Germany will lose the war'.

The beginning of 1941 is a pivotal date in war propaganda. Laval was eliminated from the Vichy government and his supporters joined Radio-Paris, which was reorganised under the direction of the Propaganda Abteilung. Vichy propaganda began to create the image of a quiet, predominantly rural France, united around its venerable leader. Its radio and newsreels ignored foreign countries, notably Germany, which was never mentioned. Only three countries seemed to exist: France, Spain and Switzerland, countries whose traditions, habits and economy (seen as mainly rural) were often compared. Outside Europe existed only the French empire and her colonies appeared in one third of the issues of the French Newsreels; two documentaries devoted to the Empire, *Fidelity of the Empire* and *Imperial Railway*, were shown throughout the southern zone. It might be tempting to conclude that Vichy aimed at making the French put their faith in Empire, but the opposite thesis seems closer to the truth. First, there were more documentaries devoted to the colonies in 1938 or 1939 than there were in 1941. Secondly, in 1941 audiences were shown only the most superficial aspects of the colonial countries (landscapes, habits of the natives), whereas, before the war, the movies had emphasised the mutual assistance and close unity between France and the Empire. France, described by Vichy broadcasting and pictured by Vichy newsreels, was a closed, introverted country which looked mainly at itself. Four themes regularly appeared almost every week: (1) Pétain, his life, his speeches, his travels; (2) French traditions; (3) the youth, its education, its regeneration through sport and open-air life; and (4) the workers, especially the countrymen and craftsmen. The newsreel emphasis was supported by propaganda documentaries (also shown in commercial cinema programmes) made by the *French Legion of the Combatants* (a conservative grouping of Pétain's supporters more or less equivalent to the Spanish Falange and distinct from the French Fascist or Nazi parties): *The Bread*; *Traditions*; *Great Pastoral*; *The Fine Work* and *Symphony of the Work*. The Vichy message is easily summarised: thanks to Pétain the class struggle in France has ended and everybody now does his best to go back to the peace and harmony of the old France; youth prepared to succeed their elders [see also Elizabeth Strebel's discussion of documentary films, below, pp. 275–8].

Radio-Paris ridiculed the sleepy, reactionary pastoral vision of the Vichy propaganda. In contrast to National Broadcasting the Paris-men took their listeners seriously. In November 1940 they produced an entirely new concept in French broadcasting, 'Compass-Card'. Listeners were requested to write to the programmes and give their opinion; their letters were read and commented on at length. The programme proved to be so popular that it was transmitted twice a week at the prime time of 7.45 p.m. Other Radio-Paris programmes offered practical advice to workers, the unemployed and families. These talks were cleverly conceived, providing practical information of how and when to find a job, intercut with Fascist slogans. Even reluctant people were obliged to listen to propaganda slogans if they wanted to get the particulars connected with their own problems. Vichy dealt with starvation and unemployment by promoting a rural dream; Paris offered a solution in the modernisation of France according to the German model. It was claimed endlessly that the German factories were healthy and well-equipped, workers earned good wages, and then the needs of the families and, particularly, children were satisfied. These talks were clearly intended to make the unemployed voluntarily seek jobs in Germany. Radio-Paris was also critical of Vichy's old-fashioned 'revolution'. One Parisian ploy was to disclose facts illustrating that Vichy preferred to be stagnant. National Broadcasting seldom spoke of the persecution against the Jews and this provided an opportunity for the Paris-men to illustrate Vichy's hypocrisy and expand upon the admitted anti-Semitism of the collaborationists. One programme, 'The Jews against France' had the speakers tracking down the Jews. When the Germans decided to confine the foreign Jews to two concentration camps, Radio-Paris urged its listeners to denounce hiding Jewish families, drawing attention to those who had escaped arrest and broadcasting reports on the dangerous people who had been captured. Paris was not inferior to Berlin in anti-Semitism. The Paris-men did not conceal that they were pro-Nazi; 'Compass-Card' always began with a pro-Nazi slogan, 'For a clean France in a unified Europe' and many of its programmes sought to prove that 'new Europe – is in the making'. In July 1941 a French-speaking German journalist, Dr Friedrich, was entrusted with a twice-weekly talk celebrating the Reich and its Führer; including, naturally, the success of the Reichswehr in the Balkans and in North Africa.

The World Newsreels supported the Radio-Paris propaganda line in presenting the capture of Greece in mid-May and featured stories of its occupation four times during the following months. The war and foreign news were featured on the screen and on the radio in Northern France; there was a significant exception. During the winter of 1940 and spring of 1941 it was hard to detect any reference to the Soviet Union. Russia did not seem to exist until June 1941 and many Frenchmen were extremely surprised when they were told that Hitler had attacked Stalin. From June to December 1941 the media paid more and more attention to war on the Eastern Front. What did the World Newsreels tell occupied France? The first issues gave few precise details; German troops were seen in motion but audiences got most of their information from the commentator who denounced the Bolsheviks. The message changed in the middle of July (issue no. 51, 18 July). The spectators did not need to rely upon the enthusiastic commentaries since they were direct witnesses. They saw a crowd of emaciated and poorly clothed people who could not be anything but Russians; they smiled and applauded as they welcomed the German soldiers who had liberated them from the Bolshevik oppression. A few weeks later audiences saw Russian prisoners; long, endless files of ragged, defeated and exhausted men. At the same time Radio-Paris interviewed French and German journalists just back from the front, who enthusiastically described the victorious Nazi conquest. The Eastern campaign strongly influenced the development of propaganda in France. The struggle of the Paris-men for a German-ruled Europe appeared to be triumphant. Vichy propagandists could no longer ignore that outside world, and the Russian war was slowly introduced on the southern screens. From November 1941 it had been regularly inserted in the French Newsreels, sometimes treated as the most important topic (40 per cent of issue no. 48, 22

November). But this was no more than the coverage of important events.

Vichy was also affected in another way by the competition with Radio-Paris in that Vichy's peaceful vision of rural France was tempered now by unexpected hints of social conflicts. In August 1941 General Secretary of Information Marion went as far as to criticise in a radio broadcast the 'selfish bosses' whose egoism induced the workers to become Communist. Vichy's National Broadcasting adopted some of the worst aspects of Radio-Paris, especially in its incitement to hatred. From September to December the Freemasons were attacked almost daily on the radio; Vichy radio sometimes resorted to racial prejudice in denouncing the Jews. There was nothing, however, in Vichy propaganda, which could be compared to the shameful racial prejudices propagated by Radio-Paris.

The BBC had difficulty in answering the two competing French broadcasting systems. Some Anglo-French speakers would have liked to denounce French racism and its effects; others thought that many Frenchmen distrusted the foreign Jews (the 'wops') and trusting Pétain (owing to the silence of National Broadcasting on the Jews) believed there was no anti-Semitic persecution in Vichy France. London was reduced to enumerating what had been stolen by the occupiers and transported back to Germany. The BBC's dominant propaganda theme of late 1941 was: 'The Nazis sack France, they will enslave you'. The Political Wartime Executive chose not to criticise Vichy. An important change occurred in the winter of 1941, as the Germans began to lose ground in Russia. Now London was in a position to broadcast news censured by the continental stations. Instead of simply repeating that Germany was going to lose the war, the BBC now detailed the defeats suffered by the Nazi forces trapped in the depths of the Russian winter by the Soviet defence.

During 1942 little news about Russia was reported on the French wireless; the Nazi-dominated World Newsreels gave some brief information but most of the time they referred only to the daily life of the soldiers without showing scenes of the front. Vichy's French Newsreels were even more cautious, in that only 16 of their 1942 issues referred to the Eastern Front. Germany needed increased help; Laval was recalled to the Vichy government because he would support German demands for workers from France. A few Frenchmen had enlisted in the 'Legion of the French Volunteers', fighting in Russia. (A documentary film, *Fort Cambronne*, was devoted to the 'Legion'.) The 'Legion' was sometimes mentioned by Radio-Paris, but French troops were of little importance; the Reich wanted workers, not soldiers. By 1942 propaganda necessarily focused on the necessity to send French workers to Germany. A new daily programme, 'The Sound Gazette', was set up on Radio-Paris with a clever format of mixing talks, music, dialogues and interviews. Broadcast at the peak hour of 9 p.m., 'The Sound Gazette' stressed day after day the idea that France must collaborate with Germany. Reluctant though they were, the Vichy-men were obliged to create a similar programme, 'Work-radio', less enthusiastically touted for economic collaboration. Three arguments were used to persuade the listeners: (1) it was fine to work in Germany (a documentary film, *Workers of France*, illustrated how well off the French were in German towns and factories); (2) if young people would go to work in Germany the Germans would release the French military prisoners. This was the incredible German bargain known as 'the relief' programme: one prisoner released for every two workers recruited. Families were interviewed on the radio; women said how hard it was to feed a large family with no husband at home, mothers pleaded for their sons and children for their fathers; and (3) Germany must win otherwise the Bolsheviks would overwhelm Europe. On 22 June 1942 Laval said in a broadcast speech: 'I desire the victory of Germany' and proclaimed the necessity of a French mobilisation to back the defender of Europe. London's immediate reaction was the statement that the Nazis were in a bad position if they were reduced to seeking help from a humiliated and occupied country. The BBC also worked against the 'relief' programme, informing its French listeners that German cities and industry were regularly bombed, more and more civilians were being killed and that there were severe shortages in many districts. Thanks to the Resistance movement, London knew where and when local campaigns were started to recruit workers. The Anglo–French BBC speakers urged their listeners to resist the German temptations. London's counter-propaganda became more precise and thus more effective at a time when the two French radio networks began to conceal more and more bad news.

After the Allied landings in Morocco, Vichy, which had previously avoided attacking the British directly, changed its position. It was difficult to tell the truth: this would have proved that the Germans had been quickly and easily expelled from North Africa. Little was said about the current events, but long radio talks were delivered against the men who were destroying the Empire. Vichy had by then lost its control over the newsreels to Paris and National Broadcasting itself was being guided by Laval's collaborationists. Continuing to celebrate Pétain and promote rural life, the Vichy-men were obliged to integrate programmes transmitted from Paris or made in Vichy by collaborationists. One such programme entitled 'The Jewish Problem' brought to National Broadcasting listeners a trite, violent anti-Semitism which was unknown previously. According to the hour of the day, listeners heard aggressive talks against the 'wops', decadent Americans, Gaullists in the hire of Bolsheviks, as well as soothing speeches on agriculture. The Paris-men also had difficulty in coping with the dramatically changed situation. In October 1942 Stalingrad was described as a gigantic battle in which the Soviets were said to play their final card. The presentation of the Russian war by *France-Newsreels* (the unified newsreels made by the Paris-men and the German censors) illuminated the waverings of the German propagandists. The Eastern Front was regularly mentioned during the Autumn 1942, but the information became less and less precise. Then, from December 1942 to February 1943 the impression was that military operations had been reduced to nothing. The end of the Battle of Stalingrad was never mentioned. However, in March 1943, the French audiences saw refugees from the Caucasus, who joined the German troops in order to escape the Bolshevik oppression. Soon after Russia vanished. The newsreels, as well as Radio-Paris no longer spoke of the war shifting emphasis to the Bolshevik threat.

During this period audiences saw a few documentary films denouncing the 'hidden forces' of Communism and Freemasonry which would destroy France if the Germans did not win the war. The collaborationists focused on Communism; talks against the French Communist party and its allegiance to the Soviet Union were broadcast systematically in April 1943. Other talks were inserted in the news bulletins during the spring and the summer. The threat of Bolshevism was used to justify the levies of workers ordered by the Germans. From September 1942, men of fighting age were liable for impressment by the occupying forces; Vichy, instead of resisting the call-up, decided in February 1943 to regulate it. National Broadcasting ignored the levy. Radio-Paris, on the contrary, tried to justify the German policy by claiming that the young men were stupid people, 'horrible idiots', who needed to be 'trained, drilled' by the Germans (this talk was broadcast on 29 April 1943). The Paris-men were now extremely vulnerable and the BBC countered easily with the argument that it was better to enter the underground forces than be forced to work in Germany. Armed French Resistance developed in 1943 largely as a response to the German labour demands. London was more and more effective in giving notice of impending levies, informing the listeners of the progress of the Resistance and publicising Resistance attacks on the Nazi occupation forces.

During the months before the Liberation, the British Political Warfare Executive's radio propaganda took the initiative; the collaborationist French stations were now on the defensive. The BBC urged young people, civil servants and soldiers to 'take to the Maquis', it warned French civilians of bombings and, after the Normandy landing in June 1944, told them of the progress of the Allied forces. Under the leadership of Philippe Henriot, Vichy's National Broadcasting was now fully subordinated to the occupiers. Both French radio stations and the newsreels developed the same point of view during the final months of the occupation. The destructive nature of the Allied bombings was exploited; criticism of the Resistance was equally important, as the Maquis were presented as ruffians, outlaws who had taken up arms to sack the country and who were manoeuvred by the Bolsheviks. The Vichy collaborationists fielded a small crew of debaters whose leaders were Jean-Herold Paquis and Henriot himself. As they had nothing precise to say, the pro-Nazi speakers used an excellent technique: they attacked the BBC-men, unveiling and exploiting the political disagreements between the Gaullists, the Communists and the other Resistance parties, while pointing out the contradictions between the aims of the Russians and those of the Allies. Henriot personally addressed the BBC speakers and made them answer. Even if his talks were pure polemic, his conviction and skilfulness obliged his Anglo–French counterparts to hold a dialogue with him. The conflicts of propaganda had been reduced to the simplest terms – for or against Germany – but it was at a time when it was no longer possible to hesitate in making a decision.

What was the effect of this barrage of propaganda directed against the French people? The effects of propaganda are hard to describe. The first difficulty is the lack of evidence. There are four sources: (1) the reaction of the parties involved in the propaganda-war to counter propaganda campaigns of the other parties. When Pétain, in the speech he delivered on 1 January 1942, complained about the attacks of Radio-Paris, he made the listeners suspect that some people were influenced by the collaborationists and their criticism of Vichy; (2) the immediate effects of (or the lack of response to) a propaganda campaign; (3) the opinions on propaganda expressed during the war; and (4) the opinions expressed by the contemporaries after the war.

I shall start with the last source, more precisely with an investigation on the effects of radio propaganda made by J.L. Crémieux-Brilhac and G. Bensimon in 1973–4. Objections were raised suggesting that recollections, 30 years after the war, cannot be reliable. Furthermore, owing to the failure of Vichy and of the collaborationists, the sample respondents were tempted to overestimate the interest they felt in the BBC programmes. These objections are valid. The investigators knew it was virtually impossible to define the role of radio influence in prompting people to resist the Germans, but their aim was to evaluate the 'image' of broadcasting more than the actual influence of the radio programmes. The witnesses studied in the research were men and women of more than 40 years old, who lived in various regions of France during the war. The social origin and social status of the respondent were taken into account. Some of the findings are most illuminating.

(1) According to the respondents, the radio played a prominent part in the life of the French during the war. We cannot say positively that radio *was* important but there was a general recalled belief in its importance and power.

(2) Eighty-seven per cent of the respondents claimed that they listened regularly to the radio. Some of them began to listen to BBC London as early as 1940. The BBC was received clearly in the north and north-west throughout the war; it was more difficult to pick it up in the south. The two French radio stations were clearly received, although it was sometimes difficult to catch National Broadcasting in the western districts (a detail attested by contemporary sources).

(3) The BBC had the largest radio audience. Whereas civil servants were particularly keen, doctors and priests were diffident.

(4) The neutral Swiss broadcasting station of Sottens, with its four daily news bulletins, had the second largest public, just behind London.

(5) Two-thirds of the respondents listened to Philippe Henriot from time to time; Clergymen and the members of the upper class most often enthused about him.

(6) A few respondents said that BBC talks led them to demonstrate in the streets, boycott the collaborationists, hide to escape the work levies and join to the Maquis.

Other sources appear to document some of these conclusions. The diary of the journalist Pierre Limagne, published shortly after the war, proved that he used to listen to the four radio stations (including Sottens) almost every day and that the news broadcasts were a prominent part of his life. In all the monographs on France during the war we find a paragraph (based on police-reports, newspapers and post-war interviews) devoted to the importance of news broadcasts. A report sent to Berlin in August 1940 by the *Oberbefehlshaber des Heeres in Frankreich* already expressed concern about the influence of the BBC. A little later, on 1 December, Radio-Paris violently attacked those who listened to London. Severe penalties were promised for BBC listeners, beginning with jail in October 1940 and ending with death in December 1943. The Germans went so far as to try to seize the wireless sets in some districts – an effort which was ineffective. A great many French still remember grave, tense people sitting silently in back rooms, behind the drawn blinds of the shops, waiting for the moment when the distant-sounding voice would say 'London calling'; on every previous day, the same voice had filled with hope the apparent emptiness of the night. Vichy was so worried about the impact of the BBC broadcasts that, despite its claim to 'independence' it welcomed German radio experts entrusted with jamming London's frequencies. On their side the London-men feared Radio-Paris, or at least some of its speakers for, in June 1944, they ordered the French Resistance to kill Philippe Henriot.

There was a strong belief, on both sides of the Channel, in the power of propaganda. Is it possible to go further and try and evaluate the impact of the radio and films? In limited, well defined, cases the impact looks perfectly clear. In December 1940, London told the French not to leave their homes on 1 January 1940. People complied with this order and they did the same on several occasions. London ordered the loyal Frenchmen to write the Victory V on the walls of France; the newspapers were subsequently filled with complaints about the V painted everywhere. There is no shortage of evidence that propaganda provoked immediate responses. More important evidence is that many workers enlisted for work in Germany in 1941 when Radio-Paris propaganda was at its best. On the contrary there were fewer and fewer recruits when the BBC counter-attacked, as in 1943 when more than 100,000 workers avoided the German requisitions. How many of them had been convinced by the BBC? The question will never be answered. It can be argued also that the workers went to Germany in 1941 because there was no peril at the time – and similarly stopped going when the Allied bombings became very dangerous. In other words the impact of propaganda is likely to be subsidiary or supplementary to other factors.

In dealing with potential media effects during World War II, more attention must be paid to information. Different radios competed; their rivalry became a channel for reaching more people with more information than was available in other non-occupied countries. The French case involves an interaction between a change in the use of the media, as a result of war propaganda, and a response by audiences which were previously under-informed. To a large extent the most important effect of World War II propaganda in France was the introduction of broadcasting as a major source of information and entertainment.

Sources

The records (National Broadcasting, Radio-Paris, French BBC) and newsreels (World Newsreels, French Newsreels, France Newsreels) still available are kept in the Archives of the Institut National de l'Audiovisuel, tour les Mercuriales, 40 rue Jean Jaurès, 93170, Bagnolet, tel. 362.12.12. The series of *French Newsreels* and *France Newsreels* is also available in Gaumont Archives, 1 quai Gabriel Peri, 94, Joinville.

Bibliography

General

Amouroux, Henri, *La Grande Histoire des Français sous l'occupation*, 4 vols. (Paris, 1977–9)
Aron, Robert, *Histoire de Vichy* (Paris, 1954)
Cotta, Michèle, *La Collaboration, 1940–1944* (Paris, 1964)

Farmer, Paul, *Vichy Political Dilemma* (London, 1955)
Fortune, G. and W., *Hitler-divided France* (London, 1943)
Humbreit, Hans, *Der Militarbefehlshaber in Frankreich, 1940–1944* (Boppard am Rhein, 1968)
Jackel, Eberhard, *Frankreich in Hitlers Europa* (Stuttgart, 1966)
Lochner, L.P., *The Goebbels Diaries, 1942–1943* (New York, 1948)
Michel, Henri, *Vichy, Année 40* (Paris, 1966)
Ory, Pascal, *La France allemande (1933–1945). Paroles du collaborationnisme français* (Paris, 1977)
Paxton, Robert O., *Vichy France, Old Guard and New Order 1940–1944* (New York, 1972)

Public Opinion and Propaganda

Albrecht, Gerd, *Nazionalsozialistische Filmpolitik* (Stuttgart, 1969)
Audiat, Pierre, *Paris pendant la guerre (juin 1940–août 1944)* (Paris, 1946)
Baudot, Marcel, 'L'Opinion publique devant l'invasion de la Russie' *Revue d'Histoire de la Deuxième guerre mondiale*, no. 64 (October 1964), p. 63–80
L'Opinion publique sous l'occupation, l'exemple d'un département français, 1939–1945 (Paris, 1966)
Dejonghe, Etienne, 'Le Nord isolé: occupation et opinion (mai 1940–mai 1942)', *Revue d'histoire moderne et contemporaine*, vol. 26 (January 1979), pp. 48–98
George, Alexander L., *Propaganda Analysis. A study of inferences made from Nazi Propaganda in WWII* (Evanston, 1959)
Limagne, Pierre, *Ephémérides de quatre années tragiques, 1940–1944*, 3 vols. (Paris, 1945–7)
Luirard, Monique, *Le Forez et la Révolution Nationale* (Saint Etienne, 1972)
La Région stéphanoise dans la guerre et dans la paix (Saint Etienne, 1980)
Nobecourt, R.G., *Les Secrets de la propagande en France occupée* (Paris, 1962)
Polonski, Jacques, *La Presse, la propagande et l'opinion publique sous l'occupation* (Paris, 1946)
Zeman, Z.A.B., *Nazi Propaganda* (London, New York, 1965)

Radio

Amaury, Phillippe, *De l'information et de la propagande d'Etat. Les deux premières expériences d'un 'ministère de l'information' en France* (Paris, 1969)
Commission consultative des dommages et des réparations, *Emprise allemande sur la pensée française*, vol. IV: *Radio* (Paris, 1947)
Crémieux-Brilhac, J.L., 'Les Émissions françaises de la BBC pendant la guerre', *Revue d'Histoire de la Deuxième Guerre mondiale*, no. 1 (November 1950), pp. 73–95
Crémieux-Brilhac J.L. and Bensimon G., 'Les Propagandes radiophoniques et l'opinion publique en France de 1940 à 1944', *Revue d'Histoire de la Deuxième Guerre Mondiale*, no. 101 (January 1976), pp. 3–18
Drechster, Karl, 'Les émetteurs clandestins français de Goebbels en mai-juin 1940', *Recherches internationales à la lumière du marxisme*, vol. 23 (1961), pp. 299–312
Dunan, Elisabeth, 'La *Propaganda Abteilung* de France', *Revue d'Histoire de la Deuxième Guerre mondiale*, no. 4 (October 1951), pp. 19–32
Kries, Ernst and Speir, Hans, *German radio Propaganda. Report on home broadcasts during the War* (London, New York, 1944)
Lean, E.T., *Voices in the darkness. The story of the European radio War* (London, 1943)

Lefebure, Antoine, *Le Rôle et l'influence de la radio en France pendant la guerre* (unpublished MA, University of Paris, 1972)

Miquel, Pierre,*Histoire de la radio et de la télévision* (Paris, 1972)

Pevsner, Max, 'Les Thèmes de la propagande allemande avant le 22 juin 1941', *Revue d'Histoire de la Deuxième Guerre mondiale*, no. 64 (October 1966), pp. 29–38

Rolo, Charles, *Radio Goes to War* (London, 1943)

Rouffet, Michel, *La Lutte des autorités allemandes d'occupation contre l'influence de la propagande ennemie par voie de radio, 1940–1944* (unpublished MA, University of Paris, 1974)

Schumann, Maurice, *La Voix du couvre-feu* (Paris, 1964)

Ici Londres. Les voix de la liberté, 1940–1944, 5 vols. (Paris, 1975)

Touzeau, Jacques, *La Propagande radiophonique en France pour la Relève et le Service du travail obligatoire* (unpublished MA, University of Nanterre, undated)

Cinema

Bazin, André, *Le Cinéma de l'occupation et de la Résistance* (Paris, 1975)

Bertin-Maghit, Jean-Pierre, *Le Cinéma français sous Vichy. Les films français de 1940 à 1944, signification, fonction sociale* (Paris, 1980)

Bost, J.L., 'Four Years of French Cinema under the Occupation', *The Cine-technician*, no. 52 (January 1945)

Chirat, Raymond, *Catalogue des films français de long métrage. Films de fiction, 1940–1950* (Luxembourg, 1981)

Commission consultative des dommages et réparation, *Emprise allemande sur la pensée française*, vol. II: *Industries cinématographiques* (Paris, 1947)

Ehrlich, Evelyn J. *Effects of the German Occupation on the French Film Industry* (unpublished PhD, New York University, 1977)

Garçon, François, *La Société française à travers le film, 1940–1944* (unpublished PhD, University of Nanterre, 1981)

Gutman, Nelly, *Le Cinéma français sous l'occupation* (unpublished MA, Ecole des Hautes Etudes, Paris, 1972)

Leglise, Paul, *Histoire de la politique du cinéma français*, vol. II: *Le cinéma entre les Républiques, 1940–1946* (Paris, 1977)

Maine, Paul, *La Propagande nazie par le cinéma en France, 1939–1945* (unpublished MA, University of Nanterre, 1972)

Oms, Marcel, (ed.), '*Le Cinéma de Vichy*', *Cahiers de la Cinémathèque*, no. 10 (July 1973)

Parker, Daniel, *La Démoralisation de la jeunesse par le cinéma* (Paris, 1942)

Pevsner, Max, 'Les Actualités cinématographiques de 1940 à 1944', *Revue d'Histoire de la Deuxième Guerre mondiale*, no. 64 (October 1966), pp. 88–96

Regent, Roger, *Cinéma de France, de la Fille du puisatier aux enfants du Paradis* (Paris, 1948)

Sadoul, Georges, *Le Cinéma pendant la guerre, 1939–1945* (Paris, 1954)

Siclier, Jacques, *La France de Pétain et son cinéma* (Paris, 1981)

Strebel, Elizabeth G., 'French Cinema 1940–1944 and its Socio-psychological Significance: a Preliminary Probe', *Historical Journal of Film, Radio and Television*, vol. 1 (January 1981), pp. 33–46

13 VICHY CINEMA AND PROPAGANDA

Elizabeth Strebel

Probably no period of Modern French History has aroused more passion and controversy than France at the time of the Vichy Government and Nazi Occupation. In the last few years, there has been a flurry of scholarship assessing the role of the cinema in France during these 'black years' (as they are called by the French) from the collapse in 1940 to the 1944 Liberation. Current studies on the subject by Jean Pierre Bertin-Maghit, Jacques Siclier and Francis Courtade[1] differ dramatically in their methodological approaches as well as in their conclusions. There are two major questions to be answered. First, to what extent did the cinema shape and reflect socio-political attitudes in France from 1940 to 1944? And, secondly, did the French cinema serve the propaganda interests of either Vichy or the Nazi occupiers?[2]

It is a major premise that propaganda need not only comprise blatant political messages, but may also constitute more subtle statements ('softcore') of social integration, arguably all the more powerful because of their very indirectness.[3] This study will treat documentary as well as feature films, 'hardcore' propaganda and seemingly apolitical feature films of escape and diversion. Films will be treated as complex texts, giving closest attention to specific cinematic codes, structures and symbols most relevant to the socio-political context.

For years the basic starting point for any exploration of the French Cinema 1940–4 was Roger Régent's memoire *Cinéma de France sous L'Occupation*, published in 1948. Thorough and detailed as this book is, a remarkable account by a witness to the period, it ultimately suffers from falling under the spell of the general 'myth of the Resistance'. This myth, which dominated political and cultural thought in France from the Liberation to the early 1970s, held roughly that collaboration was the domaine of relatively few, shame-faced, aberrant Frenchmen and that by far the vast majority of French were resisters at heart if not in deed. What this meant in terms of evaluating the French films of the period is that allegedly the bulk of French film production did not serve the cause of pro-Vichy, much less pro-German, propaganda and that those films which did were rare exceptions.[4]

The tumultuous political events of 'May 68' in France led to a re-evaluation of the myth of the Resistance. But it was the release in Paris in 1970 of Marcel Ophul's explosive four-hour documentary *The Sorrow and the Pity* (*Le Chagrin et la Pitié*) that shattered the myth once and for all in terms of popular consciousness.[5] Fuel to the fire of auto-critique was added by the appearance of the French translation in 1973 of Robert Paxton's probing study of collaborationism, *Vichy France, old Guard and New Order 1940–1944*.[6] It was in the light of these events that several new studies were published devoted to Vichy cinema.

The first was a short but useful study, *Cinéma de Vichy*, put out by the *Cinémathèque* of Toulouse, which eminated from a colloquium organised by the *Congrès Indépendant du Cinéma International* on this topic in the summer of 1972. The most valuable in the collections of articles is René Noell's monograph devoted to the Cinema of Perpignan from 1939 to 1944.[7] In addition to giving a microcosmic view of what cinema going was like in a small town during the war years, information on film distribution and relative propularity (French, German and American), Noell's article provides insight into the fine mechanism by which propaganda was disseminated. One can discover, for example, that *Jew Süss* opened at the Castillet, one of Perpignan's major cinema houses, one month before the *Journal Officiel* registered the Statute of Jews on 14 June and that the film was revived each year thereafter until it was projected for free in 1944 by the Office of German Placement.[8] One can also learn that it was at a gala organised for the profit of the *Secours National* that the citizens of Perpignan saw the film *Philippe Pétain, sa Vie, son œuvre*, and that tickets of one franc were distributed in all the cinema houses to enable the public to participate in the Week of the Prisoners of War, organised by the COIC (*Comité d'Oganisation de l'Industrie Cinématographique*).[9]

All of the articles in *Cinéma de Vichy* reflect the spirit of auto-critique sparked by *The Sorrow and the Pity* and editor Marcel Oms acknowledges his debt to the Ophuls film. It appears that the consensus of the colloquium was that French films from 1940 to 1944 admirably expressed the ideology of Pétain's National Revolution. As Pierre Cadars put it, 'The Popular Front was a long way off and in the films herb tea henceforth replaced red wine and the workers in their caps and the pimps yielded their place to young girls with flowers, debonnaire clergymen and exemplary mothers.'[10]

Francis Courtade continued the re-evaluation in a chapter entitled 'La Fiancée des Ténèbres' in his book *Les malédictions du cinéma français* (1978).[11] Citing the articulated intentions of Raoul Ploquin Director of the comité d'Organisation des Industries Cinématographiques to try to aspire to the 'high level of such films as *Jew Süss* and *The Young Hitlerien*' to further the cause of New French Politics, Courtade goes on to show the ways in which French film of the period did succeed in propagandising Pétainist ideology. He points to specific films which exhibit an exaltation of land, rural existence, work, country, family, rigidly traditional family morality, the regenerative spirit of youth, all fundamental themes of the Vichy National Revolution. Devoting only one chapter to the issue, Courtade was unable to delve into either the complexity of the films or the competing visions of Vichy but he made a sound beginning in unravelling the story of cinematographic propaganda in this period. Jean Pierre Bertin-Maghit was the first historian to attempt a full-scale study and a rigorous analysis of a large percentage of the Vichy films. In his *Le cinéma français sous Vichy* (1980) he used a semiological approach to investigate 125 of the 220 films produced from 1940 to 1944. There are two sections in his book: (1) the structures within films and (2) the conceptions of the world proposed by the films. Bertin-Maghit is very interested in assessing the extent to which feature film production was propagandistic. Drawing on Jacques Ellul's demarcation of varieties of propaganda, in the initial section of the book Bertin-Maghit postulates the notion of a propaganda of integration, which implies a subtle promotion of the values of the dominant group in power. His intentions and his effort in tracking down such a large number of films scattered through diverse archives are admirable. Unfortunately, the vast amount of work Bertin-Maghit obviously has done does not really lead to greater understanding either of the films themselves or of the times, for his film analysis is limited focusing on one aspect of narrative structure, the evolution in the relationship of amorous couples. In the end, he devises elaborate categories of centrifugal and centripetal structure, which give an impressive aura of scientific veracity. However, when all is translated into lay terms, his hieroglyphics roughly come down to the old 'Boy-meets-Girl, Boy-loses-Girl, Boy-gets-Girl' syndrome (whether or not through endogenous or exogenous causes), all of which is probably equally applicable to every Hollywood film of the thirties and forties as well. Here is a prime example of semiological introversion run amuck.

The much shorter second section of the book is much more useful. Its sociological orientation sets up tallies of diverse social classes, socio-professional groups and locations (Paris, city, country) represented in all the films under review. Noting the preponderant representation of the bourgeoisie, particularly those based in Paris, and socio-political categories of artists, those without profession and the unemployed, Bertin-Maghit observes that there has been no essential change from French films of the thirties to those of the forties.[13] However, he argues, in conclusion, French films 1940–4 do rework certain 'dramatic unities desired by spectators of the thirties to imperceptibly interject them in the mold of Pétainist ideology'.[14] This conclusion, re-echoing the Toulouse Colloquium and Francis Courtade, seems to be tacked on to the end somewhat precipitously and artificially, having little to do with the semiological model building which occupies the bulk of the book.

Jacques Siclier, journalist, cinema critic for *Le Monde*, author of a number of books on the cinema, seems to offer a direct response to Bertin-Maghit in his *La France de Pétain et son cinéma* (1981). As announced rather defiantly in the blurb on the book's jacket, Siclier sets out to be 'resolutely subjective, anti-intellectual, anti-university, anti-Parisian and naturally anti-structuralist'. He writes from the point of view of witness to the times. Having grown up in Troyes in the forties, an avid cinema buff, he claims to have seen virtually all of the 220 French films of the period when they were first released. Besides the obvious dangers of being a witness to an epoch with 40 years hindsight (even though he did rescreen many of the films), there is also the problem that the impact of various films in Troyes is not necessarily what it was in Perpignan or Paris.

Siclier is the first to delve into the important question of the role of Continental, the Paris-based production company which was directed and financed by the Germans. Moreover, Siclier's filmographies and narrative summaries of the 220 films of the period at the end of his book are invaluable. Still, his off-the-cuff approach does at times lead to sloppiness and missed opportunities.[15]

The only point on which Siclier and Bertin-Maghit agree is that French films of the forties seem to be an extension of those of the thirties. However, for Siclier this means (in dramatic contrast to Bertin-Maghit) that there was absolutely no question of propaganda. Hitting out in an attempt at new revisionism, Siclier writes, 'Imagine a French *Jew Süss*'.[16] Siclier further argues that the whole reason why French feature films of the period were so removed from reality was to escape having to make propaganda. Here of course is a rather narrow and restricted definition of the term propaganda with which, notably, Dr Goebbels would have found it hard to concur.[17]

One of the weaknesses with all these studies is that they have underestimated the extent of cinematic propaganda on French screens by according relatively little attention to documentary film, which rose to prominence in the period; they also underestimated the important links between documentary film and feature film. They have tended to dismiss any sort of influential role for the German-controlled Continental, because its films were so diverse and seemingly devoid of overt propaganda. Another shortcoming that these studies share is their simplistic ahistoric view of the Vichy Regime; clearly it was much more than the slogan so often associated with the Maréchal Pétain: *Travail*, *Patrie*, *Famille*. Robert Paxton has demonstrated that Vichy was characterised not by unanimity but by its competing visions.[18] Thus far no attempt had been made to link the films of the period with specific events like the 1942 Jewish deportations or with specific Vichy legislation. Finally, attempting to survey as many films as possible, often the full richness and complexity of the films themselves is lost.

The role played by documentary film in Vichy France has been virtually neglected.[19] And yet this period saw the biggest output of documentary films in French cinema history – nearly 400 for the four year period. The growth of the documentary was promoted first of all by a Decree of 12 April 1941, which formally restricted the number of feature films to one per programme. The time normally allotted to the usual second feature film could now be devoted to documentary shorts. Such a practice had been operative in the Occupied Zone since 26 October 1940, just as it had in Germany from January 1936 for obvious propagandistic purposes.

Relatively few of these 400 documentaries can be considered 'hard-core' propaganda. It does seem significant that there was a concentration of obviously hard-core propaganda films, particularly those of an anti-Semitic nature, between April and October 1942, concurrent with the formation of the new Laval Government of 26 April 1942. This was the period marked by the beginning of the first massive Jewish deportations in July and the extension of the

Occupation to the whole of France in October.

The documentaries most closely tied to right-wing Parisian radical and National Socialist ideology were, as could be expected, co-productions. An example of one such co-production was the 50-minute *Le Péril juif*, a joint Franco–German venture of the *Institut d' Etude des Questions Juives*. This film was in fact a specially edited and adapted French version of *Der Ewige Jude* (1940) which outlined 'the Jewish problem' and explained 'the reasons for and necessity of measures for the protection and defence against the 'eternal danger of Jewish racism'[20]. Its commercial release was in Paris at the César on 6 July 1942, ten days before the infamous roundup of some 13,000 Jews at the Vélodrome d'Hiver in preparation for their mass deportation to the East. The critical timing of the film's release demonstrated a concerted effort to prepare the Roman Catholic French public for this potentially traumatic event.

The distinguishing characteristic of this film is that it popularised the Nazi dogma that even 'assimilated Jews conserved the characteristic of their ancestral race, physical type, spirit, mentality, absolute repugnance for productive labour in the fields, workshops and factories'.[21] This notion was designed to wean the French away from the traditional form French anti-Semitism, which, bolstered by the Catholic Church's acceptance of conversion, had always supported assimilation. The thrust of the film fostered the necessity of racial separateness, the absolute impossibility of assimilation and the urgent need for a solution to the Jewish 'problem'. The film is a montage of diverse footages: Nazi footage of impoverished Warsaw ghetto Jews emphasising their supposed innate slovenliness, Yiddish feature-film footage of the Festival of Purim commemorating the 'Jewish massacre of Persians', extracts from the Hollywood film, *The House of Rothschild* (Twentieth Century, 1934) designed to illustrate the international monetary and political power of Jews and newsreel shots and still photographs of the American Jews Bernard Baruch and Henry Morgenthau, the French Popular Front leader Léon Blum, and the British War Secretary, Leslie Hore-Belisha. International Bolshevik conspiracies were represented by Karl Marx, Rosa Luxemburg and Bela Kuhn. The concluding images of the film, intended to haunt and disturb the viewer long after having left the theatre, were pictures of animals being slaughtered according to the Kosher ritual of food preparation. From physical revulsion over the suffering of the beasts there was intended to be a transference of revulsion to those who were responsible for this inhumane slaughtering.

Another hardcore documentary propaganda film of the period which dealt with the Jewish question was *Les Corrupteurs*, a 29-minute film which appeared in September 1942. This film was produced by the exclusively French production company, *Societé Nova Films* directed by Robert Muzard. It had been founded earlier that year for the cinematographic dissemination of radical right-wing propaganda. The specific focus of *Les Corrupteurs* dealt with the manner in which Jews had exercised a nefarious control over France's Press, Radio and, most particularly, Cinema. There were three parts to the film.[22] The first showed how a young man had been driven to become a criminal by the influence of Jewish-American gangster films. The second part narrated the story of a young girl who wanted to become a film star, but fell into the hands of the Jewish producers and was forced to become a prostitute. The third section documented the ruin of small investors who were fleeced by Jewish bankers. The second part's notion of the sexual defilement of the pure Aryan girl (forced prostitution) again reflects National Socialism rather than traditional French anti-Semitism. The rape scene is dramatically central to Veit Harlan's *Jew Süss* and the insatiable sexual appetite of the Jew was a frequently propagandised image on the part of the Nazis. *Les Corrupteurs* finishes with 'a vibrant appeal from Maréchal Pétain warning the French against the Jewish Danger'. What is striking about this documentary is that it was paired with the popular Henri Decoin feature *Les Inconnus dans la maison* for its commercial run.[23] This pairing is significant in that the major preoccupations of the documentary (the nefarious influence of the cinema and the theme of Jewish sexual defilement of an Aryan girl) find a direct echo in the feature film. This serves to render the propaganda doubly potent and suggests premeditation.

Among other hard-core propaganda films which figured in this critical period of April–October 1942 were Nova Films' *Monsieur Girouette* (June 1942) with its Pétainist attack on 'swing', 'alcoholism', 'bolshevism' and other forms of 'moral decadence' and Nova's *Les Forces Occultes* (September 1942) which railed against Freemasons and Third Republic Parliamentarians. *François vous avez la mémoire courte* (April 1942) was a 35-minute documentary issued by the Secretary General of Information, which presented a montage of footage documenting Bolshevik influence from the Russian Revolution through to the period of the Popular Front. Finally, *La terre qui renaît* (July 1942), produced by a company with the suspicious-sounding name of La France Européenne (indicating most probably close German ties), was basically a film of 'agricultural propaganda' with the *de rigueur* lashing out against Jews common to most of the hard-core propaganda.[24]

At the same time, commercial cinema programmes included a host of 'soft-core' or indirect propaganda films. One such film was *Jardin sans fleurs* (July 1942) put out by the *Commissariat d'Etat à la Famille*, showing the unhappiness of childless couples and the barrenness of abandoned villages due to the crisis of depopulation.[25] Another example was *Croisade de l'Air Pur* (July 1942), sponsored by the company Artisans d'Art du Cinéma, which dealt with the Maréchal's pet project of sending a million urban children on vacation in the pure air of the country.[26] The vast majority of the period's documentary films were seemingly apolitical and non-propagandistic. But were they? Although it is difficult to locate and view the surviving films of the period, fairly detailed descriptions of them are to be found in the Corporative Review *Le Film*. From these descriptions and from documentaries, like those of Georges Rouquier, one finds France depicted as an essentially pre-industrial, predominantly rural, almost medieval, society. Representative was *Manosque pays de Jean Giono*, a documentary film which focused on the milieu of the novelist and playwright who in classic works such as *Régain* (1930) had extolled the virtues of rural life.[27] The descriptions in *Le Film* indicate that films abounded on the forests, rivers, mountains and rural artisans of France. When a documentary film did deal with Paris, it dealt with historical rather than contemporary Paris. In *A travers Paris* one visited the architectural wonders of Paris's past glories – Cluny, Notre Dame, La Sainte Chapelle – not the contemporary urban setting.[28] When a documentary involved itself with tourism, the projected visit is not the Côte d'Azur and its Casinos but the Benedictine Abbey of *Solesme*.

A great common theme of many of the documentaries is a celebration of artisanal labour. *Petits artisans, grands artistes* explores the workshops of goldsmiths and woodworkers, stressing the precision of handwork, craftsmanship, professionalism, weight of tradition, an aura of little change since the days of guilds and journeymen.[29] One of the most prolific production companies of documentary shorts in this period called itself indicatively *Artisans d'art du cinéma*. Between 1940 and 1942 of the 216 documentaries made, Artisans d'Art was responsible for 24.[30] In addition to the already mentioned *A travers Paris* and the soft-core propaganda film *Croisade de l'air pur*, this company put out films on very old cottage-type industries like the silk and the glass industry.

The whole preoccupation with artisanal labour can be linked to the Vichy traditionalists who, as Paxton has shown, made a concerted effort to foster associations of independent artisans as a vehicle for reasserting pre-industrial values. Their influence, illustrated by the production and distribution of documentary film propaganda, appears to be extensive.

The case of documentary film-maker Georges Rouquier is curious and revealing. Nothing in Rouquier's social background or political preferences would suggest that he should be in the least sympathetic to Vichy ideology. Indeed, his youthful participation in the Left-wing Ciné-Club of Léon Moussinac, *Les Amis de Spartacus*, would point to quite the contrary. Yet Rouquier's documentaries of the forties, particularly *Le Tonnelier* (1942) and *Le Charron* (1943), exude admiration for artisanal labour. In *Le Tonnelier* we lovingly follow the process by which M. Valentin, the barrel-maker painstakingly shapes planks into staves, assembles them with iron bands and heats the boards forcing them to take on the shape of a barrel, just as barrel-makers have done with the same skill and care for centuries. In a subsequent film, *Le Charron*, the notion of the continuity of artisanal trade from generation to generation is underscored by a central scene where the old cartwright drops his hammer, grips his side in pain, and his son picks up where the father left off. Whatever Rouquier's intentions in making these films, and it was probably as John Weiss has put it, less 'the evils of industrialism' and more 'the strength of French resources of skill and ingenuity',[31] the resonances with Vichy traditionalist policy points to the complexity of what one defines as propaganda at this moment in history. At another point in time, a film on wheel-making with lingering shots of a crucifix on the cartwright's cottage would perhaps be politically neutral, at this point in time, such a film and all the others like it must be seen as constituting a propaganda of social integration whether wittingly or unwittingly. (See also Pierre Sorlin's treatment of documentaries, above, Ch. 12).

It has generally been assumed that producers of feature films in the Vichy period made escapist and fanatical films to avoid having to making propaganda films. However, most feature films of other periods and of other national cinemas are similarly escapist and often fantastical, having little to do with social realities or the lives of average individuals. Most of cinema history has dealt with the pleasures and passions of the aristocracy and upper bourgeoisie. In this respect, a certain continuity between French films of the thirties and forties is hardly surprising or revealing. There are however many different kinds of fiction and escape, and it is revealing to try and interpret form and structure in fiction films for an understanding of more subtle forms of propaganda.

Three topics involving French feature films produced between 1940 and 1944 are particularly relevant to the question of propaganda: (1) the influence of the Continental, (2) the image of Jews and the nature of French anti-Semitism and (3) the image of the Family and Vichy's Moral Order.

Any study of the extent to which film production was influenced by pro-Vichy or pro-German propaganda must take into account the role played by the French production company, Continental. This was the Paris-based UFA subsidiary directed by the German Alfred Greven, who took his orders directly from Goebbels. The Continental was responsible for 30 of the 220 French films made between 1940 and 1944, more than any other single production company. A fair number of Continental's films were well-made and highly successful at the box office.[32] Indeed, one such film *La Symphonie Fantastique* (1941), directed by Christian Jacques on the life of Hector Berlioz, aroused the ire of Goebbels and even led to a confrontation between Goebbels and Greven. As Goebbels recorded in his diaries on 15 May 1942,

> The film is of excellent quality and amounts to a first-class national fanfare. I shall unfortunately not be able to release it for public showing. I am very angry to think that our own offices in Paris are teaching the French how to represent nationalism in pictures.[33]

Four days later Goebbels continued in the diaries,

> Greven has an entirely wrong technique in that he has regarded it as his task to raise the level of the French movie. That is wrong.

> It isn't our job to supply the Frenchmen with good pictures and it is especially not our task to give them movies that are beyond reproach in their nationalistic tendency. If the French people on the whole are satisfied with light, corny stuff, we ought to make it our business to produce such cheap trash. It would be a case of lunacy for us to promote competition against ourselves. We must proceed in our movie policies as the Americans do in their policies toward the North and South American continents. We must become the dominating movie power in the European continent . . . After I talked to him for a long time, Greven realized the wisdom of this course and will pursue it in the future.[34]

These comments, practically the only ones in the diaries devoted to French cinema, reveal that Goebbels was seemingly more interested in profit motives, economic hegemony, at the most cultural imperialism, than actively promoting propaganda via French cinema. Since the French were satisfied with 'light corny stuff', a staple diet of such films would be more than enough to ensure German domination.

The intentions of Alfred Greven are another story, since Goebbels obviously had much more to occupy his mind than French films, and the Continental was, as Siclier has pointed out, Greven's whole life. To his credit, Siclier has been the first to try to document the role of Greven, and yet he remains as mysterious a figure at the end as at the beginning of his investigation. Siclier was satisfied that Continental had no propagandistic movies, citing script-writer Charles Spaak's memories: 'At the Continental, one did not make propaganda. Were the cinematographers so virtuous? Were they so ferociously anti-German? No, quite simply they were never asked to engaged in any propaganda.'[35] Siclier has a very narrow definition of the term propaganda. Continental's seemingly heterogeneous production may in fact be more consciously insidious than Siclier believes. At the end of his book he presents a 1945 list of the *Centrale Catholique du Cinéma* of morally undesirable French films of the Vichy years.[36] All films were classified from the point of view of moral acceptability. The rating scale went from 1 to 6, 1–3 being acceptable, 4 being either restricted to adults or ill-advised, 5 being proscribed absolutely and 6 being proscribed because essentially pernicious from a social, moral or religious perspective. When this rating scale is applied exclusively to the films of the Continental, we find that 11 films or a third of its production were deemed morally unacceptable. The Centrale Catholique awarded only two 6s in rating the 220 films, both of which went to films produced by Continental *Le Corbeau* and *La Vie de plaisir*. Of seven films which received a rating of 5, three were produced by the Continental.

All of this would suggest that Continental was promoting films of a different sort of moral fabric to that of the rest of the French film production. Certainly the images of prostitution, alcoholism, anticlericalism in *La Vie de plaisir* and the focus on the abortionist Doctor Germain and the raw sensuality of Ginette Leclerc in *Le Corbeau* were quite antithetical to that which Maréchal Pétain had in mind for his Révolution Nationale. It must also be pointed out that it was the Continental that was responsible for many of the most popular of the *film noir* genre, the crime thrillers and 'whodunits', like the films of Clouzot, *Le Dernier des Six* (Clouzot was scriptwriter), *L'Assassin habite au 21*, *Le Corbeau*, films based on the works of Georges Simenon *Cécile est morte* and *Les Caves du Majestic* and the film *L'Assassinat du Père Noël*. Why would the German-backed, allegedly apolitical, Continental want to disseminate films that were morally suspect from the Catholic viewpoint, involving narratives that centred around crime and gangsters, all running quite obviously counter to Vichy's dreams of moral regeneration? There are two possibilities. One reason could be purely economic, the fact that this sort of film was more popular at the box office. But then again, highly moralistic films like *Les Visiteurs du soir*, with its black and white conflicts and triumph of pure, ideal love, as opposed to carnal love, were also popular successes. The second possibility is that unconsciously or even consciously an attempt was being made to subtly undermine Pétain's authority by promoting films which ran counter to the objectives of the National Revolution and sowed the seeds of social disintegration. Supporting this notion is the fact that three Continental films with the worst ratings *Val d'Enfer* (5), *Le Corbeau* (6) and *La Vie de plaisir* (6) were all made in 1943 after Goebbels' admonition to Greven that he should avoid making films that would encourage French nationalism.

Le Corbeau, in particular, with its narrative centring on anonymous letters of denunciation which threaten to undermine the entire social fabric of a small provincial village, has been singled out as fostering social disintegration. In the Clouzot trial after the war it was brought out that the script for this film had been written in 1937 and therefore the film could not possible be construed as propaganda. The point here is that in the thirties no producer could be found for the script, but in the forties willing support for such a venture came from the German-backed company.

Although the archives and records of Continental are no longer extant, we can, however, infer a fair amount of complicity between Continental and proponents of Paris-based Radical Right groups by the pairing of Continental's *Les Inconnus dans la maison* and the aformentioned Nova Film *Les Corrupteurs*. It is to this particular pairing and its significance that we turn as we discuss the image of Jews in French Cinema of the forties and the question of anti-Semitic propaganda in feature film.

To discuss the image of Jews and the nature of anti-Semitism in French cinema of the Vichy period, it is useful to have a point of reference. This has been provided by Pierre Sorlin's recent study of French Cinema's depiction of Jews in the thirties.[37] Sorlin's methodology is based on an analysis of the indicators of Jewishness. He asks the question how do we learn that a character is a Jew, through a verbal clue, a name or accent, or a visual clue, or a stereotypical association with money or business, and what does this reveal about French anti-Semitism? Sorlin concludes that 'the majority of the movies projected a softened version of the old anti-Semitism prompting the spectators to distrust but hardly hate the Jews.'[38]

Depiction of Jews in the cinema of the Vichy period was of course problematic, due to the legislation which denied Jews the right to pursue professional careers within the cinema. It was one thing for Jewish scriptwriters and set designers to collaborate anonymously and clandestinely, but such continued participation was impossible for Jewish actors and actresses. Perhaps one must count as Jewish references dark figures who are the embodiments of evil, pitted against tall, blond heros and heroines like the dwarf and Morolt in *L'Eternel retour*. Such indicators are ambivalent. One prominent film in which a Jew is central to the narrative is Decoin's *Les Inconnus dans la maison*, and it is revealing to analyse this film (produced by Continental) in some detail.

The narrative of this film deals with a murder which has been committed presumably by one of the members of a gang of bored teenagers. The accused Emile Manu is defended by Hector Loursat (played by Raimu), an erstwhile lawyer of great talents, who had taken to drink when his wife deserted him. Suspensefully, the identity of the real murderer is kept to the end of the film when Loursat unmasks the real guilty one as another gang member, Ephraim Luska. The name Ephraim indicates Jewishness, the surname Luska implies some sort of Eastern European origin. It is interesting to note this reference at a time when foreign, as distinct from French, Jews were being deported.

Another very revealing aspect of the film is the major piece of evidence Loursat uses to convict Luska. To establish a motive, he first asks all the male gang members if they were in love with Nicole, the lone female member of the gang, who also happens to be Loursat's daughter. All answer affirmatively with the exception of Luska. Loursat then produces a still photo of the entire gang. All the youths except Luska are seen gazing directly at the camera, where Luska is seen lecherously oggling Nicole. This carries with it the notion of the insatiable sexual appetite of the Jew noticeably absent from traditional anti-Semitism and from the filmic portrait of Jews in the thirties. As if to further underscore separateness, Luska, upon realising that his pretence is up, hurls himself to the floor of the courtroom in a wildly emotional and physical display which contrasts dramaticially with the stiff, rigid stance of the other youths, who have been primed by their parents on proper courtroom deportment. The script for *Les Inconnus dans la maison* (written by Clouzot) was based on a novel by Simenon which was written in 1939 and published in 1940.[39] This film illustrates the complexity and difficulty surrounding definition and identification of cinematographic propaganda. Finally, what of the image of the family and moral order of Pétain's Vichy government? Bertin-Maghit has explored the treatment of couples in feature film, but this does not seem very relevant to Vichy notions of propaganda. What does seem much more pertinent is an examination of the cinematographic treatment of the family, since one of Vichy's major preoccupations was with a strengthening of the family. Pétain had gone as far as to decree 'the right of families takes precedence over the state as well as over the rights of individuals'.[40] Although Vichy family theorists blamed the Third Republic for its anti-family climate of high divorce, legalised prostitution and general atmosphere of moral decadence, Vichy Family legislation was in fact an extension of the Daladier Code of 1939 which aimed at correcting the alarmingly low birthrate by such measures as tightening anti-abortion legislation and by providing incentives for increasing family size.

What is the image of the French family as offered by the French cinema of the period? Contrary to what has already been written – Courtade's 'hymn to the family' and Cadars' 'mamans exemplaires' – the actual narratives and images are involved with family disintegration. The films of the period do not deal with ideal families but rather skilfully lead us to the assumption that the institution of the family should be strengthened by focusing on the disastrous results of families in dissolution; they also accept the reality of the demographic crisis of the low birth rate and try to rectify it.

The first aspect of the disintegration of the family is the striking absence of small children (with notable exceptions such as *Nous les Gosses*). When we do see small children they are detestable (Roland in *Le Corbeau*), monstrous (the childlike dwarf of *L'Eternel Retour*) or unloved (Pierrot in *L'Assassin a Peur la Nuit*). There is no more striking image of the lack of love between parents and children than in *L'Assassin a Peur la Nuit*. Pierrot, after dangling precariously from a cliff overlooking the quarry, is greeted with a box on the ears from his father, just after his rescue, presumably because he has caused so much trouble.

Teenagers appear more often in films of the period, but again it is the lack of communication between parents and children which is at the forefront. Raimu's (Loursat's) great courtroom speech at the end of *Les Inconnus dans la maison*, redolent with Vichy rhetoric, becomes more pursuasive since it follows upon images of disaffection between parents and children, not the least poignant of which has been Nicole's pleading for the love and attention of her alcohol-ravaged father, Loursat himself.

At the same time, films in which we have pregnant women and births abound, *Les Ailes blanches*, *Andorra ou les hommes d'Airain*, *Le Bal des passants*, *Vénus aveugle*, *Les Caves du Majestic*, *La Femme perdue*, *Val d'Enfer*, *La Nuit merveilleuse*, *Lucrèce*, *Jeannou*, *Graine au vent*, *La Fille du puisatier*, *La Vie de plaisir*, *Le Corbeau*, *Le Moussaillon*. What is particularly striking is that many of the pregnancies involve illegitimate children (*La Fille du puissatier*, *Le Val d'Enfer*, *La Femme perdue*, *Le Corbeau*, *Les Ailes blanches*, *Les Caves du Majestic*, *Andorra ou les hommes d'Airain*, *La Vie de plaisir*). There is a subtle difference in the treatment of illegitimate children between the films put out by Continental and other production companies. With the films of

Continental, *Le Val d'Enfer*, *Le Corbeau* and *Les Caves du Majestic*, illegitimacy is presented as an accepted fact of life. With the other films, a resolution of the moral problem of illegitimacy is demanded, and narratives are structured so that an illegitimate child is hidden, concealed, and at the very end of the film brought back into the family fold either through marriage or acceptance on the part of a family patriarch.

Abortion figures prominently in a number of films, notably in *Les Ailes blanches*, where Lucette contemplates abortion but goes ahead and has the child, in *Le Corbeau* where Dr Germain is accused of being an abortionist because at deliveries he saves mothers as opposed to babies, but most prominently in *Le Bal des passants*. In this film, Fabienne, who believes her husband is deceiving her, has an abortion. When she learns that she has been wrong about her husband, she becomes pregnant again. The reprehensible abortionist, desirous of blackmail, ends up revealing the abortion to Fabienne's husband. Repulsed by her dastardly act, he leaves for five years, only to forgive her and be reunited with his ever-faithful wife and daughter at the end of the film. In all these films, abortion is presented as an absolute taboo.

The inability to have children is a preoccupation with a number of films. Ultimately most of these films find resolution by having the woman become a substitute mother. In *Le Voile bleu* Louise Jaurraud gives birth to a little boy who doesn't live. Since her husband has been killed at the Front in 1914 she becomes a governness and, as such, a substitute mother for a number of children, whose parents are too busy to pay attention to them. In *Vénus aveugle*, Clarisse is so distraught at the death of her child Violette and her maternal instinct is so great, that she begins caring for a doll, until she becomes a surrogate mother to a child whose own mother has abandoned her. In only two films of the period is the inability to have children left unresolved *L'Appel du bled* and *La Grande Meute*. However, as far as we can tell, these films had little popularity.

Promotion of fecundity and a strengthening of family and the moral order were central preoccupations of French feature film at this time. Wherever there was a conflict between the two, fecundity prevailed unquestionably as the more important of the two. It is of course impossible to ascertain how much of an impact cinematographic family propaganda, as compared with all the other Vichy incentives and programmes for increasing family size, had on the French populace. But by the end of the war, the French birthrate was considerably higher than it had been for a century.

We have seen that the case of cinematographic propaganda in Vichy France is very complex indeed. It cannot be reduced to the neat and tight formula of *Travail, Patrie, Famille*. The cinematographic propaganda of the period is multiple and diverse, reflecting the competing visions within Vichy. There is the 'hard-core' propaganda of the Parisian-based French Radicals, sympathetic to the Nazis, particularly concentrated in the critical period of April–October 1942. There is the 'soft-core' propaganda of the Vichy traditionalists, with extensive influence on both documentary and feature film production throughout the entire period. Sometimes within a given film like *Les Inconnus dans la maison*, one can find both of these propaganda lines co-existing. There is the output of Continental *versus* the rest of French feature film industry, with their respectively conflicting moralities. There is the contrast within the output of Continental between the early films which are more supportive of French nationalism and the Vichy regime as opposed to the films after 1942 containing subtle efforts to undermine the social fabric of French society. There is the conscious propaganda, the explanations of which appear proudly and defiantly in the trade journal *Le Film*, while there is also the unwitting propaganda of those like Georges Rouquier, whose documentaries quite unintentionally admirably serve the cause of integration to Vichy ideals. Very often, more subtle forms of propaganda, the socially integrative kind, are transmitted in totally unexpected ways, as where the notion of strengthening the family is communicated by numerous films that focus on the drama of families in dissolution. Although it is, of course, difficult to measure the impact of these competing propagandas, it is clear that whether subtly or unsubtly, consciously or unconsciously, the French, who flocked to the cinemas in greater numbers than ever before in those 'black years', were getting a good deal more from the silver screens than just the escape and diversion for which they undoubtedly so longed.

Notes

1. Jean Pierre Bertin-Maghit, *Le Cinéma français sous Vichy, les films français de 1940 à 1944* (Paris, 1980), Jacques Siclier, *La France de Pétain et son cinéma* (Paris, 1981), Francis Courtade, *Les Malédictions du cinéma francais, une historie du cinéma Français Parlant (1928–1978)*, (Paris, 1978).

2. See Elizabeth Strebel, 'French Cinema, 1940–1944, and its Socio-Phychological Significance', *Historical Journal of Film, Radio and Television*, vol. 1. no. 1. (March, 1981).

3. Here, as with Bertin-Maghit, we are indebted to the categorisation of different forms of propaganda of Jacques Ellul in his *Propagandes* (Paris, 1962). This has been translated by Konrad Kellen and Jean Lerner (Vintage Books, 1973).

4. Habitually cited films of collaboration are the Abel Gance film *Vénus Aveugle*, which he dedicated to Maréchal Pétain, Marcel Pagnol's *La Fille du puisatier*, featuring one of the Marechal's celebrated talks to the nation and the films of Jean-Paul Paulin. Clouzot's *Le Corbeau* and Delannoy's *L'Eternel retour* were vigorously attacked as pro-Nazi immediately after the Liberation, but there is by no means unanimity on the signification of these films in historical retrospect.

5. A discussion of films dealing with and exploding myths of Resistance prior to and after the release of *Le Chagrin et la pitié* is to be found in Siclier, *La France de Pétain et son cinéma*, pp. 241–54.

6. Robert O. Paxton, *Vichy France, Old Guard and New Order 1940–1944* (New York, 1972). This work has been singularly invaluable in terms of my perceptions and understanding of Vichy France.

7. René Noell, 'Les Années Grises' (39–41), pp. 5–11 and 'Les Années Noires', pp. 13–19, *Cinéma de Vichy*, Perpignan, Cahiers de la Cinémathèque (1972).

8. Ibid., p. 10.

9. Ibid., p. 11.

10. Pierre Cadars, 'Redécouverte du Cinéma de Vichy', *Cinéma de Vichy*, p. 27.

11. Courtade, *Les Malédictions du cinéma français*, p. 181–225.

12. Ibid., p. 203

13. Bertin-Maghit, *Le Cinéma français sous Vichy*, p. 102.

14. Ibid., p. 136.

15. As an example of Siclier's sloppiness, on p. 38, Siclier correctly cites the fact that *Les Corruptuers*, an anti-Semitic documentary short, was distributed with Decoin's *Les Inconnus dans la maison*, whereas on p. 61, he incorrectly states that it was the short *Forces occultes* which accompanied the Decoin feature film, thus missing the opportunity of pointing out the very close thematic ties between the two films.

16. Siclier, *La France de Pétain et son cinéma*, p. 69.

17. Goebbels in fact strongly believed that the best propaganda was the least obvious.

18. Paxton, *Vichy France, Old Guard and New Order 1940–1944*, p. 139.

19. One of the first to address himself seriously to the role of documentary film in the Vichy years is John Weiss in 'An Innocent Eye? The Career and Documentary Vision of Georges Rouquier up to 1945', *Cinema Journal*, vol. 20 no. 2 (spring, 1981), pp. 36–61.

20. This film was described in *Le Film*, basically the only trade journal of the period. '*Le Péril juif*', *Le Film*, 8 August 1942.

21. Ibid., p. 12.

22. '*Les Corrupteurs*', *Le Film* 9 September 1942, p. 14.

23. This pairing would suggest complicity between Nova Film and the German-directed Continental, which produced the feature film.

24. '*La Terre qui renaît*', *Le Film* 4 July 1942, p. 12.

25. '*Jardin sans fleurs*', *Le Film* 4 July 1942, p. 12.

26. '*Croisade de l'air pur*', *Le Film* 4 July 1942, p. 12.

27. '*Manosque, pays de Jean Giono*', *Le Film* 9 October 1943, p. 12.

28. '*A travers paris*', *Le Film* 25 April 1942, p. 11.

29. '*Petits artisans, grands artistes*', *Le Film*, 29 August 1942, p. 10.

30. Siclier publishes a list of all these documentaries and their producers and directors that appeared in *Le Nouveau Film* (January, 1943). See Siclier *La France de Pétain et son cinéma*, pp. 439–44.

31. Weiss, 'An Innocent Eye? The Career and Documentary Vision of Georges Rouquier up to 1945', p. 51.

32. Among Continental's films which did very well at the box office were *Le Corbeau*, *Le Val d'Enfer* and *Les Inconnus dans la maison*.

33. Louis P. Lochner, *The Goebbels Diaries 1942–1943* (New York, 1948), p. 215.

34. Ibid., p. 221.

35. Siclier, *La France de Pétain et son cinéma*, p. 67.

36. Siclier, *La France de Pétain et son cinéma* pp. 445–57. Apparently the Catholic Central attempted to rate films during the Occupation period and their efforts were often suppressed by the Germans.

37. Pierre Sorlin, 'Jewish Images in the French Cinema of the 1930s', *Historical Journal of Film, Radio and Television*, vol. 1, no. 2, (October, 1981), pp. 139–50.

38. Ibid., p. 148.

39. Siclier uses this as an argument against any propagandistic intentions in *Les Inconnus dans la maison*.

40. Paxton, *Vichy France, Old Guard and New Order 1940–1944*, p. 166.

PART FOUR: JAPANESE PROPAGANDA

14 JAPANESE DOMESTIC RADIO AND CINEMA PROPAGANDA, 1937–1945: AN OVERVIEW*

Gordon Daniels

Long before the creation of the modern Japanese state censorship and propaganda had a significant role in politics and cultural life. From the early seventeenth century Chu Hsi Confucianism was the ideology of government, and moralistic exhortation was an important aspect of administration.[1] Placards and edicts instructed all Japanese to be diligent and loyal and to behave in ways appropriate to their social status.[2] By the eighteenth century literary and theatrical censorship was detailed and effective, and did much to create the special conventions of the *kabuki* theatre.[3] Pre-modern censors sought to protect the regime and public morals, and as eductional standards rose official control of publications became increasingly important.

In 1868, following the Meiji Restoration, Japan's new government began an energetic programme of Westernisation. This reached its political climax with the proclamation of the new constitution in 1889. Like earlier rulers, Japan's modernisers saw propaganda and censorship as valuable tools of government, not only to strengthen the state but to spread ideals of modernisation and national unity. As a result, Japan's economic and political advance was accompanied by the development of official propaganda and press censorship.[4] Thus it was natural that new media, such as radio and cinema, would be subject to censorship and become vehicles for official policy.

As early as 1896 Japanese government officials began research into wireless telegraphy, and within seven years they had successfully transmitted a message to the colony of Taiwan. In 1915 the Wireless Telegraphy Law (*Musen Denshinhō*) was promulgated and after World War I the establishment of broadcasting stations became a practical possibility. In December 1923 the Ministry of Communications instituted Regulations on Private Radio-Telephonic Broadcasting Facilities (*Hōsōyō Shisetsu Musen Denwa*

* This article first appeared in the *Historical Journal of Film, Radio and Television*, vol. 2, no. 2 (October 1982) and appears by kind permission of the Editor.

Kisoku), the basic legal framework for the new medium. According to this, stations were to be private non-profit making organisations, largely financed by licence fees. All programme content would require government approval, and no entertainment programmes were to be permitted during working hours.[5] The first head of Tokyo's pioneer station Gotō Shimpei regarded radio as an essentially serious medium. On the eve of the first broadcast he claimed that radio could improve the level of popular culture, and help commerce and industry by spreading economic information. Other leaders, such as Communications Minister Adachi Kenzō, noted the important role which the BBC had played in the General Strike, and emphasised radio's political importance.[6] These broad notions of broadcasting's social and political power led to the abandonment of plans for private stations. In their place the government created the Japan Broadcasting Corporation (*Nippon Hōsō Kyōkai* – NHK) as a 'privately owned government sponsored monopoly'.[7] Shares were owned by important newspaper companies and private individuals but the central control agency was the Ministry of Communications. The appointment and dismissal of officials, programme planning, changes of rules and financial arrangements all required approval from the Ministry.[8] Initially NHK operated stations in Tokyo, Osaka and Nagoya, but it soon began to construct a nationwide network. In 1928 seven stations were in use and the present Emperor's enthronement ceremonies were covered by radio. Programmes included plays and traditional music but by and large their content was deeply serious. Foreign language courses, stock market reports and radio exercises soon became regular items and less than one-fifth of radio time was devoted to entertainment.[9]

As NHK's significance increased there was much conflict between ministries for control of its organisation. From the beginning the Communications Ministry was in command, but the Home Ministry, which controlled the police and maintained political orthodoxy, mounted a powerful challenge. As educational broadcasting developed the Ministry of Education also sought a voice in NHK policy. After many battles the Communications Ministry remained in control but in 1933 the Central Broadcasting Council was created as an advisory and co-ordinating body. This included the Deputy Ministers of Communications, Home Affairs and Education, and in 1934 equivalent officials from the Army, Navy and Foreign ministries became members.[10] In 1935 NHK helped to found the national Dōmei News Agency. This supplied radio with most of its news and information. In 1936 the government founded an Information Committee under cabinet control to coordinate propaganda activities.[11] In these years of military expansion the tightening of official controls was a marked feature of Japanese broadcasting: pre-transmission censorship was applied to all programmes and prevented the transmission of all of the following.

(1) Items that impaired the dignity of the Imperial House.
(2) Items that disturbed public order and desirable customs.
(3) Items referring to diplomatic or military secrets.
(4) Items referring to confidential proceedings in the Diet.
(5) Items relating to the contents of preliminary investigations prior to public trials and others prohibited from Government announcements.
(6) Items deemed to impair the honour of Government and public offices or of the Army and Navy or items deemed to impair the credit of an individual or groups of individuals.
(7) Items deemed to be political speeches or discussions.
(8) Items deemed to be advertisements of business or individuals.
(9) Items deemed to cause marked disturbance of public sentiments.[12]

Japan's invasion of Manchuria, in September 1931, had provided a great stimulus to broadcasting and the outbreak of war in China (in 1937) was an even greater influence. Furthermore experience gained during this conflict was put to good use during World War II. The campaign in China soon spread from skirmishes to a major struggle and popular interest increased rapidly. In surveys carried out by NHK, relatives of servicemen showed a deep interest in all information regarding the scene and conditions of war.[13] NHK responded with a wide variety of appropriate programmes. There were more frequent news bulletins, including special late night transmissions to rural areas where electric power was not available during the working day. There were also commentaries on the fighting and statements of Japan's objectives. The premier and other ministers began to appear before the microphone. But perhaps most important were programmes which attempted to link men at the front with their families at home. In 1938 NHK broadcast special programmes based upon a particular town or prefecture which expressed support for local men at the front. These shows often contained folk songs and other regional elements and were transmitted to China as well as to domestic audiences.[14]

Although the government was clearly in control of radio during the China incident it was often prone to strange miscalculations. At first NHK broadcast casualty lists, but this was soon prohibited after military intervention.[15] If this was one lesson for the future, radio preparation for air raids was another. In November 1937 Chinese planes approached the shore of south west Japan and air-raid warnings were broadcast. The importance of radio to air defence and propaganda led to an official campaign to spread radio ownership. Cheap sets were manufactured and more offices were opened for the purchase of licences.[16] In 1939 there was a nationwide poster drive encouraging ownership, and loudspeakers were erected in hundreds of railway stations, parks, squares and other public places. Listening was given further stimulus by broadcasts of quality material such as traditional stories, which were only indirectly patriotic. As a result of these campaigns between 1938 and 1940 license holders (Appendix 14.1) increased from 4,165,729 to 5,668,031.[17] In 1941, a new Current Affairs Broadcasting Planning Council was created. This was dominated by officials of the Army, Navy and Communications Ministries and planned all programmes relating to war propaganda.

In 1940, as German military successes transformed the war in Europe, Japanese foreign policy moved closer to that of the Axis Powers. This shift of interest from war in China to a wider world was soon reflected in radio. In particular Japan's Foreign Minister, Arita Hachirō, began to broadcast on major themes of policy. On 29 July he broadcast a 'special lecture' on the 'International Situation and the Position of the Japanese Empire'. In this he claimed that 'Japan and other East Asian nations were in a position racially and economically to adopt a policy of mutual assistance'. He advocated 'coexistence, co-prosperity and stabilization'.[18] This was regarded by many as one of the first official declarations of plans to create a Co-prosperity Sphere. Following Foreign Minister Matsuoka's visit to Berlin and the signing of the Tripartite Pact, Matsuoka appeared on radio voicing the pact's virtues and the following day Prime Minister Konoe reinforced the case for the new Axis alliance.

1940 was also a time of important changes in Japan's political structure. After much argument all political parties were dissolved and were replaced by the Imperial Rule Assistance Association. This so-called 'new structure' was explained and advocated over the radio by the premier and other important leaders.[19]

As a wider war appeared increasingly likely, structures of government supervision and control were further developed. The Cabinet Information Bureau was established in December 1940 and took over many of the Communications Ministry's remaining powers over radio. The new Bureau declared its aim to be 'The establishment of a military state through the unity and solidarity of the public' with the goal 'of raising morale by radio particularly among farmers and young people'. Its second role was to 'make known abroad the Emperor's true intent' and in particular 'broadcasts to China and Micronesia' were to be expanded.[20] On the domestic service a 'Government Hour' was reserved every night for appearances by ministers and civil servants to explain topics of the day. At the school level broadcasts increasingly integrated education with war propaganda.

When Japan entered World War II in December 1941 her broadcasting authorities were well prepared. Special wartime schedules had been planned and provision had already been made for broadcasts from the Diet and the premier's residence. On 7 December representatives of NHK were summoned to the Army Ministry to receive an announcement that war with Britain and the United States had begun. At 7 a.m. the next day the following simple message was broadcast: 'Announcement by the Army and Navy Departments of Imperial Headquarters – at dawn, December 8th the Imperial Army and Navy entered into hostilities with British and American forces in the Western Pacific'.[21] Existing schedules were abandoned to be replaced by repeated readings of the Imperial Rescript declaring war, the playing of military marches, news programmes and readings from Ōkawa Shūmei's *Bei-Ei Tō-A Shinryakushi* (*History of American and British Aggression in East Asia*).[22] The theme of the moment was the need to repel Western aggression in the Far East and to emancipate Asians who lived under European colonial rule or dominance. On the first day of the war there were fifteen extra news bulletins. On the same day Miyamoto Yoshino of the Cabinet Information Bureau broadcast proclaiming:

> Now is the time for all people to rise for the nation. The government and people must be united. One hundred million Japanese must join hands and help each other to go forward. The government will inform the people over the radio of where our nation will go and how they should behave. All the people of Japan please gather round the radio. We expect you to wholeheartedly trust the government's announcements over the radio because the government will take all responsibility and will give you the complete truth. Please obey all instructions which the government issues over the radio.[23]

As this exhortation indicated, the radio was to be used for the transmission of many detailed instructions, as well as for broader attempts to raise public morale. In every city, town and hamlet 'neighbourhood associations' had been created to assist in propaganda, savings, salvage and rationing. Each of their regular meetings was timed to coincide with a special radio broadcast which gave instructions on important duties and issues of the day.[24]

Although radio's chief role was to support Japan's forward policy, war with the West brought new dangers. Japan's government assumed that Allied air raids were a serious possibility and this had significant consequences for radio. Firstly, it was feared that enemy bombers would use Japanese radio broadcasts for navigation purposes. To counter this danger Japan's second radio channel, which had been founded for quality broadcasts, was closed down. All broadcasts on the remaining channel were then centralised, and transmitted from Tokyo. In addition, special studios were established in the Defence General Headquarters and local Army and Navy Headquarters. The studio at the premier's residence was placed at the disposal of the Cabinet Information Board with staff on permanent call. The Government anticipated bomb damage to studios, and emergency facilities were constructed in schools and other public buildings.

During air raids all broadcasts were to be suspended, while as a further security measure all frequencies were to be unified. This also aimed to centralise authority. However these technical changes created confusion and soon a group frequency system was introduced. At night five frequencies were used, each one in an area which corresponded to an armed-forces region. At later stages in the war the number of such regions was reduced to four, then increased to six and eight.

During these months of technical precautions and adjustments NHK transmitted a wide variety of programmes which enunciated three principles of policy: Japan had been compelled to declare war on the Anglo–American powers to survive and maintain her prestige; the main cause of war was the enemies' ambition to conquer the world; Japan's purpose was 'to establish a new world order to assist all nations to take their rightful place in a spirit of universal brotherhood'.[25] To assist in co-ordinating programme policy a new tripartite Programming Conference was created consisting of the Cabinet Information Bureau, the Ministry of Communications and NHK. As a result changes in schedules were soon introduced. Hours of broadcasting were expanded by one and a half hours to end at 11.30 p.m; the 'Government Hour' continued. 'Record of Victories' was a new series and a wide range of poets and novelists were commissioned to produce literary works on martial and East Asian themes. Such series as 'Our Determination' and 'The People's Resolve' featured both cultural dignitaries and anonymous farmers, housewives and students who presented the impression of a united nation.[26] Even where the content of programmes remained largely unchanged new titles were introduced; for example, 'Woman's Hour' was renamed 'Home at War Hour'. Many young Japanese listened to special programmes in groups and afterwards pledged themselves to support the war. In the first months of conflict NHK broadcast a great deal of martial music and patriotic celebration but even music was subjected to ideological restrictions. On 2 January 1942 jazz and 'sensual' Western music were forbidden and thus removed from broadcasting schedules. This foreign music was replaced by Japanese melodies and traditional Japanese war songs. An increasing number of songs were hurriedly composed and broadcast to celebrate some victory or military exploit[27] such as 'The Occupation of Thailand', 'The Attack on the Philippines' and 'The Annihilation of the British Eastern Fleet'. This was a euphoric period when Japanese military successes surprised even optimistic citizens. A succession of victories in South East Asia and the Pacific made it unnecessary to distort or fabricate news to any great extent. Radio spokesmen for the Imperial Army and Navy became popular personalities and were as popular as successful military commanders. Interest in radio advanced as never before. In 1943 7,346,929 families had licences, and in 1944 radio listening reached its wartime peak.[28]

Yet the more serious aspects of war were never far away. People were often urged to be ready for special emergency radio announcements and on 18 April 1942 the United States launched its first symbolic air attack led by General James Doolittle on the Japanese mainland. On this occasion a warning was broadcast by radio, though it was too late to be effective. Even before this, a particularly sombre announcement had been made (months after the event) of the loss of the crew of a midget submarine which had been sunk while attempting to attack Pearl Harbor. On this occasion the enthusiastic marches of the first phase of war were replaced by melancholy music.[29] As Japan's fortunes declined radio was increasingly the vehicle for musical laments.

Despite the overwhelming presence of war news and information in Japanese programmes, appeals to patriotism were also made at a higher level. This policy may have stemmed from a recognition that part of the population constituted a sophisticated audience. It may also have reflected pride in Japan's high level of cultural achievement. In 1942 NHK created a new prize for radio drama and in the following year created a permanent company of radio actors. The prize clearly had reasonably high standards for in its first year no First Prize was awarded. The play *Ame Kakeru Yume* ('A Dream soaring through Heaven'), awarded the Second Prize, was devoted to a conspicuously human subject which had little connection with war, the difficulties of a village without a resident doctor.[30]

By 1943 war news, however delayed or restricted, was increasingly serious. Battlefields were far from the mainland but American submarine and air activity created shortages of food and raw materials. In response to these needs, broadcasting was reshaped to add impetus to production. Now broadcasts began at 5.40 a.m. and ended at 9.30 p.m. so as to coincide with workers' daily schedules. A special series 'To Industrial Soldiers' was broadcast each morning to encourage factory workers who left their homes early. The food shortage was countered with an increasing number of programmes for farmers, such as 'Farmers' Hour'. Vegetable gardening by civilians was also encouraged in an increasing number of programmes in the 'Home at War Hour' series.[31]

One of NHK's greatest strengths lay in the mounting of coordinated campaigns to emphasise and re-emphasise a particular aspect of the war. For example within a single day songs, literary works, drama, talks and symposia would all be transmitted to describe and enthuse about a special aspect of Japan's struggle.[32] As in radio's early days, Japanese broadcasters assumed that their audience could accept a surprising degree of seriousness. On 21 October 1943 large numbers of university students paraded in the Meiji Shrine Stadium on the eve of going to war, undeniably an occasion of great poignancy. NHK broadcast this sad occasion presumably hoping that it would strengthen national resolve.[33]

Throughout these years the Japanese population accepted a high level of propaganda and exhortation, but by 1944 they appeared to be tiring of this wearisome fare. Now the government recognised that life was becoming too austere to provide meaningful incentives to work. Furthermore entertainment in all fields was suffering from shortages of supplies and manpower. In response to this, in May the government recognised the need for a new radio strategy. The emphasis now turned to raising morale by entertainment.[34] In theory these new programmes were attempts to evoke patriotic feelings by emphasising Japanese culture; in practice they were often more popular than crude propaganda. As the realities of war became clearer, superficial slogans were ineffective and it was impossible to impress wounded soldiers with trite optimism. One of the most impressive series of the period was a series of cultural talks for convalescents which presented information on the more complex and beautiful aspects of Japanese traditional culture. The history of art, Zen Buddhism and the tea ceremony featured in these talks, and the series was so successful that it continued in the early months of peace.[35] Other patriotic programmes of an impressive character were readings from famous literary works. Yoshikawa Eiji's fictionalised account of the swordsman and artist Mivamoto Musashi (read by the famous actor Tokugawa Musei) was tremendously popular and continued for over a year.[36] The final year of war also saw the mounting and broadcasting of prestige productions which also achieved great popularity. On New Year's Day 1945 the famous *kabuki* play *Kanjinchō* (on the same theme as Kurosawa's film *The Men Who Tread On The Tiger's Tail*, 1945) was broadcast with a distinguished cast of 34 actors.[37] Amid shortages and air raids this marked a brief and popular flowering of rewarding entertainment. Even masterpieces of Western, albeit German and Austrian, culture were broadcast in 1944; such operas as 'The Marriage of Figaro' and 'Tannhäuser' featured in this series and were reported to be popular.

Parallel with this temporary burst of quality the more serious and practical aspect of broadcasting continued. In the summer of 1944 American B–29 bombers attacked Western Japan and by November Tokyo was within range of American bases in the Mariana islands. In response to this immediate danger, an increasing number of programmes covered aspects of civil defence and air raid precautions. Recordings of American bombs exploding and American aircraft noise often illustrated such talks.[38] More important than the spread of civil defence propaganda was the special position of radio in Japan's air raid warning system. When serious air raids began broadcasts were the only effective source of information and in a very direct sense NHK's broadcasts became essential for human survival. Whenever radar or observers noted approaching enemy aircraft the local radio station was informed. The message was then relayed to Tokyo, from there messages were sent to all stations which were ordered to switch to the previously agreed group frequency system.[39] Stations in the area concerned would continue to transmit their normal programmes until the warning became 'immediate', then programmes would be suspended. In 1945 air raid warnings and alerts became more and more frequent and normal programmes were increasingly disrupted. In the aftermath of raids government propagandists broadcast ambiguous reports which attempted to minimise the psychological damage of the raids. 'Though severe damage was inflicted on urban buildings, fires were successfully extinguished through the efforts of public authorities and civilians' was a typical formula of the time. No close detail was ever given regarding areas which had been damaged. By 1944 fear of further damage to public morale was acute, and even significant earthquake damage was excluded from radio news.[40]

Although broadcasting was largely exempt from the impact of economic difficulties its audience ultimately suffered as the production of new sets declined drastically. In 1943 receiver production reached 565,000 sets but in the following year valves were in short supply. Output fell to 72,862 sets and in 1945 less than 3,000 receivers were manufactured in eight months. Replacements and spares were almost impossible to obtain so that many sets went out of use. In this critical time when radio was vital for survival, advisers visited households helping them to repair and convert their sets to use fewer valves (radiotubes). NHK also sent staff with receiving equipment to areas where sets had been destroyed to facilitate group listening. This shortage of effective sets combined with flight and evacuation led to a large loss of audiences in the final months of war.[41]

When islands within Metropolitan Japan, such as Iwo Jima and Okinawa, became battlegrounds a new form of propaganda was employed. Special broadcasts were beamed to beleaguered garrisons. These included inspirational messages from government leaders, such as the head of the Cabinet Information Bureau, and more plaintive appeals from members of servicemen's families. Special songs such as one commemorating the defence of Iwo Jima were broadcast to men at the front. The fall of Iwo Jima and the loss of Okinawa were commemorated in special programmes of mourning, with the Prime Minister praising the sacrifices of those who had died.[42] Although defeat was unmentionable on Japanese radio, the increasingly desperate nature of Japan's position was impossible to conceal. Yet the Japanese authorities appeared to believe that poignant news could inspire resolve. In the spring and summer of 1945 outside broadcasts from *kamikaze* bases were frequent. Pilots were interviewed and the sounds of their aircraft were conveyed by radio to the civilian population.[43]

Following the dropping of atomic bombs on Hiroshima and Nagasaki and the entry of the Soviet Union into the Far Eastern war, the Japanese government moved reluctantly to accept the allies' surrender terms. On 13 August the Cabinet decided to surrender but this decision brought new dangers. There was fear that patriotic elements in the armed forces, and right-wing civilian groups, might continue armed resistance or even attempt a *coup* against the government. Prince Konoe was convinced that defeat might stimulate a Communist revolution. In this delicate situation only an unprecedented broadcast – a direct message from the Emperor – could hope to maintain national unity. On 14 August everyone was warned to listen to 'an important broadcast' at noon on the following day. At that time many gathered in groups to listen to radios in public places, the Emperor's broadcast declared that due to

> the general trends of the world and the actual conditions in our empire we have decided to effect a settlement of the present situation by an extraordinary measure. We have instructed our government to inform the United States, Great Britain, the

> Soviet Union and China of our acceptance of their joint declaration.[44]

Emotive terms such as 'surrender' and 'defeat' were carefully omitted from the Emperor's text. To have spoken frankly could have created the very disturbances which the broadcast sought to avoid.

NHK's next and final phase of propaganda sought to ensure that the armistice could be converted into a stable surrender. Some broadcasters looked even further into the future and sought to begin mental preparations for the post-war world. At first the Emperor's message was repeated and Cabinet Ministers explained its significance. Soon there were more positive attempts to influence the popular mind. After two days the new Prime Minister, Prince Higashikuni, spoke over the radio urging co-operation between government and people. On 20 August he cautioned against any rash action, which was a euphemism for resistance to allied invasion forces. This message was repeated on the hour for five hours. By this time the censorship apparatus was loosened. Attention now turned to food production with more programmes on agriculture and gardening. Special entertainment programmes were prepared for farming families. 'Children's Hour' returned to the air as did the weather forecast and performances by the NHK Symphony Orchestra. General Douglas MacArthur landed in Japan on 30 August. The surrender was signed on 2 September. Japan's war was at an end.[45]

Retrospectively one sees how, within a rigid framework of censorship and control, Japanese radio played a complex and responsive role during eight years of war. In the China conflict it linked servicemen and their families; after Pearl Harbor it stirred enthusiasm for the war; from the spring of 1942 some defeats were concealed and in the following year it emphasised increasing production; in 1944 high quality entertainment replaced austerity as a significant element in broadcasting. In the final year of war radio played a crucial role in warning people of air attacks. Heroic suicide pilots featured in an increasing number of programmes, and radio sought to maintain national morale, but in August 1945 it helped prepare Japan for surrender and the post-war world. Japanese radio may well have been crass in its chauvinism and dishonest in its presentation of events, but in its concern for national unity, production and Japanese tradition it reflected major enduring themes in Japanese modernisation.

In the same year that the Japanese carried out their first experiments in wireless the first moving pictures were shown in Tokyo. In 1896 an Edison Kinetoscope was imported from the United States and in the following year a theatre in Kanda, Tokyo, began showing films with Lumière equipment.[46] By the end of the Russo–Japanese war Japanese cameramen were taking film at home and abroad and by 1908 Japanese feature films, of a primitive sort, were being created. Like much that was modern and Western the cinema was of great interest to forward-looking Japanese, and by 1912 the important Nikkatsu film company had begun its activities. As in most countries production was dominated by fiction films, while European and American films were widely shown in Japanese cinemas. In the inter-war years the Japanese cinema developed rapidly, but this growth coincided with official unease at the development of left-wing thought in intellectual and labour circles. As early as 1911 the Tokyo police had taken action against the French film *Jigoma* on account of its potential for corrupting the young, and in 1925 the Home Ministry introduced a nationwide system of government film censorship. As in the control of radio, Home Ministry officials were principally concerned with possible damage which might be inflicted on the Imperial House. In fact films which made light of Western monarchies were also regarded as subversive. Other areas of life protected by the censors were the armed forces, and 'the social order', and, as in most countries, although eroticism disturbed the censors, it was a less important concern than political and military matters.[47] Thus well before the invasion of Manchuria the Japanese government had a well-developed system of censorship as well as directives which restricted the filming of the Imperial family.

Just as radio's popularity was greatly enhanced by interest in foreign wars so the cinema benefitted from military adventures. In particular public interest in warfare in exotic surroundings gave a great stimulus to the development of newsreels and news cinemas in the 1930s.[48] In these same years, although feature and documentary films were overwhelmingly the product of private companies, government influence steadily increased. Immediately after the outbreak of the China incident the Home Ministry issued clear guidelines for war films. They were to raise morale, not criticise the army, show no bloody or pitiful scenes of war, and to do nothing to lower the morale of conscripts and their families.[49] Parallel to these negative regulations went an increasing tide of opinion, both private and official, in favour of 'national policy' films which would support Japan's international position. In 1933 the *Osaka Mainichi* newspaper film division responded to the Manchurian crisis by making *Hijōji Nippon* (*Japan in Time of Emergency*), which in some respects set the pattern for much Japanese film propaganda.[50] The script of the film was a long address by the nationalistic General Araki Sadao. This extolled Japan's virtues, her mission in Asia, and with appropriate film sequences showed the corrupting influence which Western culture brought to Japanese society. Western influence was equated with decadence, laziness and lack of national pride. This film also presented a geopolitical theme which was often to be repeated in Japanese propaganda; this was the notion of the encirclement of Japan by hostile countries and in particular the threat which the Soviet Union posed to Japan, Korea and Manchuria. Feature films of a policy character became much more numerous after the outbreak of the war in China when the costs of an ever-expanding war made it imperative to secure greater and greater sacrifices from the Japanese people. Among these were many films which set out to show the suffering, comradeship and courage of the Imperial Army. In the words of *The Cinema Yearbook of Japan* for 1938 many films which treated the China incident were 'no more than cheap sensational films of poor quality without any artistic value', but there were marked exceptions.[51] Tasaka Tomotaka's *Gonin no Sekkōhei* (*Five Scouts*), released in early 1938, was perhaps the first impressive film set against the background of the China war.[52] This was a simple story of a patrol carried out by five soldiers. One fails to return, is mourned, and finally reappears. Then the soldiers move on to another engagement. Westerners might view this as a melancholy tale presented in an austere manner but it corresponded closely to Japanese ideas of the arduous nature of war and the stoical behaviour of Japanese troops. By 1940 such films had virtually become a genre in themselves; the most outstanding was perhaps Tasaka's *Mud and Soldiers* (*Tsuchi to Heitai*) (1940), described by the United States' Office of Strategic Services (OSS) as:

> Probably the most comprehensive treatment of war . . . the prize-winning picture of 1940 describes the Hangchow landing in the China campaign. The film is the life story of a squad; dull

days on the transport, landing at dawn, days of marching in the mud, nights in the trenches soaked in water, and drenched by pouring rain, cold food, cold lodging, monotony, hardship, blisters, lice and dirt. As the war goes on the men in the squad get acquainted with each other. They hear about each other's families. They read letters from home together, crack jokes, and when wounded rescue each other from the enemies' fire. But inevitably the squad grows smaller and smaller. They show each other last kindnesses, cremate the body of each fallen comrade, often at the risk of life, and take the ashes along for the eventual shipment home. Throughout the film there are several battles, several deaths, several rest periods, but always the mud of the road – an endless road with only rare glimpses of beauty such as a lotus in a pond, a sunset, a clump of trees to remind them of home. It ends with a rest stop in an abandoned Chinese village.[53]

Another major theme of Japanese films in the years 1937–40 was Japan's mission in Asia. This was illustrated in numerous feature films illustrating the interrelationships of Japanese and Chinese and their cooperation against various enemies. In Watanabe Kunio's *Nessa no Chikai* (*Vow of the Desert*) Japanese were shown cooperating in the building of a road west from Peking. At a more personal level there was a romance between the Japanese director and a Chinese girl. The villains were Communist terrorists who sought to sabotage the road and the romance. The director is murdered by a Communist terrorist but finally the Communist is converted to the Pan–Asian ideal.[54] A much more popular, ingenious and successful film on a Pan–Asian theme was Fushimizu Osamu's *Shina no Yoru* (*China Night*) (1940). Again a Sino–Japanese romance formed the central element of the plot. In this case a Japanese naval officer has a dignified relationship with a war orphan in Shanghai. Much of the interest in this film lay in the conflict between worthy and unworthy Japanese, with a naval officer protecting the orphan from molestation. As a result of these adventures the Chinese girl abandons her hatred of Japanese and becomes a supporter of their Pan–Asian aims.[55] Japanese propagandists recognised that their austere forms of propaganda were not equally acceptable in all countries and the ending of the film was modified for audiences in Malaya and the Philippines.

The picture as shown in China ends with the wedding of China to

> Japan. For Japanese audiences it goes further. Before the marriage is consummated the hero is called to duty. He leaves his bride, is wounded by her countrymen, and loses his life on the battlefront. On learning the news she commits suicide by drowning. Here the picture ends for Japanese audiences. As shown in Malaya and the Philippines the news of the death proves false, and although wounded in the battle with Communist guerrillas, he returns just as she is about to throw herself into the river and saves her. The film thus ends on a happy symbolic note of Japan rescuing China, saving China from Communism, and the two living happily ever after.[56]

It would be wrong to think that the era of the China war only produced films which were concerned with war, or romance in the shadow of war. Before Pearl Harbor it was still possible to produce films which reflected other aspects of Japan's political and military difficulties. In the 1930s there was considerable interest in the British documentary movement and some films, in this vein, linked the arduous life of the virtuous peasant (which elsewhere might inspire a radical film) with Japan's overseas expansion. In 1941, after three years planning, Yamamoto Kajirō (assisted by the young Kurosawa) made *Uma* (*Horse*) a semi-documentary story of a peasant girl who rears a colt until it is two years old. Set in a cold, austere region of highland Japan much of the film's quality lay in its skilful depiction of the seasons, agricultural labour, and the growth of the horse, the central object in the story, destined to be bought by the Imperial Army.[57]

The increasing number of links between politics and filmmaking were the products of conscious changes in official policy. Knowledge of the role of cinema in Germany played a part in Japanese policy and in 1939 a Film Law (*Eiga–hō*) was passed which subjected virtually every aspect of the industry to a system of government licenses. From this time on no one could work in the industry without government approval.[58] In view of this it is hardly surprising that few Japanese actors or directors carried out acts of resistance against government policy. The difficulties of Japan's economic position could also be used to justify various forms of indirect control which were as potent as the overt clauses of the Film Law. In 1937 the Japanese economy was placed on a war footing with a policy of restricting all inessential imports. This measure, combined with a policy of reducing foreign influences, justified the exclusion of an increasing number of American films and the increasing dominance by home productions of Japanese screens.[59] Foreign films were deemed inessential; raw film was also in short supply. This genuine shortage could easily be used to prevent the supply of film to any director who was considered undesirable. By 1940 government control had extended beyond control of production to rules about programming in individual cinemas. It was made compulsory to show newsreels and documentary films, heavily coloured by 'national policy', as part of all programmes. Furthermore, a national routing of films around two planned circuits was enforced by government order.[60]

One more significant organisational change took place between the outbreak of war in Europe and the attack on Pearl Harbor. As a result of government pressure existing newsreel companies, owned by the major newspaper groups were amalgamated in 1940 into one single Japan Film Company (*Nippon Eigasha*) which dominated all newsreel production during the war years.

Needless to say many of the films which had been produced during the China war continued to be shown after Pearl Harbor. This was particularly true of cinemas in outlying or conquered territories. However, documentaries gained an unprecedented importance in the early war years. Many of these were the products of special service film units which were attached to army and navy forces in the field or at sea. Perhaps the most successful of these were records of Japanese victories in the opening months of the war. In the past documentary films had been regarded as uncommercial and unlikely to be profitable but some of the new campaign films attracted large audiences.[61] Not only were victories attractive experiences but most of them had been won in exotic and romantic surroundings; even these documentaries retained the seriousness which marks Japanese propaganda.

In 1942 the army in the Philippines produced *Tōyō no Gaika* (*Victory Song of the Orient*) which was not only shown in cinemas but in many schools, public halls and community centres. Like numerous Japanese documentaries it began with an ideological statement. The colonial buildings of Manila (now peaceful and orderly after the Japanese occupation) were shown as an indication of imperialist influence. Then American posters, stores, buildings and fashions were shown as symbols of the corrupting influence of the West and, implicitly, the damage which had been inflicted on oriental culture. Much of the remainder of the film depicted the campaign to destroy the last American redoubts in the Bataan peninsula. Yet this version of the campaign showed no military action. Japanese soldiers were shown providing health care for Filipino villagers, but much of the film was a detailed and slow-moving depiction of the many services necessary to a modern army in a major campaign. Transport, medical servies, communications, food supplies and the movement of reinforcements were all shown as if to convey the complex and scientific character of Japan's forces. There was some light relief in shots of soldiers playing volleyball but the bulk of the film was almost a didactic tract indicating the skilful organisation of the Imperial Army. At times, artillery fire is heard but the enemy first appear as prisoners of war. Large piles of captured equipment are shown, the Americans' cowardice and failure to commit suicide is criticised, and the film ends with an ill-organised victory parade of civilians and troops in Manila.[62] Like much Japanese propaganda in the early stages of war this film implicitly linked Japan's crusade with modernity, and presented war as slow, arduous and hardly glamorous. Similar films depicting campaigns in Burma (*Biruma Senki*) and Malaya (*Marei Senki*) were also produced by army units; the latter being notable for its depiction of General Yamashita demanding surrender from the defeated General Percival. This film also showed the East pitted against the West and depicted 'an exhibition of British Commonwealth troops of many nationalities providing a guard of honour for General Yamashita as he drove to his headquarters in Singapore.[63]

As in most countries, Japanese wartime propagandists often sought to combine the romance of history with a contemporary message. In particular, films were made of historical events which could present the Pan–Asian ideal as something with deep historic roots. Incidents in the history of Sino–Western relations were a useful basis for such propaganda. A typical film of this genre was *Doreisen* (*Slaveship*) which described the treatment of Chinese coolies in a Peruvian ship.[64] This ship was forced by a storm to take shelter in Yokohama harbour. After numerous coolies had escaped from its hull and pleaded for help from the Japanese, the Japanese liberated them and allowed them to return to their own country. The theme of Sino–Japanese friendship was obvious, and it was easy to forget that in fact a British diplomat had pleaded with the Japanese to treat the Chinese with humanity. The events of the Opium War provided a more credible basis for an anti-Western film based upon history; while Pan–Asianism was also projected in an epic, shot in Mongolia, depicting the career of Ghengis Khan.[65]

Yet, as in the field of radio, the cinema at times produced propaganda of high quality, whose connection with the war was far from direct. Mizoguchi Kenji's lengthy treatment of the eighteenth-century story of the 47 loyal retainers (*Genroku Chūshingura*) was in a sense history, for it depicted a true story, but it was also an incident which had become almost mythical. This film was an excellent evocation of life in the eighteenth century, of the relations between lords and their loyal followers. Implicitly it supported the samurai ethic which the government claimed existed in the Imperial Army. Yet there was no overt ideological statement in this film and violence – as opposed to plots and schemes – had a very small part in its action.[66]

Perhaps the success of war documentaries had an influence on the pattern of feature films which were made in the years which followed Japan's initial victories. The conquest of Hong Kong and the attack on Singapore were reconstructed with actors playing the part of soldiers and marines.[67] Of these reconstructions perhaps the most ambitious and successful was *Hawai Marei Oki Kaisen* (*The War at Sea from Hawaii to Malaya*) which was made in 1942 at the suggestion of the Navy to commemorate the anniversary of Pearl Harbor.[68] Like the documentary *Horse* this was made by Yamamoto Kajirō and mingled documentary and reconstruction in impressive ways. Many shots in the early sections of the film depict the intensive drill, physical exercise and training of trainee naval pilots, shot at an important base north of Tokyo. One critic has stated that these shots are dishonest for they carefully exclude all the violence and harshness usually associated with discipline in the Japanese armed forces.[69] Nevertheless these sequences effectively symbolise the notion that the modern military skills of the pilot are based on discipline and physical strength. This theme was often part of Japanese propaganda which emphasised the importance of men against weapons or machines. A second more social theme of this film is that of the virtues of life in the Japanese countryside. The cadet returns to a 'typical' farmhouse where everyone behaves with dignity and restraint; where women are subordinate and all the sterling values of tradition are maintained. Inevitably the climax of this film is the attack upon Pearl Harbor where shots of real aircraft are combined with the clever use of models to depict American installations. Ties with Germany are perhaps symbolised by the use of Wagner's 'Ride of the Valkyries' as music to accompany the raid. Americans, via their radio programmes, are depicted as decadent, pleasure-loving, and insignificant enemies. Yet as in the morose depictions of the China incident the ending is poignant as the camera dwells for some time upon a plane which plunges into the sea.

As the war progressed and conditions became more serious new themes were treated by Japanese directors; perhaps, as in radio, there was need to escape from the jingoism of the early war years. One contributor to a new variety of feature film was Kurosawa whose *Ichiban Utsukushiku* (*The Most Beautiful*) (1944) depicted an aspect of the war which was characteristic of 1943 and after. This film is set in an optical factory where Japanese women live and work together. Many shots show their diligent work of grinding, polishing, and checking lenses. The women are also shown participating in military drill, designed to improve their industrial morale. Besides dwelling upon a typically Japanese group the film shows the various personal problems which threaten the unity and effectiveness of the group and hence the war effort. One girl becomes ill and her departure temporarily depresses her fellow workers. However with redoubled efforts they increase production. Another girl falls from a roof and is sent to hospital. Again morale falters, but a third woman, a natural leader, determines to rally her fellow workers. Homesickness often depresses the girls; one allows a machine to run out of control. When the supervisor visits her home and leaves the factory, again spirits flag. One girl allows a defective lens to pass through the factory without adequate checks. This errant worker finally works through the night until she locates the defective lens. Her sacrifice is greeted with acclaim and the community is restored to a measure of happiness.[70]

Some wartime Japanese films had little overt connection with propaganda. Kurosawa's *Sugata Sanshirō* dealt with *jūjitsu* – and showed an American sailor abusing a rickshaw driver – but its connection with the war was marginal.[71] In the later years of war shortages of raw film and damage to studios made all large-scale filmmaking increasingly difficult.

Beyond the world of feature films and full length documentaries the making of short documentary films was of considerale importance. Many shorter documentaries inadvertently depicted the decline in Japan's position and the changing mood of her war effort. At first documentaries depicted modern aspects of the military forces, indications that Japan was a leader in various military developments. *Divine Soldiers of the Skies* (*Sora no Shimpei*) (1942) depicted the training of parachute units and the capture of Palembang by paratroops. But by 1944 America's superiority in air warfare was becoming clear and civil defence became an important theme for filmmakers with new documentaries illustrating the effects of blast as well as how to cope with incendiaries by simple methods.[72]

Yet perhaps the best guide to the changing character of Japanese film propaganda can be seen in the weekly newsreels which were shown in all cinemas throughout the war.[73] Understandably the early months of war produced newsreels of victories, but even these sequences had a distinctive mood. Often great emphasis was placed on the happy reception given to Japanese troops by Burmese, Malays and Indonesians. Similarly a rapid return to law and order was noted. Furthermore imperial princes were often shown visiting newly conquered territories as if to symbolise the extension of benign imperial rule. In the treatment of the populations of occupied lands much attention was devoted to the economic and technical help which Japanese were bringing to these former European colonies, while at times the close racial links between Japanese and South-east Asians were mentioned.

From the beginning of the war newsreels, like radio talks, were used for the direct presentation of government propaganda and this became increasingly apparent in 1943 and 1944. The Minister of Agriculture appeared in front of the cameras to urge increased production. The Minister of Finance appealed for national savings, but most dramatic of all was a newsreel in February 1944 which urged women to emulate their American counterparts and enter factories to increase war production. Later there were impressive shots of women driving trains and working on modern assembly lines.

As on radio, the possibility of defeat was never mentioned in the cinema, but the realities of war could not be concealed, even from the tightly censored newsreels. As the allied blockade tightened it became increasingly difficult to obtain footage from South-East Asia and domestic items became more and more dominant. At times the apparent openness of the censors' minds added to an impression of approaching disaster. In 1943 the miserable spectacle of students marching in a rain-sodden stadium before leaving for the forces was shown on the newsreels.[74] To anyone not immersed in Japanese military values such scenes could only have depressed, not reinforced, public morale. Similarly there was no attempt to conceal Axis defeats in Western Europe, when such footage was available. Mussolini's rescue by Hitler which was a clear indication of Italian weakness appeared on every Japanese screen. The newsreels often echoed radio programmes as the closing months of war were depicted as the era of suicide pilots and grim austerity. In a sense propaganda had come full circle. The sombreness of war which had been clear in the classic feature films of the China incident was again the dominant theme in Japanese film propaganda.

From the beginning of the China incident Japanese films were deeply influenced by censorship and directives of government policy. Despite this, and the concealment of the physical horrors of war, much early propaganda conveyed the true atmosphere of combat with its dirt, loneliness and suffering. China also provided exotic scenery for films which proclaimed the ideal of Sino–Japanese friendship, and implicitly Pan–Asian harmony. Historical films were also used to recount the vices of western imperialism and the shared interests of the peoples of China and Japan. Following the outbreak of war with Britain and the United States the anti-colonial message had even greater strength, and was a more attractive theme than generalised hostility to the West. The Pacific War brought a new genre of Japanese propaganda, 'the record of victory'. In contrast to the China incident the Pacific War brought clear victories and the enemy was easily identifiable. As Japan's series of triumphs came to an end her directors reconstructed past victories and emphasised war production and civil defence.

Despite an overwhelming mood of seriousness Japanese film propaganda was varied, often professional, and surprisingly imaginative. Like radio it ranged from high culture to conveying simple information and despite tight censorship sometimes conveyed the mood of war with surprising accuracy. All Japan's best directors and actors co-operated with the wartime regime. This ensured that some propaganda possessed an artistic quality which reflected Japan's cultural sophistication.

Throughout the war years the Japanese government made effective use of these two major tools of mass media, cinema and radio, to support national morale and provide essential information for its home population. The study of the content of this propaganda effort, as it developed in response to the changing fortunes of the war, provides important insights into the manner in which Japan's traditional values supported national unity, even as the demands of a modern state at war were being met.

Appendix 14.1: Radio Receiving Licences (1924–1945) in Japan

Year	Number of licences	Rate of dissemination (%)
1924	5,455	0.1
1925	258,507	2.1
1926	361,066	3.0
1927	390,129	3.2
1928	564,603	4.7
1929	650,479	5.4
1930	778,948	6.1
1931	1,055,778	8.3
1932	1,419,722	11.1
1933	1,714,223	13.4
1934	1,979,096	15.5
1935	2,422,111	17.9
1936	2,904,823	21.4
1937	3,584,462	26.4
1938	4,165,729	29.4
1939	4,862,137	34.4
1940	5,668,031	39.2
1941	6,624,326	45.8
1942	7,051,021	48.7
1943	7,346,929	49.5
1944	7,437,688	50.4[a]
1945	5,728,076	39.2

Note: a. Peak year.

Source: History Compilation Room, Radio and Television Culture Research Institute, NHK *History of Broadcasting in Japan*, pp. 402–3 (Tokyo, 1967).

Appendix 14.2: Number of Cinemas (1930–1945) in Japan

Year	Number of cinemas	Year	Number of cinemas
1930	1,392	1938	1,875
1931	1,449	1939	2,018
1932	1,460	1940	2,363
1933	1,498	1941	2,466[a]
1934	1,538	1942	2,157
1935	1,586	1943	1,986
1936	1,627	1944	1,759
1937	1,749	1945	1,237

Note: a. Peak year.

Source: History Compilation Room, Radio and Television Culture Research Institute, NHK *History of Broadcasting in Japan*, p. 405 (Tokyo, 1967).

Notes

Japanese names are given in the Japanese order – the family name first, followed by the given name, e.g. Kurosawa Akira.

1. Hall, John W. (1979) The Confucian teacher in Tokugawa Japan, in: Nivison, David S. & Wright, Arthur F. (eds.) *Confucianism in Action*, pp. 268–301 (Stanford University Press).
2. Yokoyama Toshio (1978) Tourism, dandyism and occultism: the quest for national identity in nineteenth century Japan, *Proceedings of the British Association for Japanese Studies*, Vol. III, Part 1, pp. 1–15.
3. Shively, D.H. (1968) *Bakufu* versus *Kabuki*, in: Hall, John W. & Jansen, Marius B. (eds.) '*Studies in the Institutional History of Early Modern Japan*, pp. 231–61 (Princeton University Press).
4. Altman, Albert A. (1975) *Shimbunshi*: the early Meiji adaptation of the Western style newspaper, in: Beasley, W.G. (ed.) *Modern Japan: Aspects of History, Literature and Society*, pp. 52–66 (London).
5. History Compilation Room, Radio and Television Culture Research Institute, Nippon Hōsō Kyōkai (ed.) *50 Years of Japanese Broadcasting*, p. 16 (Tokyo, 1977).
6. Ibid., pp. 21–4.
7. Office of Strategic Services, Research and Analysis Branch, *Public Information in Japan* , p. 31 (R and A Report No. 2362) (Washington, DC, 20 August 1945) (National Archives, Washington, DC).
8. History Compilation Room, Radio and Television Culture Research Institute, Nippon Hōsō Kyōkai (ed.) *History of Broadcasting in Japan*, p. 81 (Tokyo, 1967).
9. OSS, *Public Information in Japan*, p. 38.
10. *History of Broadcasting in Japan*, pp. 76–7.
11. Ibid., p. 77.
12. Ibid., p. 79.
13. Nippon Hōsō Kyōkai (ed.) (1977) *Hōsō 50-nen-shi*, p. 115 (Tokyo).

14. Ibid., pp. 116 and 122.
15. Ibid., p. 118.
16. Ibid., pp. 125–6.
17. *History of Broadcasting in Japan*, pp. 402–3.
18. *50 Years of Japanese Broadcasting*, p. 86.
19. Ibid., p. 87.
20. Ibid., pp. 87–8.
21. *Hōsō 50-nen-shi*, p. 139.
22. Ishida Takeshi (1968) *Hakyoku to Heiwa (1941–1952)*, p. 2 (Tokyo).
23. *50 Years of Japanese Broadcasting*, pp. 91–2.
24. *Hōsō 50-nen-shi*, p. 138.
25. *50 Years of Japanese Broadcasting*, pp. 94–5.
26. *Hōsō 50-nen-shi*, p. 146.
27. Shillony, Ben-Ami (1981) *Politics and Culture in Wartime Japan*, p. 144 (Oxford University Press), and *Hōsō 50-nen-shi*, pp. 147–8.
28. *History of Japanese Broadcasting*, pp. 402–3.
29. *Hōsō 50-nen-shi*, pp. 149–50.
30. Ibid., p. 150.
31. Ibid., p. 161.
32. E.g. Office of Strategic Services, *Transportation and Communications in Japan*, p. 209 (R & A 3123) Assemblage 54 (12 May 1945) (National Archives, Washington, DC).
33. *Hōsō 50-nen-shi*, p. 162.
34. Ibid., pp. 167–8.
35. Ibid., p. 162.
36. Ibid., p. 161.
37. Ibid., p. 164.
38. Ibid., p. 166.
39. *50 Years of Japanese Broadcasting*, p. 108.
40. Ibid., p. 109.
41. *Hōsō 50-nen-shi*, p. 172.
42. Ibid., pp. 168–70, 175–8.
43. Ibid., pp. 178–9.
44. The background to the surrender is described in Butow, Robert, J.C. (1954) *Japan's Decision to Surrender* (Stanford University Press). The text of the Emperor's broadcast is reproduced on p. 248.
45. *Hōsō 50-nen-shi*, pp. 195–7.
46. Anderson, Joseph L. & Richie, Donald (1959) *The Japanese Film Art and Industry*, p. 22 (Tokyo and Rutland, Vermont). The most detailed account of the origins of the Japanese cinema in Tanaka Junichirō (1975) *Nihon Eiga Hattatsu-shi*, Vol. 1 (Tokyo).
47. Kinema Junposha (1976) *Nihon Eiga Shi*, pp. 16–17 and 38–9 (Tokyo).
48. Yamamoto Fumio (1970) *Nihon Masu Komyunikeeshon-shi*, p. 193 (Tokyo).
49. *Nihon Eiga Shi*, p. 78.
50. A copy of this film is available in the Motion Picture Division of the National Archives, Washington, DC.
51. The International Cinema Association of Japan (ed.) (1938) *Cinema Year Book of Japan 1938*, p. 15 (Tokyo).
52. Nikkatsu Film Company. (A copy of this film is held in the Film Centre of the National Museum of Modern Art (*Kindai Bijutsukan*) (Tokyo).
53. Nikkatsu Film Company (held in the Film Centre, Museum of Modern Art Tokyo). Office of Strategic Services, Research and Analysis Branch, *Japanese Films, a Phase of Psychological Warfare*, p. 12 (Report 1307) (Washington, DC, 30

March 1944) (National Archives, Washington, DC).

54. Ibid., p. 6.

55. Tōhō Film Company (available in the Museum of Modern Art, Tokyo).

56. *Japanese Films, a Phase of Psychological Warfare*, p. 15.

57. Tōhō (Museum of Modern Art, Tokyo).

58. Tanaka Junichiro (1975) *Nihon Eiga Hattatsu-shi*, Vol. 3, pp. 13–15 (Tokyo).

59. For the sudden fall of film imports in 1937 see *Cinema Yearbook of Japan 1938*, p. 53.

60. *Nihon Masu Komyunikeeshon-shi*, p. 218.

61. Ibid., pp. 217–18.

62. (Motion Picture Division, National Archives, Washington, DC).

63. Nippon Eigasha, 1942 (Imperial War Museum, London).

64. Daiei, 1943, dir. Marune Santarō.

65. *Ahen Sensō* (Tōhō, 1943, dir. Makino Masahiro) and *Jingisukan* (Daiei, 1943, dir. Matsuda Sadaji) (Museum of Modern Art, Tokyo).

66. Kōa, 1941–2 (Museum of Modern Art, Tokyo).

67. E.g. *Singapōru no Sōkōgeki* (Daiei, 1943, dir. Shima Kōji).

68. Tōhō, 1942 (Imperial War Museum, London).

69. Satō Tadao (1970), *Nihon Eiga-shi*, pp. 246–247 (Tokyo).

70. Tōhō (Museum of Modern Art, Tokyo).

71. Tōhō, 1943 (Museum of Modern Art, Toyko).

72. Nippon Eigasha see *Nihon Eiga-shi*, pp. 97–8 and Satō Tadao (1977) *Nihon Kiroku Eigazō-shi*, pp. 115–17 (Tokyo).

73. For a brief analysis of Japanese newsreels see Daniels, Gordon (1981) Tradition and modernity in Japanese film propaganda, *Nippon Nyūsu 1940–1945*, in: O'Neill, P.G. (ed.) *Tradition and Modern Japan*, pp. 151–5 (Tenterden, Kent).

74. *Newsreel Issue 177* (27 October 1943) see Mainichi Shimbunsha (ed.) (1977) *Nippon Nyūsu Eigashi*, p. 345 (Tokyo).

15 JAPANESE OVERSEAS BROADCASTING: A PERSONAL VIEW

Namikawa Ryō

Nippon Hōsō Kyōkai (NHK), the Japan Broadcasting Corporation was established in 1925 and began overseas broadcasting in 1935. As part of its domestic service it established links with broadcasting services in Europe and North America. Although this provided an opportunity for broadening the horizons of Japanese listeners, the potential clash of Japanese and Western cultures raised serious problems for the NHK staff. Most of these exchanges were station-to-station programmes, consisting of greetings and music. NHK would transmit musicals from the Takarazuka and Kabuki-za theatres, as well as pieces for the stringed instruments *koto* and *shamisen*, traditional music representative of Japanese culture. International goodwill was the motive for such exchanges but an example of difficulties associated with one such exchange indicates the potential such East–West exchanges possessed for creating misunderstanding.

When Admiral Tōgō Heihachirō died in 1934 and was being mourned by the nation, the American National Broadcasting Company broadcast a special memorial programme on 5 June, which included eulogies by US naval leaders and music by the NBC Symphony Orchestra conducted by Arturo Toscanini. One of the pieces of music featured was the popular Japanese melody entitled 'Kappore', which was a well-known comic dance tune. This created a feeling of great unease amongst Japanese listeners, especially the NHK staff monitoring the programme. It was being relayed direct from the United States and the NHK staff could not easily take the programme off the air. Concern, bordering on shock, continued to mount as the short programme neared its end and the orchestra began to play the Japanese national anthem. The anthem shares the fundamental construction of Oriental music which is 12 bars, like New Orleans blues. European music is generally 16 bars. Toscanini, probably felt that he could not finish the Japanese national anthem at the end of bar 12, so he extended it to the 16th bar![1]

I was a member of the international programme staff on duty at

NHK. I turned pale. A telephone call came at once from the Tokyo Metropolitan Police with the order 'Come!' I ran to the detective sergeant's room at police headquarters to apologise. The sergeant cried 'You traitor', and I was slapped violently about the face. In Japan there was a great crime called *Fukeizai*, which meant blasphemy to the Emperor and I was judged to have committed this crime by allowing the programme to go out over the domestic service. After that incident whenever I saw that world-famous maestro on television or in a movie, his face overlapped the terrible face of the police detective.[2]

NHK began daily one-hour shortwave broadcasts on 1 June 1935 beamed at Hawaii and the West Coast of America in Japanese and English. Broadcasts to other areas soon began and in the late 1930s NHK's daily output rose to five hours using 16 languages.[3] At the outbreak of the Pacific war in December 1941, NHK's shortwave programmes were expanded to ten transmissions, using 16 languages for a total of 24 hours and 40 minutes a day, increasing programmes for the war-front in China, Thailand, French Indo-China, the Dutch East Indies and the Philippines.[4] In February 1942, programmes for Germany and Italy were added.[5] By December 1942 the overseas broadcasting of NHK had been increased to 13 transmissions in 22 languages for a total of 30 hours and 30 minutes. In 1943, it was expanded to 14 transmissions in 24 languages for a total of 30 hours and 55 minutes. In November 1943, the output was increased to 15 transmissions in 24 languages for a total of 32 hours and 35 minutes using three transmitters of 50 kilowatts. Thus overseas broadcasts were expanded with the escalation of the war. And the *Kokusai-bu* was promoted to be the *Kokusai-kyoku* of NHK;[6] that is, from International Section to Division, then to Overseas Department. To protect the transmitters from enemy bombardment, three underground studios were built under the *Hōsō-Kaikan* (Broadcasting House) in the centre of Tokyo and under the *Daiichi Seimei Biru* (First Life Insurance Company Building) near the Imperial Palace. (This building was later used as MacArthur's GHQ.) To prepare for possible damage by enemy bombing, two other shortwave transmitting stations were completed at Nazaki and Yamata. As for the *Tōa-hōsō* (Eastern Asia Broadcasting Chain),[7] two shortwave stations (Tama and Ashigara) were to be built in the low hills near Tokyo, although work on the Ashigara station was not completed before the Japanese surrender. Tama underground station was completed, and the young people of Japan now regard its big underground tunnels as the lifeless remains of the follies of the war effort.

When the war broke out, NHK had a staff of 6,000 with more than 100 men and women in the Overseas Section, including producers, writers, typists, announcers, directors and their assistants. Among them were about ten *Nisei* (American-born Japanese) announcers. Sons and daughters of Japanese parents were automatically Japanese, including the children of Japanese born and living in America. This legal complication and their own private feelings had a devastating effect on the destiny of Nisei living in Japan during the war. Where did loyalty lie when the US and Japan were at war? 'Tokyo Rose' (who worked first as typist and then announcer at NHK) was one of these cases. NHK's programmes were planned and produced taking into consideration the differences of character, nationality, history and the life-style of the listeners and the strategic objectives of Japan. In drawing up its programmes, NHK overseas section followed the patterns of the overseas programmes of the BBC, that is news, eye-witness accounts, talks, discussions, dramas, music and entertainment, using Marconi steel tapes, Telefunken discs and Japanese-manufactured discs. It also adopted the dynamic style of the programmes from Germany and the brisk announcements of San Francisco and the confident speech of the 'Voice of America'.

To guide the activities of the mass media, the Cabinet Information Bureau was established on 6 December 1940.[8] It consisted of five divisions and 17 sections, 550 officials in all. The division and section chiefs were selected from each government ministry, and the officials of each section were chosen from among civil public organisations (newspaper publishing companies, NHK, motion picture production corporations, book and magazine publishing corporations). The Cabinet ordered public organisations to recommend staff for the Bureau and the Cabinet accepted them after consultations with the various ministries. I was selected by NHK as an official of the Radio Section of the Bureau. The Radio Section consisted of three officials, that is, one chief, one official for domestic programmes and myself for the international programmes. Our duties were general guidance for NHK, and liaison between the staff of *Daihonei* (Japanese Imperial Headquarters) and to smooth out the frequent conflicts arising between the Army, Navy and NHK. My everyday work brought me constant anguish, because the army and navy's attitudes were quite often severe and simply trampled over the ideas and feeling of NHK.

For the oversight and direction of NHK's overseas broadcasting, a committee was established of relevant members of the ministries – Army, Navy, Foreign, Home, Great Asian and Communications – as well as NHK and the Dōmei News Agency. They met every morning at the Bureau under the chairmanship of the Chief of the Third Division (Foreign Affairs) and exchanged information and discussed the policies for treating the news as well as the points of emphasis. The committee's decisions were delivered immediately to all relevant sections of the Bureau. (The chief of the Third Division, Iguchi Sadao, became Ambassador to the USA after the war.[9])

Aside from the Cabinet Information Bureau, the Information Departments of the Army and Navy had primary responsibility for strategic information. The Navy Information Department dealt with both the planning and execution of military propaganda, while in the Army Information Department[10] the responsibilities were divided into different channels. The 8th Section of the Daihonei handled only the planning of publicity; the Army Information Department dealt with the actual execution. Overseas propaganda was the duty of the 8th section of the *Sambō Honbu* (General Staff), which consisted of one chief (General or field officer, section leader, captain or commander), deputy (commander or lieutenant commander) and two or three officers, noncommissioned officers, several junior officials and several employees. The 8th section controlled the Surugadai 'detached office' (prisoners of war working in overseas broadcasting, plus about 30 employees) and the monitoring centre (listening to enemy broadcasts and radio telegraphy); it was composed of one lieutenant commander, two officers below the rank of major and about 200 Nisei employees.

The Daihonei had absolute power over all national activities and controlled all domestic and foreign communications. The Japanese people were strictly forbidden to possess shortwave receiving sets and thus were totally ignorant of the manner in which the war progressed, leading eventually to total defeat. NHK, however, was listening to the broadcasts of the BBC as well as North American stations such as San Francisco. NHK staff knew the truth and found itself in the position of having to tell their own nation lies about

Japanese war achievements; NHK felt a grave responsibility to its nation as well as to foreign listeners. All Japanese believed the Daihonei propaganda that Japan was winning the war and that the Allies were withdrawing from the Far East. After suffering extraordinarily heavy losses at the naval Battle of Midway on 5 June 1942, Japan was compelled to continue false reporting of the war results. In wide areas of the South and China, Japan had to maintain the fictional achievements of the Japanese army and navy, and the pressures on NHK's overseas broadcasting became stronger than ever to cover over the real course of events. In South America, many Japanese shortwave listeners continued to believe that Japan had been victorious, even after the Emperor had declared the surrender in August 1945.[11]

We at NHK knew of the gap between the achievements of Japan and the USA but we could not give any hint of defeat on the air. The truth about all these matters was hidden from the nation by the Daihonei and the mass media. One reason why the Japanese were struck dumb with surprise, bewildered and aghast at the time of surrender was the strict concealment of the facts by Daihonei and the mass media. If the mass media had carried news closer to the facts, a large part of the nation would have been able to assess the situation and such alarm and indescribable anxiety would not have been caused by the Emperor's sudden announcement ordering, in so many words, unconditional surrender. Hatred of authority, of militarism and earnest aspirations for democracy erupted and this national feeling continues to this day. The de-control of news and opposition to militarism became a fundamental national commitment; the atomic bombing of Hiroshima and Nagasaki hardened this anti-war feeling.

Prisoners of war in South-east Asia and in the South Pacific totalled more than 100,000, and the Daihonei issued instructions to the ministries to use prisoners in seven fields of work, including propaganda. Three Allied officers were selected and sent to Tokyo where they were assigned to the overseas broadcasting section of NHK. They were Charles Cousens (Australian, former writer and announcer), Wallace Ince (American, announcer) and Norman Reyes (Philippino, announcer). They wore suits and were treated the same as Japanese employees. Many books written after the war said that they were treated violently, but the fact is that they were subjected to no force, either physically or mentally. Of course it may have been painful for them to be prisoners; their Japanese coworkers were sympathetic and even compassionate toward them as a result of the traditional fighting ethic of *Bushidō*. Some prisoners tried to affect lack of feeling in their announcing but they were genuine radio men who seemed to enjoy being in front of the microphone. Lieutenant Commander Charles Cousens was ordered by the Chief of the Army staff of the Daihonei to co-operate in the work of overseas broadcasting. I witnessed that impressive scene. Tsuneishi Shigetsugu, at that time Lt Colonel of the 8th Section of the Daihonei, transmitted the official order to Cousens. This stated, 'If you do not want to do this, you must return to the prison camp. Think about it and decide.' Everything went in a military way. Cousens' attitude was extremely fine and soldierlike. His dignified attitude never collapsed throughout the war. His soldierly and gentlemanly manner was long the subject of talk in NHK.[12]

At the beginning of 1943, just before the Japanese retreat from Guadalcanal and the German's crushing defeat at Stalingrad, Colonel Tsuneishi instructed Sawada Shinnojō, the chief of the 2nd Section of NHK, to form the *Zensen-han* (Front line unit), composed of Nisei, Charles Cousens, Wallace Ince and Norman Reyes, to operate a series of 'strategic broadcasts'. This project was under the direction of the 8th Section of the Daihonei; the Information Bureau of the Cabinet could not interfere in the content of the programmes. Sawada independently selected a team of about ten members which included Hideo Mitsushio as its leader, Kenneth (Kenkichi) Oki, graduate of New York University, Kenichi Ishii, and Shinichi Oshitari, a musician and graduate of the American University; Miss June Suyama, Miss Kuth, Sumi Hayakawa and other girls worked as typists and announcers. The manuscripts written by the members were not subjected to censorship for the army trusted them. Even Colonel Tsuneishi had confidence in this team which was responsible for producing a 75-minute programme called 'Zero Hour'. Directed at the Allied forces in South-east Asia and the South Pacific, it began at 6 o'clock every evening.[13] The opening announcement, 'This is Zero Hour from far Japan', by the Philippino Norman Reyes was followed by 'Strike up the Band' and fifteen minutes of classic music, five minutes of news, fifteen minutes of popular music, another five minutes' news, a short talk or fifteen minutes of Jazz and so on. Messages were read from war prisoners mailed to Tokyo from various parts of the Japanese occupied South Pacific, records were played by 'Orphan Ann' (Ikuko Toguri – better known as 'Tokyo Rose' to her listeners), news taken from US shortwave broadcasts and edited by the American, Wallace Ince, and 'Jazz stories' by Norman Reyes were also inserted.

The following are excerpts from scripts kept in the National Archives in Washington. They were recently copied by Akira Suzuki, a former staff member of TBS (Tokyo Broadcasting System).

ZERO HOUR

1st voice: This is the Zero Hour calling in the Pacific, and for the next 75 minutes we're going to take you through music as you like it, sweet and hot and otherwise, music from all over the world, and a thought for the day, sometimes even two thoughts for the day. First, let's have the fighting news for the fighting men.

(News)

5th voice/woman, 'Tokyo Rose': Hello you fighting orphans in the Pacific! How's tricks? This is 'after her weekend Ann' back on the air strict under [. . .] hour. Reception O.K? Well it [should] be because this is 'all request night'. And I've got a pretty nice programme for my favourite little family, the wandering Marine [. . .] of the Pacific islands. The first request is made by none other than the boss and guess what? He wants Bonney Baker, and 'My resistance is so low'. Now, what taste you have sir, she said. (Music). And now, that Hot Ruby Carr, our second request is sent in by [. . .] request number twenty nine. He wants Tony Martin, of all people, to help him forget the mosquitos and dirty rifles. Well, you know obliging Annie. Tony Martin and 'Now It Can Be Told'. (Music). This is Monday, washday for some, lots of cleaning for some and for the others, just another day for play. Let's all get together and forget those washday blues, with Kay Kaiser, Sonney Mason and all the playmates, so come join the parade you boneheads! (Music). Well, well, a new telegram, signed just M.S.S. and he wants a song also from our famous melody, R.L. Hum, well, Miss Bonnie Baker with the usual in the background, and the song, 'Shhh-baby's Asleep'. Quiet now everyone. (Music).

(Omission)

1st voice: This is the Zero Hour calling in the Pacific. We've just had it sweet, and in a moment we're going to have it hot. But in the meantime there are these news highlights.

2nd voice: Honolulu was alive with rumours, all of them wrong. It was rumoured that the closely guarded navy command where the president stayed was to be the site of a meeting with Churchill or Chiang Kai-Shek or both. Actually the whole affair was an American huddle. To the reporter who asked the president about an Anglo–American meeting, Roosevelt replied that Churchill is not in Honolulu, nor is he expected in Waikiki. A Churchill conference, he said, is a question for future determination. Roosevelt said he will report to the nation on his Pacific trip, his first war journey. He said he has no time for political campaigning in the usual sense, but said that he will report to the people from time to time.

Roosevelt ordered the seizure of Midwest truck companies involved in an eight-day strike, and that they would be operated by the Office of Defence Transportation until the dispute was settled. The War Labour Board, which found itself powerless to solve the controversy in which one hundred eight companies refused to pay a directed seven cents an hour wage increase, and twenty-five thousand drivers went on strike.

The Australian war brides have arrived in San Francisco, forming the largest contingent of Australian wives of American servicemen. There were 296 wives carrying 72 babies. Australian sources have announced that there's plenty more, a larger number than there were in 1942. Already some babies of these brides have travelled to the United States. Another batch of 134 brides are awaiting transportation, and 200 others have applied for permit to enter the United States.

1st voice: You have just heard the news highlights for tonight. This is the Zero Hour calling in the Pacific. We've had it sweet and now . . .

3rd voice: Hey boss! What are we gonna [do] about Watanabe?

1st voice: Have we received any pictures from the International Red Cross?

3rd voice: That's just what I'm worried about . . .

1st voice: Six thirty P.M. and here again to American Fighting men in the Pacific, once again the music from homeland brings you 'Swinging music for Syncopating Smoothies' . . .

(Music)

How'd you like to be back in Los Angeles tonight, dancing at Coconut Grove with your best girl? How would you like to be parked with her in Griffith Park listening to the radio?

How'd you like to go the corner drug store tonight, and get an ice cream soda?

I wonder who your wives and girl friends are out with tonight. May be with a 4F or a war plant worker making big money while you are out here fighting and knowing you can't succeed.

Wouldn't you California boys like to be at Coconut Grove tonight with your best girl? You have plenty of Coconut Groves, but no girls.

As one can see the programme's soft tone and humour aimed to stimulate war-weariness, nostalgia and pessimistic view of war. I do not know whether this can be regarded as 'strategic broadcasting', and it is hardly likely that this sort of programme was effective in actually reducing the fighting spirit of the Allies in the South Seas. American newspapers reported that Japan's war-weariness campaign seemed to be talked about by soldiers in some places, but Colonel Tsuneishi himself recognised that it was only the first step in Japan's strategy. The war developed so rapidly that 'Zero Hour' could not achieve its intended effect. 'Tokyo Rose' later participated in the unit. Her husky and sexy voice fitted exactly the mood of the aching heart, lovesickness and solitude of the orphan she was meant to portray. The messages from prisoners of war mailed to the station from Japanese-occupied areas of the South Pacific, however, did have an effect and were received with great concern by their families. The International Red Cross co-operated in this project. Many letters came to NHK after the war thanking it for this programme. The way of speaking and the contents of 'Zero Hour' were soft and dreamy, not like the threatening manner of speaking adopted by 'Lord Haw Haw' in Germany and Ezra Pound in Italy. I think the reason for this difference in the nature of propaganda may lie in the difference in the traditional and national characters of the nations.

At times friction occurred between the Daihonei and the *Jōhō-kyoku* (Cabinet Information Bureau), although none became public. The Information Bureau was unwilling to use prisoners of war and Nisei as announcers, but in the name of 'strategy' the army gave NHK no chance to oppose it. The Information Bureau concentrated its efforts on domestic propaganda and general publicity of world policies, especially relating to the self-determination of peoples and the independence of oppressed nations.

Many of the officials of the Information Bureau were liberals. Tanomogi Shinroku, the first Chief of the Overseas Department of NHK, was a humanist who had been a journalist on the *Rafu Shimpō (Los Angeles Times)*. Satō Taiichirō, the chief of the section, had an American wife. Miyamoto Yoshio, chief of the radio section of the Information Bureau and Mizutani Shirō, an official of that section, were devoted Christians. I translated Upton Sinclair's novels and had written a long article, entitled 'Hitler Burned the Reichstag' for the leading magazine *Bungei Shunjū*; the police were watching me. The war overwhelmed us all, however, and the feeling of patriotism that gripped the nation drove us into a desperate war effort, in which our careers and individuality were so powerless that we could not help but feel distress at our inability to resist the current of ultra-nationalism. The entire nation was ordered by the Emperor to fight on. Everyone was drafted into national mobilisation, but many people must have been unable to see any prospect of victory.

I was ordered to write manuscripts for overseas broadcasting to encourage self-determination and independence among the Chinese people and about revolution in the European colonies in South-East Asia; the programmes were based on the history of Asia and the heroic words of brave revolutionaries. I wrote one item every week from the history of the Opium War of 1840–42 and the Compton Church Rebellion of 1846 to the present day, quoting from books and documents. Many of my manuscripts were published as a book with the title of *One Hundred Years' Humiliation*. It was very strange that very often our overseas broadcasting, especially in Chinese, formed a common front with the Yenan Communist Party's propaganda, at least judging from the manuscripts, against the 'warlordism of Chiang Kai-shek'. Together we agitated for resistance against the capitalist warmonger, quoting from the Socialist thought of Sun Yat-sen. The persistent urging of the South-east Asian nations to seek self-determination and independence succeeded especially in Indonesia and Vietnam. This success has been confirmed recently by the political leaders of the now-independent nations, both in meetings I have had with them and in their writing. I also wrote the script for a two-hour movie entitled *Invisible Battlefield*, produced by the Daiei Movie Company and directed by the famous Chiba Taiju. The leading actress was Kuga Yoshiko, who made her debut in this film. This movie was awarded a prize by the Government Information Bureau. I believe this long documentary was the only movie describing the broadcasting activities of Japan during World War II. In the end, though, the Daiei Company, NHK and the Government Information Bureau burned all copies of the film before General MacArthur arrived at Atsugi airfield in August 1945. No part of that film has been found in the film archives in Washington. The movie consisted of three parts. The first part dealt with the activities of the Overseas Broadcasting Department of NHK. Many of the announcers and writers appeared. The second part covered propaganda put out by the *Tōa-Hōsō* (East Asia Radio Corporations Chain) and the last part described the death-defying radio troops with their microphones and loudspeakers.

In addition to NHK's overseas broadcasting, several East and South-east Asian organisations formed part of Tōa-Hōsō:

(1) *NHK* (Japan Broadcasting Corporation).

(2) *Taiwan Broadcasting Corporation.* Ten medium-wave stations served the Japanese living in Formosa (Taiwan). Important news was received regularly from NHK in Japanese. This corporation sent programmes in Japanese to the Philippines, Malaya, the Dutch East Indies and Singapore by shortwave, and dispatched front-line radio troops. Co-operating with the Shanghai stations, this corporation beamed the strategic campaign to Hainan and the Philippines.

(3) *Korean Broadcasting Corporation.* The first broadcasting network was in Japanese, and the second in Korean.

(4) *Manchurian Telegram and Telephone Company.* The first network was in Japanese, and the second in seven languages. This corporation had a radio agreement with the German and Italian radio corporations and exchanged programmes.

(5) *North China Broadcasting Corporation.* The central station was in Peking, other stations were in big cities in North China.

(6) *Central China Broadcasting Corporation.* The central station was in the capital, Nanking, for the Japanese and Chinese. In Shanghai there were three stations. One had been built by Hitler's government and the programmes were in German and English; there were brief news broadcasts in French. When Germany fell this station came under the control of the main Shanghai station and continued in German and English under the Japanese chief. One station broadcast only in English and was managed by Nisei. The last and the largest station broadcast in

Japanese and Chinese. These three stations in Shanghai broadcast commercial messages.

The above-mentioned corporations formed part of the Tōa-Hōsō Chain and had annual conferences about co-operation, programme coordination and equipment.

Next, in the occupied areas, the stations were as follows:

(1) *Manila and the local stations.* Medium wave for the local islands. Some received 'Zero Hour' from Tokyo. Five stations received programmes mainly from the Manila station.

(2) *Hongkong radio stations.* Medium wave for the Japanese and Chinese; shortwave broadcasts were aimed at Chungking.

(3) *Saigon shortwave and medium-wave stations.* Shortwave was used for propaganda to India, Burma and Australia. Japanese from Tokyo co-operated with underground members of the Independent League of India.

(4) *Malaya radio stations.* The Singapore 500-watt short wave station was built by the Japanese in March 1942. In Malaya district there were six medium-wave stations, seven stations in Sumatra district. On the Malaya Peninsula there were several medium wave stations operating in seven languages. Singapore added a 50 kilowatt shortwave transmitter in December 1943 for the concentrated campaign against India, Burma, Chungking, Australia and the islands of the South Pacific. It was also beamed to North and South America. The propaganda aimed at the countries of South America was fairly effective. The Japanese there heard news from the Singapore shortwave transmitter.

(5) *Dutch East Indies stations.* The Jakarta 1 kilowatt transmitter opened in March 1942, and there were seven medium-wave stations in full operation. In the Celebes and Borneo areas occupied by the Japanese Navy six medium-wave stations were built. The Bandung 10 Kilowatt shortwave station started in January 1943 and attracted listeners in India, Australia and North America.

(6) *Burma radio stations.* Members of NHK were sent to Burma. When the Japanese army occupied Rangoon, all equipment at the radio station had been destroyed, and through the superhuman efforts of the NHK staff, on 15 July 1942 the station was completed under bombardment and gunfire, and radio propaganda to Burma and India was started up. The radio war

aimed at India is said to have been particularly appalling. The chief of the station was Matsuuchi Norizō, a famous baseball commentator in Japan.

Besides the news and talks, the programmes broadcast by these stations in the occupied area included a great deal of entertainment. There were folk songs and traditional folk dramas played by local musicians, actors and actresses, and special programmes not actually related to the war were broadcast for women and children. Many first-class musicians, painters, novelists and dramatists came from Japan and worked on these programmes co-operating with local radiomen, artists, teachers and residents. Even now, some 40 years later, in Burma, Thailand and Indonesia one can hear the old Japanese songs which the broadcasts had taught local children and young people.

In December 1944 I was appointed chief of the three stations of Shanghai. When I went to that international city, the situation there was confused because the Chinese realised that Japan was about to be defeated. One of my missions was to settle the friction between the Japanese army and navy. One evening before the surrender of Japan, someone at the radio station managed by Nisei broadcast the American national anthem. I was summoned by the army information office and I was in danger of being subjected to trial by courtmartial; the 'criminal' was never found out.

There is a touch of irony in the role played by Tōa-Hōsō when it received the important message in the Emperor's own voice instructing the Japanese to surrender unconditionally. His speech was relayed from NHK in Tokyo by Tōa-Hōsō on shortwave. In Shanghai, the circumstances were complicated because the Japanese army across the vast Chinese mainland was still declaring, 'One Million Men of the Emperor's army in China are ready to fight on'. The main Japanese strategy during the war was to draw the American army to the Chinese mainland where all Japanese army forces would ambush the American forces, but that shortwave broadcast from Tokyo performed a miracle. When they heard the Emperor's message, the army and navy surrendered. It was also a miracle that, in all occupied areas in East Asia, no disturbance occurred among Japanese soldiers, much less any mutiny.

The four years of war in the Pacific had ended. On 15 August 1945, the day Japan surrendered, I was in the central radio station in Shanghai. Just after the voice of the Emperor had been broadcast,

I wrote an outline of the Emperor's message and added my apology to the Chinese people. The announcers, including Chinese, Americans and Germans, gathered around me and asked, 'What kind of music shall be broadcast after the news?' They went through the records and decided and I agreed. It was 'Way down upon the Swannee River'. We could not repress our tears, hearing the melody. To us Foster's music sounded like a mixture of deep sorrow and warm humanity. We felt as though hatred and despair had been swept away.

Notes

(Notes by Kitayama Setsuro.)

1. Tanomogi Shinroku writes, 'the American partner was NBC. Music was performed by the NBC (radio) orchestra'. (*Hoso* Magazine, September, 1934). On the 'Kappore' incident, *Nihon Hōsōshi* (1951 edition of NHK history) says the 'Kappore' disc was selected by an NBC staff member as appropriate music for the occasion. The broadcast was made in the early morning New York time, and 10.00 to 10.16 p.m. JST. *Tokyo Asahi Shinbun*, (6 June, 7 June, 1934), p. 870. There is still a difference of opinion over whether it was disc music or a live performance, but NBC say it was one of two discs broadcast.

2. The author, born at Matsue in Shimane Prefecture in 1905, graduated from the Faculty of Law, Tokyo University in 1929. He joined NHK's International section in 1931.

3. *Ihon ōsō yōkai ō*, no. 395 (17 October, 1941) shows that Radio Tokyo broadcast a total of 43 hours and five minutes in frequency hours, and 22 hours and 55 minutes in programme hours, in seven transmissions and in 16 languages, according to programmes revised and approved on 22 September 1941. Transmission began on 1 October.

4. On 20 Decembeer 1941, programmes were expanded. According to *Ihon ōsō yōkai ō*, no. 412 (13 February, 1942), programme hours were 24 hours and 15 minutes. Although the *Jōhō Kyoku document does not mention it, it is certain that the official language of the Philippines, Tagalog*, was added at the start of the war.

5. It was beamed from 5.00 to 5.20 p.m. to Berlin and Rome on 50 kilowatts. This was in addition to the regular European service broadcast in English, German, Japanese, Italian and French; the programmes went out from 3.55 to 7.30 a.m.

6. It was 1 September 1942 that *Kokusai-bu* was promoted to be the *Kokusai Kyoku*. The *Kokusai Kyoku* was renamed *Kaigai Kyoku* in July, 1944. (*Kokusai ka* had been expanded to a *bu* in June, 1939, i.e. International Section to Division, then to Department, and then to Overseas Department.)

7. A major part of the domestic service was relayed to other parts of East Asia on shortwave through the *Tōa-Hōsō* network.

8. The *Jōhō Kyoku* was inaugurated on 6 December, 1940, an outgrowth from *Jōhō bu*. Peter De Mendelssohn (*Japan's Political Warfare*, London, 1944) uses the title 'Cabinet Information Board'. At the start of the *Jōhō Kyoku*, two out of the five division chiefs and five out of the 17 section chiefs were men in uniform. (*Senzen no Jōhō Kyoku Yōran*). Lucy D. Meo, in her book *Japan's Radio War on Australia 1941–1945* (Cambridge/Melbourne, 1978), uses the term 'Cabinet Board

of Information'; History Compilation Room, Radio and Television Culture Research Institute, Nippon Hōsō Kyokai (ed.), *The History of Broadcasting in Japan* (Tokyo, 1967) uses the term 'Information Bureau' (p. 148).

9. Iguchi Sadao, division chief and foreign affairs spokesman, served in the post from 27 November 1943 to 30 August 1945. His predecessor was Hori Kōichi, who had been the division chief since 18 November 1941.

10. *Rikugun Hōdōbu*; De Mendelssohn calls Maj.-Gen. Nakao Yahagi 'former Chief of the Army Press Section, Imperial Headquarters'.

11. The *Daihonei* announced (and NHK dutifully reported) that in the major naval battle of Midway (5 June 1942) the US Navy had lost 2 carriers, a heavy cruiser, one submarine and 150 aircraft, which was close to the truth with the only exaggeration being with reference to the carriers of which the US lost only one. The real deception was the reported Japanese loss of one carrier sunk and one damaged and only 35 aircraft. The actual losses (and the lost naval battle) were 4 carriers, 1 heavy cruiser, 1 battleship and 1 heavy cruiser seriously damaged, 1 destroyer damaged and over 322 aircraft lost. A similar deception took place concerning the Battle of the Philippine Sea which the Daihonei also announced as a great victory having sunk virtually the entire American fleet, a fleet which was shortly to arrive off the Japanese coast. The Japanese view of the war is ably expressed by Lt-Colonel Tsuneishi Shigetsugu in his recent book *Dai Tō-a Sensō Hiroku Shinri Sakusen no Kaisō* (Tokyo, 1978); also see Tominaga Kengo, *Daihonei Happyō no Shinso Shi* (Tokyo, 1970), p. 78. In order to prevent any leaks of the naval disaster, the survivors were held incommunicado with the wounded brought ashore after dark. The experience is described in M. Fuchida and M. Okumiya, *Midway: the Battle that Doomed Japan* (US Naval Institute, 1957).

12. L.D. Meo, in *Japan's Radio War on Australia, 1941–1945*, describes him as Major C.H. Cousens.

13. Initially, according to my data, 'Zero Hour' was broadcast from 7.25 to 7.45 p.m. In August 1943, it was broadcast from 6.40 p.m. but still was a 20-minute programme. I believe that 'Zero Hour' was expanded to a 75-minute programme from 6.00 to 7.15, starting on 1 February, 1944 – the peaktime. From 5 April 1945 'Zero Hour' was broadcast from 6.00 to 7.00 until the surrender.

NOTES ON CONTRIBUTORS

Erik Barnouw was Chief of the Motion Picture, Broadcasting and Recorded Sound Division at the Library of Congress until retirement in 1981. Professor Emeritus of Dramatic Arts, Columbia University, he had a long and varied career in broadcasting. He is the author, among other works primarily on the mass media, of *A History of Broadcasting in the United States* (3 vols. Oxford University Press, 1966–70). He is a member of the editorial board of the *Historical Journal of Film, Radio and Television.*

Thomas Cripps is Professor of History at Morgan State University, Baltimore, Maryland. A prolific writer in the history of the cinema, his major contribution has been *Slow Fade to Black: The Negro in American Film* (Oxford University Press, 1977); a second volume, covering the period from 1940 is soon to appear. He also wrote the script of *Black Shadows on the Silver Screen* (Post-Newsweek television, 1975), an award-winning film, and is a member of the editorial board of the *Historical Journal of Film, Radio and Television.*

David Culbert is Associate Professor of History at Louisiana State University at Baton Rouge. Amongst his wide range of publications are *News for Everyone: Radio and Foreign Affairs in Thirties America* (Greenwood Press, 1976) and *Mission to Moscow* (edited with introduction, University of Wisconsin Press, 1980). He is editor-in-chief of the forthcoming multi-volume *Film and Propaganda in America: A Documentary History* and a member of the *Historical Journal of Film, Radio and Television*'s editorial board.

Gordon Daniels is a Senior Lecturer in Modern Far Eastern History in the Centre of Japanese Studies, University of Sheffield. He has written widely on Japan during World War II. His most recent publication is *A Guide to the Reports of the United States Strategic Bombing Survey* (Royal Historical Society, London, 1981).

Sergei Drobashenko is Deputy Director of the Film Art Institute of the State Film Archive of the USSR. A prolific writer in the history of Soviet film, his most recent work is *Istoriya sovetskogo dokumental'nogo fil'ma* (The History of Soviet documentary film) (Moscow, 1980).

David Ellwood is a Lecturer in Contemporary History at the University of Bologna. He is Joint Editor of *The Politics of European Liberation* (Leicester University Press forthcoming) and author of *L'alleato nemico. La politica dell' occupazione anglo-americana in Italia 1943–46* (Milan, 1977).

Peter Kenez is Professor of History at Stevenson College, University of California, Santa Cruz. He is the author of *Civil War in South Russia, 1918* (University of California Press, 1971) and *Civil War in South Russia, 1919–20* (University of California Press, 1977). At present he is completing a study of the rise of the Soviet propaganda system, 1917–32.

Namikawa Ryō, a graduate of the Faculty of Law of Tokyo University, joined the International Section of Japan Broadcasting Corporation (NHK) in 1931, becoming a member of the Cabinet Information Bureau during World War II. He had a distinguished post-war academic career as Professor of Drama and English Literature at Nihon University, Tokyo, which included his translation of *Upton Sinclair's Works* (1952–6).

Rémy Pithon is an historian at the University of Lausanne in Switzerland. He specialises in the social and ideological aspects of the French cinema of the 1930s and 1940s. He has published a number of articles in specialist journals.

Nicholas Pronay is Senior Lecturer in Modern History at the University of Leeds. A member of the editorial board of the *Historical Journal of Film, Radio and Television*, his most recent publications include (with Frances Thorpe) *British Official Films in the Second World War. A Descriptive Catalogue* (Clio Press, 1980) and (with D.W. Spring) *Propaganda, Politics and Film 1918–45* (Macmillan, 1981). Chairman of the Inter University History Film Consortium and Director of Television and Film for the Historical Association, he has also written two highly praised BBC Further

Education Television series on various aspects of the political impact of the cinema in the 1930s and 1940s.

Gianni Rondolino is Professor of Film History at the University of Turin and co-editor of *Il Nuovo Spettatore* (Turin). His publications include *Dizionario del cinema italiano 1945–1969* (Einaudi, Turin, 1969), *Roberto Rossellini* (La Nuova Italia, Florence, 1973), *Storia del cinema d'animazione* (Einaudi, Turin, 1974), *Storia del cinema* (3 vols., Utet, Turin, 1977), *Dizionario del cinema italiano*. I: *I registi* (Bolaffi, Turin, 1979), *Luchino Visconti* (Utet, Turin, 1981).

K.R.M. Short is Senior Lecturer in History at Westminster College, Oxford. Secretary General of the International Association for Audio-Visual Media in Historical Research and Education (IAMHIST), he is the Editor of the *Historical Journal of Film, Radio and Television*. His publications include *Feature Films as History* Croom Helm/University of Tennessee, 1981) and (with Karsten Fledelius) *History & Film: Methodology, Research, Education* (Eventus, Copenhagen, 1980)

Pierre Sorlin is Professor at the University of Saint-Denis where he teaches contemporary history with reference to the audiovisual media. His publications on film are: *Sociologie du Cinéma* (Paris, 1977); *La Révolution figurée* (Paris, 1979) and *The Film in History* (Oxford, 1980).

Elizabeth Strebel is an Adjunct Assistant Professor in the Cinema Department of the State University of New York. Her publications include *French Social Cinema of the Nineteen Thirties* (Arno Press, New York, 1980) and several articles on French film and politics in historical and film journals, including the *Journal of Contemporary History*, the *Historical Journal of Film, Radio and Television* and *Sight and Sound*.

Philip Taylor is Lecturer in International History at the University of Leeds. Author of *The Projection of Britain: British Overseas Publicity and Propaganda, 1919–39* (Cambridge University Press, 1981) he is a specialist in the area of British propaganda. In collaboration with M.L. Sanders, he also wrote *British propaganda in the First World War* (Macmillan, 1982).

David Welch is Lecturer in Modern History at the Polytechnic of Central London. Author of *Propaganda and the German Cinema, 1933–45* (Oxford University Press, 1983) he is a specialist in German history and Political Propaganda in the twentieth century. He is currently editing *The Power of Nazi Propaganda* (Croom Helm, 1983).

INDEX